Table of Contents

Ratios and Proportional Relationships

▶ **Understand ratio concepts and use ratio reasoning to solve problems.**

The Number System

Expressions and Equations

▶ Apply and extend previous understandings of arithmetic to algebraic expressions.

▶ Reason about and solve one-variable equations and inequalities.

▶ Represent and analyze quantitative relationships between dependent and independent variables.

Geometry

▶ **Solve real-world and mathematical problems involving area, surface area, and volume.**

Statistics and Probability

▶ Develop understanding of statistical variability.

▶ Summarize and describe distributions.

Introduction

Core Standards for Math offers two-page lessons for every content standard in the *Common Core State Standards for Mathematics.* The first page of each lesson introduces the concept or skill being taught by providing step-by-step instruction and modeling and checks students' understanding through open-ended practice items. The second page includes multiple-choice practice items as well as problem-solving items.

Common Core State Standards for Mathematics: Content Standards

Content Standards define what students should understand and be able to do. These standards are organized into clusters of related standards to emphasize mathematical connections. Finally, domains represent larger groups of related standards. At the elementary (K–6) level, there are ten content domains. Each grade addresses four or five domains. The table below shows how the domains are placed across Grades K–6.

	Grade Levels						
Domains	**K**	**1**	**2**	**3**	**4**	**5**	**6**
Counting and Cardinality (CC)	•						
Operations and Algebraic Thinking (OA)	•	•	•	•	•	•	
Numbers and Operations in Base Ten (NBT)	•	•	•	•	•	•	
Measurement and Data (MD)	•	•	•	•	•	•	
Geometry (G)	•	•	•	•	•	•	•
Numbers and Operations—Fractions (NF)				•	•	•	
Ratios and Proportional Relationships (RP)							•
The Number System (NS)							•
Expressions and Equations (EE)							•
Statistics and Probability (SP)							•

The lessons in ***Core Standards for Math***are organized by content standard. The content standard is listed at the top right-hand corner of each page. The entire text of the standards is provided on pages 261–265. The lesson objective listed below the content standard number indicates what part of the standard is emphasized in the lesson. You may choose to have students complete all the lessons for a particular standard or select lessons based on the more focused objectives.

Name Isaac

Lesson 1

COMMON CORE STANDARD CC.6.RP.1

Lesson Objective: Model ratios.

Model Ratios

Daniel is growing tulips and daffodils in a pot. For every 3 tulips he plants, he plants 1 daffodil. How many daffodils will he plant if he plants 12 tulips?

Step 1 Make a model and write the ratio. The ratio of tulips to daffodils is 3:1.

○ = 1 tulip
● = 1 daffodil

Step 2 Model the number of daffodils Daniel will plant if he plants 6 tulips.

Step 3 Use the model and ratio to make a table. The table shows that for every 3 tulips, there is 1 daffodil.

Tulips	3	6	9	12
Daffodils	1	2	3	4

Step 4 Find 12 tulips on the table. The number of daffodils is 4.

Step 5 Write the new ratio. The new ratio is 12:4.

So, if Daniel plants 12 tulips, he will plant 4 daffodils.

Write the ratio of triangles to squares.

1. 2 : 3

2. 4 : 7

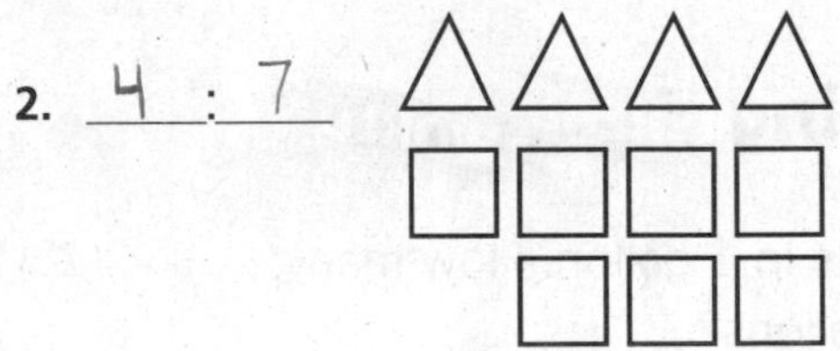

Draw a model of the ratio.

3. 5:1

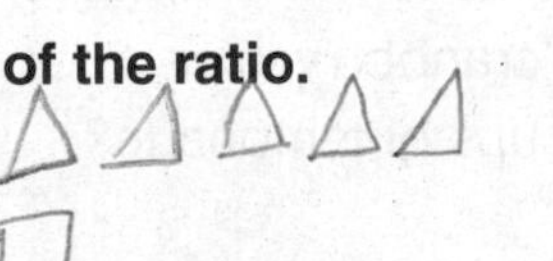

4. 3:4

Complete the table.

5. 1 table for every 5 students

Students	5	10	15	20
Tables	1	2	3	4

6. 7 pencils for every 1 student

Students	1	2	3	4
Pencils	7	14	21	28

Name Isaac

Lesson 1
CC.6.RP.1

1. For every team competing in a robotics competition, there are 4 students. How many students are on 3 teams?

Ⓐ 1
Ⓑ 3
Ⓒ 7
Ⓓ 12

2. Jillian uses 3 tablespoons of whipped cream for each bowl of dessert that she prepares. Which model could be used to describe the ratio of tablespoons of whipped cream to the number of bowls of dessert?

Ⓐ 3 red counters and 1 yellow counter
Ⓑ 2 red counters and 1 yellow counter
Ⓒ 4 red counters and 1 yellow counter
Ⓓ 2 red counters and 4 red counters

3. John has 2 comic books. Leroy has 3 comic books. What model shows the ratio of the number of John's comic books to the number of Leroy's comic books?

Ⓐ 
Ⓑ 
Ⓒ
Ⓓ

4. In every classroom in Millview Middle School, there are 2 computers. How many computers are in 4 classrooms?

Ⓐ 2
Ⓑ 4
Ⓒ 6
Ⓓ 8

Problem Solving

5. There are 4 quarts in 1 gallon. How many quarts are in 3 gallons?

12 quarts

6. Martin mixes 1 cup lemonade with 4 cups cranberry juice to make his favorite drink. How much cranberry juice does he need if he uses 5 cups of lemonade?

20 cups

Name Isaac

Lesson 2

COMMON CORE STANDARD CC.6.RP.1

Lesson Objective: Write ratios and rates.

Ratios and Rates

A **ratio** is a comparison of two numbers by division.
Ratios can compare parts of a whole or compare one part to the whole.
A **rate** is a ratio that compares two numbers that have different units.

The picture shows a group of school supplies. One part is pencils. The other part is notebooks. Write the ratio of pencils to notebooks. Write the ratio using words, as a fraction, and with a colon.

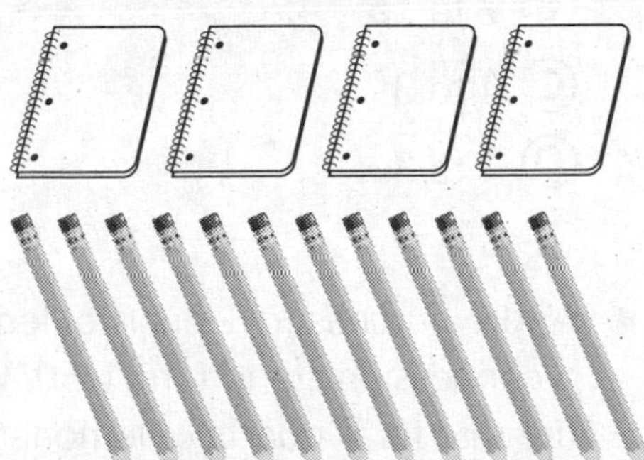

Write the number of pencils first, and then write the number of notebooks.

12 to 4	$\mathbf{\frac{12}{4}}$	**12:4**
number of pencils to number of notebooks	$\frac{\text{number of pencils}}{\text{number of notebooks}}$	number of pencils : number of notebooks

You could also write a ratio comparing part to whole. Write the ratio of notebooks to school supplies, three ways.

4 to 16	$\mathbf{\frac{4}{16}}$	**4:16**
number of notebooks to number of school supplies	$\frac{\text{number of notebooks}}{\text{number of school supplies}}$	number of notebooks : number of school supplies

Write each ratio three ways.

1. Write the ratio of circles to squares.

5 to 7  $\frac{5}{7}$ 5 : 7

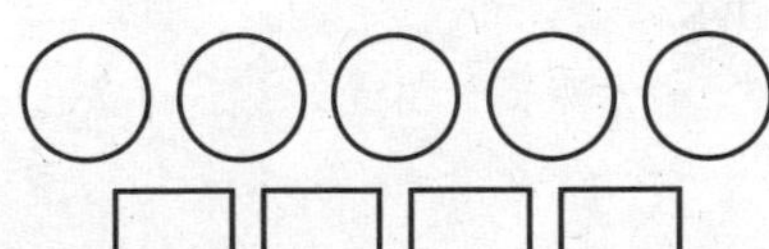

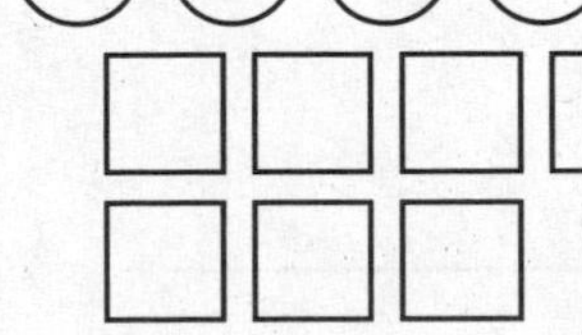

2. Write the ratio of squares to shapes.

7 to 12 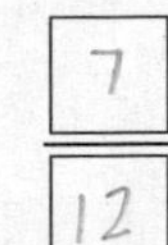 $\frac{7}{12}$ 7 : 12

Name ____________________

Lesson 2
CC.6.RP.1

1. At Fabric World, ribbon is sold at a rate of \$2 for 1 yard. What rate gives the cost for 8 yards of fabric?

   (A) \$2:1 yard
   (B) \$8:4 yards
   (C) \$10:1 yard
   (D) \$16:8 yards

2. Brenda planted 8 daisies, 3 pansies, 5 zinnias, and 6 marigolds in her garden. What is the ratio of zinnias to daisies?

   (A) 5:22
   (B) 5:8
   (C) 6:5
   (D) 8:3

3. Ashley has 4 pairs of low-top sneakers, 7 pairs of high-top sneakers, 3 pairs of sandals, and 1 pair of boots. What is the ratio of the pairs of low-top sneakers to the total number of pairs of shoes?

   (A) 4 to 15
   (B) 7 to 15
   (C) 4 to 3
   (D) 1 to 3

4. Andre purchased 1 quart of lemonade from a concession stand for \$1.50. Which shows the rate for 6 quarts of lemonade?

   (A) $\frac{\$0.25}{6 \text{ quarts}}$
   (B) $\frac{\$1.50}{1 \text{ quart}}$
   (C) $\frac{\$7.50}{1 \text{ quart}}$
   (D) $\frac{\$9.00}{6 \text{ quarts}}$

Problem Solving REAL WORLD

5. Gemma spends 4 hours each week playing soccer and 3 hours each week practicing her clarinet. Write the ratio of hours spent practicing clarinet to hours spent playing soccer three different ways.

   ____

6. Randall bought 2 game controllers at Electronics Plus for \$36. What is the unit rate for a game controller at Electronics Plus?

   ____

Name ______________________________

Lesson 3

COMMON CORE STANDARD CC.6.RP.2

Lesson Objective: Use unit rates to make comparisons.

Find Unit Rates

When comparing prices of items, the better buy is the item with a lower unit price.

Determine the better buy by comparing unit rates.

A 12-ounce box of Wheat-Os costs $4.08, and a 15-ounce box of Bran-Brans costs $5.40. Which brand is the better buy?

Step 1 Write a rate for each.

Wheat-Os

$\frac{\$4.08}{12\text{ oz}}$ ←

Since you are looking for the lower cost per ounce, write cost over ounce.

→ $\frac{\$5.40}{15\text{ oz}}$

Bran-Brans

Step 2 Write each rate as a unit rate.

$\frac{\$4.08 \div 12}{12\text{ oz} \div 12} = \frac{\$0.34}{1\text{ oz}}$

Divide the numerator and denominator by the number in the denominator.

$\frac{\$5.40 \div 15}{15\text{ oz} \div 15} = \frac{\$0.36}{1\text{ oz}}$

Step 3 Choose the brand that costs less.

$\frac{\$0.34}{1\text{ oz}}$ (circled)

$0.34 is less than $0.36.

$\frac{\$0.36}{1\text{ oz}}$

So, Wheat-Os are the better buy.

Determine the better buy by comparing unit rates.

1. 20 pens for $1.60 or 25 pens for $2.25

a. Write a rate for each.

__________ and __________

b. Write each rate as a unit rate.

__________ and __________

c. Which is the better buy?

____

2. 13 berries for $2.60 or 17 berries for $3.06

a. Write a rate for each.

__________ and __________

b. Write each rate as a unit rate.

__________ and __________

c. Which is the better buy?

____

1. Juan paid $2.52 for 12 ounces of peanuts. What is the unit rate?

Ⓐ $\frac{\$0.21}{1 \text{ ounce}}$
Ⓑ $\frac{\$2.52}{12 \text{ ounces}}$
Ⓒ $\frac{\$4.76}{1 \text{ ounce}}$
Ⓓ $\frac{\$30.24}{12 \text{ ounces}}$

2. Dora used the grocery ads to list apple prices at four stores.

Gordon's: 4 pounds for $3.32
Greenwise: 2 pounds for $1.62
PJ's: 3 pounds for $2.37
Tosko: 5 pounds for $4.50

Which store charges the **least** amount per pound?

Ⓐ Gordon's
Ⓑ Greenwise
Ⓒ PJ's
Ⓓ Tosko

3. Robert compared the cost of popcorn at 4 movies theaters.

Cinema World: 33 ounces for $5.61
Tons of Movies: 27 ounces for $5.13
Parkside Theater: 28 ounces for $5.04
Landview Cinema: 32 ounces for $4.80

Which movie theater charges the **least** amount per ounce?

Ⓐ Cinema World
Ⓑ Tons of Movies
Ⓒ Parkside Theater
Ⓓ Landview Cinema

4. Dmitri bought 28 ounces of trail mix for $3.92. What is the unit rate?

Ⓐ $\frac{\$0.14}{1 \text{ ounce}}$
Ⓑ $\frac{\$3.92}{28 \text{ ounces}}$
Ⓒ $\frac{\$7.14}{1 \text{ ounce}}$
Ⓓ $\frac{\$109.76}{28 \text{ ounces}}$

Problem Solving REAL WORLD

5. Sylvio's flight is scheduled to travel 1,792 miles in 3.5 hours. At what average rate will the plane have to travel to complete the trip on time?

____

6. Rachel bought 2 pounds of apples and 3 pounds of peaches for a total of $10.45. The apples and peaches cost the same amount per pound. What was the unit rate?

____

Name ______________________________

Lesson 4

COMMON CORE STANDARD CC.6.RP.3a

Lesson Objective: Use a multiplication table to find equivalent ratios.

Equivalent Ratios and Multiplication Tables

To find equivalent ratios, you can use a multiplication table or multiply by a form of 1.

Write two ratios equivalent to 10:14. Use a multiplication table.

Step 1 Find 10 and 14 in the same row.

Step 2 Look at the columns for 10 and 14.

Choose a number from each column. Make sure that the numbers you choose are in the same row. — 5 and 7 — 30 and 42

Step 3 Write the new ratios. — 5:7 — 30:42

×	1	2	3	4	5	6	7	8	9
1	1	2	3	4	5	6	7	8	9
2	2	4	6	8	10	12	14	16	18
3	3	6	9	12	15	18	21	24	27
4	4	8	12	16	20	24	28	32	36
5	5	10	15	20	25	30	35	40	45
6	6	12	18	24	30	36	42	48	54
7	7	14	21	28	35	42	49	56	63
8	8	16	24	32	40	48	56	64	72
9	9	18	27	36	45	54	63	72	81

Use multiplication or division.

Step 1 To multiply or divide by a form of 1, multiply or divide the numerator and denominator by the same number.

Multiply $\frac{10 \times 3}{14 \times 3} = \frac{30}{42}$ **Divide** $\frac{10 \div 2}{14 \div 2} = \frac{5}{7}$

Step 2 Write the new ratios. $\frac{30}{42}$ $\frac{5}{7}$

Solve.

1. Write a ratio that is equivalent to 6:16.

   a. Find 6 and 16 in the same row.

   b. Choose a pair of numbers from a different row, in the same columns as 6 and 16. _____ and _____

   c. Write the equivalent ratio. 6:16 = _____:_____

×	1	2	3	4	5	6	7	8	9
1	1	2	3	4	5	6	7	8	9
2	2	4	6	8	10	12	14	16	18
3	3	6	9	12	15	18	21	24	27
4	4	8	12	16	20	24	28	32	36
5	5	10	15	20	25	30	35	40	45
6	6	12	18	24	30	36	42	48	54
7	7	14	21	28	35	42	49	56	63
8	8	16	24	32	40	48	56	64	72
9	9	18	27	36	45	54	63	72	81

2. Write two ratios equivalent to $\frac{5}{9}$.

   ____

3. Write two ratios equivalent to $\frac{8}{6}$.

   ____

Name ________________________

Lesson 4
CC.6.RP.3a

1. In Natalia's class, there are 10 boys and 14 girls. Which ratio is equivalent to $\frac{10}{14}$?

   Ⓐ $\frac{10}{21}$
   Ⓑ $\frac{5}{7}$
   Ⓒ $\frac{5}{6}$
   Ⓓ $\frac{17}{14}$

2. In Abraham's last basketball game of the season, the ratio of free throws he made to the free throws he attempted was $\frac{12}{18}$. Which is an equivalent ratio?

   Ⓐ $\frac{2}{18}$
   Ⓑ $\frac{6}{12}$
   Ⓒ $\frac{4}{6}$
   Ⓓ $\frac{12}{9}$

3. Of the 24 students in a class, 8 said they have at least two siblings. Which ratio is equivalent to $\frac{8}{24}$?

   Ⓐ $\frac{4}{24}$
   Ⓑ $\frac{6}{24}$
   Ⓒ $\frac{4}{12}$
   Ⓓ $\frac{12}{28}$

4. There are 21 sedans and 12 sports utility vehicles on the lot of a car dealership. Which ratio is equivalent to $\frac{21}{12}$?

   Ⓐ $\frac{7}{4}$
   Ⓑ $\frac{24}{12}$
   Ⓒ $\frac{21}{9}$
   Ⓓ $\frac{7}{2}$

Problem Solving REAL WORLD

5. Tristan uses 7 stars and 9 diamonds to make a design. Write two ratios that are equivalent to $\frac{7}{9}$.

   ____

6. There are 12 girls and 16 boys in Javier's math class. There are 26 girls and 14 boys in Javier's choir class. Is the ratio of girls to boys in the two classes equivalent? Explain.

   ____

Name ______________________________

Lesson 5

COMMON CORE STANDARD CC.6.RP.3a

Lesson Objective: Solve problems involving ratios by using the strategy *find a pattern.*

Problem Solving • Use Tables to Compare Ratios

Use tables of equivalent ratios to solve the problem.

Kevin's cookie recipe uses a ratio of 4 parts flour to 2 parts sugar. Anna's recipe uses 5 parts flour to 3 parts sugar. Could their recipes make the same cookies?

Read the Problem	Solve the Problem
What do I need to find? I need to find out if the ratio of ________ to ________ in Kevin's recipe is equivalent to the ratio in ______________________.	Make a table of equivalent ratios for each recipe.
What information do I need to use? I will use the ________ of ________ to ________.	
How will I use the information? I will make ________ to compare the ________.	

Kevin's Recipe

Flour	4	8	12	16	20
Sugar	2	4	6	8	10

Anna's Recipe

Flour	5	10	15	20	25
Sugar	3	6	9	12	15

Find an amount of flour that is in both tables.

____

Write the ratio for Kevin's recipe. $\frac{20}{\square}$

Write the ratio for Anna's recipe. $\frac{20}{\square}$

Are the ratios the same? ________

So, their recipes ______________ make the same cookies.

1. Sherona takes a 6-minute break after every 24 minutes of study. Benedict takes an 8-minute break after every 32 minutes of study. Are their ratios of study time to break time equivalent?

____

2. Micah buys 10 pens for every 2 pencils. Rachel buys 12 pens for every 3 pencils. Are their ratios of pens to pencils bought equivalent?

____

Name ______________________

Lesson 5
CC.6.RP.3a

1. The table shows the basketball standings for teams in an intramural league.

Basketball Standings

Team	Wins	Losses
Bears	15	10
Stars	12	9
Wildcats	6	5
Knights	8	6

Which basketball teams have equivalent ratios of wins to losses?

(A) Stars and Knights
(B) Wildcats and Stars
(C) Knights and Wildcats
(D) Bears and Stars

2. The number of comedy and action films that 4 friends have in their DVD collections is recorded in the table.

DVD Collections

Friend	Comedy	Action
Winston	12	5
Chang	10	15
Ricardo	3	11
Shaneka	8	12

Which 2 people have equivalent ratios of comedy films to action films?

(A) Winston and Chang
(B) Winston and Ricardo
(C) Ricardo and Shaneka
(D) Chang and Shaneka

Problem Solving REAL WORLD

3. Out of the people who called in during a radio station poll, 9 out of 25 chose pop as their favorite type of music, 1 out of 5 callers chose rock, 6 out of 75 callers chose classical, and 18 out of 50 callers chose R&B. Which pair of ratios are equivalent? Explain how you know.

____

____

____

____

____

____

____

Name ____________________

Lesson 6

COMMON CORE STANDARD CC.6.RP.3a

Lesson Objective: Use tables to solve problems involving equivalent ratios.

Algebra • Use Equivalent Ratios

You can find equivalent ratios by using a table or by multiplying or dividing the numerator and denominator by the same number.

Kate reads 5 chapters in 2 hours. At this rate, how many chapters will she read in 6 hours?

Step 1 Make a table of equivalent ratios.

		$5 \cdot \mathbf{2}$	$5 \cdot \mathbf{3}$
Chapters read	5	10	15
Time (hours)	2	4	6
		$2 \cdot \mathbf{2}$	$2 \cdot \mathbf{3}$

Step 2 Find 6 hours in the table. Find the number of chapters that goes with 6 hours: 15

Step 3 Write the new ratio: $\frac{15}{6}$

The ratios $\frac{5}{2}$ and $\frac{15}{6}$ are equivalent ratios. So, Kate will read 15 chapters in 6 hours.

Julian runs 10 kilometers in 60 minutes. At this pace, how many kilometers can he run in 30 minutes?

Step 1 Write equivalent ratios with a missing value.

$$\frac{10}{60} = \frac{\blacksquare}{30}$$

Step 2 Divide the numerator and denominator by 2 to write the ratios using a common denominator.

$$\frac{10 \div 2}{60 \div 2} = \frac{\blacksquare}{30}$$

The denominators are the same, so the numerators are equal to each other.

$$\frac{5}{30} = \frac{\blacksquare}{30} \rightarrow \blacksquare = 5$$

So, Julian can run 5 kilometers in 30 minutes.

Use equivalent ratios to find the unknown value.

1. $\frac{4}{5} = \frac{\square}{20}$

	$4 \cdot 2$	$4 \cdot 3$	$4 \cdot 4$
4		12	
5	10		20
	$5 \cdot 2$	$5 \cdot 3$	$5 \cdot 4$

2. $\frac{\square}{12} = \frac{2}{3}$

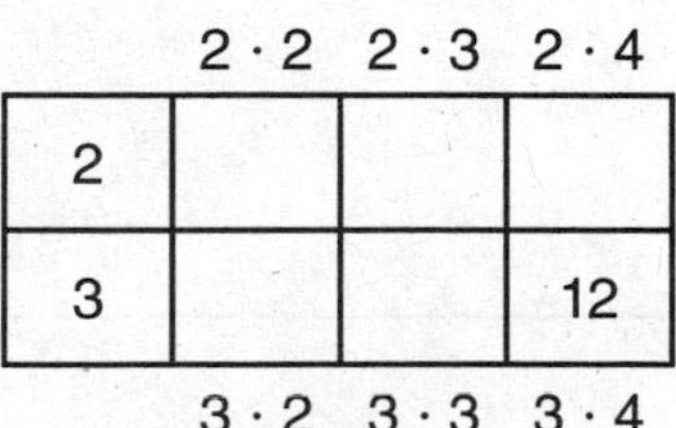

	$2 \cdot 2$	$2 \cdot 3$	$2 \cdot 4$
2			
3			12
	$3 \cdot 2$	$3 \cdot 3$	$3 \cdot 4$

3. $\frac{24}{27} = \frac{\square}{9}$

4. $\frac{3}{7} = \frac{9}{\square}$

5. $\frac{8}{10} = \frac{\square}{5}$

6. $\frac{30}{45} = \frac{6}{\square}$

Name ____________________

Lesson 6
CC.6.RP.3a

1. Kelsey can make 3 loaves of bread with 7 cups of flour. How many loaves of bread can she make with 21 cups of flour?

Ⓐ 7
Ⓑ 9
Ⓒ 63
Ⓓ 147

2. Antonio burns 75 calories for every 15 minutes he rides his bicycle. At that rate, how many calories will Antonio burn if he rides his bicycle for 60 minutes?

Ⓐ 4 calories
Ⓑ 150 calories
Ⓒ 225 calories
Ⓓ 300 calories

3. Jung-Su reads 35 pages of a novel in 2 hours. At that rate, how many pages will he read in 6 hours?

Ⓐ 70
Ⓑ 105
Ⓒ 210
Ⓓ 420

4. Dwayne hikes 60 miles in 3 days. At that rate, how many days does it take him to hike a total of 240 miles?

Ⓐ 12
Ⓑ 14
Ⓒ 15
Ⓓ 19

Problem Solving REAL WORLD

5. Honeybees produce 7 pounds of honey for every 1 pound of beeswax they produce. Use equivalent ratios to find how many pounds of honey are produced when 25 pounds of beeswax are produced.

____

6. A 3-ounce serving of tuna provides 21 grams of protein. Use equivalent ratios to find how many grams of protein are in 9 ounces of tuna.

____

Name ______________________________

Lesson 7

COMMON CORE STANDARD CC.6.RP.3a

Lesson Objective: Use a graph to represent equivalent ratios.

Algebra • Equivalent Ratios and Graphs

Jake collects 12 new coins each year. Use equivalent ratios to graph the growth of his coin collection over time.

Step 1 Write an ordered pair for the first year. Let the *x*-coordinate represent the number of years: 1. Let the *y*-coordinate represent the number of coins: 12.

Ordered pair: (1, 12)

Step 2 Make a table of equivalent ratios.

Coins	12	24	36	48	60
Year	1	2	3	4	5

Step 3 Write ordered pairs for the values in the table.

(1, 12), (2, 24), (3, 36), (4, 48), (5, 60)

Step 4 Label the *x*-axis and *y*-axis.

Step 5 Graph the ordered pairs as points.

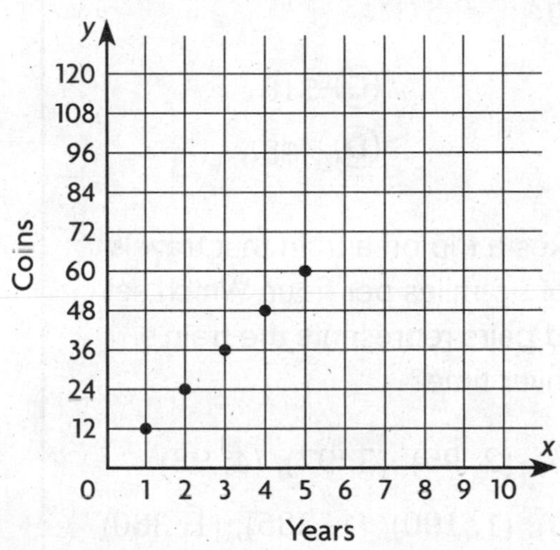

The point (1, 12) represents the year Jake started his collection. It shows that he had 12 coins after 1 year.

Use the graph for 1–5.

1. Helen walks at a rate of 3 miles in 1 hour. Write an ordered pair. Let the *y*-coordinate represent miles and the *x*-coordinate represent hours. (___, ___)

2. Complete the table of equivalent ratios.

Miles	3			12	
Hours			3		5

3. Write ordered pairs for the values in the table.

(___, ___), (___, ___), (___, ___), (___, ___), (___, ___)

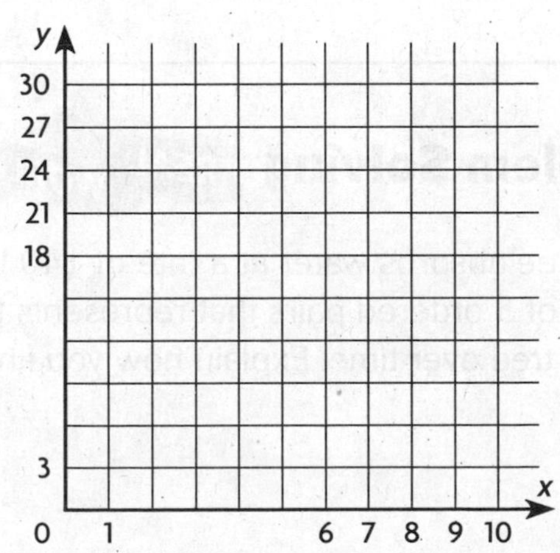

4. Label the graph. Graph the ordered pairs.

5. What does the point (2, 6) represent on the graph?

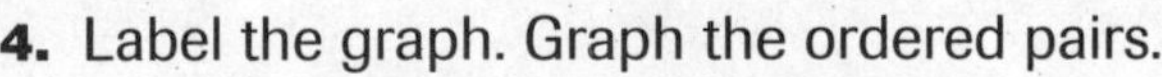

Name ______________________________

1. The graph shows the amount of money Timothy earns from his tutoring job.

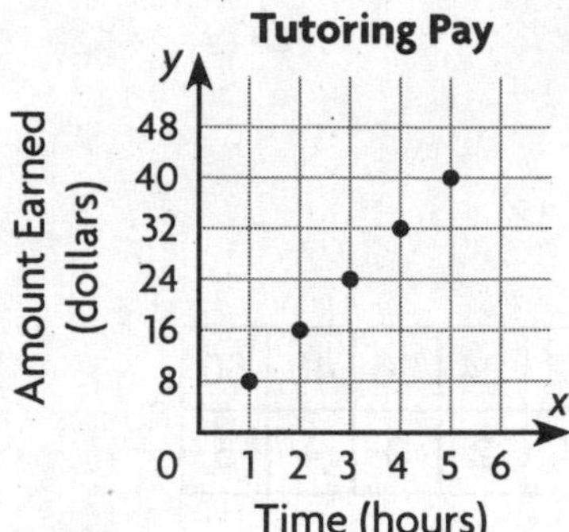

How much does Timothy earn for 4 hours of tutoring?

Ⓐ $32 Ⓒ $16
Ⓑ $24 Ⓓ $8

2. Shawn takes a trip on a train that travels at a rate of 95 miles per hour. Which set of ordered pairs represents the train's distance over time?

Ⓐ (1, 95), (2, 96), (3, 97), (4, 98)
Ⓑ (1, 95), (1, 190), (1, 285), (1, 380)
Ⓒ (1, 95), (2, 95), (3, 95), (4, 95)
Ⓓ (1, 95), (2, 190), (3, 285), (4, 380)

3. The graph shows the rate at which a helicopter travels over time.

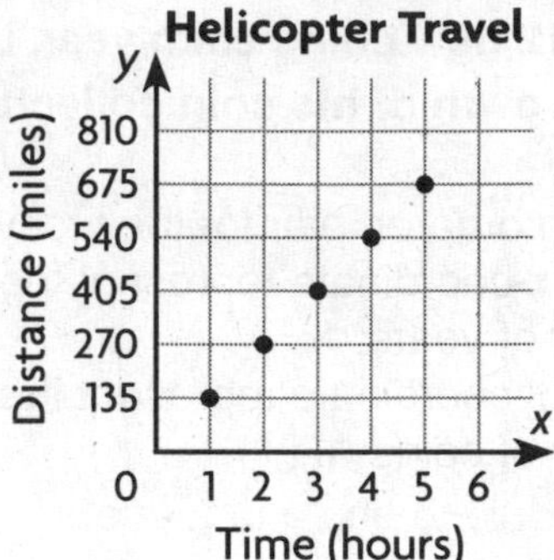

How far does the helicopter travel in 7 hours?

Ⓐ 1,080 miles Ⓒ 143 miles
Ⓑ 945 miles Ⓓ 135 miles

4. Mrs. Carter is charged $0.50 per minute for international phone calls. Which set of ordered pairs represents the cost of an international phone call for different numbers of minutes?

Ⓐ (1, 0.5), (1, 1), (1, 1.5), (1, 2), (1, 2.5)
Ⓑ (1, 0.5), (3, 1), (5, 1.5), (7, 2), (9, 2.5)
Ⓒ (2, 2), (4, 4), (8, 8), (16, 16), (32, 32)
Ⓓ (1, 0.5), (10, 5), (50, 25), (100, 50)

Problem Solving REAL WORLD

5. A tree absorbs water at a rate of 140 liters per day. Use a table to list a set of 5 ordered pairs that represents the amount of water absorption of the tree over time. Explain how you know your answer is correct.

Name ______________________________

Lesson 8

COMMON CORE STANDARD CC.6.RP.3b

Lesson Objective: Solve problems using unit rates.

Algebra • Use Unit Rates

You can find equivalent ratios by first finding a unit rate.

Marcia makes bracelets to sell at craft fairs. She sold 14 bracelets for $154. How much could she expect to earn if she sells 25 bracelets?

Step 1 Write equivalent ratios.

$$\frac{\text{money}}{\text{bracelets}} \rightarrow \frac{\$154}{14} = \frac{\blacksquare}{25} \leftarrow \frac{\text{money}}{\text{bracelets}}$$

Step 2 Since 25 is not a multiple of 14, use the known ratio to find a unit rate.

$$\frac{\$154 \div \boxed{14}}{14 \div 14} = \frac{\blacksquare}{25}$$

$$\frac{\$\boxed{11}}{1} = \frac{\blacksquare}{25}$$

Marcia earns $11 per bracelet.

Step 3 Write an equivalent ratio by multiplying the unit rate's numerator and denominator by the same value. Since 1 · 25 = 25, multiply by 25 over 25.

$$\frac{\$11 \cdot \boxed{25}}{1 \cdot \boxed{25}} = \frac{\blacksquare}{25}$$

Step 4 Since the denominators are equal, the numerators are also equal.

$$\frac{\boxed{\$275}}{25} = \frac{\blacksquare}{25}$$

So, Marcia would earn $275 if she sells 25 bracelets.

Use a unit rate to find the unknown value.

1. $\frac{120}{20} = \frac{300}{\blacksquare}$

a. Find the unit rate: $\frac{120 \div \square}{20 \div 20} = \frac{300}{\blacksquare}$

b. $\frac{\square}{1} = \frac{300}{\blacksquare}$

c. $\frac{6 \cdot 50}{1 \cdot \square} = \frac{300}{\blacksquare}$

d. $\blacksquare$ = ________

2. $\frac{\blacksquare}{100} = \frac{90}{15}$

$\blacksquare$ = ________

3. $\frac{90}{\blacksquare} = \frac{44}{22}$

$\blacksquare$ = ________

4. $\frac{45}{10} = \frac{\blacksquare}{54}$

$\blacksquare$ = ________

Name ____________________

Lesson 8
CC.6.RP.3b

1. If 5 bags of oranges weigh 35 pounds, how many pounds do 2 bags of oranges weigh?

   Ⓐ 7 pounds
   Ⓑ 10 pounds
   Ⓒ 14 pounds
   Ⓓ 70 pounds

2. The table shows the numbers of calories in 4 ounces of several types of fruit juice.

Calories in 4 Ounces of Juice

Type of Juice	Calories
Apple	60
Grape	76
Orange	56

How many calories are there in 5 ounces of apple juice?

   Ⓐ 300 calories
   Ⓑ 75 calories
   Ⓒ 15 calories
   Ⓓ 12 calories

3. On a map of Arizona, 2 inches represent 54 miles. The map distance from Yuma to Sentinel is 3 inches. What is the actual distance, in miles, between the cities?

   Ⓐ 81 miles
   Ⓑ 45 miles
   Ⓒ 27 miles
   Ⓓ 9 miles

4. If 7 bags of empty aluminum cans weigh 21 pounds, how many pounds do 15 bags of empty aluminum cans weigh?

   Ⓐ 3 pounds
   Ⓑ 5 pounds
   Ⓒ 45 pounds
   Ⓓ 105 pounds

Problem Solving

5. To stay properly hydrated, a person should drink 32 fluid ounces of water for every 60 minutes of exercise. How much water should Damon drink if he rides his bike for 135 minutes?

   ____

6. Lillianne made 6 out of every 10 baskets she attempted during basketball practice. If she attempted to make 25 baskets, how many did she make?

   ____

Name ______________________________

Lesson 9

COMMON CORE STANDARD CC.6.RP.3c

Lesson Objective: Use a model to show a percent as a rate per 100.

Model Percents

A **percent** is a ratio that compares a number to 100. It represents part of a whole.

Model 54% on the 10-by-10 grid. Then write the percent as a ratio.

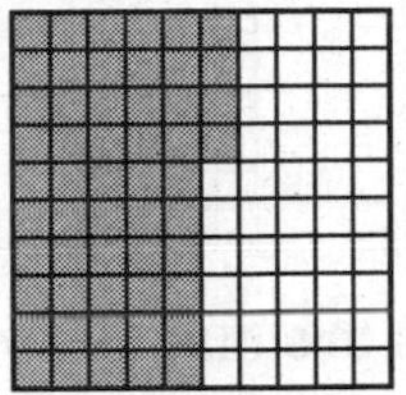

Step 1 The grid represents 1 whole. It has 100 equal parts. To show 54%, shade 54 of the 100 equal parts.

Step 2 A ratio can be written as a fraction. Write the number of shaded parts, 54, in the numerator. Write the total number of parts in the whole, 100, in the denominator.

shaded ⟶ 54
total ⟶ 100

So, 54% is 54 out of 100 squares shaded, or $\frac{54}{100}$.

Model the percent and write it as a ratio.

1. 19%

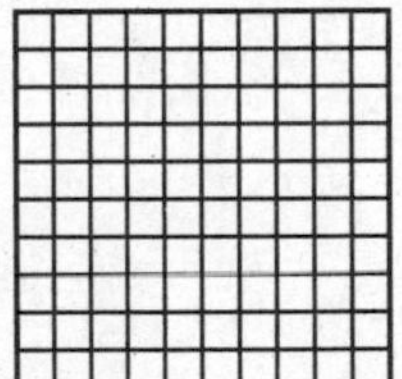

ratio: __________

2. 80%

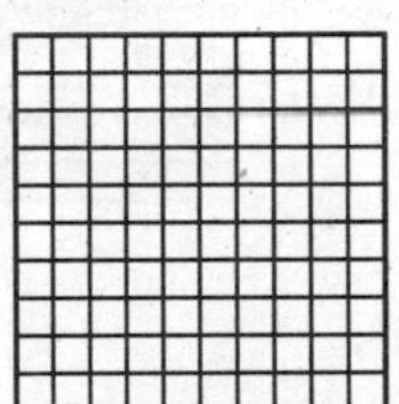

ratio: __________

3. 66%

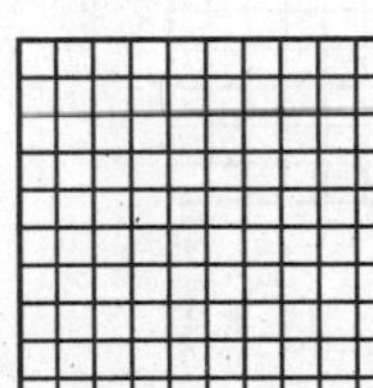

ratio: __________

4. 3%

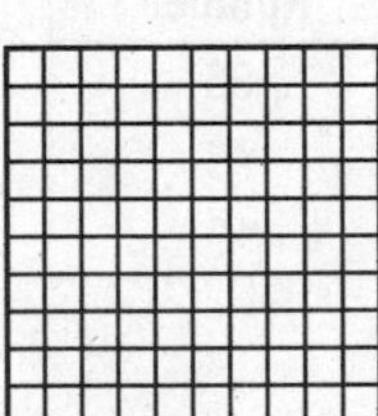

ratio: __________

5. 31%

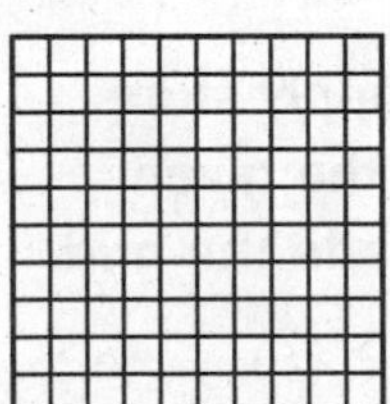

ratio: __________

6. 25%

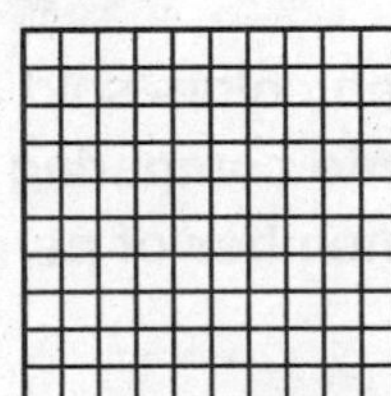

ratio: __________

Name ______________________

1. The model shows the part of muffins in a delivery that are blueberry.

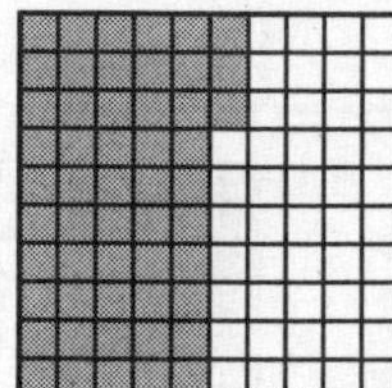

What is this number written as a percent?

Ⓐ 3.5%
Ⓑ 5.3%
Ⓒ 35%
Ⓓ 53%

2. What ratio represents the shaded part?

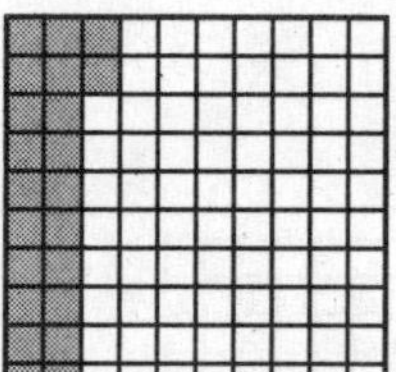

Ⓐ $\frac{22}{50}$
Ⓑ $\frac{11}{50}$
Ⓒ $\frac{1}{5}$
Ⓓ $\frac{1}{22}$

3. Which model shows 17% shaded?

Ⓐ 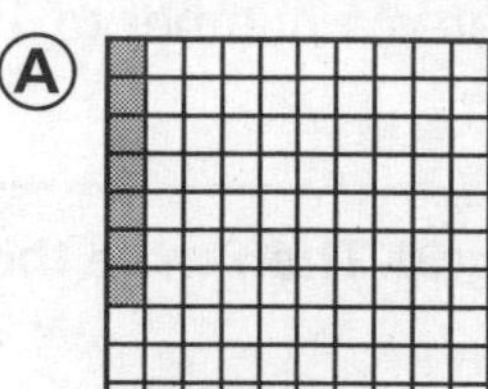

Ⓑ 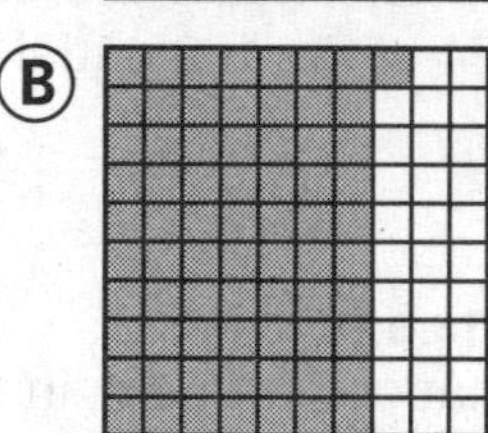

Ⓒ 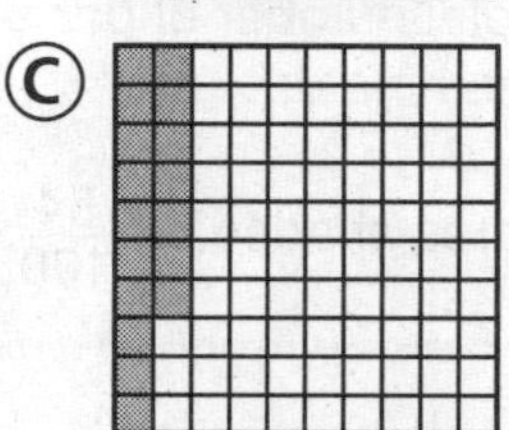

Ⓓ 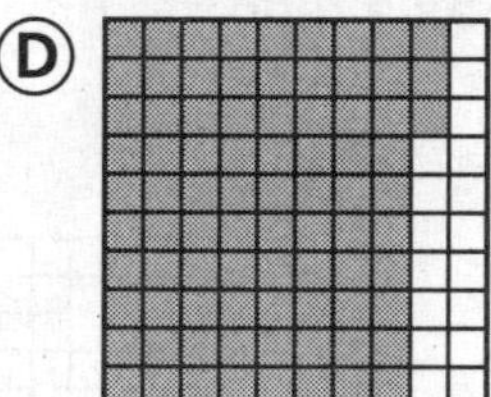

Problem Solving

Pens Sold	
Color	Number
Blue	36
Black	49
Red	15

The table shows the pen colors sold at the school supply store one week. Write the ratio comparing the number of the given color sold to the total number of pens sold. Then shade the grid.

4. Black

______ 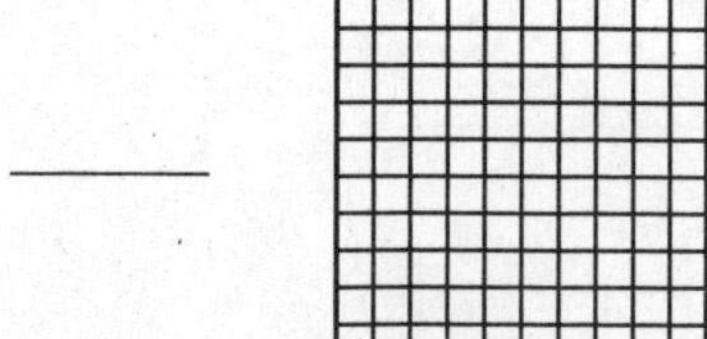

5. Not blue

______ 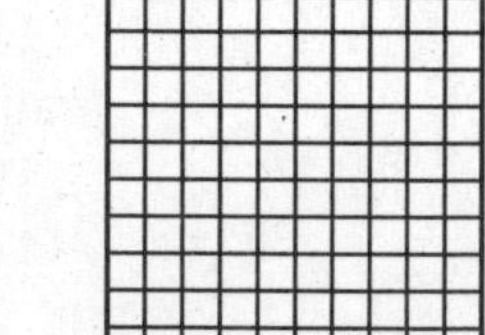

Name ______________________________

Lesson 10

COMMON CORE STANDARD CC.6.RP.3c

Lesson Objective: Write percents as fractions and decimals.

Write Percents as Fractions and Decimals

You can write a percent as a decimal and a fraction.

Write 140% as a decimal and as a fraction in simplest form.

Step 1 Write 140% as a decimal by dividing 140 by 100. This results in the decimal point moving two places to the left.

$140\% = 140 = 1.40$

Step 2 Write 1.40 as a fraction by writing the 1 as a whole number and the decimal as a fraction. The 40 after the decimal point represents 40 hundredths. So, write 40 in the numerator and 100 in the denominator.

$1.40 = 1\frac{40}{100}$

Step 3 Simplify.

$1\frac{40}{100} = 1\frac{2}{5}$

So, $140\% = 1.40 = 1\frac{2}{5}$.

Write the percent as a decimal and as a fraction in simplest form.

1. 75% ____________
2. 44% ____________
3. 128% ____________
4. 5% ____________
5. 464% ____________
6. 38% ____________
7. 7% ____________
8. 0.6% ____________
9. 234% ____________
10. 0.9% ____________
11. 72% ____________
12. 8% ____________

1. Lowell works weekends at an ice cream parlor. Last week, his boss gave him a 3% raise. What is this number written as a decimal?

Ⓐ 0.003
Ⓑ 0.03
Ⓒ 0.3
Ⓓ 3.0

2. From 1997 to 2009, the number of households in the United States using the Internet increased about 346%. Which fraction is equivalent to 346%?

Ⓐ $\frac{346}{1,000}$
Ⓑ $\frac{36}{100}$
Ⓒ $\frac{173}{50}$
Ⓓ $\frac{173}{5}$

3. A cell phone manufacturer found that, on average, 1.25% of every 100 cell phones produced by the company's factory had a defective antenna. What decimal is equivalent to 1.25%?

Ⓐ 0.0125
Ⓑ 0.125
Ⓒ 1.25
Ⓓ 12.5

4. Ava went to a restaurant for dinner and left an 18% tip for her server. What is this number written as a decimal?

Ⓐ 0.18
Ⓑ 1.8
Ⓒ 18
Ⓓ 180

Problem Solving REAL WORLD

5. An online bookstore sells 0.8% of its books to foreign customers. What fraction of the books are sold to foreign customers?

____

6. In Mr. Klein's class, 40% of the students are boys. What decimal represents the portion of the students that are girls?

____

Name ______________________________

Lesson 11

COMMON CORE STANDARD CC.6.RP.3c

Lesson Objective: Write fractions and decimals as percents.

Write Fractions and Decimals as Percents

You can write fractions and decimals as percents.

To write a decimal as a percent, multiply the decimal by 100 and write the percent symbol.

0.073 = 7.3% ← To multiply by 100, move the decimal point two places to the right.

To write a fraction as a percent, divide the numerator by the denominator. Then write the decimal as a percent.

To write $\frac{3}{8}$ as a percent, first divide 3 by 8.

$$\begin{array}{r} 0.375 \\ 8\overline{)3.000} \\ -24 \\ \hline 60 \\ -56 \\ \hline 40 \\ -40 \\ \hline 0 \end{array}$$

So, $\frac{3}{8}$ = 0.375.

0.375 = 37.5% ← To write 0.375 as a percent, multiply by 100 and write the percent symbol.

Write the decimal or fraction as a percent.

1. 0.45 ______
2. 0.6 ______
3. 2.34 ______
4. $\frac{7}{8}$ ______
5. $\frac{19}{50}$ ______
6. 0.03 ______
7. $1\frac{11}{16}$ ______
8. $\frac{51}{10}$ ______

Name ______________________________

Lesson 11

CC.6.RP.3c

1. In a litter, 2 out of 8 kittens are male. What percent of the kittens in the litter are female?

   (A) 25%

   (B) 28%

   (C) 75%

   (D) 82%

2. How is the decimal 1.7 expressed as a percent?

   (A) 0.17%

   (B) 1.7%

   (C) 17%

   (D) 170%

3. The Totally Clean Toothpaste Company advertises that $\frac{9}{10}$ of all people surveyed prefer their toothpaste. What percent of the people surveyed prefer Totally Clean Toothpaste?

   (A) 900%

   (B) 90%

   (C) 9%

   (D) 0.9%

4. On Friday, 0.325 of the students in Keisha's math class were absent. What percent of the students were absent?

   (A) 0.325%

   (B) 3.25%

   (C) 32.5%

   (D) 325%

Problem Solving REAL WORLD

5. According to the U.S. Census Bureau, $\frac{3}{25}$ of all adults in the United States visited a zoo in 2007. What percent of all adults in the United States visited a zoo in 2007?

   ____

6. A bag contains red and blue marbles. Given that $\frac{17}{20}$ of the marbles are red, what percent of the marbles are blue?

   ____

Name ______________________________

Lesson 12

COMMON CORE STANDARD CC.6.RP.3c

Lesson Objective: Find a percent of a quantity.

Percent of a Quantity

You can use ratios to write a percent of a quantity.

Find 0.9% of 30.

Step 1 Write the percent as a rate per 100. $0.9\% = \frac{0.9}{100}$

Step 2 Multiply by a fraction equivalent to 1 to get a whole number in the numerator. $\frac{0.9}{100} \times \frac{10}{10} = \frac{9}{1{,}000}$

Step 3 Write the multiplication problem. $\frac{9}{1{,}000} \times 30$

Step 4 Multiply. $\frac{9}{1{,}000} \times 30 = \frac{27}{100} = 0.27$

So, 0.9% of 30 is 0.27.

Find the percent of the quantity.

1. 8% of 90 ________

2. 20% of 80 ________

3. 95% of 340 ________

4. 33% of 28 ________

5. 200% of 8.5 ________

6. 125% of 70 ________

7. 0.25% of 120 ________

8. 0.4% of 50 ________

9. 45% of 70 ________

10. 155% of 30 ________

11. 75% of 124 ________

12. 0.8% of 1,000 ________

13. James correctly answered 85% of the 60 problems on his math test. How many questions did James answer correctly?

____

14. A basketball player missed 25% of her 52 free throws. How many free throws did the basketball player make?

____

Name ___________________________

1. In a crate of 1,500 light bulbs, it is estimated that 4% are defective. How many of the 1,500 light bulbs in the crate are likely to be defective?

   Ⓐ 600
   Ⓑ 400
   Ⓒ 60
   Ⓓ 40

2. Carly is a catcher on the school softball team. By the end of the season, she had played in 45% of the 40 games the team played. In how many games did Carly **not** play?

   Ⓐ 24
   Ⓑ 22
   Ⓒ 20
   Ⓓ 18

3. Malik gets an allowance of $9 each week from his parents for doing chores around the house. He saves 25% of his allowance. How much does Malik save each week?

   Ⓐ $0.02
   Ⓑ $0.23
   Ⓒ $2.25
   Ⓓ $22.50

4. In a recent survey about the types of transportation used for vacation, 36% of the 200 people surveyed chose airplanes, 53% chose automobiles, 2% chose trains, and the remainder chose boats. How many people chose boats?

   Ⓐ 182
   Ⓑ 140
   Ⓒ 72
   Ⓓ 18

Problem Solving REAL WORLD

5. The recommended daily amount of vitamin C for children 9 to 13 years old is 45 mg. A serving of a juice drink contains 60% of the recommended amount. How much vitamin C does the juice drink contain?

   ____

6. During a 60-minute television program, 25% of the time is used for commercials and 5% of the time is used for the opening and closing credits. How many minutes remain for the program itself?

   ____

Name ______________________________

Lesson 13

COMMON CORE STANDARD CC.6.RP.3c

Lesson Objective: Solve percent problems by applying the strategy *use a model.*

Problem Solving • Percents

Use a model to solve the percent problem.

Lucia is driving to visit her parents, who live 240 miles away from her house. She has already driven 15% of the distance. How many miles does she still have to drive?

Read the Problem	Solve the Problem
What do I need to find? ______________________ ______________________ ______________________	Use a bar model to help. Draw a bar to represent the total distance. Then draw a bar that represents the distance driven plus the distance left. 100% total distance: 240 miles distance driven: ? 15%
What information do I need to use? ______________________ ______________________ ______________________	The model shows that 100% = ______ miles,
How will I use the information? ______________________ ______________________ ______________________ ______________________	so 1% of 240 = $\frac{240}{100}$ = ______ miles. 15% of 240 = 15 × ______ = ______ So, Lucia has already driven ______ miles. She still has to drive 240 − ______ = ______ miles.

1. At a deli, 56 sandwiches were sold during lunchtime. Twenty-five percent of the sandwiches sold were tuna salad sandwiches. How many of the sandwiches sold were not tuna salad?

____

2. Mr. Brown bought a TV for $450. He has already paid 60% of the purchase price. How much has he already paid and how much does he have left to pay?

____

Name ______________________________

1. Ricardo has saved 83% of the money he needs to buy a new skateboard that costs $150. How much **more** does he need to save to buy the skateboard?

   Ⓐ $25.50
   Ⓑ $67
   Ⓒ $83
   Ⓓ $124.50

2. Deanna has 80 books in her collection. If 60% of the books are fiction, how many of the books are nonfiction?

   Ⓐ 60
   Ⓑ 48
   Ⓒ 32
   Ⓓ 20

3. Michele has visited 30 lighthouses in Virginia and Maryland. Twenty percent of the lighthouses were in Virginia. How many **more** lighthouses did she visit in Maryland than in Virginia?

   Ⓐ 6
   Ⓑ 18
   Ⓒ 20
   Ⓓ 24

4. Quincy is using 320 pieces of stone tile to make a red, white, and blue mosaic. If 20% of the pieces are blue and 35% are white, how many pieces are red?

   Ⓐ 64
   Ⓑ 112
   Ⓒ 144
   Ⓓ 176

Problem Solving REAL WORLD

5. Of 450 lunches sold at school on Thursday, 40% were hamburgers and the rest were pizza. How many **more** pizza lunches were sold than hamburgers? Explain how you found your answer.

____

____

____

____

____

____

Name ______________________________

Lesson 14

COMMON CORE STANDARD CC.6.RP.3c

Lesson Objective: Find the whole given a part and the percent.

Find the Whole From a Percent

You can use equivalent ratios to find the whole, given a part and the percent.

54 is 60% of what number?

Step 1 Write the relationship among the percent, part, and whole. The percent is 60%. The part is 54. The whole is unknown.

$$\text{percent} = \frac{\text{part}}{\text{whole}}$$

$$60\% = \frac{54}{■}$$

Step 2 Write the percent as a ratio.

$$\frac{60}{100} = \frac{54}{■}$$

Step 3 Simplify the known ratio.

- Find the greatest common factor (GCF) of the numerator and denominator.

$$60 = \mathbf{2} \times \mathbf{2} \times 3 \times \mathbf{5}$$
$$100 = \mathbf{2} \times \mathbf{2} \times \mathbf{5} \times 5 \longrightarrow \text{GCF} = \mathbf{2} \times \mathbf{2} \times \mathbf{5} = 20$$

- Divide both the numerator and denominator by the GCF.

$$\frac{60 \div 20}{100 \div 20} = \frac{54}{■}$$

$$\frac{3}{5} = \frac{54}{■}$$

Step 4 Write an equivalent ratio.

- Look at the numerators. *Think:* 3 × 18 = 54
- Multiply the denominator by 18 to find the whole.

$$\frac{3 \times \mathbf{18}}{5 \times \mathbf{18}} = \frac{54}{■}$$

$$\frac{54}{90} = \frac{54}{■}$$

So, 54 is 60% of 90.

Find the unknown value.

1. 12 is 40% of ______
2. 15 is 25% of ______
3. 24 is 20% of ______
4. 36 is 50% of ______
5. 4 is 80% of ______
6. 12 is 15% of ______
7. 36 is 90% of ______
8. 12 is 75% of ______
9. 27 is 30% of ______

Name ______________________________

Lesson 14
CC.6.RP.3c

1. 9 is 15% of what number?

Ⓐ 24
Ⓑ 60
Ⓒ 85
Ⓓ 135

2. A train is traveling from Orlando, Florida to Atlanta, Georgia. So far, it has traveled 75% of the distance, or 330 miles. How far is the train ride from Orlando to Atlanta?

Ⓐ 247 miles
Ⓑ 255 miles
Ⓒ 405 miles
Ⓓ 440 miles

3. Carmen has saved 80% of the money she needs to buy a new video game. If she has saved $36, how much does the video game cost?

Ⓐ $28.80
Ⓑ $45
Ⓒ $63.80
Ⓓ $80

4. The sixth graders at Amir's school voted for the location of their class trip. The table shows the results.

Class Trip Votes

Location	Percent
History museum	25%
Art museum	35%
Aquarium	40%

If 126 students voted for going to the art museum, how many sixth graders are at Amir's school?

Ⓐ 161
Ⓑ 315
Ⓒ 360
Ⓓ 504

Problem Solving REAL WORLD

5. Michaela is hiking on a weekend camping trip. She has walked 6 miles so far. This is 30% of the total distance. What is the total number of miles she will walk?

____

6. A customer placed an order with a bakery for cupcakes. The baker has completed 37.5% of the order after baking 81 cupcakes. How many cupcakes did the customer order?

____

Name ______________________________

Lesson 15

COMMON CORE STANDARD CC.6.RP.3d

Lesson Objective: Use ratio reasoning to convert from one unit of length to another.

Convert Units of Length

To convert a unit of measure, multiply by a conversion factor. A **conversion factor** is a rate in which the two quantities are equal, but are expressed in different units.

Convert to the given unit. 2,112 ft = ______ mi

Customary Units of Length
1 foot (ft) = 12 inches (in.)
1 yard (yd) = 36 inches
1 yard = 3 feet
1 mile (mi) = 5,280 feet
1 mile = 1,760 yards

Step 1 Choose a conversion factor.

1 mile = 5,280 feet, so use the conversion factor $\frac{1 \text{ mile}}{5{,}280 \text{ feet}}$.

Step 2 Multiply by the conversion factor.

$2{,}112 \text{ ft} \times \frac{1 \text{ mi}}{5{,}280 \text{ ft}} = \frac{2{,}112 \cancel{\text{ft}}}{1} \times \frac{1 \text{ mi}}{5{,}280 \cancel{\text{ft}}} = \frac{2{,}112}{5{,}280} \text{ mi} = \frac{2}{5} \text{ mi}$

So, 2,112 ft = $\frac{2}{5}$ mi.

When converting metric units, move the decimal point to multiply or divide by a power of ten.

14 dm = ______ hm

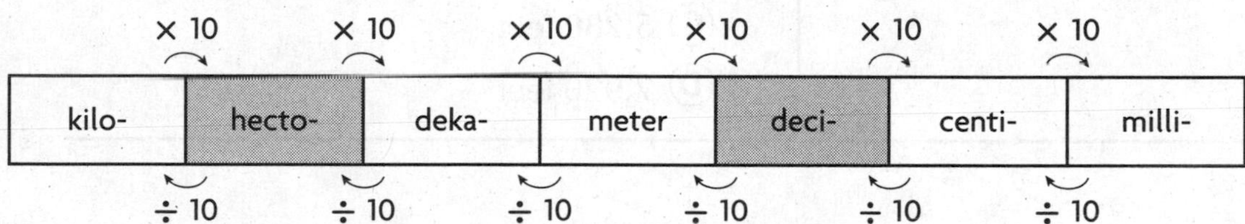

Step 1 Start at the given unit.

Step 2 Move to the unit you are converting to.

Step 3 Move the decimal point that same number of spaces in the same direction. Fill any empty place-value positions with zeros.

So, 14 dm = 0.014 hm.

Convert to the given unit.

1. 4.5 miles = ____________ yards

2. 0.8 hectometers = ____________ millimeters

3. 48 inches = ____________ feet

4. 45 centimeters = ____________ dekameters

Name ______________________________

Lesson 15
CC.6.RP.3d

1. April is making necklaces using beads that are 6 millimeters in diameter. What is the diameter of each bead in centimeters?

Ⓐ 0.6 centimeter
Ⓑ 0.06 centimeter
Ⓒ 0.006 centimeter
Ⓓ 0.0006 centimeter

2. Adam's porch is 8 yards long. What is the length of his porch in inches?

Ⓐ 24 inches
Ⓑ 96 inches
Ⓒ 288 inches
Ⓓ 384 inches

3. Cho ran a race that was 5 kilometers long. What was the length of the race in meters?

Ⓐ 0.005 meter
Ⓑ 50 meters
Ⓒ 500 meters
Ⓓ 5,000 meters

4. The distance from Caleb's house to his school is 1.5 miles. What is the distance in feet?

Ⓐ 1,760 feet
Ⓑ 2,640 feet
Ⓒ 5,280 feet
Ⓓ 7,920 feet

Problem Solving REAL WORLD

5. The giant swallowtail is the largest butterfly in the United States. Its wingspan can be as large as 16 centimeters. What is the maximum wingspan in millimeters?

____

6. The 102nd floor of the Sears Tower in Chicago is the highest occupied floor. It is 1,431 feet above the ground. How many yards above the ground is the 102nd floor?

____

Name ______________________________

COMMON CORE STANDARD CC.6.RP.3d

Lesson Objective: Use ratio reasoning to convert from one unit of capacity to another.

Convert Units of Capacity

Capacity is the measure of the amount that a container can hold. When converting customary units, multiply the initial measurement by a conversion factor.

Convert to the given unit. 35 c = ______ qt

Customary Units of Capacity
8 fluid ounces (fl oz) = 1 cup (c)
2 cups = 1 pint (pt)
2 pints = 1 quart (qt)
4 cups = 1 quart
4 quarts = 1 gallon (gal)

Step 1 Choose a conversion factor.

1 quart = 4 cups, so use the conversion factor $\frac{1 \text{ quart}}{4 \text{ cups}}$.

Step 2 Multiply by the conversion factor.

$35 \text{ c} \times \frac{1 \text{ qt}}{4 \text{ c}} = \frac{35 \cancel{\text{c}}}{1} \times \frac{1 \text{ qt}}{4 \cancel{\text{c}}} = \frac{35}{4} \text{ qt} = 8\frac{3}{4} \text{ qt}$

You can rename the fractional part using the smaller unit.

$8\frac{3}{4}$ quarts = 8 quarts, 3 cups

So, 35 c = $8\frac{3}{4}$ qt, or 8 qt, 3 c.

When converting metric units, move the decimal point to multiply or divide by a power of ten.

26 cL = ______ hL

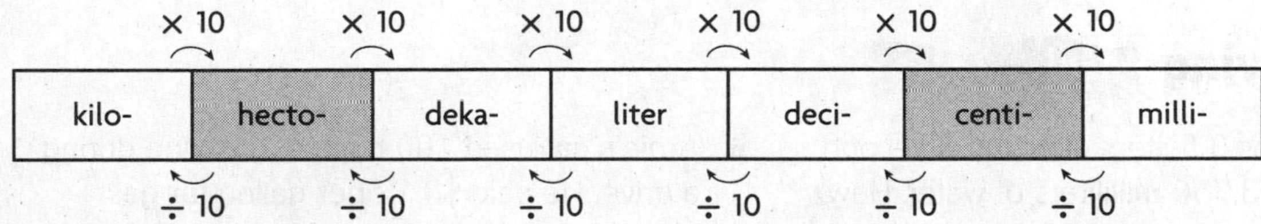

Step 1 Start at the given unit.

Step 2 Move to the unit you are converting to.

Step 3 Move the decimal point that same number of spaces in the same direction. Fill any empty place-value positions with zeros.

So, 26 cL = 0.0026 hL.

Convert to the given unit.

1. 0.72 kiloliters = ____________ deciliters

2. 78 qt = ______ gal, ______ qt

3. 52 liters = ____________ hectoliters

4. 5 pints = __________ cups

Name ________________________________

1. Jason made 36 pints of lemonade for the class picnic. How many gallons of lemonade did he make?

(A) 9 gallons
(B) 6 gallons
(C) $4\frac{1}{2}$ gallons
(D) $2\frac{1}{2}$ gallons

2. Chandelle filled her bathtub with 15 gallons of water. How many pints of water did she put in the tub?

(A) 30 pints
(B) 60 pints
(C) 90 pints
(D) 120 pints

3. Edmund has a pitcher that holds 2 quarts of liquid. How many cups can the pitcher hold?

(A) 4 cups
(B) 8 cups
(C) 16 cups
(D) 32 cups

4. Mrs. Ruiz bought **six** 2-liter bottles of juice. How many dekaliters of juice did she buy?

(A) 0.012 dekaliter
(B) 0.12 dekaliter
(C) 1.2 dekaliters
(D) 120 dekaliters

Problem Solving REAL WORLD

5. A bottle contains 3.5 liters of water. A second bottle contains 3,750 milliliters of water. How many more milliliters are in the larger bottle than in the smaller bottle?

6. Arnie's car used 100 cups of gasoline during a drive. He paid $3.12 per gallon for gas. How much did the gas cost?

____

Name ___________________________

Lesson 17

COMMON CORE STANDARD CC.6.RP.3d

Lesson Objective: Use ratio reasoning to convert from one unit of weight or mass to another.

Convert Units of Weight and Mass

In the customary system, weight is the measure of the heaviness of an object. When converting customary units, multiply the initial measurement by a conversion factor.

Convert to the given unit. 19 lb = ______ oz

Customary Units of Weight
1 pound (lb) = 16 ounces (oz)
1 ton (T) = 2,000 pounds

Step 1 Choose a conversion factor.

16 ounces = 1 pound, so use the conversion factor $\frac{16 \text{ ounces}}{1 \text{ pound}}$.

Step 2 Multiply by the conversion factor.

$19 \text{ lb} \times \frac{16 \text{ oz}}{1 \text{ lb}} = \frac{19 \cancel{\text{lb}}}{1} \times \frac{16 \text{ oz}}{1 \cancel{\text{lb}}} = \frac{304}{1} \text{ oz} = 304 \text{ oz}$

So, 19 lb = 304 oz.

In the metric system, mass is the measure of the amount of matter in an object. When converting metric units, move the decimal point to multiply or divide by a power of ten.

3.1 dag = ______ mg

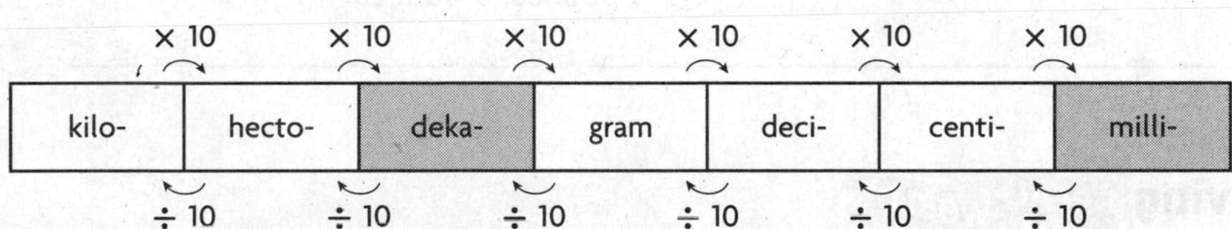

Step 1 Start at the given unit.

Step 2 Move to the unit you are converting to.

Step 3 Move the decimal point that same number of spaces in the same direction. Fill any empty place-value positions with zeros.

So, 3.1 dag = 31,000 mg.

Convert to the given unit.

1. 43.2 dg = ____________ hg
2. 4,500 pounds = ______ tons
3. 3.5 grams = __________ milligrams
4. 3 pounds = __________ ounces

Name ______________________________

1. Mr. Connell's car weighs 1.5 tons. What is the weight of his car in pounds?

   Ⓐ 2,000 pounds
   Ⓑ 2,500 pounds
   Ⓒ 3,000 pounds
   Ⓓ 4,000 pounds

2. How many grams are equivalent to 102 milligrams?

   Ⓐ 10.2 grams
   Ⓑ 1.02 grams
   Ⓒ 0.102 gram
   Ⓓ 0.0102 gram

3. Lonnie has a box of cereal with a mass of 347 grams. What is the mass in centigrams?

   Ⓐ 3.47 centigrams
   Ⓑ 34.7 centigrams
   Ⓒ 3,470 centigrams
   Ⓓ 34,700 centigrams

4. Li Mei is mailing a package. The package weighs 35 ounces. What is the weight of the package in pounds and ounces?

   Ⓐ 2 pounds
   Ⓑ 2 pounds, 3 ounces
   Ⓒ 3 pounds, 5 ounces
   Ⓓ 4 pounds, 3 ounces

Problem Solving REAL WORLD

5. Maggie bought 52 ounces of swordfish selling for $6.92 per pound. What was the total cost?

____

6. Three bunches of grapes have masses of 1,000 centigrams, 1,000 decigrams, and 1,000 grams, respectively. What is the total combined mass of the grapes in kilograms?

____

Name ___________________________

Lesson 18

COMMON CORE STANDARD CC.6.RP.3d

Lesson Objective: Transform units to solve problems.

Transform Units

To solve problems involving different units, use the relationship among units to help you set up a multiplication problem.

Green peppers are on sale for $1.80 per pound. How much would 2.5 pounds of green peppers cost?

Step 1 Identify the units.

You know two quantities: pounds of peppers and total cost per pound. You want to know the cost of 2.5 pounds.

$$\$1.80 \text{ per lb} = \frac{\$1.80}{1 \text{ lb}}$$

Step 2 Determine the relationship among the units.

The answer needs to be in dollars. Set up the multiplication problem so that pounds will divide out.

$$\frac{\$1.80}{1 \text{ lb}} \times 2.5 \text{ lb} = \frac{\$1.80}{1 \cancel{\text{lb}}} \times \frac{2.5 \cancel{\text{lb}}}{1} = \$4.50$$

Step 3 Use the relationship.

So, 2.5 pounds of peppers will cost $4.50.

Solve.

1. If 2 bags of cherries cost $5.50, how much do 7 bags cost?

   a. What are you trying to find?

   ____

   b. Set up the problem.

   ____

   c. What is the cost of 7 bags?

   ____

2. The area of a living room is 24 square yards. If the width is 12 feet, what is the length of the living room in yards?

   a. What is the width in yards?

   ____

   b. Set up the problem.

   ____

   c. What is the length in yards?

   ____

Name ______________________________

Lesson 18
CC.6.RP.3d

1. Sofia knitted a rectangular afghan that has an area of 24 square feet. If the length of the afghan is 2 yards, what is the width in feet?

   Ⓐ 12 feet
   Ⓑ 8 feet
   Ⓒ 6 feet
   Ⓓ 4 feet

2. A house painter uses 6 gallons of paint per day. How many gallons does the painter use in a 5-day workweek?

   Ⓐ 11 gallons
   Ⓑ 16 gallons
   Ⓒ 24 gallons
   Ⓓ 30 gallons

3. A rectangular football field, including both end zones, is 120 yards long. The field has an area of 57,600 square feet. What is the width of the field in feet?

   Ⓐ 480 feet
   Ⓑ 360 feet
   Ⓒ 160 feet
   Ⓓ 53 feet

4. Lucy's car gets 32 miles per gallon of gasoline. How many miles can she drive on 4 gallons of gas?

   Ⓐ 256 miles
   Ⓑ 128 miles
   Ⓒ 24 miles
   Ⓓ 8 miles

Problem Solving REAL WORLD

5. Green grapes are on sale for $2.50 a pound. How much will 9 pounds cost?

   ____

6. A car travels 32 miles for each gallon of gas. How many gallons of gas does it need to travel 192 miles?

   ____

Name ______________________________

Lesson 19

COMMON CORE STANDARD CC.6.RP.3d

Lesson Objective: Solve problems involving distance, rate, and time by applying the strategy *use a formula.*

Problem Solving • Distance, Rate, and Time Formulas

Use a formula to solve the problem.

A bug crawls at a rate of 2 feet per minute. How long will it take the bug to crawl 25 feet?

Read the Problem	Solve the Problem
What do I need to find? I need to find ____________________ ____________________.	Write the appropriate formula. $t = d \div r$
What information do I need to use? I need to use the ________ the bug crawls and the ________ at which the bug crawls.	Substitute the values for d and r. $t =$ ______ ft $\div \frac{2\text{ ft}}{1\text{ min}}$
How will I use the information? First I will choose the formula ________ because I need to find time. Next I will substitute ________ for d and ________ for r. Then I will ________ to find the time.	Rewrite the division as multiplication by the reciprocal. $t = \frac{25\text{ ft}}{1} \times \frac{1\text{ min}}{2\text{ ft}} =$ ______ min

1. A family drives for 3 hours at an average rate of 57 miles per hour. How far does the family travel?

____

2. A train traveled 283.5 miles in 3.5 hours. What was the train's average rate of speed?

____

Name ______________________________

1. Sunni is riding a raft down a stream that is moving at a rate of 75 feet per minute. How far downstream does she travel in 5 minutes?

   Ⓐ 750 feet Ⓒ 225 feet
   Ⓑ 375 feet Ⓓ 15 feet

2. A sprinting cheetah covered a distance of 518 meters in 18.5 seconds. How fast was the cheetah running?

   Ⓐ 30 meters per second
   Ⓑ 28 meters per second
   Ⓒ 25 meters per second
   Ⓓ 22 meters per second

3. Tamika drove $142\frac{1}{2}$ miles at a rate of 57 miles per hour. For how long was Tamika driving?

   Ⓐ 1 hour Ⓒ 2 hours
   Ⓑ $1\frac{1}{2}$ hours Ⓓ $2\frac{1}{2}$ hours

4. The table shows data from four cyclists during a training session.

Training Session

Cyclist	Distance (in miles)	Start Time	End Time
Alisha	$35\frac{3}{4}$	2:30 P.M.	5:15 P.M.
Jose	$38\frac{1}{4}$	1:30 P.M.	4:30 P.M.
Raul	$31\frac{1}{4}$	1:50 P.M.	4:20 P.M.
Ruthie	$21\frac{3}{4}$	4:45 P.M.	6:15 P.M.

How fast did Raul travel in miles per hour?

   Ⓐ $12\frac{1}{2}$ miles per hour
   Ⓑ $12\frac{3}{4}$ miles per hour
   Ⓒ 13 miles per hour
   Ⓓ $14\frac{1}{2}$ miles per hour

Problem Solving REAL WORLD

5. The table shows data from a school exercise program. If Malinda jogs at the target rate, how far will she travel? Explain how you know.

Exercise Program Information

Type	Target Rate (kilometers per hour)	Start Time	End Time
Walking	3.5	8:30 A.M.	10:00 A.M.
Jogging	8.5	7:15 A.M.	8:30 A.M.
Biking	19.5	11:50 A.M.	2:05 P.M.

____

____

____

____

____

Name ______________________________

Lesson 20

COMMON CORE STANDARD CC.6.NS.1

Lesson Objective: Use a model to show division of fractions.

Model Fraction Division

Use fraction strips to find $\frac{1}{2} \div 3$.

Step 1 $\frac{1}{2} \div 3$ can mean divide $\frac{1}{2}$ into 3 equal parts and find how much is in each part. Find a fraction strip such that 3 of that strip make the same length as a single $\frac{1}{2}$-strip.

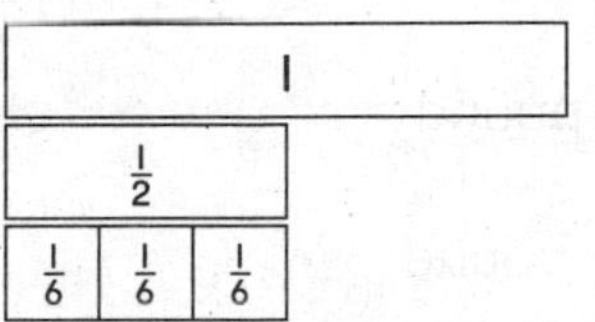

Step 2 There are three $\frac{1}{6}$-strips in $\frac{1}{2}$, so $\frac{1}{2} \div 3 = \frac{1}{6}$.

Use the model to find the quotient.

1. $\frac{2}{3} \div 6 =$ __________

$\frac{1}{3}$			$\frac{1}{3}$		
$\frac{1}{9}$	$\frac{1}{9}$	$\frac{1}{9}$	$\frac{1}{9}$	$\frac{1}{9}$	$\frac{1}{9}$

2. $\frac{1}{4} \div 2 =$ __________

$\frac{1}{4}$	
$\frac{1}{8}$	$\frac{1}{8}$

Draw a model with fraction strips. Then find the quotient.

3. $\frac{3}{4} \div 6$

$\frac{3}{4} \div 6 =$ __________

4. $\frac{2}{3} \div 4$

$\frac{2}{3} \div 4 =$ __________

Name ____________________

1. Monique made $\frac{5}{8}$ pound of trail mix and divided the mix into 4 equal portions. What is the weight of each portion?

Ⓐ $\frac{1}{8}$ pound
Ⓑ $\frac{5}{32}$ pound
Ⓒ $1\frac{1}{4}$ pounds
Ⓓ $2\frac{1}{2}$ pounds

2. Sung Lee studied for 4 hours. If he studies $\frac{2}{3}$ of an hour for each class, how many classes does he have?

Ⓐ 2
Ⓑ 3
Ⓒ 6
Ⓓ 8

3. Joanne has $\frac{9}{10}$ yard of fabric that she wants to divide into 3 equal pieces. How long should each piece be?

Ⓐ $\frac{3}{10}$ yard
Ⓑ $\frac{10}{27}$ yard
Ⓒ $\frac{3}{5}$ yard
Ⓓ $\frac{10}{13}$ yard

4. Jayson takes a total of 5 hours of swimming lessons per week. If each lesson is $\frac{5}{6}$ of an hour, how many lessons does he take per week?

Ⓐ 5
Ⓑ 6
Ⓒ 10
Ⓓ 11

Problem Solving REAL WORLD

5. Mrs. Jennings has $\frac{3}{4}$ gallon of paint for an art project. She plans to divide the paint equally into jars. If she puts $\frac{1}{8}$ gallon of paint into each jar, how many jars will she use?

____

6. If one jar of glue weighs $\frac{1}{12}$ pound, how many jars can Rickie get from $\frac{2}{3}$ pound of glue?

____

Name ______________________

Lesson 21

COMMON CORE STANDARD CC.6.NS.1

Lesson Objective: Use compatible numbers to estimate quotients of fractions and mixed numbers.

Estimate Quotients

You can use compatible numbers to help you estimate the quotient of fractions and mixed numbers.

Example 1: Estimate $19\frac{5}{7} \div 3\frac{4}{5}$ using compatible numbers.

Step 1 Find whole numbers that are close to $19\frac{5}{7}$ and $3\frac{4}{5}$ that are easy to divide mentally.

Think: $19\frac{5}{7}$ is close to 20, and $3\frac{4}{5}$ is close to 4.

Step 2 Rewrite the problem and then divide: $20 \div 4 = 5$

So, the estimated quotient is 5.

Example 2: Estimate $6\frac{1}{5} \div \frac{3}{8}$ using compatible numbers.

Step 1 Rewrite the problem using compatible numbers. $6 \div \frac{1}{2}$

Step 2 Divide. Think: How many halves are in 6 wholes? 12

So, the estimated quotient is 12.

Estimate using compatible numbers.

1. $8\frac{1}{6} \div 1\frac{7}{8}$

a. Rewrite the problem using compatible numbers.

____

b. What is the estimated quotient?

____

2. $11\frac{7}{9} \div \frac{4}{10}$

a. Rewrite the problem using compatible numbers.

____

b. What is the estimated quotient?

____

Name ______________________________

Lesson 21
CC.6.NS.1

1. Shing estimates that it takes him $\frac{4}{5}$ hour to mow a yard. Which is the **best** estimate of the number of yards he can mow in $4\frac{1}{4}$ hours?

   Ⓐ 8
   Ⓑ 6
   Ⓒ 4
   Ⓓ 2

2. Melinda has $24\frac{1}{3}$ feet of rope to cut into jump ropes that are each $8\frac{1}{6}$ feet long. Which is the **best** estimate of the number of jump ropes she can cut?

   Ⓐ 3
   Ⓑ 5
   Ⓒ 10
   Ⓓ 16

3. A car travels $83\frac{7}{10}$ miles on $2\frac{1}{4}$ gallons of fuel. Which is the **best** estimate of the number of miles the car travels on one gallon of fuel?

   Ⓐ 38 miles
   Ⓑ 42 miles
   Ⓒ 62 miles
   Ⓓ 84 miles

4. Rama has $14\frac{4}{5}$ pounds of birdseed to fill bird feeders. Each feeder holds $2\frac{7}{8}$ pounds of birdseed. About how many bird feeders can she fill?

   Ⓐ 3
   Ⓑ 4
   Ⓒ 5
   Ⓓ 6

Problem Solving REAL WORLD

5. Estimate the number of pieces Sharon will have if she divides $15\frac{1}{3}$ yards of fabric into $4\frac{4}{5}$-yard lengths.

   ____

6. Estimate the number of $\frac{1}{2}$-quart containers Ethan can fill from a container with $8\frac{7}{8}$ quarts of water.

   ____

Name ______________________________

Lesson 22

COMMON CORE STANDARD CC.6.NS.1

Lesson Objective: Divide fractions.

Divide Fractions

You can multiply by reciprocals to divide fractions.

Write the reciprocal of $\frac{1}{7}$.

To find the reciprocal of a number, switch the numerator and the denominator.

$\frac{1}{7} \to \frac{7}{1}$

Since $\frac{1}{7} \times \frac{7}{1} = 1$, the reciprocal of $\frac{1}{7}$ is $\frac{7}{1}$.

Find the quotient of $\frac{4}{5} \div \frac{1}{4}$. Write it in simplest form.

Step 1 Find the reciprocal of the second fraction.

Think: $\frac{1}{4} \times \frac{4}{1} = 1$.

The reciprocal of $\frac{1}{4}$ is $\frac{4}{1}$.

Step 2 Write a multiplication problem using the reciprocal of the second fraction.

$\frac{4}{5} \div \frac{1}{4} = \frac{4}{5} \times \frac{4}{1}$

Step 3 Multiply.

$\frac{4}{5} \times \frac{4}{1} = \frac{16}{5}$

Step 4 Simplify.

$\frac{16}{5} = 3\frac{1}{5}$

So, $\frac{4}{5} \div \frac{1}{4} = 3\frac{1}{5}$.

Find the quotient. Write it in simplest form.

1. $\frac{5}{6} \div \frac{2}{3}$ ____________

2. $\frac{3}{8} \div \frac{1}{6}$ ____________

3. $\frac{2}{3} \div \frac{1}{2}$ ____________

4. $6 \div \frac{2}{3}$ ____________

5. $12 \div \frac{3}{4}$ ____________

6. $\frac{5}{8} \div \frac{1}{2}$ ____________

7. $\frac{7}{10} \div \frac{2}{5}$ ____________

8. $\frac{5}{6} \div \frac{1}{6}$ ____________

Name ______________________________

Lesson 22
CC.6.NS.1

1. Rupali has a piece of string that is $\frac{5}{8}$ yard long. She wants to cut the string into 4 equal pieces. How long should each piece be?

Ⓐ $\frac{2}{5}$ yard

Ⓑ $\frac{5}{32}$ yard

Ⓒ $\frac{1}{8}$ yard

Ⓓ $\frac{9}{12}$ yard

2. Anna has $\frac{4}{5}$ pound of cookies. She places the cookies into bags that hold $\frac{1}{10}$ pound each. How many bags does she fill?

Ⓐ 2

Ⓑ 3

Ⓒ 8

Ⓓ 12

3. Robert bought $\frac{3}{4}$ pound of grapes and divided them into 6 equal portions. What is the weight of each portion?

Ⓐ 8 pounds

Ⓑ $4\frac{1}{2}$ pounds

Ⓒ $\frac{2}{5}$ pound

Ⓓ $\frac{1}{8}$ pound

4. Mrs. Ruiz has $\frac{11}{12}$ yard of string to hang 3 banners. She uses the same length of string to hang each banner. How much string does she use for each banner?

Ⓐ $\frac{11}{12}$ yard

Ⓑ $\frac{6}{11}$ yard

Ⓒ $\frac{4}{11}$ yard

Ⓓ $\frac{11}{36}$ yard

Problem Solving REAL WORLD

5. Rick knows that 1 cup of glue weighs $\frac{1}{18}$ pound. He has $\frac{2}{3}$ pound of glue. How many cups of glue does he have?

____

6. Mrs. Jennings had $\frac{5}{7}$ gallon of paint. She gave $\frac{1}{7}$ gallon each to some students. How many students received paint if Mrs. Jennings gave away all the paint?

____

Name ______________________________

Lesson 23

COMMON CORE STANDARD CC.6.NS.1

Lesson Objective: Use a model to show division of mixed numbers.

Model Mixed Number Division

Use pattern blocks to find the quotient of $3\frac{1}{2} \div \frac{1}{6}$.

Step 1 Model 3 with 3 hexagon blocks.

Model $\frac{1}{2}$ with 1 trapezoid block.

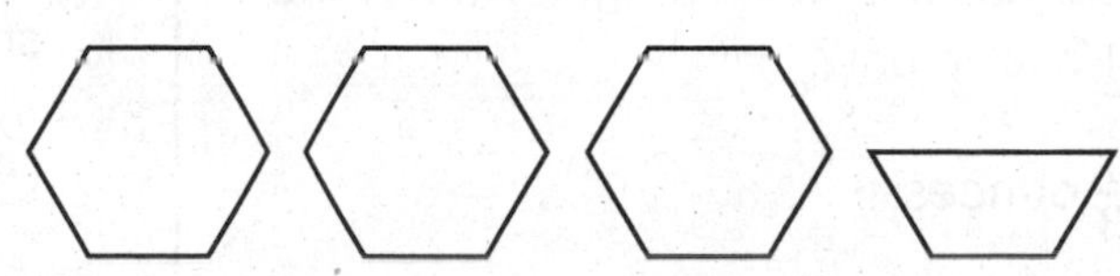

Step 2 Find a block that shows $\frac{1}{6}$.

6 triangle blocks are equal to 1 hexagon.

So, a triangle block shows $\frac{1}{6}$.

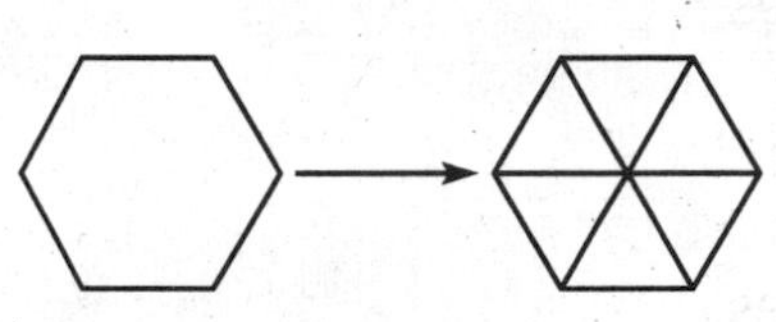

Step 3 Cover your model with triangle blocks.

Count the triangles.
There are 21 triangle blocks.

So, $3\frac{1}{2} \div \frac{1}{6} = 21$.

Use the model to find the quotient.

1. $2\frac{1}{3} \div \frac{1}{6} =$ __________

2. $2\frac{1}{2} \div \frac{1}{2} =$ __________

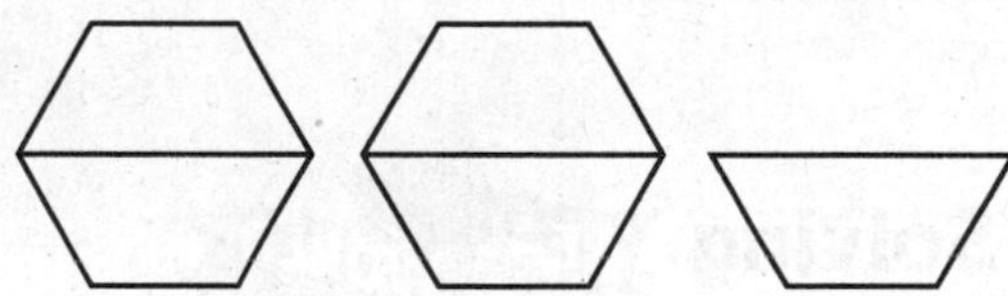

Use pattern blocks to find the quotient. Then draw the model.

3. $1\frac{1}{2} \div \frac{1}{6} =$ __________

4. $1\frac{2}{3} \div \frac{1}{3} =$ __________

Name ______________________________

Lesson 23
CC.6.NS.1

1. A box of energy bars contains 8 bars. The total weight of the bars is $10\frac{2}{3}$ ounces. If each bar has the same weight, what is the weight of one bar?

   (A) $1\frac{1}{3}$ ounces

   (B) $1\frac{2}{3}$ ounces

   (C) $2\frac{2}{3}$ ounces

   (D) $6\frac{2}{3}$ ounces

2. City workers are repaving a street that is $1\frac{1}{2}$ miles long. If they repave $\frac{1}{4}$ mile per day, how long will it take to repave the entire street?

   (A) 6 days

   (B) 4 days

   (C) 3 days

   (D) 2 days

3. Mr. Spencer has $7\frac{1}{5}$ liters of juice. He wants to pour equal amounts of juice into 3 punch bowls. How many liters of juice should he pour into each bowl?

   (A) $1\frac{4}{5}$ liters

   (B) $2\frac{2}{5}$ liters

   (C) $2\frac{4}{5}$ liters

   (D) $3\frac{1}{5}$ liters

4. Clemente has $5\frac{1}{3}$ yards of wood to construct shelves. He will use a $\frac{2}{3}$-yard piece of wood for each shelf. How many shelves can he make?

   (A) 12

   (B) 10

   (C) 8

   (D) 6

Problem Solving REAL WORLD

5. Marty has $2\frac{4}{5}$ quarts of juice. He pours the same amount of juice into 2 bottles. How much does he pour into each bottle?

   ____

6. How many $\frac{1}{3}$-pound servings are in $4\frac{2}{3}$ pounds of cheese?

   ____

Name ________________________________

Lesson 24
COMMON CORE STANDARD CC.6.NS.1
Lesson Objective: Divide mixed numbers.

Divide Mixed Numbers

To divide mixed numbers, first rewrite the mixed numbers as fractions greater than 1. Then multiply the dividend by the reciprocal of the divisor.

Find the quotient of $7\frac{1}{2} \div 2\frac{1}{2}$. Write it in simplest form.

Step 1 Write the mixed numbers as fractions. $7\frac{1}{2} \div 2\frac{1}{2} = \frac{15}{2} \div \frac{5}{2}$

Step 2 Use the reciprocal of the divisor to write a multiplication problem. $= \frac{15}{2} \times \frac{2}{5}$

Step 3 Simplify. Look for common factors in the numerators and denominators. Divide out the common factors. $= \frac{\overset{3}{\cancel{15}}}{\underset{1}{\cancel{2}}} \times \frac{\overset{1}{\cancel{2}}}{\underset{1}{\cancel{5}}}$

Step 4 Multiply and simplify the product. $= \frac{3}{1} = 3$

So, $7\frac{1}{2} \div 2\frac{1}{2} = 3$.

Find the quotient. Write it in simplest form.

1. $\frac{3}{4} \div 1\frac{1}{2}$ ________
2. $4\frac{1}{2} \div 1\frac{3}{4}$ ________
3. $8 \div 2\frac{3}{4}$ ________
4. $5\frac{5}{8} \div 1\frac{1}{2}$ ________
5. $2\frac{5}{8} \div \frac{5}{6}$ ________
6. $\frac{4}{7} \div 1\frac{2}{3}$ ________
7. $4\frac{7}{10} \div \frac{4}{5}$ ________
8. $4\frac{2}{5} \div \frac{8}{15}$ ________
9. $24 \div 2\frac{2}{3}$ ________
10. $8\frac{3}{4} \div 2\frac{1}{3}$ ________
11. $3\frac{7}{8} \div 4$ ________
12. $2\frac{5}{8} \div 3\frac{1}{2}$ ________

Name ______________________________

1. Yoon Ki drove from Phoenix to Tucson in $1\frac{1}{2}$ hours. Then she drove from Tucson to El Paso in $4\frac{3}{4}$ hours. The second part of her trip was how many times as long as the first part?

Ⓐ $7\frac{1}{8}$
Ⓑ $6\frac{1}{4}$
Ⓒ $3\frac{1}{4}$
Ⓓ $3\frac{1}{6}$

2. Tina wants to run $12\frac{3}{5}$ miles over 7 days. She wants to run the same distance each day. How far must she run each day?

Ⓐ $1\frac{4}{5}$ miles
Ⓑ $5\frac{3}{5}$ miles
Ⓒ $12\frac{16}{35}$ miles
Ⓓ $19\frac{3}{5}$ miles

3. A bookstore packs 6 books in a box. The total weight of the books is $14\frac{1}{4}$ pounds. If each book has the same weight, what is the weight of one book?

Ⓐ $\frac{5}{8}$ pound
Ⓑ $2\frac{3}{8}$ pounds
Ⓒ $8\frac{1}{4}$ pounds
Ⓓ $85\frac{1}{2}$ pounds

4. Pela has $5\frac{3}{4}$ feet of string to make necklaces. She wants to make 4 necklaces that are the same length. How long should each necklace be?

Ⓐ $1\frac{1}{4}$ feet
Ⓑ $1\frac{7}{16}$ feet
Ⓒ $1\frac{3}{4}$ feet
Ⓓ $1\frac{15}{16}$ feet

Problem Solving REAL WORLD

5. It takes Nim $2\frac{2}{3}$ hours to weave a basket. He worked Monday through Friday, 8 hours a day. How many baskets did he make?

____

6. A tree grows $1\frac{3}{4}$ feet per year. How long will it take the tree to grow from a height of $21\frac{1}{4}$ feet to a height of 37 feet?

____

Name ________________________________

Lesson 25

COMMON CORE STANDARD CC.6.NS.1

Lesson Objective: Solve problems with fractions and mixed numbers by applying the strategy *use a model.*

Problem Solving • Fraction Operations

Draw a model to solve the problem.

Naomi cuts a $\frac{3}{4}$-foot paper roll into sections, each $\frac{1}{16}$ foot long. If she discards $\frac{1}{8}$ foot of the roll, how many sections does she still have?

<table>
<tr><th>Read the Problem</th><th>Solve the Problem</th></tr>
<tr><td>What do I need to find?
The number ______________________
______________________.</td><td rowspan="3">Draw a model to solve the problem.

1 foot
1/4 | 1/4 | 1/4
1/8 | 1/8 | 1/8 | 1/8 | 1/8 | 1/8 (crossed out)
1/16 | 1/16 | 1/16 | 1/16 | 1/16 | 1/16 | 1/16 | 1/16 | 1/16 | 1/16

Show $\frac{3}{4}$. Divide $\frac{3}{4}$ into eighths.
She discarded $\frac{1}{8}$, so cross out 1 eighth.
$\frac{3}{4} - \frac{1}{8} = \frac{5}{8}$
Divide $\frac{5}{8}$ into sixteenths. There are 10 sixteenths in $\frac{5}{8}$, so she has 10 sections left.</td></tr>
<tr><td>What information do I need to use?
Naomi starts with ______________________
______________________.
Each section is ______________________.
She discards ______________________.</td></tr>
<tr><td>How will I use the information?
I will ______________________
to find ______________________
______________________.</td></tr>
</table>

1. Jeff has $\frac{2}{3}$ gallon of sherbet. He gives each of his friends one $\frac{1}{12}$-gallon scoop. There is $\frac{1}{6}$ gallon left in the carton. How many friends got sherbet?

____

2. A branch measuring $8\frac{7}{8}$ feet was cut from a tree. Crystal made $2\frac{3}{16}$ feet walking sticks from the branch. She discarded $\frac{1}{8}$ foot of the branch. How many walking sticks did she make from the branch?

____

Name ______________________________

1. Marianna divided 16 yards of fabric into $3\frac{1}{3}$-yard pieces. She has $2\frac{2}{3}$ yards of fabric left over. How many $3\frac{1}{3}$-yard pieces did Marianna make?

   (A) 51
   (B) 10
   (C) 4
   (D) 3

2. There were $12\frac{3}{4}$ cups of orange juice in a carton. Each day, Alberto drank $1\frac{1}{4}$ cups of orange juice. Today, there is $\frac{1}{4}$ cup of orange juice left. For how many days has Alberto drunk orange juice?

   (A) 20 (C) 11
   (B) 16 (D) 10

3. Gordon had $5\frac{5}{8}$ cups of milk. He used $\frac{3}{4}$ cup of milk for each batch of biscuits he made. After making biscuits, he had $\frac{3}{8}$ cup of milk left over. How many batches of biscuits did Gordon make?

   (A) 4
   (B) 5
   (C) 6
   (D) 7

4. It will take Mr. Warner $15\frac{1}{2}$ hours to install a fence. Each day, he works $1\frac{1}{3}$ hours on the fence. After he finished working on the fence yesterday, he had $3\frac{1}{2}$ hours of work left to do. For how many days has Mr. Warner worked on the fence?

   (A) 4 (C) 14
   (B) 9 (D) 15

Problem Solving REAL WORLD

5. A concession stand sells ice cream in large ice cream cones, placing $\frac{1}{16}$ gallon in each cone. One day, the stand has $\frac{3}{4}$ gallon of vanilla ice cream. At the end of the day, there is $\frac{3}{16}$ gallon of vanilla remaining. How many people ordered vanilla ice cream cones that day? Explain how you know.

____

____

____

____

____

____

Name ______________________________

Lesson 26

COMMON CORE STANDARD CC.6.NS.2

Lesson Objective: Fluently divide multi-digit numbers.

Divide Multi-Digit Numbers

When you divide multi-digit whole numbers, you can estimate to check if the quotient is reasonable.

Divide 399 ÷ 42.

Step 1 Estimate, using compatible numbers.

400 and 40 are compatible numbers because 40 divides evenly into 400.

$400 \div 40 = 10$

Step 2 Divide the original numbers.

$$\begin{array}{r} 9\text{ r}21 \\ 42\overline{)399} \\ -378 \\ \hline 21 \end{array}$$

Step 3 You can write the remainder as a fraction. Use the remainder for the numerator, and the divisor for the denominator. Simplify if possible.

$\frac{21 \div 21}{42 \div 21} = \frac{1}{2}$

$399 \div 42 = 9\frac{1}{2}$

Step 4 Compare the quotient with your estimate.

Since $9\frac{1}{2}$ is close to 10, the quotient is reasonable.

Estimate. Then find the quotient. Write the remainder, if any, with an r.

1. $17\overline{)965}$ ______________

2. $29\overline{)4{,}380}$ ______________

3. $62\overline{)1{,}178}$ ______________

Estimate. Then find the quotient. Write the remainder, if any, as a fraction.

4. $836 \div 32$ ______________

5. $1{,}392 \div 18$ ______________

6. $2{,}518 \div 48$ ______________

Name ______________________________

1. A total of 3,570 people attended 14 performances of a play. The same number of tickets were sold for each performance. How many tickets were sold for each performance?

   (A) 255
   (B) 266
   (C) 277
   (D) 288

2. Melba saved $13,992 over an 11-year period. She saved the same amount each year. How much did she save each year?

   (A) $1,400
   (B) $1,399
   (C) $1,300
   (D) $1,272

3. Tabitha's parents deposited a total amount of $7,920 into her college fund during a 36-month period. They deposited the same amount each month. What was their monthly contribution to Tabitha's college fund?

   (A) $200
   (B) $217
   (C) $220
   (D) $264

4. Factory workers packaged 2,128 books into 19 cartons. Each carton contains the same number of books. How many books are in each carton?

   (A) 100
   (B) 112
   (C) 124
   (D) 136

Problem Solving REAL WORLD

5. A plane flew a total of 2,220 miles. Its average speed was 555 miles per hour. How many hours did the plane fly?

____

6. A van is carrying 486 pounds. There are 27 boxes in the van. What is the average weight of each box in the van?

____

Name ______________________________

COMMON CORE STANDARD CC.6.NS.3

Lesson Objective: Fluently add and subtract multi-digit decimals.

Add and Subtract Decimals

Estimate 84.9 + 0.463. Then find the sum.

```
   84.9  →   85     Round each number to the nearest whole number.
+ 0.463  →  + 0     So, a good estimate is 85.
            ----
             85
```

Now line up the decimal points. Then add.

```
           Write zeros as
           placeholders.                 Regroup.          1
   84.9    ----------------→   84.900  ----------→     84.900
+ 0.463    ----------------→ + 0.463   ----------→   + 0.463
                                                     -------
                                                      85.363
```

The answer is close to the estimate. So, the answer is reasonable.

Evaluate 45.2 − (27.93 − 10.84) using the order of operations.

Perform the operations in parentheses.

```
  27.93
− 10.84
-------
  17.09
```

Subtract.

```
  45.20
− 17.09
-------
  28.11
```

So, 45.2 − (27.93 − 10.84) is 28.11.

Estimate. Then find the sum or difference.

1.
```
  62.38
+ 26.92
```
______

2.
```
  48.28
−  9.41
```
______

3.
```
  81.04
  52
+ 16.44
```
______

4.
```
  27.29
− 19.39
```
______

5. 743.5 − 462.87 ______

6. 98.01 + 52.003 ______

7. 74.9 − 16.227 ______

Evaluate using the order of operations.

8. (235.152 + 77.12) − 46.326 ______

9. 11.024 − (1.518 + 1.7) ______

Name ____________________

1. A building is 52 meters tall. The building next to it is 50.36 meters tall. What is the difference between the heights of the buildings?

   Ⓐ 1.64 meters
   Ⓑ 2.36 meters
   Ⓒ 16.4 meters
   Ⓓ 164 meters

2. There are 4.14 grams of salt in a solution. If 1.8 grams of salt are added to the solution, how many grams of salt will be in the solution?

   Ⓐ 5.94 grams
   Ⓑ 4.94 grams
   Ⓒ 4.32 grams
   Ⓓ 2.34 grams

3. A scientist is comparing the sizes of two insects. One insect is 1.33 centimeters long, and the other insect is 2.01 centimeters long. What is the difference in size between the two insects?

   Ⓐ 3.34 centimeters
   Ⓑ 1.877 centimeters
   Ⓒ 1.72 centimeters
   Ⓓ 0.68 centimeter

4. Jen's arm is 51 centimeters long. Madeline's arm is 49.2 centimeters long. What is the difference in their arm lengths?

   Ⓐ 0.18 centimeter
   Ⓑ 1.8 centimeters
   Ⓒ 2.2 centimeters
   Ⓓ 18 centimeters

Problem Solving REAL WORLD

5. The average annual rainfall in Clearview is 38 inches. This year, 29.777 inches fell. How much less rain fell this year than falls in an average year?

   ____

6. At the theater, the Worth family spent \$18.00 on adult tickets, \$16.50 on children's tickets, and \$11.75 on refreshments. How much did they spend in all?

   ____

Name ______________________

Lesson 28

COMMON CORE STANDARD CC.6.NS.3

Lesson Objective: Fluently multiply multi-digit decimals.

Multiply Decimals

When multiplying decimals, you can estimate to help you place the decimal point in the product.

Estimate $32.05 × 7.4. Then find the product.

Step 1 Estimate. Round each factor to the nearest ten or the nearest whole number.

$$\begin{array}{r} 32.05 \\ \times\ 7.4 \\ \hline \end{array} \longrightarrow \begin{array}{r} 30 \\ \times\ 7 \\ \hline 210 \end{array}$$

$32.05 is about $30, and 7.4 is close to 7.

So, the product should be close to $210.

Step 2 Multiply.

$$\begin{array}{r} 32.05 \\ \times\quad 7.4 \\ \hline 12820 \\ 224350 \\ \hline 237170 \end{array}$$

Step 3 Place the decimal point. Remember, the product is estimated to be 210. Place the decimal point so that the product is close in value to 210.

237.17

So, the product is $237.17.

Estimate. Then find the product.

1. $\begin{array}{r} 8.6 \\ \times\ 4.1 \\ \hline \end{array}$ ______________

2. 12.8 × 2.21 ______________

3. $8.65 × 9.2 ______________

Evaluate using the order of operations.

4. 19.5 × (21.04 − 18.7) ______________

5. 11.7 + (7.92 × 8.5) ______________

Name ______________________

Lesson 28

CC.6.NS.3

1. Maria works 24.5 hours each week at a bookstore. She earns $8.76 per hour. How much does Maria earn each week?

   Ⓐ $2,146.20
   Ⓑ $214.62
   Ⓒ $15.74
   Ⓓ $11.21

2. Shawna is taking violin lessons. Her violin instructor charges $33.50 per hour. If Shawna has violin lessons for 3.5 hours each week, what is the weekly cost of her lessons?

   Ⓐ $11.72
   Ⓑ $116.75
   Ⓒ $117.25
   Ⓓ $1,172.50

3. The expression 0.005×0.85 represents the number of grams of iron in a liquid. How many grams of iron are in the liquid?

   Ⓐ 4.25 grams
   Ⓑ 0.425 gram
   Ⓒ 0.0425 gram
   Ⓓ 0.00425 gram

4. Michael works 15.5 hours each week at a music store. He earns $9.48 per hour. How much does Michael earn each week?

   Ⓐ $1,469.40
   Ⓑ $146.94
   Ⓒ $24.98
   Ⓓ $6.02

Problem Solving REAL WORLD

5. Blaine exchanges $100 for yen before going to Japan. If each U.S. dollar is worth 88.353 yen, how many yen should Blaine receive?

   ____

6. A camera costs 115 Canadian dollars. If each Canadian dollar is worth 0.952 U.S. dollars, how much will the camera cost in U.S. dollars?

   ____

Name ______________________________

Lesson 29

COMMON CORE STANDARD CC.6.NS.3

Lesson Objective: Fluently divide decimals by whole numbers.

Divide Decimals by Whole Numbers

When you divide a decimal by a whole number, place the decimal point in the quotient directly above the decimal point in the dividend.

Estimate $12\overline{)60.84}$. Then find the quotient.

Step 1 Estimate the quotient, using compatible numbers.

60 and 12 are compatible numbers because 12 divides evenly into 60.

$60 \div 12 = 5$

Step 2 Use long division to divide.

$$\begin{array}{r} 5.07 \\ 12\overline{)60.84} \\ -60 \\ \hline 8 \\ -0 \\ \hline 84 \\ -84 \\ \hline 0 \end{array}$$

Place the decimal point in the quotient directly above the decimal point in the dividend.

Since 8 tenths cannot be shared among 12 groups, write 0 as a placeholder in the tenths place.

So, $60.84 \div 12 = 5.07$.

Estimate. Then find the quotient.

1. $16.48 \div 8$ ____________
2. $191.7 \div 9$ ____________
3. $4\overline{)21.64}$ ____________
4. $14\overline{)41.44}$ ____________
5. $21\overline{)49.14}$ ____________
6. $6\overline{)3.78}$ ____________
7. $92.8 \div 16$ ____________
8. $5\overline{)1.725}$ ____________
9. $11\overline{)135.3}$ ____________
10. $9\overline{)7.29}$ ____________

Name ______________________________

Lesson 29
CC.6.NS.3

1. Chester walked his neighbors' dogs to earn money. He earned $89.49 during a 3-month period. What was the average amount Chester earned each month?

   Ⓐ $298.30
   Ⓑ $29.83
   Ⓒ $28.95
   Ⓓ $27.84

2. Keyshawn's kitchen sink has leaked 36.054 liters of water during the past 6 months. What is the average amount of water leaked each month?

   Ⓐ 6 liters
   Ⓑ 6.009 liters
   Ⓒ 6.9 liters
   Ⓓ 60.09 liters

3. A piece of land measuring 112.815 square kilometers was divided and then sold in equal parts to 9 different people. How many square kilometers did each person buy?

   Ⓐ 0.12535 square kilometer
   Ⓑ 1.2535 square kilometers
   Ⓒ 12.535 square kilometers
   Ⓓ 125.35 square kilometers

4. Kai's father pays him to work in the family store. Kai earned $75.72 during a 4-week period. What was the average amount Kai earned each week?

   Ⓐ $189.30
   Ⓑ $71.72
   Ⓒ $19.43
   Ⓓ $18.93

Problem Solving

5. Jake earned $10.44 interest on his savings account for an 18-month period. What was the average amount of interest Jake earned on his savings account per month?

   ____

6. Gloria worked for 6 hours a day for 2 days at the bank and earned $114.24. How much did she earn per hour?

   ____

Name ___________________________

Lesson 30

COMMON CORE STANDARD CC.6.NS.3

Lesson Objective: Fluently divide whole numbers and decimals by decimals.

Divide with Decimals

When dividing a decimal by a decimal, rewrite the divisor as a whole number. To keep an equivalent problem, move the decimal point in the dividend the same direction and number of places.

Rewrite the problem so that the divisor is a whole number.

300.7 ÷ 1.24

300.7 is the dividend and 1.24 is the divisor.

Change the Divisor

1.24 × 100 = 124

Multiply 1.24 by 100 because 1.24 has two decimal places.

Change the Dividend

300.7 × 100 = 30,070

To keep an equivalent problem, multiply the dividend by the same number, 100.

So, 300.7 ÷ 1.24 is the same problem as 30,070 ÷ 124.

Find the quotient.

$0.55\overline{)24.2}$

Step 1

Rewrite the problem so that the divisor is a whole number.

Divisor

0.55 × 100 = 55

Dividend

24.2 × 100 = 2,420

Step 2

Divide.

$$\begin{array}{r} 44 \\ 55\overline{)2420} \\ -220 \\ \hline 220 \\ -220 \\ \hline 0 \end{array}$$

So, 24.2 ÷ 0.55 = 44.

Rewrite the problem so that the divisor is a whole number.

1. 8.9 ÷ 0.62 ____________

2. 21.05 ÷ 0.2 ____________

3. 512.3 ÷ 2.71 ____________

4. 18.62 ÷ 0.02 ____________

Find the quotient.

5. 8.75 ÷ 0.7 ____________

6. 72.24 ÷ 5.6 ____________

7. $0.21\overline{)1.3545}$ ____________

8. $2.17\overline{)18.228}$ ____________

1. Amir wants to buy a new MP3 player that costs $76.50. If he saves $8.50 each week, how many weeks will it take Amir to save enough money to buy the MP3 player?

Ⓐ 0.09
Ⓑ 0.9
Ⓒ 9
Ⓓ 90

2. Christopher drove 199.5 miles in 3.5 hours. If he drove at a constant speed, how far did he drive in one hour?

Ⓐ 5.7 miles
Ⓑ 57 miles
Ⓒ 500 miles
Ⓓ 570 miles

3. Michael earned $50.43 in 6.15 hours. How much did he earn each hour?

Ⓐ $0.82
Ⓑ $3.10
Ⓒ $4.43
Ⓓ $8.20

4. Darby wants to buy a new pair of sneakers that costs $66.50. If she saves $9.50 each week, how many weeks will it take Darby to save enough money to buy the sneakers?

Ⓐ 0.07
Ⓑ 0.7
Ⓒ 7
Ⓓ 70

Problem Solving REAL WORLD

5. If Amanda walks at an average speed of 2.72 miles per hour, how long will it take her to walk 6.8 miles?

____

6. Chad cycled 62.3 miles in 3.5 hours. If he cycled at a constant speed, how far did he cycle in 1 hour?

____

Name ________________________

Lesson 31

COMMON CORE STANDARD CC.6.NS.4

Lesson Objective: Write the prime factorization of numbers.

Prime Factorization

A number written as the product of prime numbers is called the **prime factorization** of that number. To break a number down into its prime factors, divide it by prime numbers. The first eight prime numbers are listed below.

2, 3, 5, 7, 11, 13, 17, 19

You can use a factor tree to find the prime factorization of a number.

165 → (3), 55; 55 → (5), (11)

Divide the number by the least prime factor possible. Try 2, 3, 5, and so on.

Break 55 down because it is not a prime number.

The numbers at the bottom of the branches are all prime.

You can use a ladder diagram to find the prime factorization of a number.

(5)	165
(3)	33
(11)	11
	1

165 ends in 5, so it is divisible by 5. Divide 165 by 5.

Write the quotient below 165.

The sum of the digits in 33 is divisible by 3, so divide 33 by 3.

11 is prime. Divide 11 by itself.

The bottom number is 1 and all the numbers to the left are prime.

Write the number as a product of prime factors. The factors should be in order from least to greatest.

So, the prime factorization of 165 is $3 \times 5 \times 11$.

Find the prime factorization of the number.

1. 21 ________

2. 130 ________

3. 84 ________

Name ____________________

1. The combination for the lock on Santiago's suitcase is based on the prime factorization of 315. What is the prime factorization of 315?

Ⓐ $5 \times 7 \times 9$

Ⓑ $3 \times 7 \times 15$

Ⓒ $3 \times 3 \times 5 \times 7$

Ⓓ $2 \times 3 \times 3 \times 5 \times 7$

2. The combination for Mr. Tao's briefcase is based on the prime factorization of 45. What is the prime factorization of 45?

Ⓐ 3×15

Ⓑ 5×9

Ⓒ $3 \times 3 \times 5$

Ⓓ $2 \times 3 \times 3 \times 5$

3. Manuel left out one prime factor when he wrote this prime factorization for 168.

$$2 \times 2 \times 2 \times 3 \times \blacksquare$$

What is the missing prime factor?

Ⓐ 2

Ⓑ 3

Ⓒ 5

Ⓓ 7

4. Bethaney left out one prime factor when she wrote this prime factorization for 1,092.

$$2 \times 2 \times \blacksquare \times 7 \times 13$$

What is the missing prime factor?

Ⓐ 2

Ⓑ 3

Ⓒ 7

Ⓓ 13

Problem Solving REAL WORLD

5. A computer code is based on the prime factorization of 160. Find the prime factorization of 160.

____

6. The combination for a lock is a 3-digit number. The digits are the prime factors of 42 listed from least to greatest. What is the combination for the lock?

____

Name ______________________________

Lesson 32

COMMON CORE STANDARD CC.6.NS.4

Lesson Objective: Find the least common multiple of two whole numbers.

Least Common Multiple

The **least common multiple**, or **LCM**, is the least number that two or more numbers have in common in their list of nonzero multiples.

Find the LCM of 3 and 9.

List the first ten nonzero multiples of each number:

Multiples of 3: 3, 6, 9, 12, 15, 18, 21, 24, 27, 30

Multiples of 9: 9, 18, 27, 36, 45, 54, 63, 72, 81, 90

The first three nonzero multiples that 3 and 9 have in common are 9, 18, and 27.

So, the LCM of 3 and 9 is 9.

Find the LCM.

1. 4, 10

List the first ten multiples for each number.

Multiples of 4: 4, 8, ____, 16, ____, 24,

____, ____, 36, ____

Multiples of 10: 10, ____, 30, ____, 50,

____, 70, ____, ____, 100

List the numbers that appear in both lists.

Common multiples: ____ and ____

The LCM of 4 and 10 is ____.

2. 6, 8

List the first ten multiples for each number.

Multiples of 6: ______________________

____

Multiples of 8: ______________________

____

List the numbers that appear in both lists.

Common multiples: ______________________

The LCM of 6 and 8 is ____.

3. 5, 20

____

4. 6, 15

____

5. 12, 30

____

6. 7, 14

____

7. 10, 15

____

8. 6, 18

____

Name ____________________

1. Gina purchases materials to make watches for a jewelry show. There are 6 watch faces in a pack and 9 watch bands in a pack. What is the **least** number of watches Gina can make without having any supplies left over?

   (A) 12
   (B) 16
   (C) 18
   (D) 24

2. Stefani makes team shirts to sell at the basketball games. She puts one patch in the middle of each shirt. There are 3 patches in a pack and 5 shirts in a pack. What is the **least** number of team shirts Stefani can make without having any supplies left over?

   (A) 3
   (B) 5
   (C) 8
   (D) 15

3. Max purchases materials to make dog collars for a pet show. There are 6 buckles in a pack and 8 straps in a pack. What is the **least** number of dog collars Max can make without having any supplies left over?

   (A) 12
   (B) 16
   (C) 18
   (D) 24

4. Sarah makes necklaces to sell at the craft festival. She uses one pendant for each necklace. There are 4 ribbons in a pack and 6 pendants in a pack. What is the **least** number of necklaces Sarah can make without having any supplies left over?

   (A) 8
   (B) 12
   (C) 18
   (D) 24

Problem Solving REAL WORLD

5. Juanita is making necklaces to give as presents. She plans to put 15 beads on each necklace. Beads are sold in packages of 20. What is the least number of packages she can buy to make necklaces and have no beads left over?

   ____

6. Pencils are sold in packages of 10, and erasers are sold in packages of 6. What is the least number of pencils and erasers you can buy so that there is one pencil for each eraser with none left over?

   ____

Name ____________________

Lesson 33

COMMON CORE STANDARD CC.6.NS.4

Lesson Objective: Find the greatest common factor of two whole numbers.

Greatest Common Factor

A **common factor** is a number that is a factor of two or more numbers. The **greatest common factor**, or **GCF**, is the greatest factor that two or more numbers have in common.

Find the common factors of 9 and 27. Then find the GCF.

Step 1
List the factors of each number.
Factors of 9: 1, 3, 9
Factors of 27: 1, 3, 9, 27

Step 2
Identify the common factors.
Common factors of 9 and 27:
1, 3, 9

The greatest of the common factors is 9.
So, the GCF of 9 and 27 is 9.

You can use the GCF and the Distributive Property to express the sum of two numbers as a product.

Write 9 + 27 as a product.

Step 1
Write each number as the product of the GCF and another factor.

$9 = 9 \times 1$ $\quad$ $27 = 9 \times 3$

Step 2
Write an expression multiplying the GCF and the sum of the two factors from Step 1.

$9 \times (1 + 3)$

The product $9 \times (1 + 3)$ has the same value as $9 + 27$.

So, $9 + 27 = 9 \times (1 + 3)$.

Find the GCF.

1. 18, 45 ________

2. 33, 66 ________

3. 72, 96 ________

4. 50, 80 ________

Use the GCF and the Distributive Property to express the sum as a product.

5. 18 + 24 ________

6. 15 + 75 ________

7. 36 + 54 ________

8. 16 + 20 ________

Name ________________________________

Lesson 33
CC.6.NS.4

1. Madison has 56 roses and 42 daisies to use in floral centerpieces for a party. Each centerpiece will have the same number of flowers and will contain only roses or only daisies. What is the **greatest** number of flowers that Madison can use in each centerpiece?

   Ⓐ 14 Ⓒ 7
   Ⓑ 8 Ⓓ 6

2. Manny wants to make necklaces from two pieces of jewelry wire that measure 60 inches and 36 inches. He will cut both lengths of jewelry wire into equal pieces that are as long as possible. Into what lengths should he cut the pieces of wire?

   Ⓐ 20 inches Ⓒ 4 inches
   Ⓑ 12 inches Ⓓ 3 inches

3. Mr. Gentry teaches two science classes. There are 28 students in his biology class and 21 students in his environmental science class. He divides both classes into equal-sized lab groups. Each science class has their own lab groups. What is the **greatest** number of students in each lab group?

   Ⓐ 4 Ⓒ 6
   Ⓑ 5 Ⓓ 7

4. Chauncey has two pieces of rope that measure 8 feet and 12 feet. He wants to cut the rope into equal pieces that are as long as possible. Into what lengths should Chauncey cut the pieces of rope?

   Ⓐ 8 feet Ⓒ 4 feet
   Ⓑ 6 feet Ⓓ 2 feet

Problem Solving

5. Jerome is making prizes for a game at the school fair. He has two bags of different candies, one with 15 pieces of candy and one with 20 pieces. Every prize will have one kind of candy, the same number of pieces, and the greatest number of pieces possible. How many candies should be in each prize?

   ____

6. There are 24 sixth graders and 40 seventh graders. Mr. Chan wants to divide both grades into groups of equal size, with the greatest possible number of students in each group. How many students should be in each group?

   ____

Name ______________________

Lesson 34

COMMON CORE STANDARD CC.6.NS.4

Lesson Objective: Solve problems involving greatest common factor by using the strategy *draw a diagram.*

Problem Solving • Apply the Greatest Common Factor

Use the Distributive Property and a diagram to solve.

Bethany is packing cookies for her drama club's bake sale. She has 28 oatmeal cookies and 36 peanut butter cookies to pack. Each bag will contain only one kind of cookie, and every bag will have the same number of cookies. What is the greatest number of cookies she can pack in each bag? How many bags of each kind will there be?

Read the Problem	Solve the Problem
What do I need to find? I need to find the ________ number of cookies for each _____ and the number of bags for ______________.	**Step 1** Find the GCF of 28 and 36. Use prime factorization. $28 = \mathbf{2} \times \mathbf{2} \times 7$ $\quad 36 = \mathbf{2} \times \mathbf{2} \times 3 \times 3$ Multiply common prime factors: $2 \times 2 =$ _____ GCF: _____
What information do I need to use? I need to use the number of ________ ________ and the number of ________ ______________.	**Step 2** Write 28 as a product of the GCF and another factor. $28 = 4 \times$ _____ Write 36 as a product of the GCF and another factor. $36 = 4 \times$ _____
How will I use the information? First, I can find the ______________ _____. Then I can draw a diagram showing the ______________.	**Step 3** Use the Distributive Property to write 28 + 36 as a product. $28 + 36 =$ $4 \times ($_____ + _____$)$ **Step 4** Use the product to draw a diagram of the bags of cookies. Write O for each oatmeal cookie and P for each peanut butter cookie.

O O O O	O O O O	O O O O	O O O O	O O O O			P P P P	P P P P							

So, each bag will have _____ cookies. There will be _____ bags of oatmeal cookies and _____ bags of peanut butter cookies.

1. Jacob is putting 18 nonfiction and 30 fiction books on bookshelves. Each shelf will have only fiction or only nonfiction, and every shelf will have the same number of books. What is the greatest number of books for each shelf, and how many shelves will there be for each type of book?

____

1. Kenya placed 21 apples and 28 oranges into different bowls. Each bowl held the same amount of fruit and contained only apples or only oranges. What is the **greatest** number of pieces of fruit that Kenya could have placed in each bowl?

   Ⓐ 14　Ⓒ 4
   Ⓑ 7　Ⓓ 3

2. Mr. Hill has 27 students in his class, and Mr. Young has 24 students in his class. Both classes are divided into equal-sized teams, with the **greatest** possible number of students on each team. How many teams are there in all?

   Ⓐ 3　Ⓒ 9
   Ⓑ 8　Ⓓ 17

3. Leslie baked 64 chocolate chip cookies and 88 peanut butter cookies. She wants to place the cookies in snack bags for a party. Each snack bag will contain the same number of cookies and contain only one type of cookie. If she places the **greatest** number of cookies in each snack bag, how many snack bags contain peanut butter cookies?

   Ⓐ 2　Ⓒ 8
   Ⓑ 4　Ⓓ 11

4. Caleb's bookcase holds 16 nonfiction books and 12 fiction books. Each shelf holds the same number of books and contains only one type of book. Each shelf holds the **greatest** number of books possible. How many shelves does the bookcase have?

   Ⓐ 7　Ⓒ 3
   Ⓑ 4　Ⓓ 2

Problem Solving REAL WORLD

5. Otis wants to place 75 green marbles and 60 red marbles in bags to give to his friends. Each bag should contain the same number of marbles, and all marbles in a bag should be the same color. If he places the **greatest** possible number of marbles in each bag, how many bags will have green marbles? Explain how you know.

____

____

____

____

____

____

Name ______________________________

COMMON CORE STANDARD CC.6.NS.4

Lesson Objective: Multiply fractions.

Multiply Fractions

To multiply fractions, you can multiply numerators and multiply denominators. Write the product in simplest form.

Find $\frac{3}{10} \times \frac{4}{5}$.

Step 1 Multiply numerators. Multiply denominators.

$$\frac{3}{10} \times \frac{4}{5} = \frac{3 \times 4}{10 \times 5} = \frac{12}{50}$$

Step 2 Write the product in simplest form.

$$\frac{12}{50} = \frac{12 \div 2}{50 \div 2} = \frac{6}{25}$$

So, $\frac{3}{10} \times \frac{4}{5} = \frac{6}{25}$.

To simplify an expression with fractions, follow the order of operations as you would with whole numbers.

Find $\left(\frac{5}{7} - \frac{3}{14}\right) \times \frac{1}{10}$.

Step 1 Perform the operation in parentheses. To subtract, write an equivalent fraction using a common denominator.

Multiply the numerator and denominator of $\frac{5}{7}$ by 2 to get a common denominator of 14.

$$\left(\frac{5}{7} - \frac{3}{14}\right) \times \frac{1}{10} = \left(\frac{5 \times 2}{7 \times 2} - \frac{3}{14}\right) \times \frac{1}{10}$$

$$= \left(\frac{10}{14} - \frac{3}{14}\right) \times \frac{1}{10}$$

$$= \frac{7}{14} \times \frac{1}{10}$$

Step 2 Multiply numerators. Multiply denominators.

$$= \frac{7 \times 1}{14 \times 10} = \frac{7}{140}$$

Step 3 Write the product in simplest form. Divide the numerator and the denominator by the GCF.

$$= \frac{7 \div 7}{140 \div 7} = \frac{1}{20}$$

So, $\left(\frac{5}{7} - \frac{3}{14}\right) \times \frac{1}{10} = \frac{1}{20}$.

Find the product. Write the product in simplest form.

1. $\frac{3}{4} \times \frac{1}{5}$ ____________
2. $\frac{4}{7} \times \frac{5}{12}$ ____________
3. $\frac{3}{8} \times \frac{2}{9}$ ____________
4. $\frac{4}{5} \times \frac{5}{8}$ ____________

Evaluate using the order of operations.

5. $\frac{7}{8} - \frac{5}{6} \times \frac{1}{2}$ ____________
6. $\left(\frac{4}{5} + \frac{1}{3}\right) \times \frac{5}{9}$ ____________
7. $\frac{3}{4} \times \frac{2}{5} + \frac{1}{4}$ ____________
8. $\frac{3}{10} \times \left(\frac{2}{3} - \frac{1}{6}\right)$ ____________

Name ______________________

Lesson 35

CC.6.NS.4

1. Mr. Bryon had a gas can with $4\frac{1}{4}$ gallons of gasoline in it. He used $\frac{1}{4}$ of the amount in the can to mow his lawn. How many gallons did Mr. Bryon use to mow his lawn?

   Ⓐ $\frac{15}{16}$ gallon

   Ⓑ $1\frac{1}{16}$ gallons

   Ⓒ $4\frac{1}{16}$ gallons

   Ⓓ $4\frac{1}{2}$ gallons

2. Alana bought $2\frac{5}{8}$ pounds of mixed nuts for the school picnic. Her classmates ate $\frac{3}{4}$ of the mixed nuts. How much of the mixed nuts did her classmates eat?

   Ⓐ $1\frac{31}{32}$ pounds

   Ⓑ 2 pounds

   Ⓒ $2\frac{15}{32}$ pounds

   Ⓓ $3\frac{1}{2}$ pounds

3. Kelly feeds her cat $\frac{7}{8}$ cup of food per day. How much food does she feed her cat in one week, including the weekend?

   Ⓐ $1\frac{3}{4}$ cups　Ⓒ $5\frac{5}{6}$ cups

   Ⓑ $4\frac{3}{8}$ cups　Ⓓ $6\frac{1}{8}$ cups

4. The table shows how many hours some of the part-time employees at the Pizza Shop worked last week.

   Pizza Shop

Name	Hours Worked
Conrad	$6\frac{2}{3}$
Giovanni	$9\frac{1}{2}$
Sally	$10\frac{3}{4}$

   Louisa worked $1\frac{1}{3}$ times as many hours as Giovanni worked. How many hours did Louisa work last week?

   Ⓐ $3\frac{5}{6}$ hours　Ⓒ $12\frac{2}{3}$ hours

   Ⓑ $10\frac{5}{6}$ hours　Ⓓ $14\frac{1}{3}$ hours

Problem Solving REAL WORLD

5. Jason ran $\frac{5}{7}$ of the distance around the school track. Sara ran $\frac{4}{5}$ of Jason's distance. What fraction of the total distance around the track did Sara run?

   ____

6. A group of students attend a math club. Half of the students are boys and $\frac{4}{9}$ of the boys have brown eyes. What fraction of the group are boys with brown eyes?

   ____

Name ______________________________

Lesson 36

COMMON CORE STANDARD CC.6.NS.4

Lesson Objective: Simplify fractional factors by using the greatest common factor.

Simplify Factors

Sometimes you can simplify before you multiply fractions.

Find the product of $\frac{5}{6} \times \frac{4}{15}$. Simplify before multiplying.

Step 1 Rewrite as a single fraction.

$$\frac{5 \times 4}{6 \times 15}$$

Step 2 Look for numbers in the numerator that have common factors with numbers in the denominator. Find the GCF.

$$\frac{\textcircled{5} \times \boxed{4}}{\boxed{6} \times \textcircled{15}}$$

The GCF of 5 and 15 is 5.
The GCF of 6 and 4 is 2.

Step 3 Divide.

$5 \div 5 = 1$
$15 \div 5 = 3$

$6 \div 2 = 3$
$4 \div 2 = 2$

$$\frac{\overset{1}{\cancel{5}} \times \overset{2}{\cancel{4}}}{\underset{3}{\cancel{6}} \times \underset{3}{\cancel{15}}}$$

Step 4 Rewrite the fraction with the new numbers. Multiply the numerators. Multiply the denominators.

$$\frac{1 \times 2}{3 \times 3} = \frac{2}{9}$$

So, $\frac{5}{6} \times \frac{4}{15} = \frac{2}{9}$.

Find the product. Simplify before multiplying.

1. $\frac{4}{9} \times \frac{3}{14}$ ______

2. $\frac{3}{4} \times \frac{2}{5}$ ______

3. $\frac{3}{20} \times \frac{5}{6}$ ______

4. $\frac{7}{10} \times \frac{4}{5}$ ______

5. $\frac{3}{16} \times \frac{8}{27}$ ______

6. $\frac{1}{8} \times \frac{2}{7}$ ______

Name ______________________________

Lesson 36
CC.6.NS.4

1. India has a $\frac{3}{5}$-pound bag of nuts. She uses $\frac{5}{6}$ of the bag to bake brownies. How many pounds of nuts did India use to make the brownies?

   Ⓐ $\frac{7}{8}$ pound
   Ⓑ $\frac{1}{2}$ pound
   Ⓒ $\frac{1}{6}$ pound
   Ⓓ $\frac{2}{15}$ pound

2. Otis bought a total of $\frac{7}{10}$ pound of grapes and cherries. The weight of the grapes is $\frac{2}{3}$ of the total weight. What is the weight of the grapes?

   Ⓐ $\frac{20}{21}$ pound
   Ⓑ $\frac{9}{13}$ pound
   Ⓒ $\frac{7}{15}$ pound
   Ⓓ $\frac{3}{10}$ pound

3. In a class, $\frac{2}{5}$ of the students said their favorite food is pizza. Of those students, $\frac{5}{12}$ said their favorite pizza topping is pepperoni. What fraction of the students in the class said their favorite pizza topping is pepperoni?

   Ⓐ $\frac{1}{10}$
   Ⓑ $\frac{1}{6}$
   Ⓒ $\frac{10}{17}$
   Ⓓ $\frac{2}{3}$

4. Aubrey has $\frac{3}{4}$ gallon of milk to use for two recipes. She uses $\frac{1}{12}$ of the milk for one of the recipes. How much milk does she use?

   Ⓐ $\frac{1}{4}$ gallon
   Ⓑ $\frac{1}{8}$ gallon
   Ⓒ $\frac{1}{12}$ gallon
   Ⓓ $\frac{1}{16}$ gallon

Problem Solving REAL WORLD

5. Amber has a $\frac{4}{5}$-pound bag of colored sand. She uses $\frac{1}{2}$ of the bag for an art project. How much sand does she use for the project?

   ____

6. Tyler has $\frac{3}{4}$ month to write a book report. He finished the report in $\frac{2}{3}$ that time. How much time did it take Tyler to write the report?

   ____

Name ___________________________________

Lesson 37

COMMON CORE STANDARD CC.6.NS.5

Lesson Objective: Understand positive and negative numbers, and use them to represent real-world quantities.

Understand Positive and Negative Numbers

Positive integers are to the right of 0 on the number line.
Negative integers are to the left of 0 on the number line.
Opposites are the same distance from 0, on opposite sides.

What is the opposite of ⁻3?

Step 1 Graph the integer.

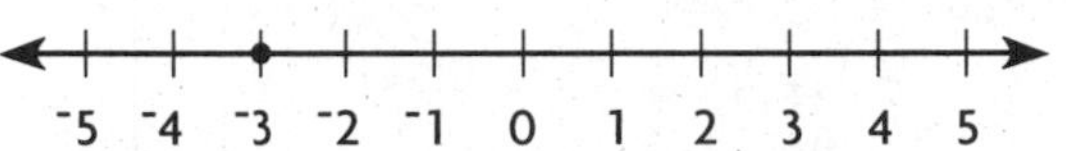

⁻3 is a negative integer. Graph it to the left of 0.

Step 2 Graph the integer and its opposite on a number line.

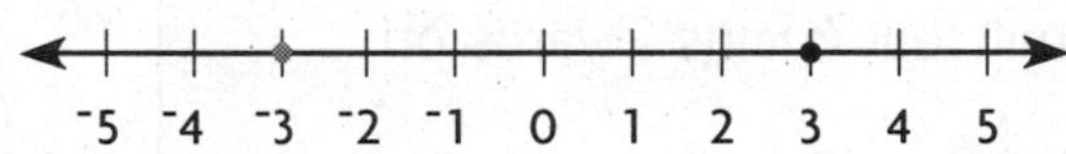

The opposite of ⁻3 is 3 places to the right of 0.

So, the opposite of ⁻3 is 3.

Graph the integer and its opposite on the number line.

1. 2 opposite: _______

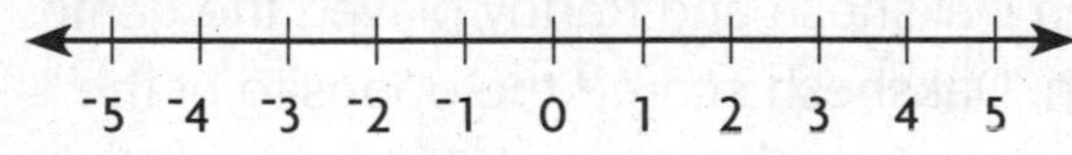

2. ⁻4 opposite: _______

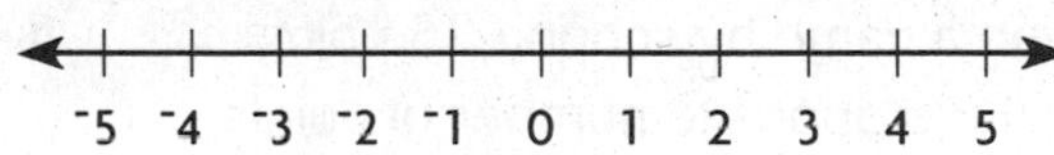

3. ⁻1 opposite: _______

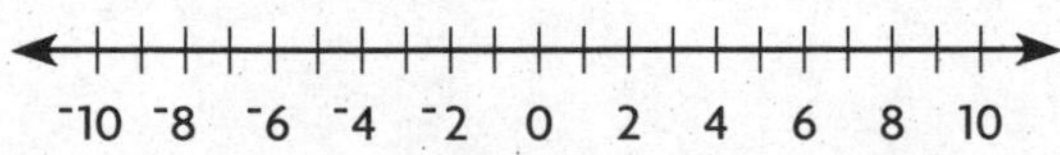

4. 7 opposite: _______

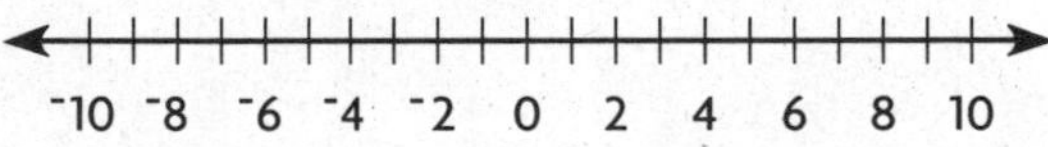

Write the opposite of the opposite of the integer.

5. ⁻18 _______

6. 90 _______

7. ⁻31 _______

Name ___________________________

Lesson 37
CC.6.NS.5

1. Which situation could be represented by the integer $^{+}6$?

   Ⓐ A football team loses 6 yards on a play.

   Ⓑ A golfer's score is 6 over par.

   Ⓒ A town is 6 feet below sea level.

   Ⓓ A video game player loses 6 points.

2. Which situation could be represented by the integer $^{-}2$?

   Ⓐ A football team gains 2 yards on a play.

   Ⓑ A golfer's score is 2 over par.

   Ⓒ A city is 2 feet below sea level.

   Ⓓ A student earns 2 bonus points on a quiz.

3. Which situation could be represented by the integer $^{+}15$?

   Ⓐ A football team gains 15 yards on a play.

   Ⓑ A $15 withdrawal is made from a bank account.

   Ⓒ A town is 15 feet below sea level.

   Ⓓ A video game player loses 15 points.

4. Maria withdrew $20 from her checking account. What integer represents the withdrawal?

   Ⓐ $^{-}20$

   Ⓑ 0

   Ⓒ 20

   Ⓓ $^{-}40$

Problem Solving REAL WORLD

5. Dakshesh won a game by scoring 25 points. Randy scored the opposite number of points as Dakshesh. What is Randy's score?

   ____

6. When Dakshesh and Randy played the game again, Dakshesh scored the opposite of the opposite of his first score. What is his score?

   ____

Name ______________________________

Lesson 38

COMMON CORE STANDARD CC.6.NS.6a

Lesson Objective: Plot rational numbers on a number line, and use a number line to identify opposites.

Rational Numbers and the Number Line

Graph $^-0.8$ and 1.3 on the number line.

Step 1 Use positive and negative integers to help you locate the decimals. 0.8 is between 0 and 1, so $^-0.8$ is between 0 and $^-1$. 1.3 is between 1 and 2.

Step 2 The number line is marked in tenths. There is a tick mark every 0.1. Count 8 tick marks to the left of 0 for $^-0.8$. Count 3 tickmarks to the right of 1 for 1.3.

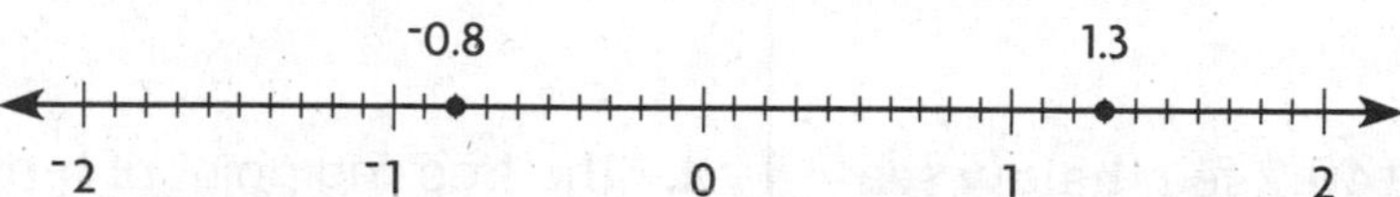

Graph $\frac{3}{5}$ and $^-1\frac{1}{2}$ on the number line.

Step 1 Use positive and negative integers to help you locate the fractions. $\frac{3}{5}$ is between 0 and 1. $1\frac{1}{2}$ is between 1 and 2, so $^-1\frac{1}{2}$ is between $^-1$ and $^-2$.

Step 2 The number line is marked in tenths. There is a tick mark every $\frac{1}{10}$. Use equivalent fractions to help you graph the points.

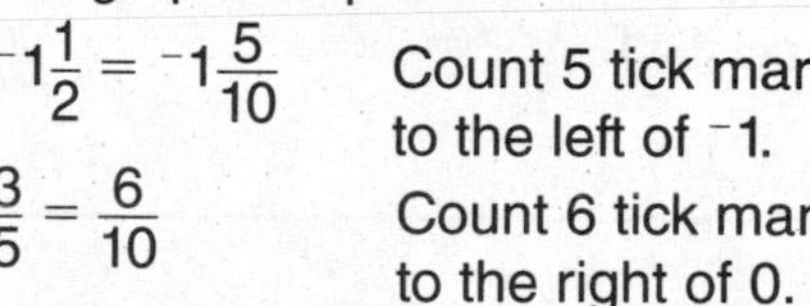

$^-1\frac{1}{2} = {}^-1\frac{5}{10}$ Count 5 tick marks to the left of $^-1$.

$\frac{3}{5} = \frac{6}{10}$ Count 6 tick marks to the right of 0.

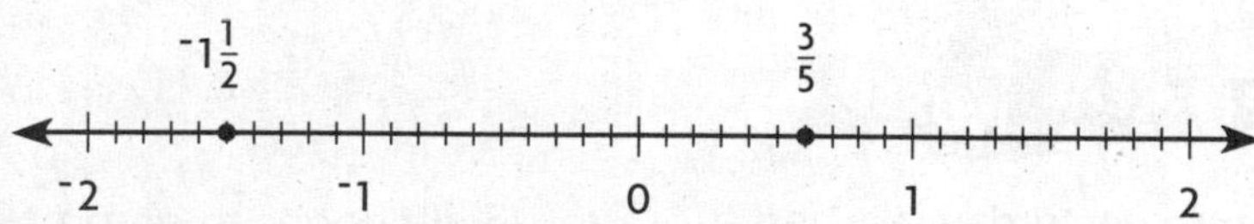

Graph the number on the horizontal number line.

1. $^-1\frac{2}{5}$

2. 0.6

3. $^-1.2$

4. $1\frac{8}{10}$

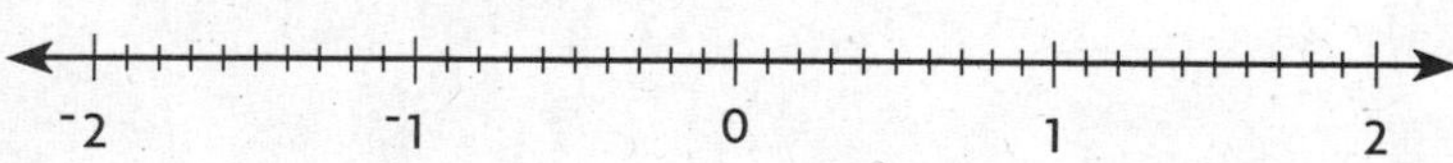

Name ______________________________

Lesson 38
CC.6.NS.6a

1. The normal low temperature during January for a town in Alaska is $^{-}8.6$°F. Between which two integers does this temperature lie?

   Ⓐ $^{-}10$ and $^{-}9$
   Ⓑ $^{-}9$ and $^{-}8$
   Ⓒ $^{-}8$ and $^{-}7$
   Ⓓ $^{-}7$ and $^{-}6$

2. A city's elevation is 140.2 feet **below** sea level. Between which two integers does this elevation lie?

   Ⓐ $^{-}141$ and $^{-}140$
   Ⓑ $^{-}140$ and 0
   Ⓒ 0 and 140
   Ⓓ 140 and 141

3. The integer $^{-}3.5$ represents a fee that was charged to Carl's bank account. Between which two integers does this number lie?

   Ⓐ 3 and 4
   Ⓑ 3 and 8
   Ⓒ $^{-}3$ and 8
   Ⓓ $^{-}4$ and $^{-}3$

4. The freezing point of bromine is about $^{-}7.2$° Celsius. Between which two integers does this temperature lie?

   Ⓐ $^{-}10$ and $^{-}9$
   Ⓑ $^{-}9$ and $^{-}8$
   Ⓒ $^{-}8$ and $^{-}7$
   Ⓓ $^{-}7$ and $^{-}6$

Problem Solving REAL WORLD

5. The outdoor temperature yesterday reached a low of $^{-}4.5$°F. Between what two integers was the temperature?

   ____

6. Jacob needs to graph $^{-}6\frac{2}{5}$ on a horizontal number line. Should he graph it to the left or right of $^{-}6$?

   ____

Name ______________________________

Lesson 39

COMMON CORE STANDARD CC.6.NS.6b

Lesson Objective: Identify the relationship between points on a coordinate plane.

Ordered Pair Relationships

You can tell which quadrant to graph a point in by looking at whether the coordinates are positive or negative.

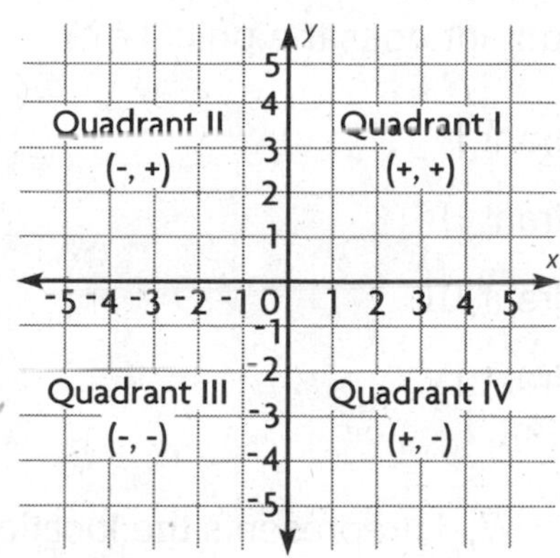

Find the quadrant for the point (4, -5).

Step 1 The *x*-coordinate is 4, a positive number. So, the point must be in Quadrant I or IV.

Step 2 The *y*-coordinate is -5, a negative number. So, the point must be in Quadrant III or IV.

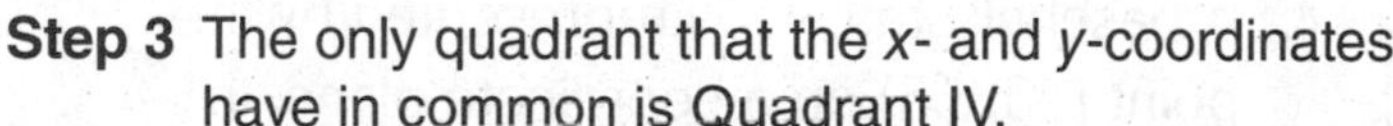

Step 3 The only quadrant that the *x*- and *y*-coordinates have in common is Quadrant IV.

So, the point (4, -5) is in Quadrant IV.

Two points are reflections of each other if the x-axis or y-axis forms a line of symmetry for the two points. This means that if you folded the graph along that axis, the two points would line up.

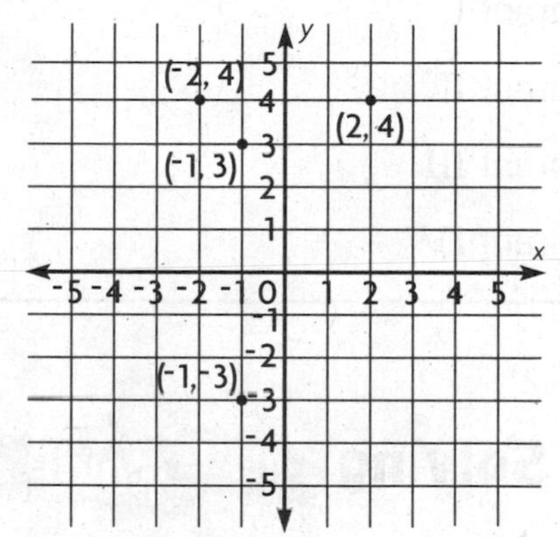

(-1, 3) and (-1, -3) are reflected across the *x*-axis. The *x*-coordinates are the same. The *y*-coordinates are opposites.

(2, 4) and (-2, 4) are reflected across the *y*-axis. The *y*-coordinates are the same. The *x*-coordinates are opposites.

Identify the quadrant where the point is located.

1. (-1, 5)

x-coordinate: -1 Quadrant: _____ or _____

y-coordinate: 5 Quadrant: _____ or _____

The point is in Quadrant _____.

2. (-3, -2)

x-coordinate: -3 Quadrant: _____ or _____

y-coordinate: -2 Quadrant: _____ or _____

The point is in Quadrant _____.

3. (2, 4)

Quadrant: _____

4. (-6, 7)

Quadrant: _____

5. (8, -1)

Quadrant: _____

6. (-7, -5)

Quadrant: _____

The two points are reflections of each other across the x- or y-axis. Identify the axis.

7. (2, 7) and (-2, 7)

axis: _____

8. (-1, 4) and (-1, -4)

axis: _____

9. (5, -6) and (5, 6)

axis: _____

10. (8, -3) and (-8, -3)

axis: _____

Name ____________________

1. The city of Dellville is represented by the point (3, ⁻2) on a coordinate plane. In which quadrant does the point lie?

Ⓐ Quadrant I
Ⓑ Quadrant II
Ⓒ Quadrant III
Ⓓ Quadrant IV

2. The point (⁻7, 1) represents the location of a fountain on a map of a park. In which quadrant does the point lie?

Ⓐ Quadrant I
Ⓑ Quadrant II
Ⓒ Quadrant III
Ⓓ Quadrant IV

3. The town of Cedarcroft is represented by the point (11, 1) on a coordinate plane. In which quadrant does the point lie?

Ⓐ Quadrant I
Ⓑ Quadrant II
Ⓒ Quadrant III
Ⓓ Quadrant IV

4. A baseball stadium is represented by the point (⁻3, ⁻5) on a coordinate plane. In which quadrant does the point lie?

Ⓐ Quadrant I
Ⓑ Quadrant II
Ⓒ Quadrant III
Ⓓ Quadrant IV

Problem Solving REAL WORLD

5. A town's post office is located at the point (7, 5) on a coordinate plane. In which quadrant is the post office located?

____

6. The grocery store is located at a point on a coordinate plane with the same *y*-coordinate as the bank but with the opposite *x*-coordinate. The grocery store and bank are reflections of each other across which axis?

____

Name ____________________

Lesson 40

COMMON CORE STANDARD CC.6.NS.6c

Lesson Objective: Convert between fractions and decimals.

Fractions and Decimals

Terminating decimals end. **Repeating decimals** do not end but have repeating digits. One way to convert a terminating decimal to a fraction or mixed number is to read the number.

Look at the decimal 5.75. The right-hand digit is in the hundredths place. Read 5.75 as "five and seventy-five hundredths."

whole number → $5\frac{75}{100}$ ← fraction

As a mixed number, the whole number is 5. The numerator is 75. The denominator is 100.

Write the fraction in simplest form using the greatest common factor.

75: 1, 3, (5), 15, (25), 75
100: 1, 2, 4, (5), 10, 20, (25), 50, 100
GCF = 25

$$5\frac{75}{100} = 5\frac{75 \div 25}{100 \div 25} = 5\frac{3}{4}$$

So, $5.75 = 5\frac{3}{4}$ in simplest form.

Identify the decimal and the fraction in simplest form for point *E*.

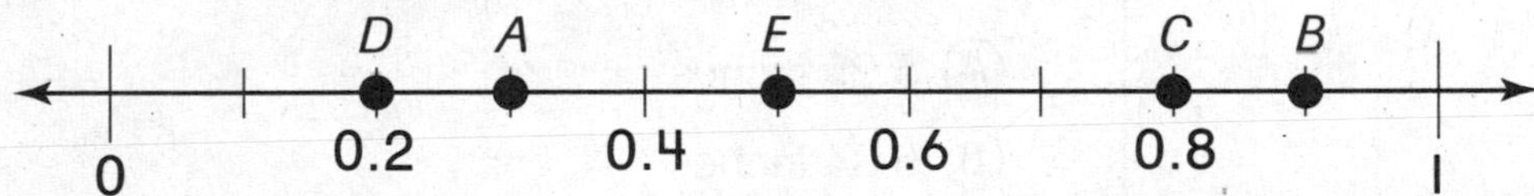

Decimal
Between 0 and 1 there are 10 spaces. So, each space represents 0.1. Point *E* is one space to the right of 0.4. Point *E* is the next tenth, or 0.5.

So, Point *E* is at $0.5 = \frac{1}{2}$.

Fraction
Read 0.5 as "five-tenths." Write $\frac{5}{10}$. Simplify by dividing the numerator and denominator by the GCF, 5.
$\frac{5 \div 5}{10 \div 5} = \frac{1}{2}$

Write as a fraction or mixed number in simplest form.

1. 0.48 ________ **2.** 0.8 ________ **3.** 0.004 ________ **4.** 3.6 ________ **5.** 4.82 ________

Identify a decimal and a fraction or mixed number in simplest form for each point.

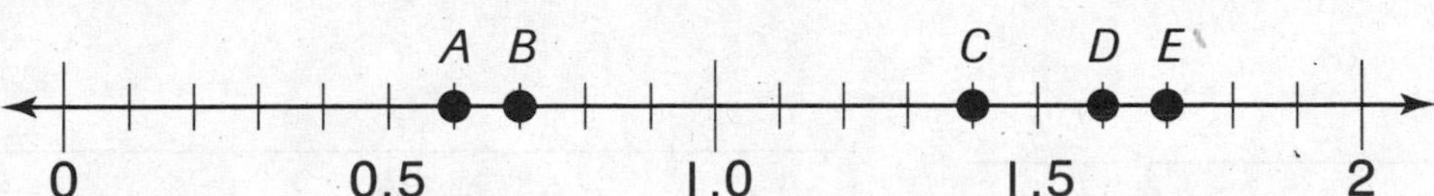

6. Point *A* ________ **7.** Point *B* ________ **8.** Point *C* ________ **9.** Point *D* ________ **10.** Point *E* ________

1. Calvin has a recipe that calls for $\frac{3}{8}$ pound of cheddar cheese. The packages he sees in the grocery store show the weights in decimal amounts. Which amount of cheese should Calvin buy?

Ⓐ $0.\overline{3}$ pound
Ⓑ 0.35 pound
Ⓒ 0.375 pound
Ⓓ $2.\overline{6}$ pounds

2. On Saturday morning, Briana and her friends walked 1.35 miles. What is this distance as a mixed number?

Ⓐ $1\frac{1}{4}$ miles
Ⓑ $1\frac{7}{20}$ miles
Ⓒ $1\frac{2}{5}$ miles
Ⓓ $1\frac{3}{5}$ miles

3. Josh's walking stick is 4.875 feet long. Which is the same length written as a mixed number?

Ⓐ $4\frac{3}{8}$ feet
Ⓑ $4\frac{3}{4}$ feet
Ⓒ $4\frac{5}{6}$ feet
Ⓓ $4\frac{7}{8}$ feet

4. Maria measured the distance between two pictures on her wall. The distance was $6\frac{3}{4}$ inches. Which is the same distance as a decimal?

Ⓐ 5.25 inches
Ⓑ 6.34 inches
Ⓒ 6.75 inches
Ⓓ 7.13 inches

Problem Solving REAL WORLD

5. Grace sold $\frac{5}{8}$ of her stamp collection. What is this amount as a decimal?

____

6. What if you scored a 0.80 on a test? What fraction of the test, in simplest form, did you answer correctly?

____

Name ____________________

Lesson 41

COMMON CORE STANDARD CC.6.NS.6c

Lesson Objective: Compare and order fractions and decimals.

Compare and Order Fractions and Decimals

You can compare fractions and decimals by rewriting them so all are fractions or decimals.

Use < or > to compare 0.77 and $\frac{7}{10}$.

Method 1

Write the fraction as a decimal. Then compare the decimals.

$$\frac{7}{10} = 10\overline{)7.0} = 0.7 \qquad \begin{array}{r} 0.7 \\ 10\overline{)7.0} \\ -7.0 \\ \hline 0 \end{array}$$

$0.77 > 0.7$

So, $0.77 > \frac{7}{10}$.

Method 2

Write the decimal as a fraction. Rewrite $\frac{7}{10}$ with a denominator of 100. Then compare the fractions.

$0.77 = \frac{77}{100}$ $\quad \frac{7}{10} = \frac{7 \times 10}{10 \times 10} = \frac{70}{100}$

$77 > 70$

So, $\frac{77}{100} > \frac{70}{100}$ and $0.77 > \frac{7}{10}$.

Order 0.08, $\frac{1}{20}$, and 0.06 from least to greatest.

Write each number as a fraction.

$0.08 = \frac{8}{100}$ $\quad \frac{1}{20} = \frac{1}{20}$ $\quad 0.06 = \frac{6}{100}$

Compare the fractions.

Compare the fractions with the same denominator.

$8 > 6$

So, $\frac{8}{100} > \frac{6}{100}$.

Compare the fractions with different denominators using common denominators.

$\frac{1}{20} = \frac{1 \times 5}{20 \times 5} = \frac{5}{100}$, $5 < 6$, so $\frac{1}{20} < \frac{6}{100}$.

So, $\frac{1}{20} < \frac{6}{100} < \frac{8}{100}$.

So, the numbers from least to greatest are $\frac{1}{20}$, 0.06, and 0.08.

Compare. Write <, >, or = in each ◯.

1. $\frac{4}{11}$ ◯ $\frac{2}{11}$
2. $\frac{5}{7}$ ◯ $\frac{5}{6}$
3. 0.27 ◯ 0.3
4. 0.9 ◯ $\frac{4}{25}$

Order from least to greatest.

5. $\frac{3}{8}, \frac{5}{16}, \frac{1}{4}$ ____________
6. $0.7, 0.82, \frac{4}{5}$ ____________
7. $2\frac{1}{6}, 1\frac{5}{12}, 2\frac{1}{4}$ ____________
8. $0.64, 0.6, \frac{5}{8}$ ____________

Name ____________________

Lesson 41
CC.6.NS.6c

1. In a survey about favorite breakfast foods, $\frac{3}{8}$ of those surveyed chose cereal, 0.125 chose yogurt, 0.1875 chose fruit, and $\frac{5}{16}$ chose toast. Which food got the **least** number of votes?

Ⓐ cereal
Ⓑ fruit
Ⓒ toast
Ⓓ yogurt

2. Sophia buys an apple that weighs 0.45 pound, a grapefruit that weighs $\frac{3}{4}$ pound, a navel orange that weighs $\frac{5}{8}$ pound, and a pear that weighs 0.5 pound. What is the order of the fruit from **least** weight to **greatest** weight?

Ⓐ pear, apple, grapefruit, navel orange
Ⓑ apple, pear, navel orange, grapefruit
Ⓒ grapefruit, navel orange, pear, apple
Ⓓ pear, navel orange, grapefruit, apple

3. The table shows the grades that four students received on their last math test.

Math Test Grades

Student	Score
Alex	0.95
Octavia	$\frac{16}{20}$
Tonya	$\frac{9}{10}$
Wilson	0.87

Which shows the students in order from **greatest** test score to **least** test score?

Ⓐ Alex, Tonya, Wilson, Octavia
Ⓑ Octavia, Wilson, Tonya, Alex
Ⓒ Tonya, Octavia, Alex, Wilson
Ⓓ Wilson, Alex, Octavia, Tonya

4. Sylvia walked 1.5 miles, Chase walked $1\frac{1}{5}$ miles, Anna walked 1.7 miles, and Anthony walked $1\frac{3}{4}$ miles. Who walked the farthest?

Ⓐ Sylvia
Ⓑ Chase
Ⓒ Anna
Ⓓ Anthony

Problem Solving REAL WORLD

5. One day it snowed $3\frac{3}{8}$ inches in Altoona and 3.45 inches in Bethlehem. Which city received less snow that day?

____

6. Malia and John each bought 2 pounds of sunflower seeds. Each ate some seeds. Malia has $1\frac{1}{3}$ pounds left, and John has $1\frac{2}{5}$ pounds left. Who ate more sunflower seeds?

____

Name ______________________________

Lesson 42

COMMON CORE STANDARD CC.6.NS.6c

Lesson Objective: Plot ordered pairs of rational numbers on a coordinate plane.

Rational Numbers and the Coordinate Plane

A **coordinate plane** is formed by two intersecting lines on a grid. The horizontal line is the *x*-axis. The vertical line is the *y*-axis. They intersect at the **origin**.

An **ordered pair** shows the horizontal and vertical distances a point is from the origin. Positive numbers in an ordered pair mean "right" for the first number and "up" for the second number. Negative numbers mean "left" for the first number and "down" for the second number.

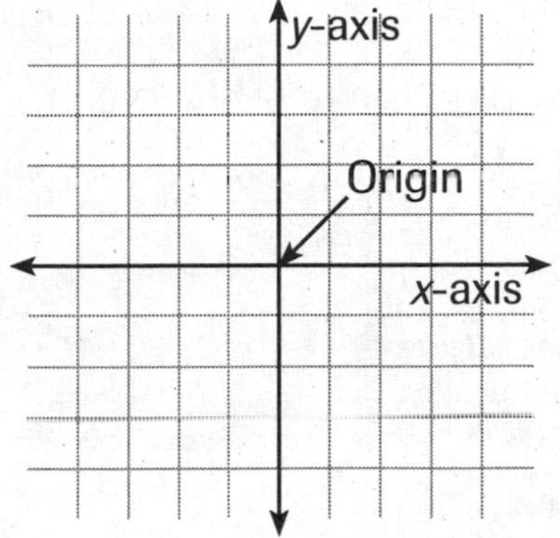

Write the ordered pair for point *K*.

Step 1 Place your finger at point *K*. Place your pencil tip at the origin.

Step 2 With your pencil tip, count how many units to the right or left of the origin point *K* is. Record that number.

Point *K* is 2.5 units right of the origin, so the first number in the ordered pair is $^{+}2.5$, or 2.5.

Step 3 With your pencil tip, count how many units down from the origin point *K* is. Record that number.

Point *K* is 3.5 units down from the origin, so the second number in the ordered pair is $^{-}3.5$.

So, the ordered pair for point *K* is $(2.5, {}^{-}3.5)$.

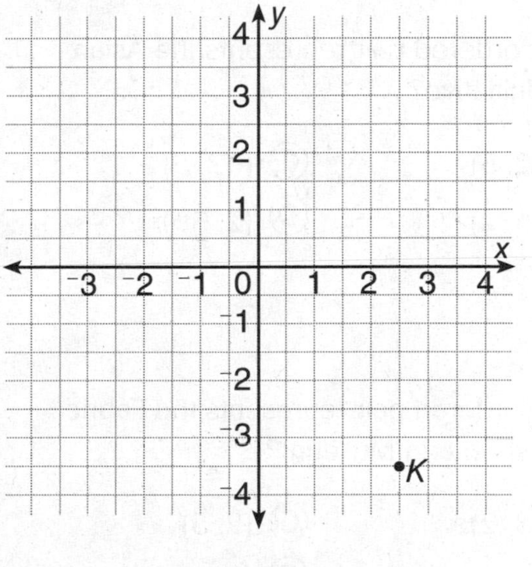

Write the ordered pair for each point.

1. point *P* ______________
2. point *Q* ______________
3. point *R* ______________
4. point *S* ______________
5. point *T* ______________
6. point *U* ______________

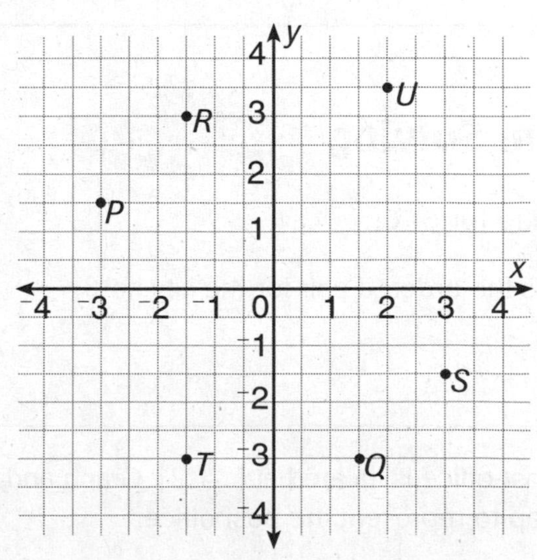

Name ______________________________

Lesson 42
CC.6.NS.6c

Use the map for 1–2.

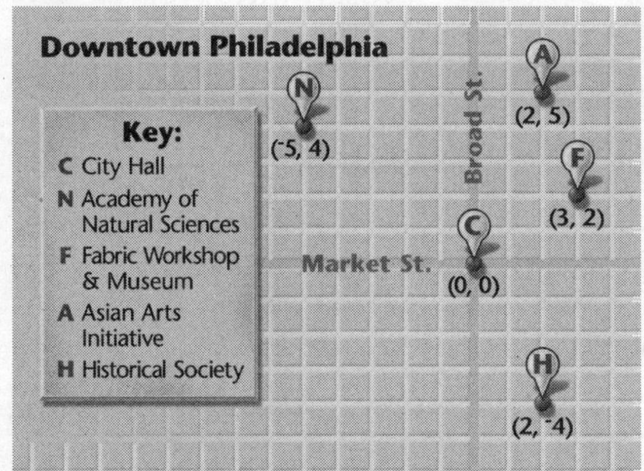

1. What ordered pair represents the Asian Arts Initiative?

Ⓐ (2, 5) Ⓒ (⁻2, 5)
Ⓑ (5, 2) Ⓓ (2, ⁻5)

2. What ordered pair represents the Fabric Workshop and Museum?

Ⓐ (3, 2) Ⓒ (2, 5)
Ⓑ (⁻5, 4) Ⓓ (2, ⁻4)

Use the coordinate plane for 3–4.

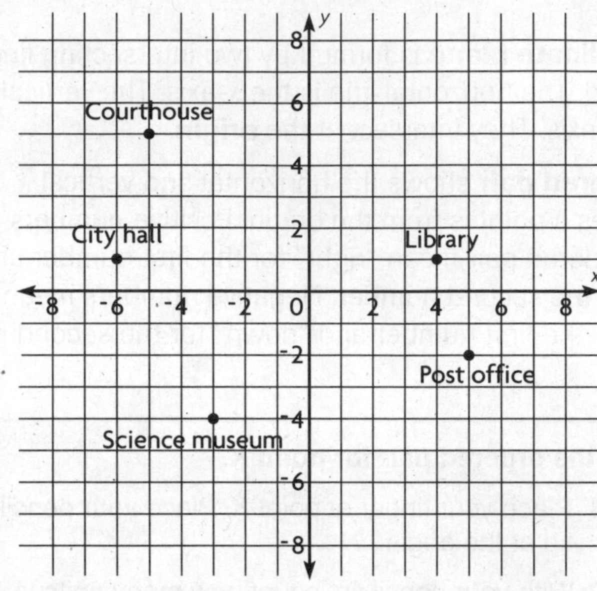

3. What ordered pair represents the library?

Ⓐ (⁻6, 1) Ⓒ (5, ⁻2)
Ⓑ (⁻5, 5) Ⓓ (4, 1)

4. What ordered pair represents the science museum?

Ⓐ (⁻2, ⁻4) Ⓒ (⁻4, ⁻2)
Ⓑ (⁻3, ⁻4) Ⓓ (5, ⁻2)

Problem Solving REAL WORLD

Use the map for 5–6.

Map of Elmwood

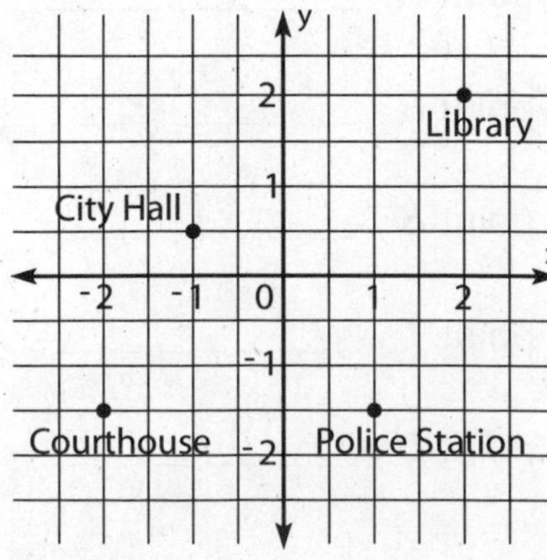

5. What is the ordered pair for the city hall?

____

6. The post office is located at $\left(-\frac{1}{2}, 2\right)$. Graph and label a point on the map to represent the post office.

Name ______________________________

Lesson 43

COMMON CORE STANDARD CC.6.NS.7a

Lesson Objective: Compare and order integers.

Compare and Order Integers

Use a number line to compare $^{-}2$ and $^{-}4$.

Step 1 Graph $^{-}2$ and $^{-}4$. Both numbers are negative integers. Graph them to the left of 0.

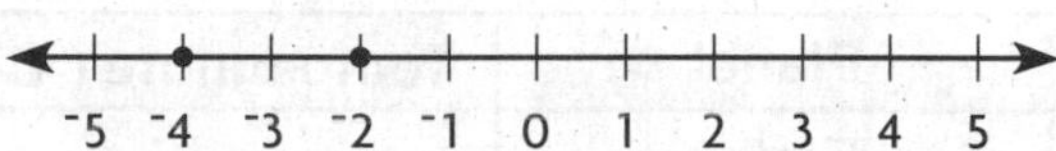

Step 2 Decide which number is greater. Numbers become greater as you move to the right on a number line.

$^{-}2$ is to the right of $^{-}4$.

So, $^{-}2$ is greater than $^{-}4$. Write: $^{-}2 > {}^{-}4$.

Order these integers from least to greatest: 3, $^{-}7$, 0, 4, $^{-}1$.

Step 1 Graph the integers on a number line.

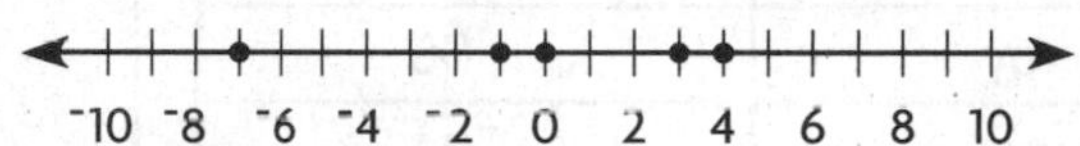

Step 2 Write the numbers in order from left (least) to right (greatest). $^{-}7$, $^{-}1$, 0, 3, 4

Compare the numbers. Write < or >.

1. 3 ◯ $^{-}6$

3 is to the _______ of $^{-}6$ on the number line,

so 3 is ___________ than $^{-}6$.

2. $^{-}4$ ◯ 2

3. 1 ◯ $^{-}5$

4. $^{-}7$ ◯ $^{-}3$

Order the numbers from least to greatest.

5. 4, $^{-}3$, $^{-}5$

_____ < _____ < _____

6. $^{-}11$, 2, 6

_____ < _____ < _____

7. 8, $^{-}7$, 4

_____ < _____ < _____

Order the numbers from greatest to least.

8. 1, $^{-}2$, 0

_____ > _____ > _____

9. $^{-}6$, 2, 5

_____ > _____ > _____

10. $^{-}3$, 3, $^{-}4$

_____ > _____ > _____

Name ____________________

Lesson 43
CC.6.NS.7a

1. The low temperatures in Harrisburg over 4 days were ⁻1°C, ⁻2°C, 4°C, and 0°C. Which list shows these temperatures written in order from **least** to **greatest**?

   Ⓐ ⁻2°C, ⁻1°C, 0°C, 4°C
   Ⓑ ⁻2°C, 0°C, ⁻1°C, 4°C
   Ⓒ ⁻1°C, ⁻2°C, 0°C, 4°C
   Ⓓ 4°C, 0°C, ⁻1°C, ⁻2°C

2. The table shows the elevation of four lakes.

Elevations of Bodies of Water

Lake	Elevation (ft)
Lake Clipson	⁻117
Lake Roney	66
Lake Harney	⁻81
Lake Campbell	97

Which lake has the **highest** elevation?

   Ⓐ Lake Clipson
   Ⓑ Lake Roney
   Ⓒ Lake Harney
   Ⓓ Lake Campbell

3. The table shows the average surface temperature of the planets in the solar system.

Average Surface Temperature of Planets

Planet	Temperature (°C)
Earth	15
Jupiter	⁻110
Mars	⁻65
Mercury	167
Neptune	⁻200
Saturn	⁻140
Uranus	⁻195
Venus	464

Which list shows the planets Mercury, Venus, Earth, and Mars written in order from **greatest** to **least** average surface temperature?

   Ⓐ Mercury, Venus, Earth, Mars
   Ⓑ Venus, Mercury, Earth, Mars
   Ⓒ Mars, Earth, Mercury, Venus
   Ⓓ Venus, Mercury, Mars, Earth

Problem Solving REAL WORLD

4. Meg and Derek played a game. Meg scored ⁻11 points, and Derek scored 4 points. Write a comparison to show that Meg's score is less than Derek's score.

   ____

5. Misha is thinking of a negative integer greater than ⁻4. What number could she be thinking of?

   ____

Name ___________________________________

Lesson 44

COMMON CORE STANDARDS
CC.6.NS.7a, CC.6.NS.7b

Lesson Objective: Compare and order rational numbers.

Compare and Order Rational Numbers

Compare 0.5 and $^{-}3$ using the number line.

Step 1 Graph the numbers. Use positive and negative integers to help you locate the decimals.
0.5 is between 0 and 1.
$^{-}3$ is negative, so it is to the left of 0.

Step 2 As you move right on the number line, numbers become greater.

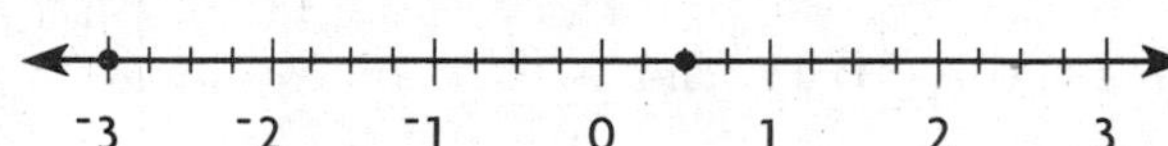

So, $0.5 > {}^{-}3$.

Compare $^{-}2\frac{1}{4}$ and $1\frac{1}{2}$ using the number line.

Step 1 Graph the numbers. Use positive and negative integers to help you locate the fractions.
$^{-}2\frac{1}{4}$ is between $^{-}2$ and $^{-}3$. $1\frac{1}{2}$ is between 1 and 2.

Step 2 As you move left on the number line, numbers become less.

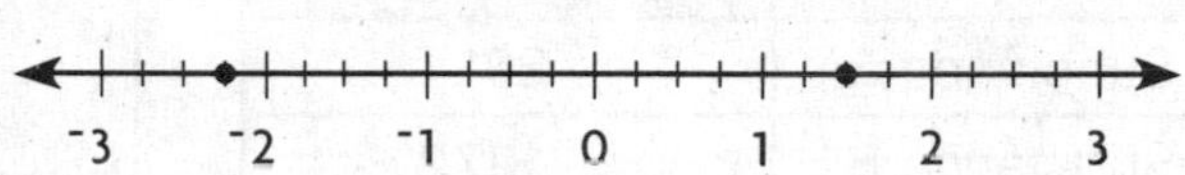

So, $^{-}2\frac{1}{4} < 1\frac{1}{2}$.

Compare the numbers. Write < or >.

1. $^{-}0.7$ ◯ $^{-}1\frac{1}{8}$
2. 0.3 ◯ $^{-}4.6$
3. $-\frac{1}{4}$ ◯ 3.2
4. $-\frac{5}{8}$ ◯ $^{-}2\frac{1}{2}$

Order the numbers from least to greatest.

5. $1.3, {}^{-}4\frac{1}{5}, {}^{-}\frac{1}{2}$

6. $^{-}2.5, {}^{-}0.9, 1$

7. $2, 2\frac{2}{3}, {}^{-}3.2$

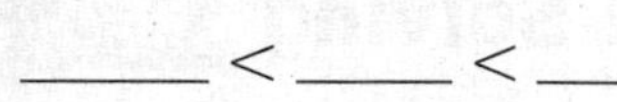

Name ______________________________

Lesson 44

CC.6.NS.7a, CC.6.NS.7b

1. The wind-chill temperatures on Sunday for four cities are $^-7.2$°F, $^-6.7$°F, $^-5.4$°F, and $^-6.1$°F. Which list shows these numbers in order from **least** to **greatest**?

Ⓐ $^-7.2, {}^-6.7, {}^-5.4, {}^-6.1$

Ⓑ $^-5.4, {}^-6.1, {}^-6.7, {}^-7.2$

Ⓒ $^-7.2, {}^-6.7, {}^-6.1, {}^-5.4$

Ⓓ $^-6.1, {}^-5.4, {}^-6.7, {}^-7.2$

2. The table shows the freezing points of four different substances.

Freezing Points

Substance	Temperature (°C)
Substance A	$^-201.7$
Substance B	$^-187.3$
Substance C	$^-159.6$
Substance D	$^-193.7$

What substance freezes at the **highest** temperature?

Ⓐ Substance A
Ⓑ Substance B
Ⓒ Substance C
Ⓓ Substance D

3. The low temperatures during one week are shown in the table.

Low Temperatures

Day	Temperature (°F)
Sunday	$^-2.1$
Monday	$^-3.8$
Tuesday	$^-2.5$
Wednesday	$^-0.4$
Thursday	$^-1.7$
Friday	$^-2.3$
Saturday	$^-1.9$

Which list shows the days arranged in order from **warmest** to **coldest** temperatures?

Ⓐ Wednesday, Thursday, Saturday, Sunday, Friday, Tuesday, Monday

Ⓑ Monday, Tuesday, Friday, Sunday, Saturday, Thursday, Wednesday

Ⓒ Wednesday, Saturday, Thursday, Sunday, Tuesday, Friday, Monday

Ⓓ Monday, Friday, Tuesday, Saturday, Thursday, Wednesday, Sunday

Problem Solving REAL WORLD

4. The temperature in Cold Town on Monday was 1°C. The temperature in Frosty Town on Monday was $^-2$°C. Which town was colder on Monday?

____

5. Stan's bank account balance is less than $^-\$20.00$ but greater than $^-\$21.00$. What could Stan's account balance be?

____

Name ______________________________

Lesson 45

COMMON CORE STANDARD CC.6.NS.7c

Lesson Objective: Find and interpret the absolute value of rational numbers.

Absolute Value

Absolute value is a number's distance from 0 on a number line. Numbers and their opposites have the same absolute value.

Find the absolute value of $^-3$ and 4.

Step 1 Graph the numbers.

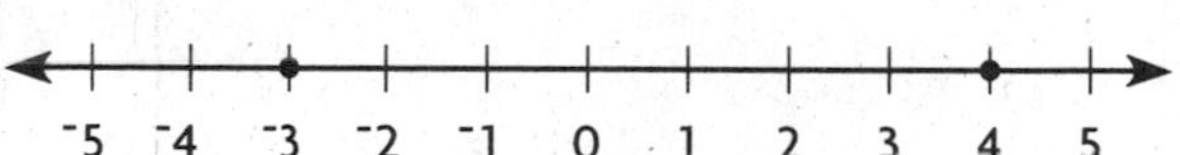

Step 2 Find each number's distance from 0.

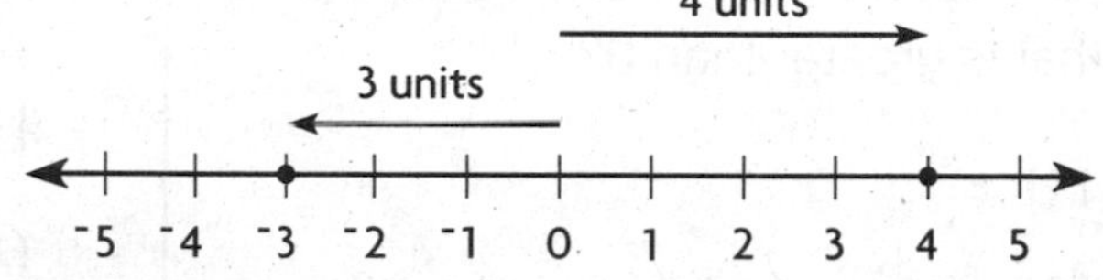

Step 3 Write the absolute value. $|^-3| = 3$ $|4| = 4$

Find the absolute value of $^-0.75$ and 2.25.

Step 1 Graph the numbers.

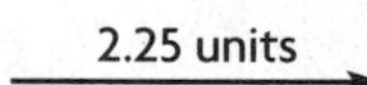

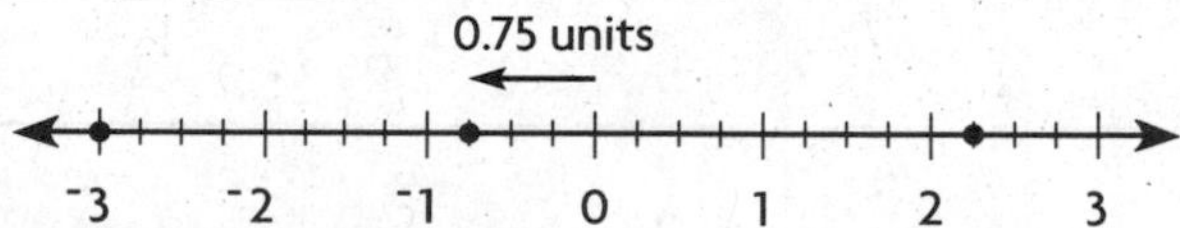

Step 2 Find each number's distance from 0.

Step 3 Write the absolute value. $|^-0.75| = 0.75$ $|2.25| = 2.25$

Find the absolute value.

1. $\left|^-3\frac{2}{3}\right|$ $^-3\frac{2}{3}$ is ____ units from 0.

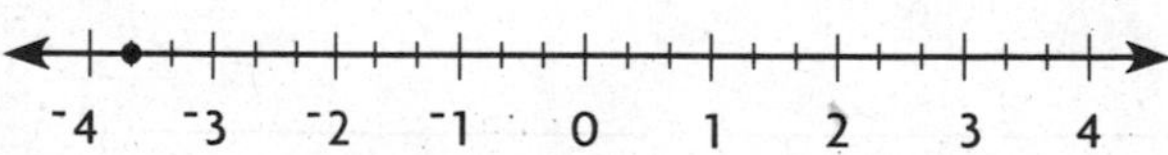

$\left|^-3\frac{2}{3}\right| =$ ____

2. $|^-2.5| =$ ____ 3. $|7| =$ ____ 4. $\left|\frac{4}{10}\right| =$ ____ 5. $|^-1| =$ ____ 6. $\left|^-1\frac{4}{5}\right| =$ ____

Name ___________________________

1. Which of the following has a value that is less than 0?

   (A) $|^-7|$
   (B) $|7|$
   (C) $^-7$
   (D) 7

2. Which of the following does **not** have a value that is greater than 0?

   (A) $|^-11|$
   (B) $^-11$
   (C) $|11|$
   (D) 11

3. The high temperature on Friday was $^-3$°C. What is the absolute value of $^-3$?

   (A) $^-3$
   (B) 0
   (C) 3
   (D) 6

4. During the first round of a board game, Alejandro lost 8 points. What does $|^-8|$ represent in this situation?

   (A) the decrease in Alejandro's score
   (B) the increase in Alejandro's score
   (C) the number of points Alejandro had at the end of the round
   (D) the number of points Alejandro had at the beginning of the round

Problem Solving REAL WORLD

5. Which two numbers are 7.5 units away from 0 on a number line?

   ____

6. Emilio is playing a game. He just answered a question incorrectly, so his score will change by $^-10$ points. Find the absolute value of $^-10$.

   ____

Name ______________________________

Lesson 46

COMMON CORE STANDARD CC.6.NS.7d

Lesson Objective: Interpret comparisons involving absolute values.

Compare Absolute Values

Use absolute value to express an elevation less than ⁻10 meters as a depth.

Step 1 Elevation indicates distance from sea level. A negative elevation means a distance below sea level.
⁻10 is 10 units below 0 on the vertical number line. This shows that the absolute value of ⁻10 is 10.

Step 2 Depth indicates distance below sea level. It is always expressed as a positive number. Use the absolute value of ⁻10 to find the depth: |⁻10| = 10

Step 3 List three elevations that are less than ⁻10 meters. Write the corresponding depths.

50
40
30
20
10
0
⁻10
⁻20
⁻30
⁻40
⁻50

Elevation (m)	Depth (m)
⁻15	15
⁻20	20
⁻30	30

So, an elevation less than ⁻10 meters is a depth greater than 10 meters.

Complete the table.

1.

Elevations Greater than ⁻13	Depth
⁻12 feet	12 feet
⁻8 feet	
	2 feet

2. Jordin's savings account balance is greater than ⁻$27. Use absolute value to describe the balance as a debt.

Jordin's balance is a debt of ________ than $27.

3. The table shows the changes in the weights of 3 dogs. Which dog had the greatest decrease in weight? How much weight did the dog lose?

Dog	Weight Change (lb)
Duffy	1.3
Buddy	⁻1.1
Dinah	⁻1.4

____

Name ______________________________

1. On February 3, 1996, a record low temperature of $^-47$°F was reached in Iowa. The temperature the next day was a little warmer. Which could have been the temperature the next day?

   Ⓐ $^-51$°F
   Ⓑ $^-49$°F
   Ⓒ $^-47$°F
   Ⓓ $^-45$°F

2. While scuba diving, Amelia explored the ocean at an elevation of $^-30$ feet. Ricardo was closer to the surface of the water than Amelia. Which describes Ricardo's depth?

   Ⓐ depth of greater than $^-30$ feet
   Ⓑ depth of greater than 30 feet
   Ⓒ depth of less than 30 feet
   Ⓓ depth of less than $^-30$ feet

3. Cynthia and Antonio are hiking. Cynthia's elevation is $^-17$ feet. Antonio is a little lower than Cynthia. Which could be Antonio's elevation?

   Ⓐ $^-20$ feet
   Ⓑ $^-15$ feet
   Ⓒ $^-10$ feet
   Ⓓ $^-5$ feet

4. Last month, Margaret's puppy had a change in weight of $^-9$ ounces. Which does **not** show a greater change in weight?

   Ⓐ loss of 10 ounces
   Ⓑ loss of 8 ounces
   Ⓒ gain of 14 ounces
   Ⓓ gain of 12 ounces

Problem Solving REAL WORLD

5. On Wednesday, Miguel's bank account balance was $^-$\$55. On Thursday, his balance was less than that. Use absolute value to describe Miguel's balance on Thursday as a debt.

   In this situation, $^-$\$55 represents a debt of

   __________. On Thursday, Miguel had a debt

   of __________ than \$55.

6. During a game, Naomi lost points. She lost fewer than 3 points. Use an integer to describe her possible score.

   ____

Name ____

Lesson 47

COMMON CORE STANDARD CC.6.NS.8

Lesson Objective: Find horizontal and vertical distances on the coordinate plane.

Distance on the Coordinate Plane

Find the distance between (4, $^-2$) and (4, 3).

Step 1 Graph the points. Points with the same *x*-coordinate are on the same vertical line. Think of the vertical line as a number line that shows the *y*-coordinates.

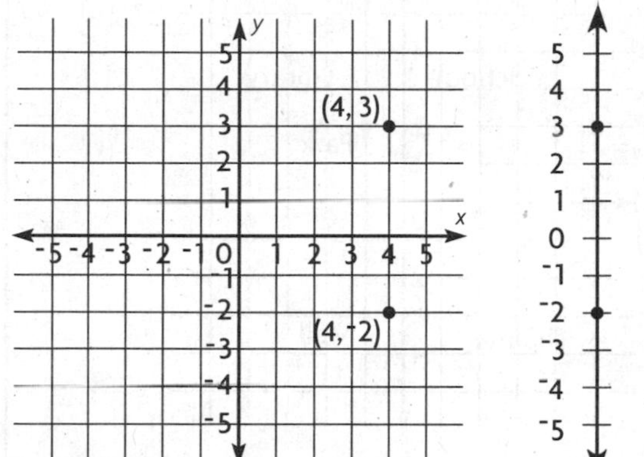

Step 2 Use absolute value to find the distances between the *y*-coordinates and 0.

$|^-2|$ shows the distance from $^-2$ to 0.

$|^-2| = 2$ units

$|3|$ shows the distance from 3 to 0.

$|^-3| = 3$ units

Step 3 Since the points are in different quadrants, add to find the total distance between the *y*-coordinates.

So, the distance between (4, $^-2$) and (4, 3) is 5 units.

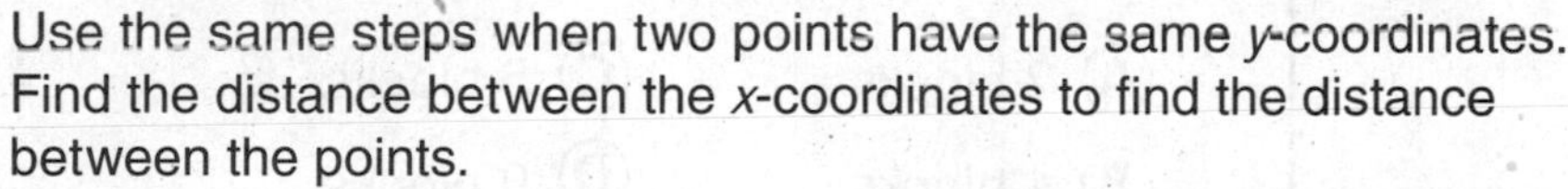

Use the same steps when two points have the same *y*-coordinates. Find the distance between the *x*-coordinates to find the distance between the points.

Graph the pair of points. Then find the distance between them.

1. (4, $^-4$) and (1, $^-4$)

   The points are on the same horizontal line.

   Distance from 4 to 0: _____ = _____

   Distance from 1 to 0: _____ = _____

   Subtract to find distance from (4, $^-4$) to (1, $^-4$):

   _____ − _____ = _____ units

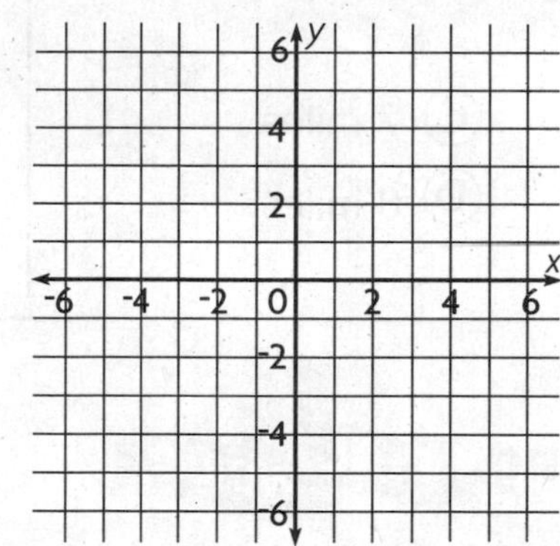

2. (2, $^-5$) and (2, 3)

   __________ units

3. ($^-1$, 3) and (5, 3)

   __________ units

4. ($^-6$, 1) and ($^-6$, $^-2$)

   __________ units

Name ______________________________

Lesson 47
CC.6.NS.8

On the coordinate plane, each unit is 1 mile. Use the coordinate plane for 1–2.

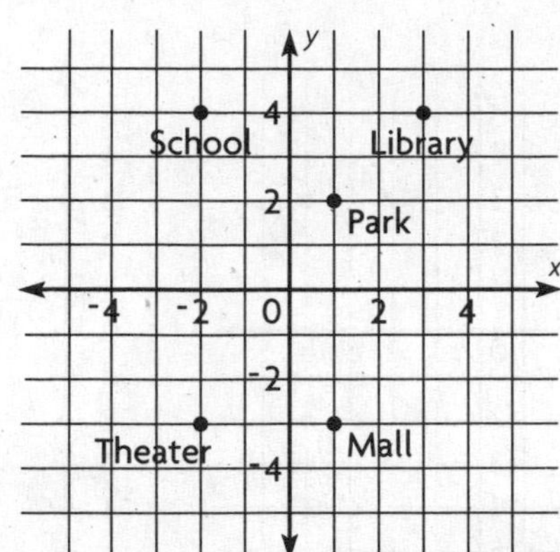

1. What is the distance from the school to the library?

   Ⓐ 1 mile Ⓑ 2 miles Ⓒ 3 miles Ⓓ 5 miles

2. What is the distance from the theater to the school?

   Ⓐ 1 mile Ⓑ 3 miles Ⓒ 7 miles Ⓓ 8 miles

Use the map for 3–4.

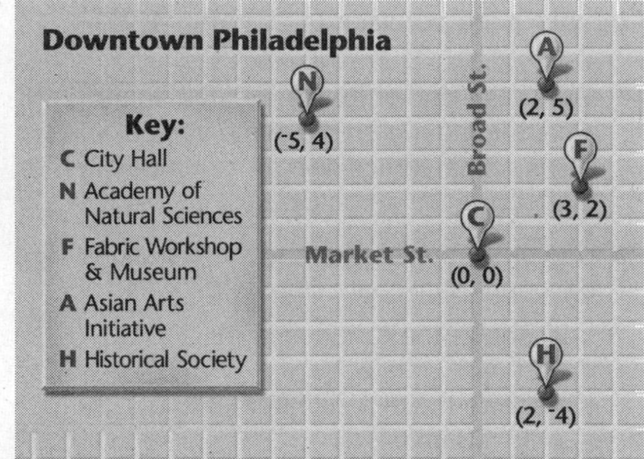

3. Lindsey is leaving the Asian Arts Initiative and wants to visit the Historical Society. How many blocks south does she need to walk?

   Ⓐ 2 blocks Ⓑ 4 blocks Ⓒ 5 blocks Ⓓ 9 blocks

4. Cesar leaves City Hall and goes to a store located at ($^-4$, 0). How many blocks west does he walk?

   Ⓐ 3 blocks Ⓑ 4 blocks Ⓒ 5 blocks Ⓓ 6 blocks

Problem Solving REAL WORLD

The map shows the locations of several areas in an amusement park. Each unit represents 1 kilometer.

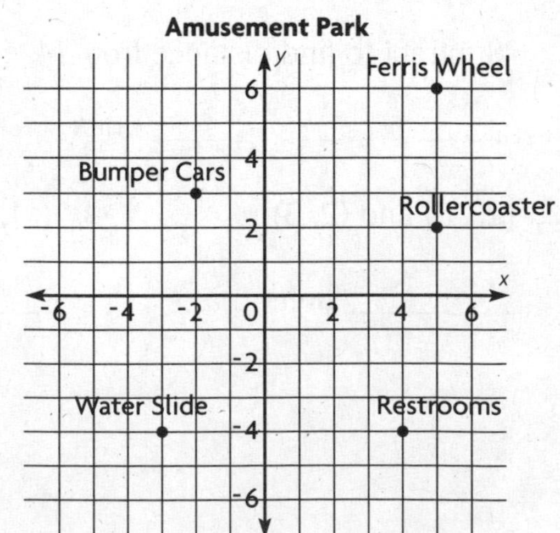

5. How far is the Ferris wheel from the rollercoaster?

   ____

6. How far is the water slide from the restrooms?

   ____

Name ______________________________

Lesson 48

COMMON CORE STANDARD CC.6.NS.8

Lesson Objective: Solve problems on the coordinate plane by using the strategy *draw a diagram.*

Problem Solving • The Coordinate Plane

Zachary is drawing a coordinate map of his town. He has graphed the police station at the point (2, −1). He is going to place the library 4 units up from the police station. What ordered pair shows where he will graph the library?

Read the Problem		
What do I need to find?	**What information do I need to use?**	**How will I use the information?**
I need to find the ____________ for the library.	The ordered pair for the ____________ is ________. The library is ______ units ______ from the police station.	I can draw a diagram to ________ the information on a coordinate plane.

Solve the Problem
Graph the point ____________.   Label it ____________.   From this point, count ______ units ________.   Graph the new point, and label it ____________.   So, the ordered pair for the library will be ________.

Solve. Graph the pairs of points on the coordinate plane.

1. Zachary has graphed the middle school at (−6, 5). He has graphed the high school 3 units to the right of the middle school. What is the high school's ordered pair?

    ____

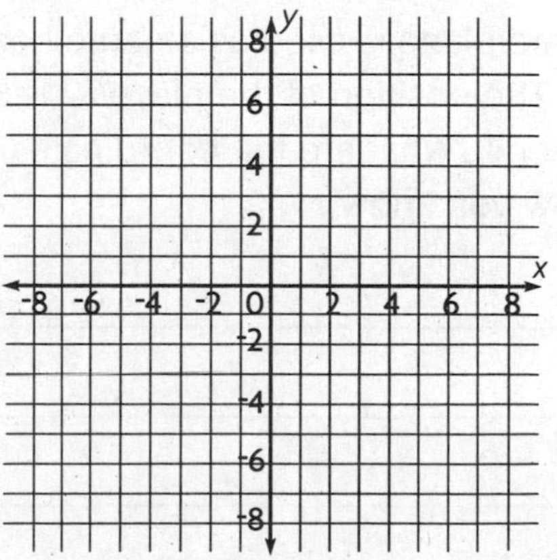

2. Zachary will graph the apartment building 2 units to the left and 5 units down from the grocery store. He has graphed the grocery store at (7, 8). Give the ordered pair for the apartment building.

    ____

Name ____________________

Lesson 48
CC.6.NS.8

1. On a map of Geston County, the post office is located at ($^-6$, 4). The fire station is located 3 units east of the post office. What ordered pair represents the location of the fire station?

   Ⓐ ($^-3$, 4)
   Ⓑ ($^-6$, 4)
   Ⓒ ($^-6$, 7)
   Ⓓ ($^-6$, 1)

2. On a map of a fair, the Ferris wheel is located at (3, 2). The carousel is located 5 units south of the Ferris wheel. What ordered pair represents the location of the carousel?

   Ⓐ ($^-2$, 2)
   Ⓑ (3, $^-3$)
   Ⓒ (8, 2)
   Ⓓ (8, 7)

3. On a map of Braxton County, the library is located at ($^-3$, $^-7$). The hospital is located 5 units west of the library. What ordered pair represents the location of the hospital?

   Ⓐ (2, $^-7$)
   Ⓑ ($^-3$, $^-2$)
   Ⓒ ($^-3$, $^-12$)
   Ⓓ ($^-8$, $^-7$)

4. On a map of a sports facility, the tennis court is located at ($^-6$, $^-1$). The basketball court is located 10 units north of the tennis court. What ordered pair represents the location of the basketball court?

   Ⓐ (4, $^-1$)
   Ⓑ (4, $^-11$)
   Ⓒ ($^-6$, 9)
   Ⓓ ($^-16$, 1)

Problem Solving REAL WORLD

5. A coordinate plane is used as a game board. The position of player 1 is at ($^-7$, 3). The position of the player 2 is 3 units down from the position of the player 1. What are the coordinates of the position of player 2? Explain how you know.

____

____

____

____

Name ______________________________

Lesson 49

COMMON CORE STANDARD CC.6.EE.1

Lesson Objective: Write and evaluate expressions involving exponents.

Exponents

An **exponent** tells how many times a number is used as a factor.

The **base** is the number being multiplied repeatedly.

For example, in 2^5, 5 is the exponent and 2 is the base.
$2^5 = 2 \times 2 \times 2 \times 2 \times 2 = 32$

Write the expression 4^5 using equal factors. Then find the value.

Step 1 Identify the base.	The base is 4.
Step 2 Identify the exponent.	The exponent is 5.
Step 3 Write the base as many times as the exponent tells you. Place a multiplication symbol between the bases.	$4 \times 4 \times 4 \times 4 \times 4$ You should have one less multiplication symbol than the value of the exponent.
Step 4 Multiply.	$4 \times 4 \times 4 \times 4 \times 4 = 1{,}024$

So, $4^5 = 1{,}024$.

Write as an expression using equal factors. Then find the value.

1. 3^4

____

2. 2^6

____

3. 4^3

____

4. 5^3

____

5. 10^4

____

6. 8^5

____

7. 11^4

____

8. 15^2

____

9. 10^7

____

____

10. 25^4

____

____

Name ______________________________

1. The bill with the greatest value ever printed in the United States had a value of 10^5 dollars. Which is another way to write that amount?

Ⓐ \$10,000
Ⓑ \$50,000
Ⓒ \$100,000
Ⓓ \$500,000

2. Carlos represented 729 with a base and an exponent. Which of the following is **not** possible?

Ⓐ The base is less than the exponent.
Ⓑ The base and the exponent are equal.
Ⓒ The base and the exponent are multiples of 3.
Ⓓ The base is an odd number and the exponent is an even number.

3. John is making a patio in his yard. He needs a total of 15^2 concrete blocks to cover the area. How many blocks does John need?

Ⓐ 30
Ⓑ 125
Ⓒ 152
Ⓓ 225

4. Which is a way to write $2 \times 2 \times 2 \times 5 \times 5$ with exponents and two bases?

Ⓐ $2^3 \times 5^2$
Ⓑ $3^2 \times 2^5$
Ⓒ $2^5 \times 5^5$
Ⓓ $2^5 \times 10 \times 5$

Problem Solving REAL WORLD

5. Each day Sheila doubles the number of push-ups she did the day before. On the fifth day, she does $2 \times 2 \times 2 \times 2 \times 2$ push-ups. Use an exponent to write the number of push-ups Shelia does on the fifth day.

____

6. The city of Beijing has a population of more than 10^7 people. Write 10^7 without using an exponent.

____

Name ____________________________________

Lesson 50

COMMON CORE STANDARD CC.6.EE.1

Lesson Objective: Use the order of operations to evaluate expressions involving exponents.

Evaluate Expressions Involving Exponents

A **numerical expression** is a mathematical phrase that includes only numbers and operation symbols.

You **evaluate** the expression when you perform all the computations.

To evaluate an expression, use the **order of operations.**

Order of Operations
1. Parentheses
2. Exponents
3. Multiply and Divide
4. Add and Subtract

Evaluate the expression $(10 + 6^2) - 4 \times 10$.

Step 1 Start with the *parentheses*. Use the order of operations for the computations inside the parentheses.

$10 + 6^2$

Find the value of the number with an *exponent*. Rewrite as multiplication:

$10 + 6^2 = 10 + 6 \times 6$

Multiply and divide from left to right:

$10 + 6 \times 6 = 10 + 36$

Add and subtract from left to right:

$10 + 36 = 46$

Step 2 Rewrite the original expression, using the value from Step 1 for the part in parentheses.

$(10 + 6^2) - 4 \times 10 = \mathbf{46} - 4 \times 10$

Step 3 Now that the parentheses are cleared, look for *exponents*.

There are no more *exponents*, so go on to the next step in the order of operations.

Step 4 *Multiply and divide* from left to right.

$46 - 4 \times 10 = 46 - 40$

Step 5 *Add and subtract* from left to right.

$46 - 40 = 6$

So, $(10 + 6^2) - 4 \times 10 = 6$.

Evaluate the expression.

1. $8^2 - (7^2 + 1)$ ____________

2. $5 - 2^2 + 12 \div 4$ ____________

3. $8 \times (16 - 2^4)$ ____________

4. $3^2 \times (28 - 20 \div 2)$ ____________

5. $(30 - 15 \div 3) \div 5^2$ ____________

6. $(6^2 - 3^2) - 9 \div 3$ ____________

Name ____________________

1. Which expression has a value of 250?

   (A) $1 + 6 \times 7 - 5^2$
   (B) $1 + 7^2 - 6 \times 5$
   (C) $(7 + 6) \times 5^2 - 1$
   (D) $(6^2 - 1) \times 7 + 5$

2. An employee placed 2^4 books onto each of 5 shelves. How many books did she place on the shelves in all?

   (A) 16
   (B) 80
   (C) 120
   (D) 245

3. A scientist placed 8 one-celled organisms into a dish. Each cell split into 2 cells every hour. The expression 8×2^6 represents the number of cells after 6 hours. How many cells were in the dish after 6 hours?

   (A) 64
   (B) 208
   (C) 512
   (D) 826

4. Which expression has a value of 35?

   (A) $7 + (2^2 - 3) + 4 \times 4$
   (B) $3 \times (7^2 - 4) \times 4 + 2$
   (C) $4^2 + 3 \times (7 - 2) + 4$
   (D) $2^2 \times 7 - (4 + 4) \times 3$

Problem Solving REAL WORLD

5. Hugo is saving for a new baseball glove. He saves \$10 the first week, and \$6 each week for the next 6 weeks. The expression $10 + 6^2$ represents the total amount in dollars he has saved. What is the total amount Hugo has saved?

   ____

6. A scientist placed fish eggs in a tank. Each day, twice the number of eggs from the previous day hatch. The expression 5×2^6 represents the number of eggs that hatch on the sixth day. How many eggs hatch on the sixth day?

   ____

Name ______________________________

Lesson 51

COMMON CORE STANDARD CC.6.EE.2a

Lesson Objective: Write algebraic expressions.

Write Algebraic Expressions

Word problems use expressions that you can write with symbols. An **algebraic expression** has at least one variable. A **variable** is a letter or symbol that represents one or more numbers. Writing algebraic expressions for words helps you solve word problems.

These are a few common words that are used for operations.

add (+)	**subtract (−)**	**multiply (×)**	**divide (÷)**
sum	difference	product	quotient
increased by	minus	times	divided by
plus	decreased by		
more than	less		
	less than		

17 more than *x*
$x + 17$

"More than" means add.
"17 more than x" means add 17 to x.

four times the sum of 7 and *n*
$4 \times (7 + n)$

"Times" means multiply.
"Sum" means add.
The words mean multiply 4 by $(7 + n)$.

A number next to a variable always shows multiplication.
For example, $\mathbf{5n}$ means the same as $\mathbf{5 \times n}$.

Write an algebraic expression for the word expression.

1. b divided by 9

____

2. c more than 5

____

3. d decreased by 29

____

4. 8 times g

____

5. p increased by 12

____

6. the quotient of k and 14

____

7. 17 less than the product of 3 and m

____

8. 2 less than the quotient of d and 16

____

Name ____________________

Lesson 51
CC.6.EE.2a

1. There are 16 ounces in 1 pound. Which expression gives the number of ounces in *p* pounds?

Ⓐ $16 + p$

Ⓑ $16 - p$

Ⓒ $16p$

Ⓓ $p \div 16$

2. The length of a swimming pool is 5 feet shorter than twice the width. Let *n* represent the width. Which expression gives the length of the swimming pool?

Ⓐ $2n + 5$

Ⓑ $2n - 5$

Ⓒ $2(n - 5)$

Ⓓ $2(n + 5)$

3. Carmen's family rents a boat at Big Lake at the rate described.

BIG LAKE BOAT
RENTAL
$200 each day
$4 for each gallon of gasoline used
19-ft

Which expression gives the total cost of the day's rental if her family uses *n* gallons of gasoline?

Ⓐ $200 - 4n$

Ⓑ $200 + 4n$

Ⓒ $(200 + 4) \times n$

Ⓓ $200n + 4$

4. There are 5,280 feet in 1 mile. Which expression gives the number of feet in *m* miles?

Ⓐ $5{,}280m$

Ⓑ $5{,}280 \div m$

Ⓒ $5{,}280 - m$

Ⓓ $5{,}280 + m$

Problem Solving REAL WORLD

5. Let *h* represent Mark's height in inches. Suzanne is 7 inches shorter than Mark. Write an algebraic expression that represents Suzanne's height in inches.

____

6. A company rents bicycles for a fee of $10 plus $4 per hour of use. Write an algebraic expression for the total cost in dollars for renting a bicycle for *h* hours.

____

Name ______________________________

Lesson 52

COMMON CORE STANDARD CC.6.EE.2b

Lesson Objective: Identify and describe parts of expressions.

Identify Parts of Expressions

Each part of an expression between the operation signs + or − is a **term**. A **coefficient** is a number multiplied by a variable, or letter.

Describe the parts of the expression $6b - 7$. Then write a word expression.

Step 1 Identify the terms.	There are two terms: $6b$ and 7.
Step 2 Describe the terms.	The first term shows multiplication: $6b = 6 \times b$ $6b$ is the product of 6 (the coefficient) and b (the variable). The second term is the number 7.
Step 3 Identify the operation separating the terms.	Subtraction gives the difference of the two terms in the expression.
Step 4 Write a word expression.	"the difference of 6 times b and 7" or "7 less than the product of 6 and b"

Identify the parts of the expression. Then write a word expression for the numerical or algebraic expression.

1. $5 \times (m - 2)$

Identify the parts. ______________________________

Describe the parts. ______________________________

____

Identify the operations. ______________________________

Write a word expression. ______________________________

2. $12 \div 2 + 7$

____

____

____

____

____

____

____

3. $8y + (2 \times 11)$

____

____

____

____

____

____

____

Name ______________________________

Lesson 52
CC.6.EE.2b

1. The baker at Sweetie Pie Cafe baked 7 cherry pies and 8 apple pies yesterday. She cut each cherry pie into 6 slices and each apple pie into 8 slices. At the end of the day, there were 5 slices of pie left unsold. The expression $(7 \times 6) + (8 \times 8) - 5$ gives the number of slices that were sold. Which describes a part in this expression?

Ⓐ the sum of 6 and 8

Ⓑ the difference of 8 and 5

Ⓒ the sum of 7 and 6

Ⓓ the product of 8 and 8

2. The cost for a group of people to go to the movies is given by the expression $9a + 5b$, where a is the number of adults and b is the number of children. What are the coefficients of this expression?

Ⓐ 9 and 5

Ⓑ a and b

Ⓒ $9a$ and $5b$

Ⓓ + and ×

3. Martin is making curtains. He buys 6 yards of fabric that cost p dollars per yard and 8 yards of fabric that cost q dollars per yard. The total amount of his purchase is given by the expression $6p + 8q$. What are the terms of this expression?

Ⓐ 6 and 8

Ⓑ p and q

Ⓒ $6p$ and $8q$

Ⓓ + and ×

4. Heidi bought 5 pepperoni pizzas and 6 cheese pizzas for a party. Each pepperoni pizza was cut into 8 pieces and each cheese pizza was cut into 10 pieces. There were 9 pieces of pizza left. The expression $(5 \times 8) + (6 \times 10) - 9$ gives the number of pieces that were eaten. Which describes a part in this expression?

Ⓐ the product of 5 and 8

Ⓑ the sum of 8 and 6

Ⓒ the difference between 10 and 9

Ⓓ the sum of 6 and 10

Problem Solving

5. Adam bought granola bars at the store. The expression $6p + 5n$ gives the number of bars in p boxes of plain granola bars and n boxes of granola bars with nuts. What are the terms of the expression?

____

6. In the sixth grade, each student will get 4 new books. There is one class of 15 students and one class of 20 students. The expression $4 \times (15 + 20)$ gives the total number of new books. Write a word expression for the numerical expression.

____

____

Name ______________________________

Lesson 53

COMMON CORE STANDARD CC.6.EE.2c

Lesson Objective: Evaluate algebraic expressions and formulas.

Evaluate Algebraic Expressions and Formulas

To evaluate an algebraic expression or formula, substitute the value for the variable. Then follow the order of operations.

Evaluate $5x + x^3$ for $x = 3, 2, 1,$ and 0.

$5x + x^3$ for $x = 3$	$5x + x^3$ for $x = 2$	$5x + x^3$ for $x = 1$	$5x + x^3$ for $x = 0$
$5 \times 3 + 3^3$	$5 \times 2 + 2^3$	$5 \times 1 + 1^3$	$5 \times 0 + 0^3$
$5 \times 3 + 27$	$5 \times 2 + 8$	$5 \times 1 + 1$	$5 \times 0 + 0$
$15 + 27$	$10 + 8$	$5 + 1$	$0 + 0$
42	18	6	0

To evaluate an expression with more than one variable, substitute each variable's value. Then follow the order of operations.

Evaluate $4c - 7 + 2d$ for $c = 2$ and $d = 5$.

$4 \times 2 - 7 + 2 \times 5$

$8 - 7 + 10$

$1 + 10$

11

So, $4c - 7 + 2d = 11$ for $c = 2$ and $d = 5$.

Evaluate the expression for x = 3, 2, 1, and 0.

1. $13 + 6x$ ____________

2. $5x + 2$ ____________

3. $2x + 3 + x^2$ ____________

4. $2x + x^2$ ____________

Evaluate the expression for the given values of the variables.

5. $7x + y + 16$ for $x = 2, y = 3$ ____________

6. $8a + 11 - 2b$ for $a = 4, b = 2$ ____________

7. $12b - 2c + 3$ for $b = 5, c = 10$ ____________

Name ______________________

1. The expression $4c$ gives the science test score that a student receives for c correct problems. What is the score for 18 correct problems?

   Ⓐ 418
   Ⓑ 184
   Ⓒ 72
   Ⓓ 22

2. The expression $180 \times (n - 2)$ gives the sum of the measures of the angles, in degrees, of a polygon with n sides. What is the sum of the measures of the angles in a polygon with 10 sides?

   Ⓐ 1,080 degrees
   Ⓑ 1,440 degrees
   Ⓒ 1,880 degrees
   Ⓓ 2,160 degrees

3. The stock clerks at Mega Brands earn \$320 each week plus \$16 per hour for any overtime. They use the expression $320 + 16h$ to find their total earnings for a week in which they worked h hours of overtime. What are the total earnings of a stock clerk who worked 4 hours of overtime last week?

   Ⓐ \$324 Ⓒ \$384
   Ⓑ \$352 Ⓓ \$484

4. The expression $500v$ gives the number of points a player earns for completing v voyages in a video game. How many points are earned for completing 8 voyages?

   Ⓐ 508
   Ⓑ 1,800
   Ⓒ 2,500
   Ⓓ 4,000

Problem Solving REAL WORLD

5. The formula $P = 2\ell + 2w$ gives the perimeter P of a rectangular room with length ℓ and width w. A rectangular living room is 26 feet long and 21 feet wide. What is the perimeter of the room?

   ____

6. The formula $c = 5(f - 32) \div 9$ gives the Celsius temperature in c degrees for a Fahrenheit temperature of f degrees. What is the Celsius temperature for a Fahrenheit temperature of 122 degrees?

   ____

Name ______________________________

Lesson 54

COMMON CORE STANDARD CC.6.EE.3

Lesson Objective: Combine like terms by applying the strategy *use a model.*

Problem Solving • Combine Like Terms

Use a bar model to solve the problem.

Each hour a company assembles 10 bikes. It sends 6 of those bikes to stores and keeps the rest of the bikes to sell itself. The expression $10h - 6h$ represents the number of bikes the store keeps to sell itself for h hours of work. Simplify the expression by combining like terms.

Read the Problem		
What do I need to find?	**What information do I need to use?**	**How will I use the information?**
I need to simplify the expression ________.	I need to use the like terms $10h$ and _____.	I can use a bar model to find the difference of the ________ terms.

Solve the Problem

Draw a bar model to subtract _____ from _____. Each square represents h, or $1h$.

10 h

h	h	h	h	h	h	h	h	h	h

h	h	h	h	h	h

6 h

_____ h

The model shows that $10h - 6h =$ _____.

So, a simplified expression for the number of bikes the store keeps is _____.

1. Bradley sells produce in boxes at a farmer's market. He put 6 ears of corn and 9 tomatoes in each box. The expression $6b + 9b$ represents the total pieces of produce in b boxes. Simplify the expression by combining like terms.

   ____

2. Andre bought pencils in packs of 8. He gave 2 pencils to his sister and 3 pencils from each pack to his friends. The expression $8p - 3p - 2$ represents the number of pencils Andre has left from p packs. Simplify the expression by combining like terms.

   ____

Name ______________________________

1. Sandwiches cost \$5, french fries cost \$3, and drinks cost \$2. The expression $5n + 3n + 2n$ gives the total cost, in dollars for buying a sandwich, french fries, and a drink for n people. Which is another way to write this expression?

Ⓐ $10n$
Ⓑ $10n^3$
Ⓒ $30n$
Ⓓ $30n^3$

2. Jackets cost \$15 and a set of decorative buttons costs \$5. The delivery fee is \$5 per order. The expression $15n + 5n + 5$ gives the cost, in dollars, of buying jackets with buttons for n people. Which is another way to write this expression?

Ⓐ $25n$
Ⓑ $25n^2$
Ⓒ $20n + 5$
Ⓓ $20n^2 + 5$

3. Dana has n quarters. Ivan has 2 fewer than 3 times the number of quarters Dana has. The expression $n + 3n - 2$ gives the number of quarters they have altogether. Which is another way to write this expression?

Ⓐ $2n^2$
Ⓑ $2n$
Ⓒ $4n^2 - 2$
Ⓓ $4n - 2$

4. Scarves cost \$12 and snowmen pins cost \$2. Shipping is \$3 per order. The expression $12n + 2n + 3$ gives the cost, in dollars, of buying scarves with pins for n people. Which is another way to write this expression?

Ⓐ $14n^2 + 3$
Ⓑ $14n + 3$
Ⓒ $17n^2$
Ⓓ $17n$

Problem Solving REAL WORLD

5. Debbie is n years old. Edna is 3 years older than Debbie, and Shawn is twice as old as Edna. The expression $n + n + 3 + 2 \times (n + 3)$ gives the sum of their ages. Simplify the expression by combining like terms. Explain how you found your answer.

____

____

____

____

Name ______________________________

Lesson 55

COMMON CORE STANDARD CC.6.EE.3

Lesson Objective: Use the properties of operations to generate equivalent algebraic expressions.

Generate Equivalent Expressions

Equivalent expressions are two or more expressions that are equal for any value of the variable in the expressions. You can use the properties of operations to write equivalent expressions.

Write an equivalent expression for 4c + 2 + c.

Step 1 Identify like terms. $4c$ and c

Step 2 Use properties of operations to combine like terms.

Commutative Property of Addition: switch 2 and c	$4c + 2 + c = 4c + c + 2$
Associative Property of Addition: group $4c$ and c	$= (4c + c) + 2$
Add $4c$ and c.	$= 5c + 2$

Use properties of operations to write an equivalent expression by combining like terms.

1. $7x + 2x + 5x$ ______________
2. $8a + 11 - 2a$ ______________
3. $12b - 8b + 3$ ______________
4. $9c - 6 + c$ ______________
5. $4p + 1 - p$ ______________
6. $8y - 2y + y$ ______________

Use the Distributive Property to write an equivalent expression.

7. $3(m + 7)$ ______________
8. $4(2t + 3)$ ______________
9. $5(9 + 6r)$ ______________
10. $8(4n - 2n)$ ______________

Name ______________________

1. Chen bought a basketball for \$23, three baseball caps, and a pair of running shoes for \$37. To find the total cost in dollars, he wrote $23 + 3d + 37 = 23 + 37 + 3d$. Which property does the equation show?

   (A) Associative Property of Addition
   (B) Commutative Property of Addition
   (C) Distributive Property
   (D) Identity Property of 1

2. Tickets for the amusement park cost \$36 each. Which expression can be used to find the cost, in dollars, of *k* tickets for the amusement park?

   (A) $(k + 30) \times (k + 6)$
   (B) $(k + 30) + (k + 6)$
   (C) $(k \times 30) \times (k \times 6)$
   (D) $(k \times 30) + (k \times 6)$

3. A restaurant owner bought *b* large bags of flour for \$45 each and *b* large bags of sugar for \$25 each. The expression $b \times 45 + b \times 25$ gives the total cost, in dollars, of the flour and sugar. Which is another way to write this expression?

   (A) $b + (45 + 25)$
   (B) $b \times (45 + 25)$
   (C) $b + (45 \times b) + 25$
   (D) $b \times (45 + b) \times 25$

4. Ramon bought 6 packs of football cards, *p* packs of hockey cards, and $4p$ packs of baseball cards. Ramon wrote this number sentence to find the total number of cards he bought.

$$(6 + p) + 4p = 6 + (p + 4p)$$

   Which property did Ramon use?

   (A) Associative Property of Addition
   (B) Commutative Property of Addition
   (C) Distributive Property
   (D) Identity Property of 1

Problem Solving REAL WORLD

5. The expression $15n + 12n + 100$ represents the total cost in dollars for skis, boots, and a lesson for *n* skiers. Simplify the expression $15n + 12n + 100$. Then find the total cost for 8 skiers.

____

6. Casey has *n* nickels. Megan has 4 times as many nickels as Casey has. Write an expression for the total number of nickels Casey and Megan have. Then simplify the expression.

____

Name ______________________

Lesson 56

COMMON CORE STANDARD CC.6.EE.4

Lesson Objective: Identify equivalent algebraic expressions.

Identify Equivalent Expressions

Use properties to determine whether $5a + 7(3 + a)$ and $12a + 21$ are equivalent.

Step 1 Rewrite the first expression using the Distributive Property. Multiply 7 and 3 and multiply 7 and *a*. $5a + 7(3 + a) = 5a + 21 + 7a$

Step 2 Use the Commutative Property of Addition. Switch 21 and $7a$. $= 5a + 7a + 21$

Step 3 Use the Associative Property of Addition to group like terms. $5a$ and $7a$ are like terms. $= (5a + 7a) + 21$

Step 4 Combine like terms. $= 12a + 21$

Compare the expressions: $12a + 21$ and $12a + 21$. They are the same.
So, the expressions $5a + 7(3 + a)$ and $12a + 21$ are equivalent.

Use properties to determine whether the expressions are equivalent.

1. $6(p + q)$ and $6p + q$

____

2. $7y - 15 + 2y$ and $9y - 15$

____

3. $1 + (8r + 9)$ and $(2 + 8) + 8r$

____

4. $0 \times 11 + 5n$ and $5n$

____

5. $16s - 4 + s$ and $12s$

____

6. $11d \times 2$ and $22d$

____

7. $10(e + 0.5g)$ and $10e + 5g$

____

8. $8m + (9m - 1)$ and $8m - 8$

____

9. $7(1 \times 2h)$ and $21h$

____

Name ______________________

Lesson 56
CC.6.EE.4

1. On Saturday, a farmer planted 10 rows of tomato plants with p plants in each row. On Sunday, she planted 6 rows of pepper plants with p plants in each row. Which expression gives the total number of plants the farmer planted this weekend?

Ⓐ $10(6 + p)$
Ⓑ $6(10 + p)$
Ⓒ $60p$
Ⓓ $16p$

2. Jacob made 8 pitchers of iced tea for the school picnic. Each pitcher filled g glasses. After the picnic, there were 2 glasses of iced tea left over. If no glasses were spilled, which expression gives the number of glasses that were drunk at the picnic?

Ⓐ $2(4g - 1)$
Ⓑ $4g(2 - 1)$
Ⓒ $2(1 - 4g)$
Ⓓ $4g(1 - 2)$

3. Jeremy's teacher buys 6 packs of thumbtacks. Each pack contains t thumbtacks. She uses 18 thumbtacks to display posters around her classroom. Which expression gives the number of thumbtacks she has left?

Ⓐ $3(6 - t)$
Ⓑ $3(t - 6)$
Ⓒ $6(t - 3)$
Ⓓ $6(3 - t)$

4. Jolene made 8 pink bracelets using b beads on each bracelet and 7 blue bracelets with b beads on each bracelet. Which expression gives the total number of beads she used?

Ⓐ $56b$
Ⓑ $15b$
Ⓒ $8(b + 7)$
Ⓓ $7(8 + b)$

Problem Solving REAL WORLD

5. Rachel needs to write 3 book reports with b pages and 3 science reports with s pages during the school year. Write an algebraic expression for the total number of pages Rachel will need to write.

____

6. Rachel's friend Yassi has to write $3(b + s)$ pages for reports. Use properties of operations to determine whether this expression is equivalent to the expression for the number of pages Rachel has to write.

____

Name ______________________________

Lesson 57

COMMON CORE STANDARD CC.6.EE.5

Lesson Objective: Determine whether a number is a solution of an equation.

Solutions of Equations

An **equation** is a statement that two mathematical expressions are equal.

Some equations include only numbers, operation signs, and an equal sign. Example: $2 + 17 = 19$

Other equations also include variables, such as x. Example: $50 - x = 37$

For an equation with a variable, a **solution** is a value of the variable that makes the equation true.

Equation: $8.6 + m = 13$	**Is $m = 5.3$ a solution?**	**Is $m = 4.4$ a solution?**
Step 1 Write the equation.	$8.6 + m = 13$	$8.6 + m = 13$
Step 2 Substitute the given number for the variable m.	$8.6 + 5.3 \stackrel{?}{=} 13$	$8.6 + 4.4 \stackrel{?}{=} 13$
Step 3 Add.	$13.9 \neq 13$ ($\neq$ means *does not equal*)	$13 = 13$
Decide whether the equation is true.	The equation is not true. So, $m = 5.3$ is **not a solution**.	The equation is true. So, $m = 4.4$ is a **solution**.

Determine whether the given value of the variable is a solution of the equation.

1. $p - 4 = 6; p = 10$

   _____ $- 4 \stackrel{?}{=} 6$

   _____ ◯ 6

   ____

2. $15.2 + y = 22; y = 6.8$

   ____

3. $n + 3 = 16; n = 12$

   ____

4. $7.4 - k = 5; k = 3.4$

   ____

5. $1\frac{1}{2} + t = 3\frac{1}{2}; t = 2$

   ____

6. $4x = 36; x = 8$

   ____

Name ______________________________

Lesson 57
CC.6.EE.5

1. Sheila scored 87 points on her science quiz. She scored 2 more points than Felicia. The equation $p + 2 = 87$ gives the number of points p that Felicia scored on her science quiz. How many points did Felicia score on her quiz?

   Ⓐ 75
   Ⓑ 79
   Ⓒ 85
   Ⓓ 89

2. After spending $3.75 on a magazine, Lorraine has $12.25 left. The equation $x - 3.75 = 12.25$ can be used to find the amount of money x Lorraine had before purchasing the magazine. Which is a solution of the equation?

   Ⓐ $x = \$16.00$
   Ⓑ $x = \$12.25$
   Ⓒ $x = \$9.00$
   Ⓓ $x = \$8.25$

3. Luke is 14 years old. He is 2 years younger than his brother Frank. The equation $f - 2 = 14$ gives Frank's age f. How old is Frank?

   Ⓐ 16
   Ⓑ 12
   Ⓒ 7
   Ⓓ 6

4. This month, Thelma's telephone bill is $43.30. It is $4.60 less than last month's bill. The equation $t - 4.60 = 43.30$ can be used to find the amount of last month's bill t. Which is a solution of the equation?

   Ⓐ $t = \$38.70$
   Ⓑ $t = \$39.60$
   Ⓒ $t = \$44.00$
   Ⓓ $t = \$47.90$

Problem Solving REAL WORLD

5. Terrance needs to score 25 points to win a game. He has already scored 18 points. The equation $18 + p = 25$ gives the number of points p that Terrance still needs to score. Determine whether $p = 7$ or $p = 13$ is a solution of the equation, and tell what the solution means.

   ____

   ____

6. Madeline has used 50 sheets of a roll of paper towels, which is $\frac{5}{8}$ of the entire roll. The equation $\frac{5}{8}s = 50$ can be used to find the number of sheets s in a full roll. Determine whether $s = 32$ or $s = 80$ is a solution of the equation, and tell what the solution means.

   ____

   ____

Name ______________________________

Lesson 58

COMMON CORE STANDARD CC.6.EE.5

Lesson Objective: Determine whether a number is a solution of an inequality.

Solutions of Inequalities

An **inequality** is a mathematical sentence that compares expressions. A **solution of an inequality** is a value for a variable that makes the inequality true.

For the inequality $a < 3$ (a is less than 3), $a = 1$ is a solution because 1 is less than 3. $a = 3$ is *not* a solution because 3 is *not* less than 3.

Inequalities use these symbols: $<$ (less than), $>$ (greater than), $\leq$ (less than or equal to), and $\geq$ (greater than or equal to).

	For the inequality $x \leq 5$, is $x = 3$ a solution?	**For the inequality $y > 8$, is $y = 3$ a solution?**
Step 1 Understand the inequality.	$x \leq 5$ means "x is less than or equal to 5." Any value that is equal to 5 or less than 5 is a solution.	$y > 8$ means "y is greater than 8." Any value that is greater than 8 is a solution.
Step 2 Decide whether the value is a solution.	3 is less than 5, so $x = 3$ is a solution.	3 is not greater than 8, so $y = 3$ is not a solution.

Determine whether the given value of the variable is a solution of the inequality.

1. $m \geq 4$; $m = 2$

   $m \geq 4$ means "m is

   ____

   ______ 4."

   $m = 2$ is ______________

2. $k < 7$; $k = 5$

   ____

3. $z \geq 12$; $z = 12$

   ____

4. $y \leq 3$; $y = 6$

   ____

5. $n > 13$; $n = 8$

   ____

6. $t < 7$; $t = 5$

   ____

Give two solutions of the inequality.

7. $x > 4$

   ________ ; ________

8. $p \leq 3$

   ________ ; ________

9. $v \geq 9$

   ________ ; ________

Name ______________________

Lesson 58
CC.6.EE.5

1. The inequality $w < 1{,}300$ represents the weight limit in pounds w of an elevator. Which is a solution of the inequality?

   Ⓐ $w = 1{,}239$
   Ⓑ $w = 1{,}304$
   Ⓒ $w = 1{,}414$
   Ⓓ $w = 1{,}575$

2. A road sign shows that motorists must travel at a speed no more than 55 miles per hour. The inequality $s \leq 55$ represents the permitted speeds s. Which is **not** a solution of the inequality?

   Ⓐ $s = 50$
   Ⓑ $s = 52$
   Ⓒ $s = 55$
   Ⓓ $s = 60$

3. Theodore must score at least 12 points to advance to the next level of a video game. The inequality $p \geq 12$ represents the possible number of points p that he can score to advance to the next level. Which is a solution of the inequality?

   Ⓐ $p = 4$
   Ⓑ $p = 0$
   Ⓒ $p = 13$
   Ⓓ $p = 9$

4. A pitcher can hold no more than 64 ounces. The inequality $p \leq 64$ represents the possible number of ounces p the pitcher can hold. Which is a solution of the inequality?

   Ⓐ $p = 61$
   Ⓑ $p = 66$
   Ⓒ $p = 68$
   Ⓓ $p = 70$

Problem Solving REAL WORLD

5. The inequality $s \geq 92$ represents the score s that Jared must earn on his next test to get an A on his report card. Give two possible scores that Jared could earn to get the A.

   ____

6. The inequality $m \leq \$20$ represents the amount of money that Sheila is allowed to spend on a new hat. Give two possible money amounts that Sheila could spend on the hat.

   ____

Name ______________________________

Lesson 59

COMMON CORE STANDARD CC.6.EE.6

Lesson Objective: Use algebraic expressions to solve problems.

Use Algebraic Expressions

You can use an algebraic expression to help solve a word problem. Use a variable to represent the unknown number.

Ina wants to serve salad at her party. She will need one head of lettuce for every 6 guests who attend. Write an expression she could use for deciding how much lettuce she needs.

Step 1 Decide what operation the problem uses.	Each head of lettuce will serve 6 people. Divide the number of guests by 6.
Step 2 Identify the unknown number.	The problem does not state how many guests will attend. Use the variable *g* for the number of guests.
Step 3 Write a word expression. Then use the word expression to write an algebraic expression.	"the number of guests divided by 6" $g \div 6$ or $\frac{g}{6}$

Ina finds out that 18 guests will attend. Evaluate the expression for this number of guests.

Step 1 Substitute 18 for *g*. $\frac{18}{6}$

Step 2 Divide. $\frac{18}{6} = 3$

So, Ina will need 3 heads of lettuce.

At her last party, Ina decorated with window stickers. For this party, she wants to use 4 times as many stickers.

1. Write an expression for the number of stickers Ina will use. (Use the variable *s* to represent the number of stickers she used at her last party.)

   ____

2. Use the expression to find the new number of stickers if she used 14 stickers for her last party.

   ____

3. Ina wants to put an equal number of stickers on each of the windows. Write an expression to show how many stickers will go on each window. (Use the variable *w* to represent the number of windows.)

   ____

4. Use the expression to find the number of stickers for each window if there are 8 windows.

   ____

Name ______________________

1. A builder needs 2 hinges to install each door. The expression $2d$ gives the number of hinges needed to install d doors. Which **best** describes the value of the variable d?

Ⓐ any positive whole number
Ⓑ a single unknown number
Ⓒ any positive number
Ⓓ any integer

2. Don wrote the expression 8 less than the product of m and 10. What algebraic expression did he write? What is the value of the expression for $m = 7$?

Ⓐ $10m + 8$; 78
Ⓑ $8m + 10$; 66
Ⓒ $10m - 8$; 62
Ⓓ $8m - 10$; 46

3. There were 3.5 inches of snow on the ground. New snow was reported to be falling at the rate of 2.5 inches per hour. What expression represents the number of inches of snow that should be on the ground after h hours? How many inches of snow should be on the ground after 8 hours?

Ⓐ $8 + 3.5h$; 16.75 inches
Ⓑ $3.5 + 2.5h$; 23.5 inches
Ⓒ $2.5 + 8h$; 30.5 inches
Ⓓ $(2.5 + 3.5) \times h$; 48 inches

4. A bicyclist travels $15h$ miles in h hours. Which **best** describes the value of h?

Ⓐ a single unknown number
Ⓑ any nonnegative number
Ⓒ any whole number
Ⓓ any integer

Problem Solving REAL WORLD

5. In the town of Pleasant Hill, there is an average of 16 sunny days each month. Write an expression to represent the approximate number of sunny days for any number of months. Tell what the variable represents.

____

6. How many sunny days can a resident of Pleasant Hill expect to have in 9 months?

____

Name ___________________________

Lesson 60

COMMON CORE STANDARD CC.6.EE.7

Lesson Objective: Write algebraic equations.

Write Equations

To write an equation for a word sentence, write the words as mathematical expressions and write = for "equals" or "is."

Write an equation for the word sentence.

Example 1 6 fewer than a number is $12\frac{2}{3}$.

Step 1 Choose a variable.
6 fewer than a number is $12\frac{2}{3}$.
Let n represent a number.

Step 2 Identify the operation.

6 fewer than n is $12\frac{2}{3}$.
"Fewer than" means subtract.

Step 3 Write an equation.

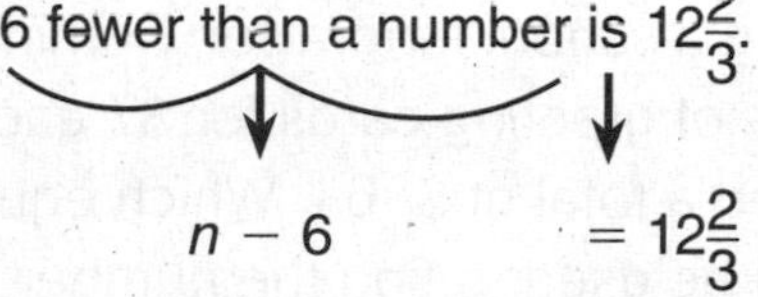

6 fewer than a number is $12\frac{2}{3}$.
$n - 6$
$= 12\frac{2}{3}$

So, the equation is $n - 6 = 12\frac{2}{3}$.

Example 2

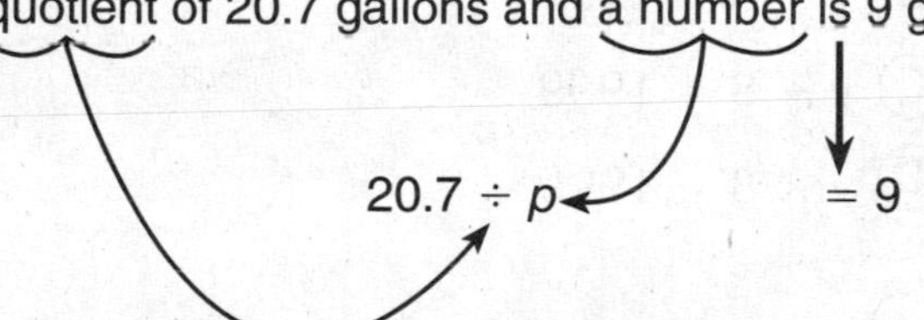

The quotient of 20.7 gallons and a number is 9 gallons.
$20.7 \div p$
$= 9$

So, the equation is $20.7 \div p = 9$.

Write an equation for the word sentence.

1. 18 more than a number is 29.

____

2. 5.2 times a number is 46.8.

____

3. 128 less than a number is 452.

____

4. Four fifths of a number equals 11.

____

5. The product of a number and 6 is 138.

____

6. The number of miles decreased by 29.8 is 139.

____

Name ______________________________

Lesson 60
CC.6.EE.7

1. Dora was born in 1981. Her son Tanner was born 25 years after Dora. Which equation could be used to find the year y in which Tanner was born?

   Ⓐ $y + 25 = 1981$
   Ⓑ $y - 25 = 1981$
   Ⓒ $y \times 25 = 1981$
   Ⓓ $y \div 25 = 1981$

2. During a school fundraiser, Dominic sold boxes of greeting cards for $7 each and earned a total of $364. Which equation could be used to find the number of boxes n Dominic sold?

   Ⓐ $n + 7 = 364$
   Ⓑ $n - 7 = 364$
   Ⓒ $n \times 7 = 364$
   Ⓓ $n \div 7 = 364$

3. A video game is on sale for $40. The sale price is $10 less than the regular price p. Which equation could be used to find the regular price of the video game?

   Ⓐ $p + 10 = 40$
   Ⓑ $p - 10 = 40$
   Ⓒ $p \times 10 = 40$
   Ⓓ $p \div 10 = 40$

4. Rowan started school in 1999. Kira started school 8 years after Rowan. Which equation could be used to find the year y in which Kira started school?

   Ⓐ $y - 8 = 1999$
   Ⓑ $y + 8 = 1999$
   Ⓒ $y \div 8 = 1999$
   Ⓓ $y \times 8 = 1999$

Problem Solving REAL WORLD

5. An ostrich egg weighs 2.9 pounds. The difference between the weight of this egg and the weight of an emu egg is 1.6 pounds. Write an equation that could be used to find the weight w, in pounds, of the emu egg.

   ____

6. In one week, the number of bowls a potter made was 6 times the number of plates. He made 90 bowls during the week. Write an equation that could be used to find the number of plates p that the potter made.

   ____

Name ______________________________

Lesson 61

COMMON CORE STANDARD CC.6.EE.7

Lesson Objective: Use models to solve addition equations.

Model and Solve Addition Equations

You can use algebra tiles to model and solve equations. Use a long rectangle to represent the variable, and a square to represent 1.

Model and solve the equation $x + 9 = 11$.

Step 1 Model the equation using algebra tiles.

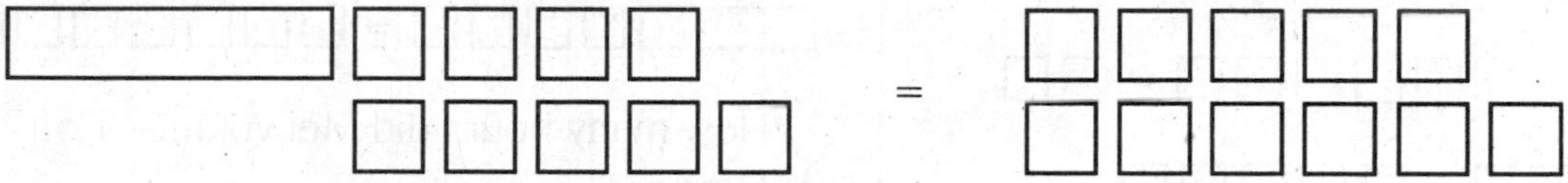

Step 2 Get the variable by itself on one side of the equation. Remove the same number of tiles from each side.

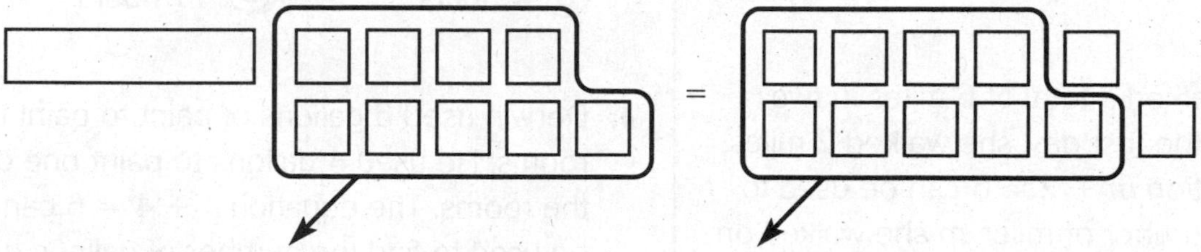

Step 3 Write the solution.

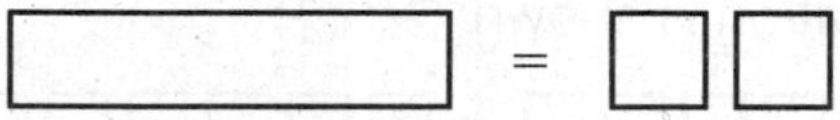

$x = 2$

Solve the equation by using algebra tiles or by drawing a picture.

1. $x + 4 = 10$

____

2. $8 = x + 2$

____

Name ______________________________

Lesson 61
CC.6.EE.7

1. Diana spent \$5 on lunch. She purchased a sandwich and a drink. The drink cost \$2. The equation $s + 2 = 5$ can be used to find the cost s of the sandwich. Which model shows the equation?

(A) [long rectangle] □□ = □□□□□

(B) [long rectangle] □□□□□ = □□

(C) [long rectangle] = □□□□□

(D) [long rectangle] = □□

2. Sophia walked a total of 6 miles in two days. On the first day, she walked 2 miles. The equation $m + 2 = 6$ can be used to find the number of miles m she walked on the second day. Which model shows the equation?

(A) [long rectangle] = □□

(B) [long rectangle] = □□□□□□

(C) [long rectangle] □□□□□□ = □□

(D) [long rectangle] □□ = □□□□□□

3. Over the weekend, Mel volunteered a total of 7 hours at an animal shelter. On Saturday, he volunteered 4 hours. The equation $h + 4 = 7$ can be used to find the number of hours h he volunteered on Sunday. The model of the equation is shown.

[long rectangle] □□□□ = □□□□□□□

How many hours did Mel volunteer on Sunday?

(A) 3 hours (C) 7 hours

(B) 4 hours (D) 11 hours

4. Derwin used 6 gallons of paint to paint two rooms. He used 4 gallons to paint one of the rooms. The equation $g + 4 = 6$ can be used to find the number of gallons g he used to paint the other room. The model of the equation is shown.

[long rectangle] □□□□ = □□□□□□

How many gallons of paint did Derwin use to paint the other room?

(A) 1 gallon (C) 6 gallons

(B) 2 gallons (D) 10 gallons

Problem Solving REAL WORLD

5. The temperature at 10:00 was 10°F. This is 3°F warmer than the temperature at 8:00. Model and solve the equation $x + 3 = 10$ to find the temperature x in degrees Fahrenheit at 8:00.

____

6. Jaspar has 7 more checkers left than Karen does. Jaspar has 9 checkers left. Write and solve an addition equation to find out how many checkers Karen has left.

____

Name ______________________________

Lesson 62

COMMON CORE STANDARD CC.6.EE.7

Lesson Objective: Use algebra to solve addition and subtraction equations.

Solve Addition and Subtraction Equations

To solve an equation, you must isolate the variable on one side of the equal sign. You can use **inverse operations**: undoing addition with subtraction or subtraction with addition. These actions are made possible by the **Addition and Subtraction Properties of Equality.**

Solve and check.

Example 1: $y + 6.7 = 9.8$

Example 2: $57 = x - 8$

Step 1 Look at the side with the variable. Subtract the number that is added to the variable, or add the number that is subtracted from the variable. Be sure to perform the <u>same</u> operation on <u>both</u> sides of the equation.

Example 1		Example 2	
$y + 6.7 = 9.8$		$57 = x - 8$	
$y + 6.7 - 6.7 = 9.8 - 6.7$	Subtract 6.7 from both sides.	$57 + 8 = x - 8 + 8$	Add 8 to both sides.

Step 2 Simplify both sides of the equation.

Example 1	Example 2
$y + 6.7 = 9.8$	$57 = x - 8$
$y + 6.7 - 6.7 = 9.8 - 6.7$	$57 + 8 = x - 8 + 8$
$y + 0 = 3.1$	$65 = x + 0$
$y = 3.1$	$65 = x$

Step 3 Check your answer in the original equation.

Example 1	Example 2
$y + 6.7 = 9.8$	$57 = x - 8$
$3.1 + 6.7 \stackrel{?}{=} 9.8$	$57 \stackrel{?}{=} 65 - 8$
$9.8 = 9.8$	$57 = 57$

So, $y = 3.1$ is the solution.

So, $x = 65$ is the solution.

Solve and check.

1. $x + 13 = 27$ ____________
2. $38 = d - 22$ ____________
3. $12.4 = a + 7.9$ ____________
4. $w - 2\frac{3}{5} = 4\frac{2}{5}$ ____________

Name ______________________________

1. The temperature rose 9 degrees between 11:00 A.M. and 4:00 P.M. yesterday. The temperature at 4:00 P.M. was 87°F. Xin Xin used the following equation to find the temperature t at 11:00 A.M.

$$t + 9 = 87$$

What was the temperature at 11:00 A.M.?

Ⓐ 68°F
Ⓑ 76°F
Ⓒ 78°F
Ⓓ 96°F

2. José used the equation $h - 125 = 75$ to find the height in feet h of a hot air balloon before it began to come down. What was the height of the hot air balloon before it began to come down?

Ⓐ 50 feet
Ⓑ 100 feet
Ⓒ 150 feet
Ⓓ 200 feet

3. Dina adds $1\frac{1}{2}$ cups of sugar to some flour to make $4\frac{1}{4}$ cups of a baking mix. She solves the equation $f + 1\frac{1}{2} = 4\frac{1}{4}$ to find the amount of flour f in the baking mix. How much flour is in the baking mix?

Ⓐ $1\frac{1}{4}$ cups
Ⓑ $2\frac{1}{4}$ cups
Ⓒ $2\frac{3}{4}$ cups
Ⓓ $5\frac{3}{4}$ cups

4. Kelsey used the equation $h - 135 = 25$ to find the height in feet h of a kite before she began to reel it in. What was the height of the kite before Kelsey began to reel it in?

Ⓐ 160 feet
Ⓑ 130 feet
Ⓒ 110 feet
Ⓓ 55 feet

Problem Solving REAL WORLD

5. A recipe calls for $5\frac{1}{2}$ cups of flour. Lorenzo only has $3\frac{3}{4}$ cups of flour. Write and solve an equation to find the additional amount of flour Lorenzo needs to make the recipe.

____

6. Jan used 22.5 gallons of water in the shower. This amount is 7.5 gallons less than the amount she used for washing clothes. Write and solve an equation to find the amount of water Jan used to wash clothes.

____

Name ______________________________

Lesson 63

COMMON CORE STANDARD CC.6.EE.7

Lesson Objective: Use models to solve multiplication equations.

Model and Solve Multiplication Equations

You can use algebra tiles or a drawing to model and solve equations. Use a rectangle to represent the variable and a square to represent 1.

Model and solve the equation $3x = 9$.

Step 1 Model the equation using rectangles and squares.

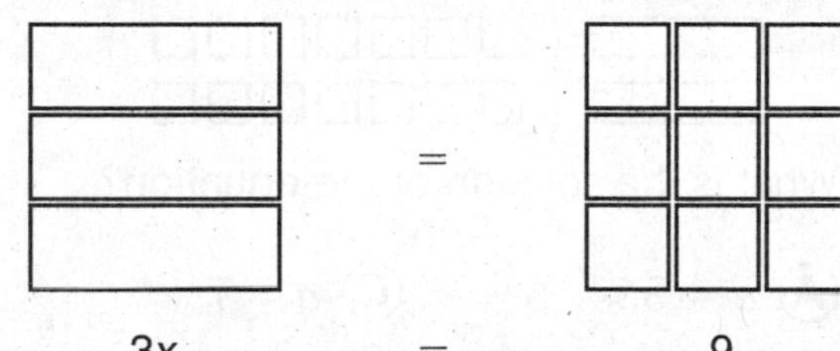

$3x = 9$

Step 2 Divide the squares into equal groups. The number of groups should be the same as the number of rectangles.

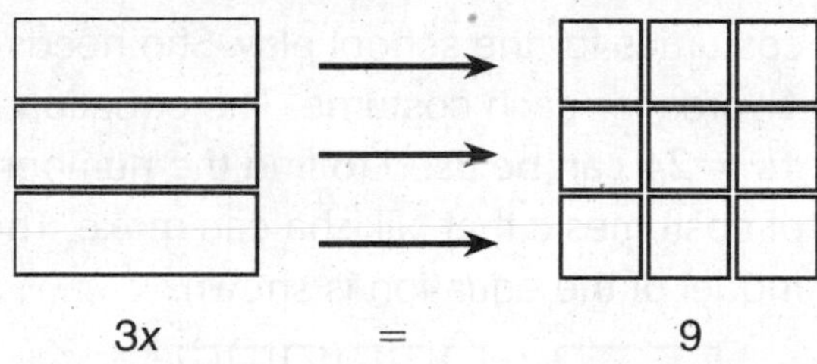

$3x = 9$

Step 3 Find the number of squares in each group.

$x = 3$

So, $x = 3$ is the solution.

Solve the equation by using algebra tiles or by drawing a picture.

1. $4x = 12$ ______

2. $2x = 16$ ______

Name ______________________________

Lesson 63
CC.6.EE.7

1. Giovanni has 20 photographs. He wants to display the same number of photographs on each of 4 pages of a photo album. The equation $4p = 20$ can be used to find the number of photographs p he will place on each page. The model of the equation is shown.

What is the solution of the equation?

Ⓐ $p = 24$ Ⓒ $p = 5$
Ⓑ $p = 20$ Ⓓ $p = 4$

2. In a basketball game, Angelique attempted 3 times as many shots as Pamela. Angelique attempted 12 shots. The equation $3s = 12$ can be used to find the number of shots s that Pamela attempted. The model of the equation is shown.

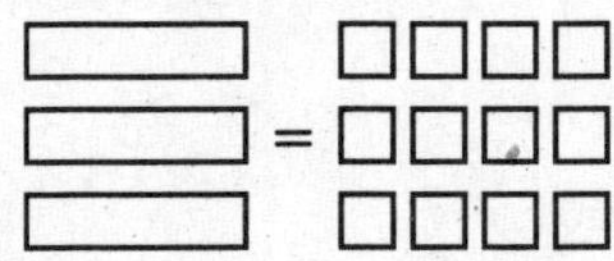

How many shots did Pamela attempt?

Ⓐ 3 Ⓒ 8
Ⓑ 4 Ⓓ 12

3. Grace's father is 35 years old. He is 5 times as old as Grace. The equation $5a = 35$ can be used to find Grace's age a. The model of the equation is shown.

What is the solution of the equation?

Ⓐ $a = 35$ Ⓒ $a = 7$
Ⓑ $a = 30$ Ⓓ $a = 5$

4. Nikisha has 24 yards of fabric to make costumes for the school play. She needs 4 yards for each costume. The equation $4c = 24$ can be used to find the number of costumes c that Nikisha can make. The model of the equation is shown.

How many costumes can Nikisha make?

Ⓐ 6 Ⓒ 18
Ⓑ 12 Ⓓ 24

Problem Solving REAL WORLD

5. A chef used 20 eggs to make 5 omelets. Model and solve the equation $5x = 20$ to find the number of eggs x in each omelet.

____

6. Last month, Julio played 3 times as many video games as Scott did. Julio played 18 video games. Write and solve an equation to find the number of video games Scott played.

____

Name ______________________________

Lesson 64

COMMON CORE STANDARD CC.6.EE.7

Lesson Objective: Use algebra to solve multiplication and division equations.

Solve Multiplication and Division Equations

A multiplication equation shows a variable multiplied by a number. A division equation shows a variable divided by a number. To solve a multiplication equation, you use the **Division Property of Equality**. To solve a division equation, you use the **Multiplication Property of Equality**. These properties state that both sides of an equation remain equal when you multiply or divide both sides by the same number.

Solve and check.

Example 1: $\frac{a}{5} = 6$ **Example 2:** $2.5x = 10$

Step 1 Look at the side with the variable. Use the inverse operation to get the variable by itself.

Example 1		Example 2	
$\frac{a}{5} = 6$	a is divided by 5.	$2.5x = 10$	x is multiplied by 2.5.
$5 \times \frac{a}{5} = 6 \times 5$	Multiply both sides by 5.	$\frac{2.5x}{2.5} = \frac{10}{2.5}$	Divide both sides by 2.5.

Step 2 Simplify both sides of the equation.

Example 1	Example 2
$\frac{a}{5} = 6$	$2.5x = 10$
$5 \times \frac{a}{5} = 6 \times 5$	$\frac{2.5x}{2.5} = \frac{10}{2.5}$
$a = 30$	$x = 4$

Step 3 Check your answer in the original equation.

Example 1	Example 2
$\frac{a}{5} = 6$	$2.5x = 10$
$\frac{30}{5} \stackrel{?}{=} 6$	$2.5 \times 4 \stackrel{?}{=} 10$
$6 = 6$	$10 = 10$

So, $a = 30$ is the solution. So, $x = 4$ is the solution.

Solve and check.

1. $3x = 42$ **2.** $4c = 48$ **3.** $12.8 = 3.2d$ **4.** $12 = 1.5w$

______ ______ ______ ______

5. $\frac{z}{6} = 9$ **6.** $\frac{d}{4} = 5$ **7.** $11 = \frac{n}{2.4}$ **8.** $12 = \frac{4}{5}k$

______ ______ ______ ______

Name ___________________________

Lesson 64
CC.6.EE.7

1. Spencer divided his baseball cards equally among 4 friends. Each friend received 16 cards. To find the number of cards *c* that Spencer had originally, he solved the equation $\frac{c}{4} = 16$. How many baseball cards did Spencer originally have?

   Ⓐ 4
   Ⓑ 32
   Ⓒ 64
   Ⓓ 72

2. Stephanie has a ball of dough that weighs 20.8 ounces. She divides the dough into 8 equal amounts to make rolls. To find the weight *w* of each amount of dough, Stephanie solves the equation $8w = 20.8$. What is the weight of each amount of dough?

   Ⓐ 2.6 ounces
   Ⓑ 12.8 ounces
   Ⓒ 28.8 ounces
   Ⓓ 166.4 ounces

3. Jenna earns $8 per hour. Her paycheck for one week was $136. The equation $8h = 136$ can be used to find the number of hours *h* she worked during the week. How many hours did she work?

   Ⓐ 17 hours
   Ⓑ 19 hours
   Ⓒ 24 hours
   Ⓓ 27 hours

4. Jasmine gave away her stuffed animal collection to 3 of her younger cousins. Each cousin got 18 stuffed animals. To find the number of stuffed animals *s* that Jasmine originally had, she solved the equation $\frac{s}{3} = 18$. How many stuffed animals did Jasmine originally have?

   Ⓐ 3
   Ⓑ 6
   Ⓒ 21
   Ⓓ 54

Problem Solving REAL WORLD

5. Anne runs 6 laps on a track. She runs a total of 1 mile, or 5,280 feet. Write and solve an equation to find the distance, in feet, that she runs in each lap.

   ____

6. DeShawn uses $\frac{3}{4}$ of a box of rice to cook dinner. The portion he uses weighs 12 ounces. Write and solve an equation to find the weight of the full box of rice.

   ____

Name ______________________________

Lesson 65

COMMON CORE STANDARD CC.6.EE.7

Lesson Objective: Solve equations involving fractions by using the strategy *solve a simpler problem.*

Problem Solving • Equations with Fractions

After driving 25 miles, Kevin has traveled $\frac{2}{3}$ of the distance from his house to his friend's house. Use the equation $25 = \frac{2}{3}d$ to find the total distance d in miles to his friend's house.

Read the Problem		
What do I need to find?	**What information do I need to use?**	**How will I use the information?**
I need to find the __________ __________ from Kevin's house to __________ __________.	I need to use the equation __________________.	I can use multiplication to change the equation to an equation with only __________, not fractions. Then I can ________ the new equation.

Solve the Problem

Step 1 Write the original equation. $$25 = \frac{2}{3}d$$

Step 2 Write a simpler equation without fractions. Multiply both sides by the denominator of the fraction.

$$3 \times 25 = (3 \times \frac{2}{3})d$$
$$75 = \frac{6}{3}d$$
$$75 = 2d$$

Step 3 Solve the simpler equation. Use the Division Property of Equality.

$$\frac{75}{2} = \frac{2d}{2}$$
$$37.5 = d$$

So, the total distance is 37.5 miles.

Solve.

1. Alyssa's cat weighs 12 pounds, which is $\frac{3}{8}$ of the weight of her dog. Use the equation $\frac{3}{8}d = 12$ to find the weight of Alyssa's dog.

____

2. Randall bought 16 baseball cards from Max, which is $\frac{2}{5}$ of Max's collection. Use the equation $16 = \frac{2}{5}c$ to find the number of cards that were in Max's collection.

____

Name ______________________________

Lesson 65

CC.6.EE.7

1. A track is $\frac{3}{4}$ mile in length. Milton jogged a total of 6 miles around the track. The equation $\frac{3}{4}n = 6$ can be used to find the number of times n he jogged around the track. How many times did he jog around the track?

   Ⓐ 2
   Ⓑ 8
   Ⓒ 18
   Ⓓ 24

2. Janae paid $12 for a shirt that was on sale. The sale price of the shirt was $\frac{1}{3}$ of the original price p. The equation $\frac{1}{3}p = 12$ can be used to find the original price of the shirt. What was the original price of the shirt?

   Ⓐ $3
   Ⓑ $4
   Ⓒ $15
   Ⓓ $36

3. Jimmy has saved $375 to purchase a new guitar. This is $\frac{3}{4}$ of the total price of the guitar. What is the price of the guitar?

   Ⓐ $125
   Ⓑ $500
   Ⓒ $1,125
   Ⓓ $1,500

4. Sylvia has read 136 pages of a novel. She has read $\frac{2}{5}$ of the novel. The equation $\frac{2}{5}p = 136$ can be used to find the number of total pages p in the novel. How many total pages are there?

   Ⓐ 340
   Ⓑ 136
   Ⓒ 68
   Ⓓ 54

Problem Solving REAL WORLD

5. Adele is taking a road trip. She has driven 160 miles, which is $\frac{5}{8}$ of the total distance she plans to travel. How far will she travel in all? Explain how you know.

____

____

____

____

____

Name ____________________

Lesson 66

COMMON CORE STANDARD CC.6.EE.8

Lesson Objective: Write algebraic inequalities.

Write Inequalities

Here are some ways to express each inequality symbol in words:

$<$	less than	under	not as much as
$\leq$	less than or equal to	at most	no more than

$>$	greater than	over	more than
$\geq$	greater than or equal to	at least	no less than

Passengers at least 12 years old pay full price for train tickets. Write an inequality to represent the situation.

Step 1 Choose a variable. Use *a* to represent "age." — a

Step 2 Choose an inequality symbol. "at least 12 years old" means "greater than or equal to 12." — $\geq$

Step 3 Write the inequality. — $a \geq 12$

Write two word sentences to represent $y < 9$.

Step 1 Identify the inequality symbol. — $<$ means "less than."

Step 2 Write a word sentence that uses the variable and integer. — *y* is less than 9.

Step 3 Write another word sentence with the same meaning. — *y* is under 9.

Write an inequality for the word sentence.

1. The distance *d* Mr. Chin drove was no more than 65 miles.

   ____

2. The amount of juice *c* in the punch is more than 3 cups.

   ____

3. The age *a* of Mia's sister is less than 8 years.

   ____

4. The temperature *t* was at least 30°F.

   ____

Write two word sentences to represent the inequality.

5. $n \geq 23$

   ____

   ____

6. $p > 16$

   ____

   ____

Name ___________________________

Lesson 66
CC.6.EE.8

1. An MP3 player can store less than 240 songs. Which inequality represents the possible number of songs *s* the MP3 player can store?

   Ⓐ $s \geq 240$
   Ⓑ $s \leq 240$
   Ⓒ $s > 240$
   Ⓓ $s < 240$

2. After-school activities are cancelled at Kurt's school if there are at least 2.5 inches of snow on the ground. Which inequality shows the number of inches of snow *s* for which after-school activities are cancelled?

   Ⓐ $s < 2.5$
   Ⓑ $s > 2.5$
   Ⓒ $s \geq 2.5$
   Ⓓ $s \leq 2.5$

3. A ship can carry no more than 6 tons of cargo. Which inequality represents the number of tons *t* that the ship can carry?

   Ⓐ $t < 6$
   Ⓑ $t > 6$
   Ⓒ $t \leq 6$
   Ⓓ $t \geq 6$

4. The repairs to Ryan's bike cost more than $50. Which inequality represents the cost of repairs *r*?

   Ⓐ $r > 50$
   Ⓑ $r < 50$
   Ⓒ $r \geq 50$
   Ⓓ $r \leq 50$

Problem Solving REAL WORLD

5. Tabby's mom says that she must read for at least 30 minutes each night. If *m* represents the number of minutes reading, what inequality can represent this situation?

   ____

6. Phillip has a $25 gift card to his favorite restaurant. He wants to use the gift card to buy lunch. If *c* represents the cost of his lunch, what inequality can describe all of the possible amounts of money, in dollars, that Phillip can spend on lunch?

   ____

Name ___________________________

Lesson 67

COMMON CORE STANDARD CC.6.EE.8

Lesson Objective: Represent solutions of algebraic inequalities on number line diagrams.

Graph Inequalities

You can graph the solutions of an inequality on a number line.

Graph the inequality $n \geq 9$.

Step 1 Determine the meaning of the inequality.
$n \geq 9$ means "n is greater than or equal to 9."

Step 2 Draw a number line and circle the number given in the inequality.

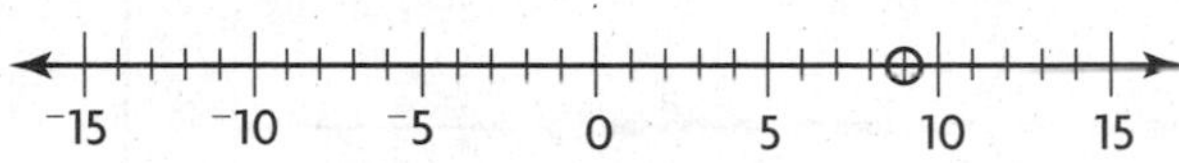

Step 3 Decide whether to fill in the circle. For $\leq$ or $\geq$, fill in the circle to show "or equal to." For $<$ or $>$, do not fill in the circle.

Since the inequality uses $\geq$, 9 is a possible solution. So, fill in the circle.

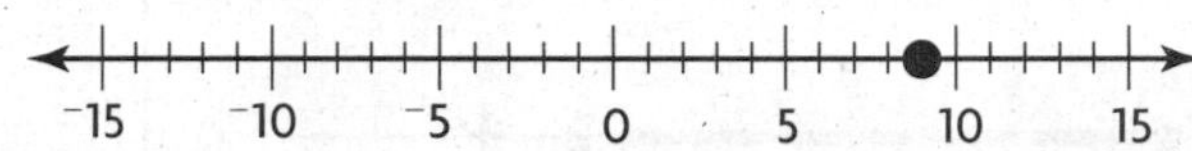

Step 4 Shade from the circle in the direction of the remaining solutions.

Since the inequality symbol is $\geq$, the shading covers all numbers greater than 9.

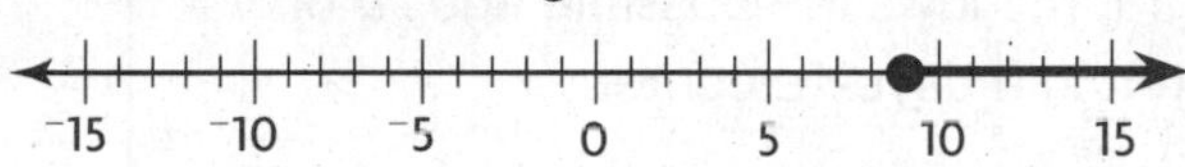

Graph the inequality.

1. $k < 8$

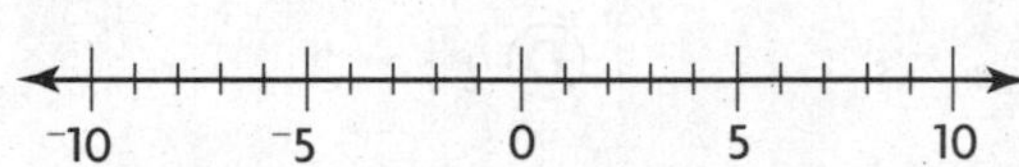

2. $r \geq 6$

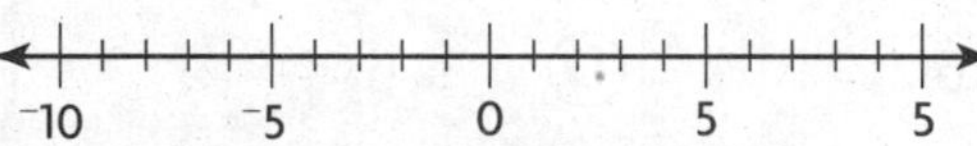

3. $w \leq 3$

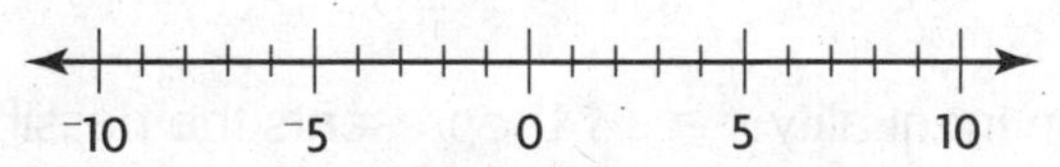

4. $x > 3$

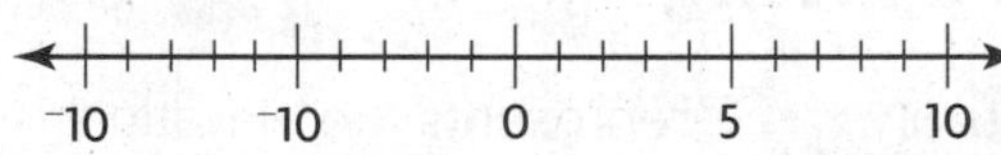

Write the inequality shown by the graph.

5. 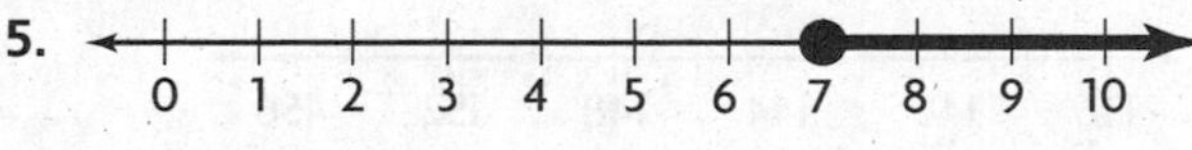

6.

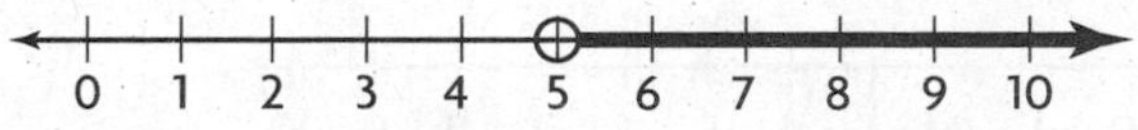

_______________ _______________

Name ____________________

Lesson 67
CC.6.EE.8

1. The East Park football team must gain at least 5 yards for a first down. The inequality $y \geq 5$ represents the number of yards y that the team must gain. Which graph represents the solutions of the inequality?

Ⓐ 0 1 2 3 4 5 6 7

Ⓑ 0 1 2 3 4 5 6 7

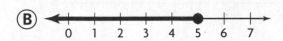

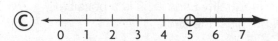

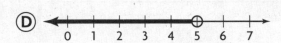

Ⓒ 0 1 2 3 4 5 6 7

Ⓓ 0 1 2 3 4 5 6 7

2. The graph shows the possible ages a of children in a daycare center.

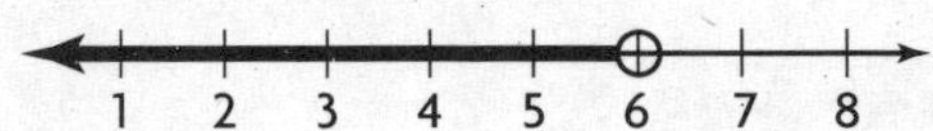

Which inequality represents this graph?

Ⓐ $a > 6$ Ⓒ $a \geq 6$

Ⓑ $a < 6$ Ⓓ $a \leq 6$

3. The inequality $a < 4$ represents the ages a of children who are admitted into the aquarium at no charge. Which graph represents the solutions of the inequality?

Ⓐ 1 2 3 4 5 6 7 8

Ⓑ 1 2 3 4 5 6 7 8

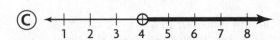

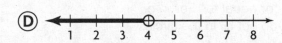

Ⓒ 1 2 3 4 5 6 7 8

Ⓓ 1 2 3 4 5 6 7 8

4. The graph shows the temperatures t in degrees Celsius for which a certain substance is frozen.

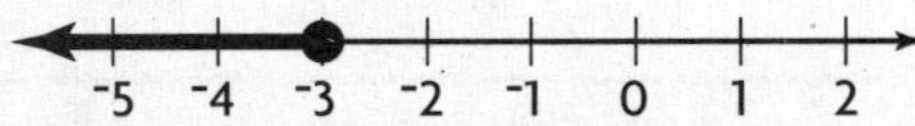

Which inequality represents this graph?

Ⓐ $t \leq {}^{-}3$ Ⓒ $t < {}^{-}3$

Ⓑ $t \geq {}^{-}3$ Ⓓ $t > {}^{-}3$

Problem Solving REAL WORLD

5. The inequality $x \leq 2$ represents the elevation x of a certain object found at a dig site. Graph the solutions of the inequality on the number line.

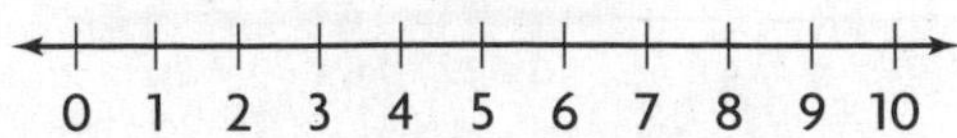

6. The inequality $x \geq 144$ represents the possible scores x needed to pass a certain test. Graph the solutions of the inequality on the number line.

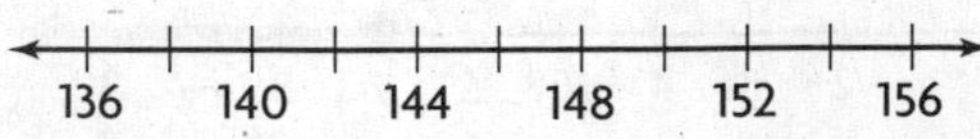

Name ____________________________

Lesson 68

COMMON CORE STANDARD CC.6.EE.9

Lesson Objective: Write an equation to represent the relationship between an independent variable and a dependent variable.

Independent and Dependent Variables

An equation with two variables shows a relationship between two quantities. The value of the **dependent variable** changes according to the value of the **independent variable.**

Sam rides the bus almost every day. He pays $2.50 for each bus ride.

Identify the dependent and independent variables in this situation. Then write an equation to represent the relationship between the total cost and the number of bus rides.

Step 1 Understand the relationship and identify variables.

Each bus ride costs $2.50. The total cost c for Sam's bus rides depends on the number of rides r he takes. The value of c will change when the value of r changes.

So, c is the dependent variable and r is the independent variable.

Step 2 Write an equation. The total cost will be $2.50 multiplied by the number of rides.

$c = 2.50 \times r$
(or $c = 2.50r$)

Use your equation to find out how much it would cost for Sam to take 4 bus rides.

Step 1 Think: 4 bus rides means $r = 4$.

Step 2 Substitute 4 for r in the equation.

$c = 2.50 \times r$
$c = 2.50 \times 4$
$c = 10.00$

So, Sam's total cost will be $10.00 for 4 rides.

Identify the dependent and independent variables. Write an equation to show the relationship between them. Then solve for the given value.

1. Janna is buying a netbook with a flash drive. The total cost c will include the price p of the netbook, plus $12.50 for the flash drive.

   Find the total cost if the price of the netbook is $375.00.

   The ______________ depends on the ______________.

   dependent variable: ______ independent variable: ______

   equation: ______ = ______ + ______

   Total cost: c = ______ + ______

   c = ______

1. Kenneth earns \$9 per hour mowing lawns. The total amount earned *t* equals the amount earned per hour times the number of hours *h*. Which equation gives the total amount earned *t* if Kenneth works *h* hours?

Ⓐ $t = 9h$
Ⓑ $h = 9t$
Ⓒ $t = 9 + h$
Ⓓ $h = 9 + t$

2. Hakeem wants to rent a bike. Bike rental costs \$1.25 per hour plus a one-time fee of \$3. Which equation represents the relationship between the number of hours *h* Hakeem rents the bike and the total cost *c*?

Ⓐ $h = 1.25c + 3$
Ⓑ $c = 1.25h + 3$
Ⓒ $h = 3c + 1.25$
Ⓓ $c = 3h + 1.25$

3. Neema purchases a gallon of milk for \$3 and some tomatoes for \$2 per pound from the grocery store. Which equation represents the relationship between the number of pounds *p* of tomatoes purchased and the total amount *a* Neema spent at the grocery store?

Ⓐ $p = 3a + 2$
Ⓑ $a = 3p + 2$
Ⓒ $p = 2a + 3$
Ⓓ $a = 2p + 3$

4. Oscar uses a 20-dollar bill to purchase an item that costs *x* dollars. Which equation represents the amount of change *y* that he should receive from his purchase?

Ⓐ $y = 20 - x$
Ⓑ $y = 20 + x$
Ⓒ $x = 20 \div y$
Ⓓ $x = 20y$

Problem Solving

6. Maria earns \$45 for every lawn that she mows. Her earnings *e* in dollars depend on the number of lawns *n* that she mows. Write an equation that represents this situation.

____

7. Martin sells cars. He earns \$100 per day, plus any commission on his sales. His daily salary *s* in dollars depends on the amount of commission *c*. Write an equation to represent his daily salary.

____

Name ______________________________

Lesson 69

COMMON CORE STANDARD CC.6.EE.9

Lesson Objective: Translate between equations and tables.

Equations and Tables

You can use tables and equations to represent the relationship between two quantities.

Use the equation to complete the table.

$y = x \div 4$

Step 1 Look at the equation to find the rule. The rule for finding y is $x \div 4$.

Step 2 Apply the rule and fill in the missing values. Divide each x-value by 4.
$44 \div 4 = 11$ $36 \div 4 = 9$ $28 \div 4 = 7$ $20 \div 4 = 5$

x	y
44	
36	
28	
20	

Write an equation for the relationship.

Input, x	30	35	40	45	50
Output, y	6	7	8	9	10

Find a pattern.
Think: "What can I do to each x-value to find its corresponding y-value?"
The y-values are less than the x-values, so try dividing or subtracting.

$30 \div 5 = 6$ $35 \div 5 = 7$ $40 \div 5 = 8$ $45 \div 5 = 9$ $50 \div 5 = 10$

The pattern is to divide x by 5 to get y. The equation is $y = x \div 5$.

Write an equation for the relationship shown in the table. Then find the missing value in the table.

1.

x	20	40	60	80
y	23	43		83

____

2.

x	3	4	5	6
y	18	24	30	

____

Use the equation to complete the table.

3. $y = 7x$

Input, x	1	2	3	4
Output, y	7			

4. $y = x - 2$

Input, x	5	8	11	14
Output, y				

Use the table for 1–2.

The table shows the number of people n seated in each section of the gym depending on the total number of people p in the gym.

Total Number of People, p	9	18	27	36
People in Each Section, n	3	6	?	12

1. Which equation could be used to find the number of people n that are seated in each section of the gym?

Ⓐ $n = 3p$
Ⓑ $n = \frac{p}{3}$
Ⓒ $n = p - 6$
Ⓓ $n = p - 12$

2. How many people n would be seated in each section if there were 27 total people in the gym?

Ⓐ 7
Ⓑ 8
Ⓒ 9
Ⓓ 10

Use the table for 3–4.

A bowling alley charges $1.50 for shoe rental and $2 per game. The table shows the total cost y of bowling x games.

Number of Games, x	Cost (dollars), y
1	3.50
2	5.50
3	?
4	9.50

3. Which equation could be used to find the total cost y of bowling x games?

Ⓐ $y = 2x + 1.5$
Ⓑ $y = 1.5x + 2$
Ⓒ $y = x + 2$
Ⓓ $y = x + 1.5$

4. What is the total cost y of bowling 3 games?

Ⓐ $7.50
Ⓑ $6.50
Ⓒ $5.00
Ⓓ $4.50

Problem Solving REAL WORLD

5. Tickets to a play cost $11 each. There is also a service charge of $4 per order. Write an equation for the relationship that gives the total cost y in dollars for an order of x tickets .

____

6. Write an equation for the relationship shown in the table. Then use the equation to find the estimated number of shrimp in a 5-pound bag.

Weight of bag (pounds), x	1	2	3	4
Estimated number of shrimp, y	24	48	72	96

____

Name ______________________________

Lesson 70

COMMON CORE STANDARD CC.6.EE.9

Lesson Objective: Solve problems involving relationships between quantities by using the strategy *find a pattern.*

Problem Solving • Analyze Relationships

The table shows the number of miles an overnight train travels. If the pattern in the table continues, how far will the train travel in 10 hours?

Overnight Train Travel Rate				
Time (hours)	1	2	3	4
Distance (miles)	60	120	180	240

Use the graphic organizer to help you solve the problem.

Read the Problem

What do I need to find?	What information do I need to use?	How will I use the information?
I need to find the ______________ the train will travel in ______ hours.	I need to find the relationship between ______ and ______________ shown in the table.	I will find a __________ in the table and use the pattern to write an __________.

Solve the Problem

Look for a pattern between the number of hours and the number of miles.

Overnight Train Travel Rate				
Time in hours, h	1	2	3	4
Distance in miles, m	60	120	180	240

1×60 $2 \times$ ___ ___ $\times$ ___ ___ $\times$ ___

Then write an equation to show the pattern.

Equation: $m =$ ___ $\times h$

To find the miles the train will travel in 10 hours, substitute 10 for h.

$m =$ ___ $\times$ ___

$m =$ ___

1. The table shows how much a restaurant pays for coffee. How much will the restaurant pay for 100 pounds of coffee?

Coffee Purchasing				
Pounds, p	5	10	30	60
Cost, c	\$20	\$40	\$120	\$240

____

Name ____________________

1. Mr. Ramirez is filling his swimming pool with water. The table shows the number of gallons of water *w* in the swimming pool after *t* minutes.

Water in Swimming Pool

Time (minutes), *t*	1	2	3	4
Water (gallons), *w*	60	120	180	240

If the pattern in the table continues, how many gallons of water *w* will be in the pool after 10 minutes?

Ⓐ 6 gallons
Ⓑ 69 gallons
Ⓒ 600 gallons
Ⓓ 2,400 gallons

2. The table shows the amount of flour *x* that a baker uses for *y* dozen cookies.

Flour Needed to Bake Cookies

Amount of Flour Used (cups), *x*	3	4	5	6
Number of Dozens, *y*	4	8	12	16

If the pattern in the table continues, how many cups of flour *x* does the baker use for 20 dozen cookies?

Ⓐ 6 cups
Ⓑ 7 cups
Ⓒ 17 cups
Ⓓ 24 cups

Problem Solving REAL WORLD

3. An employee at a home improvement store is mixing a certain shade of green paint. The table shows the number of gallons of yellow paint *y* needed for *x* gallons of blue paint.

Green Paint

Gallons of Blue Paint, *x*	2	4	6	8
Gallons of Yellow Paint, *y*	3	6	9	12

If the pattern in the table continues, how many gallons of yellow paint *y* are needed to mix with 12 gallons of blue paint to get the same shade of green paint? Explain how you know.

____

____

____

Name ______________________________

Lesson 71

COMMON CORE STANDARD CC.6.EE.9

Lesson Objective: Graph the relationship between two quantities.

Graph Relationships

You can use a graph to represent a relationship.

Graph the relationship represented by the table to find the unknown value of *y*.

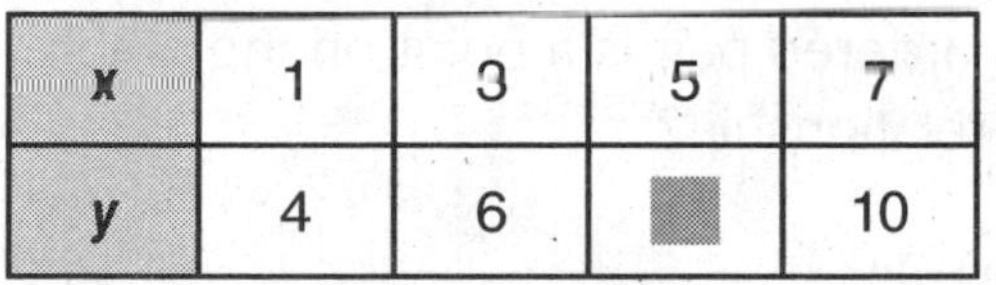

x	1	3	5	7
y	4	6	■	10

Step 1 Write ordered pairs that you know.

(1, 4), (3, 6), (7, 10)

Step 2 Plot the points.

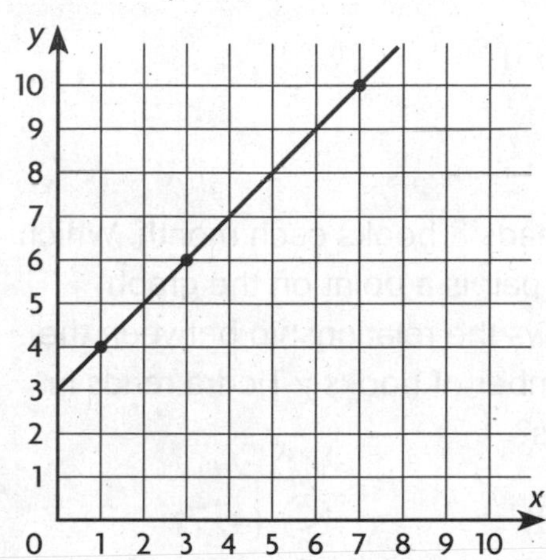

Step 3 Find the unknown *y*-value. Use a ruler to draw a line through the points. Find the *y*-value that corresponds to an *x*-value of 5.

So, when the *x*-value is 5, the *y*-value is 8.

Graph the relationship represented by the table to find the unknown value of *y*.

1.

x	1	2	3	4	5
y	3	4	■	6	7

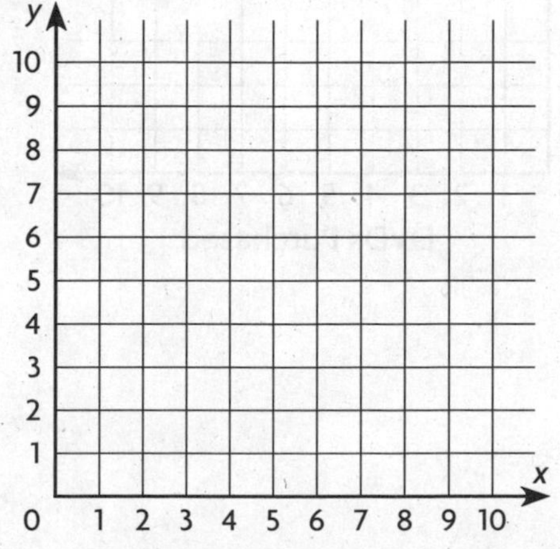

____

2.

x	2	4	6	8	10
y	8	7	■	5	4

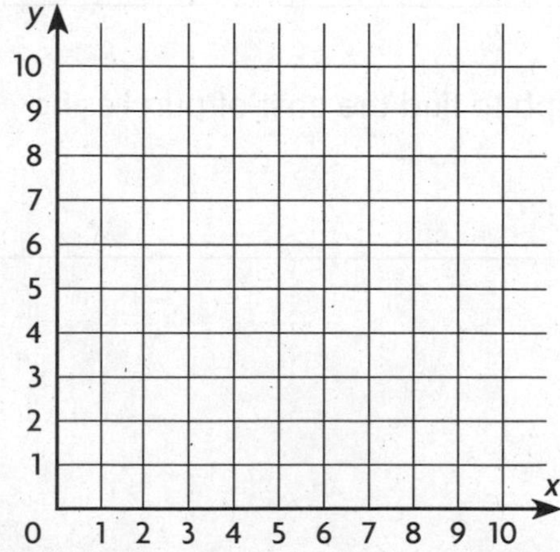

____

1. Nicholas drives at a rate of 60 miles per hour. He lets *x* represent the time in hours and *y* represent the number of miles driven. Which ordered pair is a point on the graph of the relationship?

   Ⓐ (60, 1)
   Ⓑ (4, 240)
   Ⓒ (3, 120)
   Ⓓ (2, 60)

2. DVDs cost $15 each. Mariah graphs the relationship that gives the cost *y* in dollars of buying *x* DVDs. Which ordered pair is a point on the graph of the relationship?

   Ⓐ (0, 15) Ⓒ (3, 45)
   Ⓑ (2, 3) Ⓓ (15, 3)

3. Posters cost $7 each. Rafael graphs the relationship that gives the cost *y* in dollars of buying *x* posters. Which ordered pair is a point on the graph of the relationship?

   Ⓐ (3, 10)
   Ⓑ (5, 15)
   Ⓒ (8, 52)
   Ⓓ (9, 63)

4. Tiedra reads 3 books each month. Which ordered pair is a point on the graph that shows the relationship between the total number of books *y* Tiedra reads in *x* months?

   Ⓐ (9, 3) Ⓒ (4, 7)
   Ⓑ (5, 15) Ⓓ (3, 1)

Problem Solving REAL WORLD

5. Graph the relationship represented by the table.

DVDs Purchased	1	2	3	4
Cost ($)	15	30	45	60

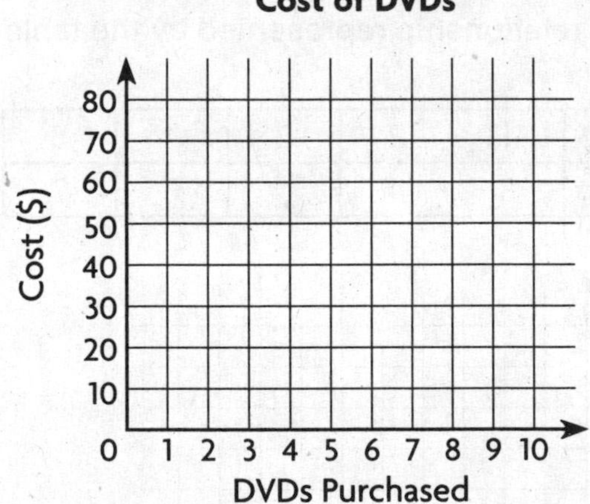

6. Use the graph to find the cost of purchasing 5 DVDs.

____

Name ________________________________

Lesson 72

COMMON CORE STANDARD CC.6.EE.9

Lesson Objective: Translate between equations and graphs.

Equations and Graphs

You can make a table of values for any equation. Use the table to write ordered pairs. Plot points to help you graph the equation. The graph of a **linear equation** is a straight line.

Graph the linear equation.

$y = x + 1$

$y = 3x - 2$

Step 1 Find ordered pairs that are solutions of the equation.

Choose four values for x. Substitute each value for x in the equation and find the corresponding value of y. Use easy values for x, such as 1, 2, 3, 4.

x	x + 1	y	Ordered Pair
1	1 + 1	2	(1, 2)
2	2 + 1	3	(2, 3)
3	3 + 1	4	(3, 4)
4	4 + 1	5	(4, 5)

x	3x − 2	y	Ordered Pair
1	3 · 1 − 2	1	(1, 1)
2	3 · 2 − 2	4	(2, 4)
3	3 · 3 − 2	7	(3, 7)
4	3 · 4 − 2	10	(4, 10)

Step 2 Graph the equation.

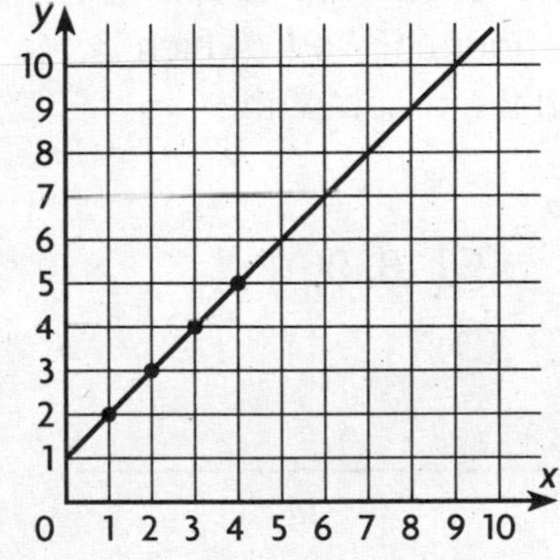

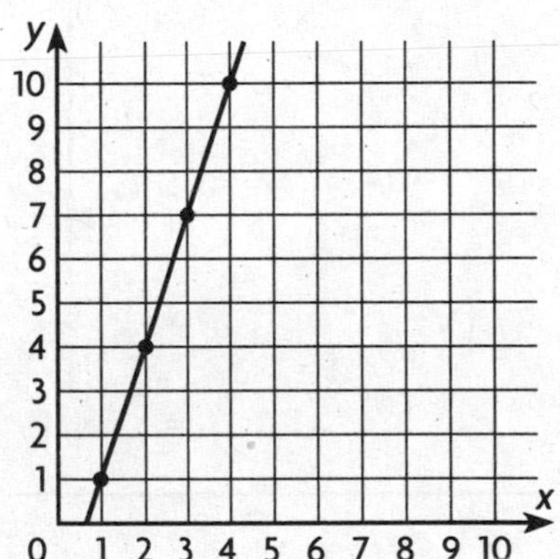

Graph the linear equation.

1. $y = x - 1$

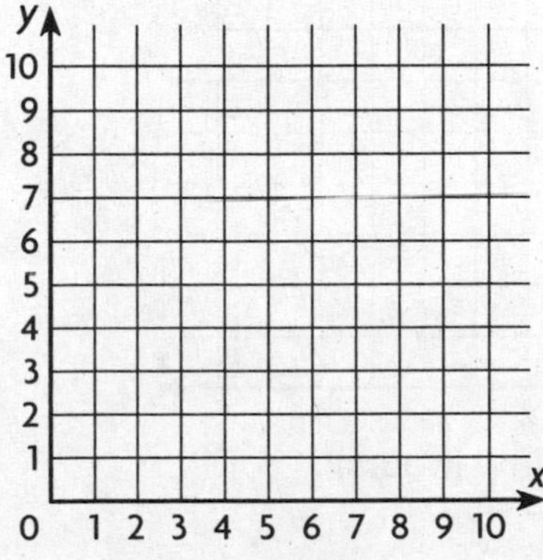

2. $y = 2x - 1$

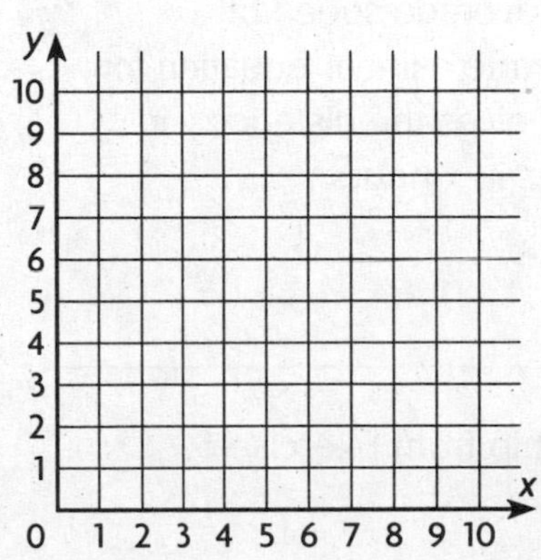

Name ____________________

Lesson 72
CC.6.EE.9

1. The graph shows the distance y a cyclist traveled over a period of time x in hours.

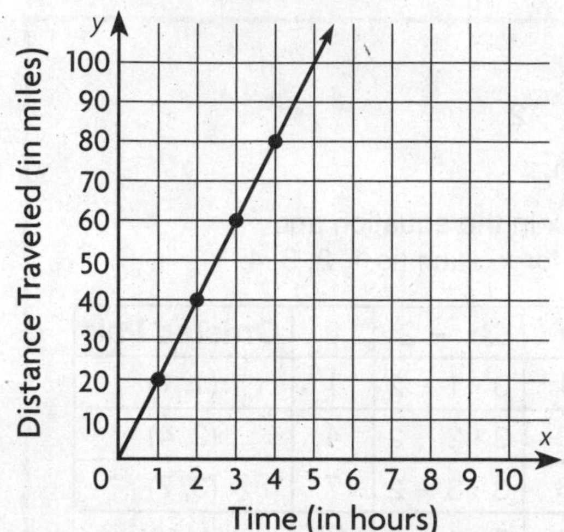

Which linear equation represents the relationship shown by the graph?

Ⓐ $y = x + 19$

Ⓑ $y = x + 20$

Ⓒ $y = \frac{x}{20}$

Ⓓ $y = 20x$

2. The linear equation $y = 5x$ represents the cost y in dollars of x pounds of dog food. Which ordered pair lies on the graph of the equation?

Ⓐ (3, 15) Ⓒ (2, 3)

Ⓑ (3, 10) Ⓓ (2, 12)

3. The linear equation $p = 10n$ represents the total number of points p scored on a quiz if n questions are correct. Which ordered pair lies on the graph of the equation?

Ⓐ (10, 1) Ⓒ (5, 2)

Ⓑ (7, 70) Ⓓ (4, 15)

4. Rod earns $12 per hour at his summer job. The linear equation $y = 12x$ represents his earnings y for x hours of work. Which ordered pair lies on the graph of the equation?

Ⓐ (0, 12) Ⓒ (8, 96)

Ⓑ (4, 16) Ⓓ (12, 1)

Problem Solving REAL WORLD

5. Dee is driving at an average speed of 50 miles per hour. Write a linear equation for the relationship that gives the distance y in miles that Dee drives in x hours.

____

6. Graph the relationship from Exercise 5.

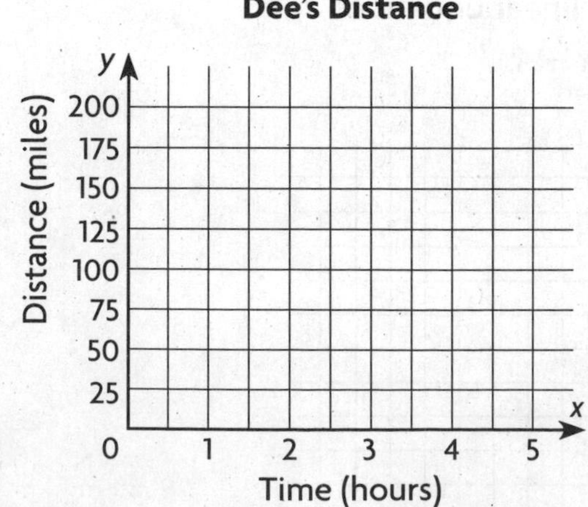

Name ____________________

Lesson 73

COMMON CORE STANDARD CC.6.G.1

Lesson Objective: Find the area of parallelograms.

Algebra • Area of Parallelograms

The formula for the area of a parallelogram is the product of the base and height.

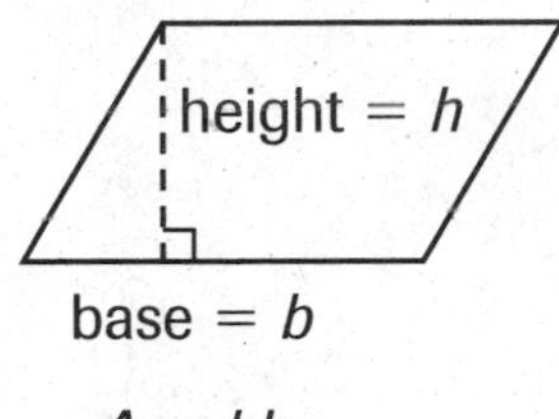

$A = bh$

The formula for the area of a square is the square of one of its sides.

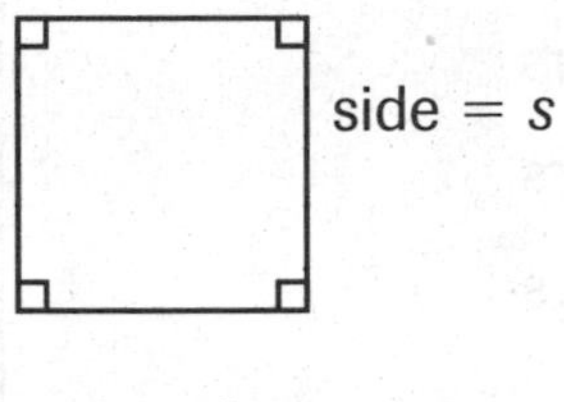

$A = s^2$

Find the area.

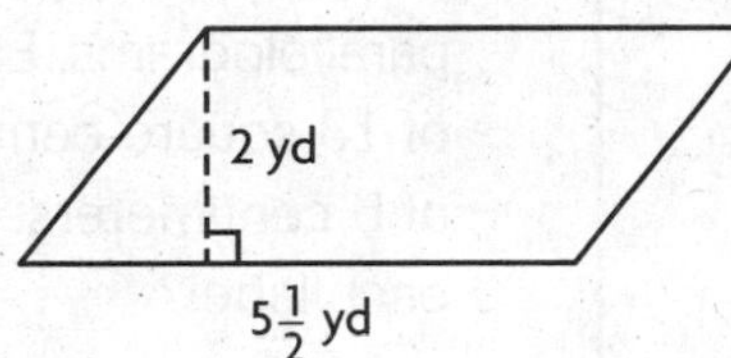

Step 1 Identify the figure. The figure is a parallelogram, so use the formula $A = bh$.

Step 2 Substitute $5\frac{1}{2}$ for b and 2 for h. $A = 5\frac{1}{2} \times 2$

Step 3 Multiply. $A = 5\frac{1}{2} \times 2 = \frac{11}{2} \times \frac{2}{1} = 11$

So, the area of the parallelogram is 11 yd².

Find the area.

1.

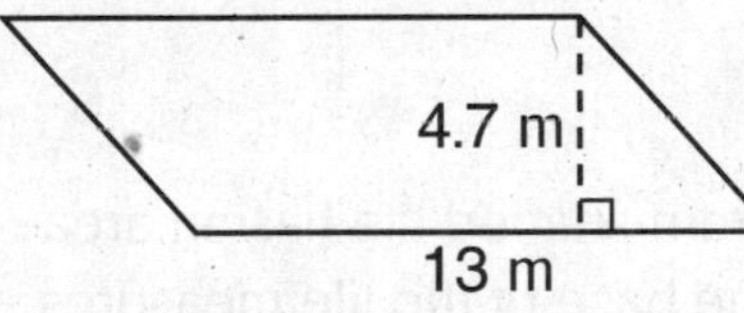

Figure: ____________________

Formula: $A =$ ______

$A =$ ______ $\times$ ______ $=$ ________ m²

2.

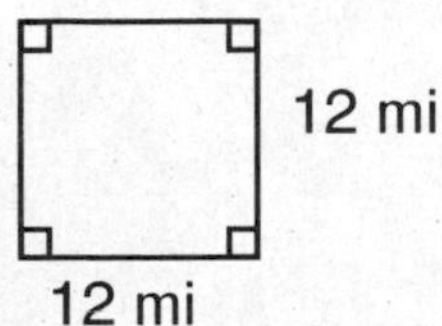

____________________ mi²

3.

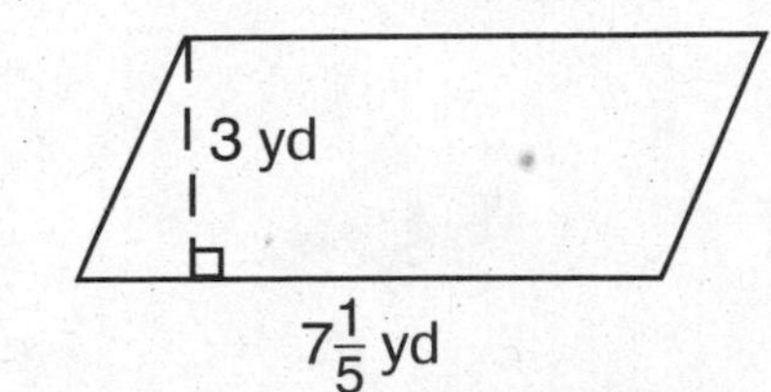

____________________ yd²

Name ______________________

1. The roof on Mrs. Vega's house is shaped like a parallelogram. The base of the roof is 16.7 meters and the height is 9 meters. What is the area of the roof?

Ⓐ 7.7 square meters
Ⓑ 25.7 square meters
Ⓒ 114.4 square meters
Ⓓ 150.3 square meters

2. Nishelle's backyard is in the shape of a parallelogram. The parallelogram has an area of 224 square feet and a base of 14 feet. What is the height of the parallelogram?

Ⓐ 8 feet
Ⓑ 16 feet
Ⓒ 238 feet
Ⓓ 3,136 feet

3. The windows in an office building are shaped like parallelograms. The base of each window is 1.8 meters and the height is 1.5 meters. What is the area of each window?

Ⓐ 1.35 square meters
Ⓑ 2.7 square meters
Ⓒ 3.3 square meters
Ⓓ 6.6 square meters

4. Leeza is making labels in the shape of parallelograms. Each label has an area of 18 square centimeters and a base of 6 centimeters. What is the height of each label?

Ⓐ 3 centimeters
Ⓑ 24 centimeters
Ⓒ 48 centimeters
Ⓓ 108 centimeters

Problem Solving REAL WORLD

5. Ronna has a sticker in the shape of a parallelogram. The sticker has a base of 6.5 cm and a height of 10.1 cm. What is the area of the sticker?

____

6. A parallelogram-shaped tile has an area of 48 in.^{2}. The base of the tile measures 12 in. What is the measure of its height?

____

Name ______________________

Lesson 74

COMMON CORE STANDARD CC.6.G.1

Lesson Objective: Investigate the relationship among the areas of triangles, rectangles, and parallelograms.

Explore Area of Triangles

You can use grid paper to find a relationship between the areas of triangles and rectangles.

Step 1 On grid paper, draw a rectangle with a baco of 8 units and a height of 6 units. Find and record the area of the rectangle.

$A =$ **48 square units**

Step 2 Cut out the rectangle.

Step 3 Draw a diagonal from the bottom left corner up to the top right corner.

Step 4 Cut the rectangle along the diagonal.

You have made 2 **triangles**.

- Are the triangles congruent? **yes**
- How does the area of one triangle compare to the area of the rectangle?

The area of the triangle is half the area of the rectangle.

If l is the length and w is the width, you can use a rectangle to find the area of a triangle.

Find the area of the triangle.

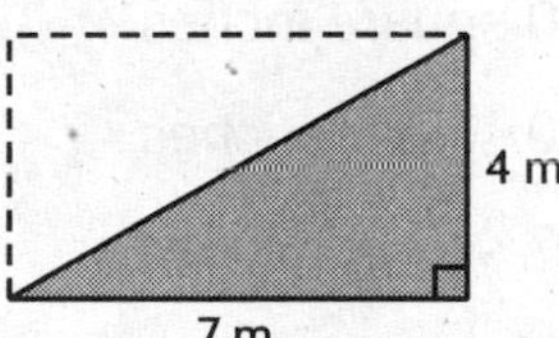

Area of rectangle: $A = lw = 7 \times 4 = 28 \text{ m}^2$

Area of triangle: $A = \frac{1}{2} \times \text{area of rectangle} = \frac{1}{2} \times 28 = 14 \text{ m}^2$

So, the area is **14** square meters.

Find the area of the triangle.

1.

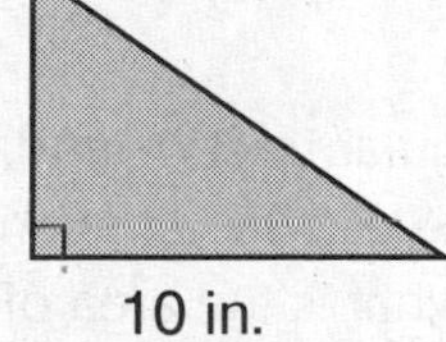

____

2.

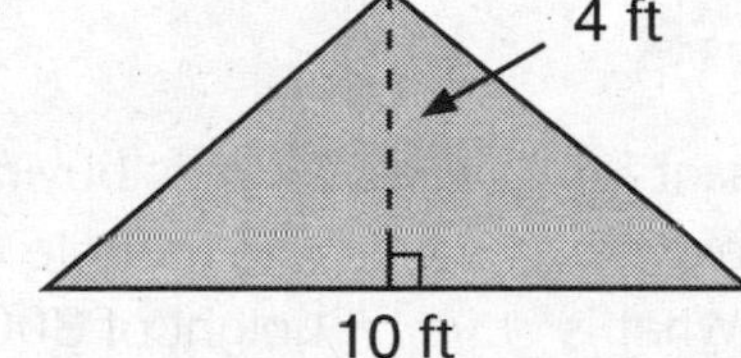

____

3.

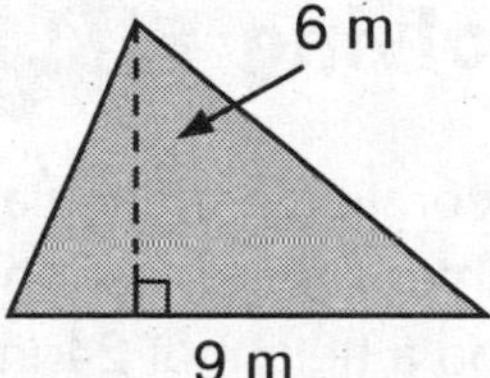

____

Name ______________________________

1. A diagram of part of a Navajo rug is shown.

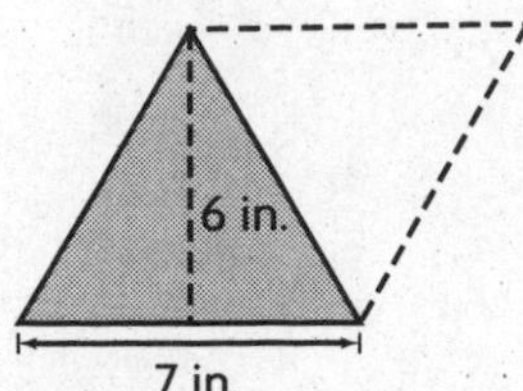

What is the area of the shaded triangle?

Ⓐ 13 square inches
Ⓑ 21 square inches
Ⓒ 35 square inches
Ⓓ 42 square inches

2. A rectangular school flag has a base of 25 inches and a height of 32 inches. The flag is divided into 2 congruent triangles formed by 2 sides and a diagonal of the flag. What is the area of each triangle?

Ⓐ 800 square inches
Ⓑ 400 square inches
Ⓒ 57 square inches
Ⓓ 41 square inches

3. A diagram of a patch on Max's quilt is shown.

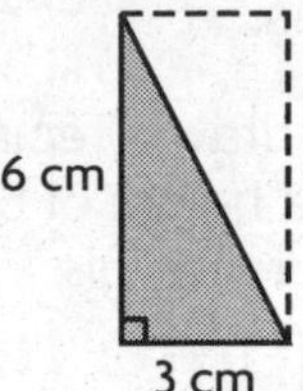

What is the area of the shaded triangle?

Ⓐ 2 square centimeters
Ⓑ 3 square centimeters
Ⓒ 9 square centimeters
Ⓓ 18 square centimeters

4. Kendra is sewing a pattern of parallelograms on her backpack. Each parallelogram has a base of 5 centimeters, a height of 18 centimeters, and is divided into two congruent triangles. What is the area of each triangle?

Ⓐ 45 square centimeters
Ⓑ 46 square centimeters
Ⓒ 90 square centimeters
Ⓓ 92 square centimeters

Problem Solving REAL WORLD

5. Fabian is decorating a triangular pennant for a football game. The pennant has a base of 10 inches and a height of 24 inches. What is the total area of the pennant?

____

6. Ryan is buying a triangular tract of land. The triangle has a base of 100 yards and a height of 300 yards. What is the area of the tract of land?

____

Name ______________________________

Lesson 75

COMMON CORE STANDARD CC.6.G.1

Lesson Objective: Find the area of triangles.

Algebra • Area of Triangles

To find the area of a triangle, use the formula
$A = \frac{1}{2} \times \text{base} \times \text{height}$.

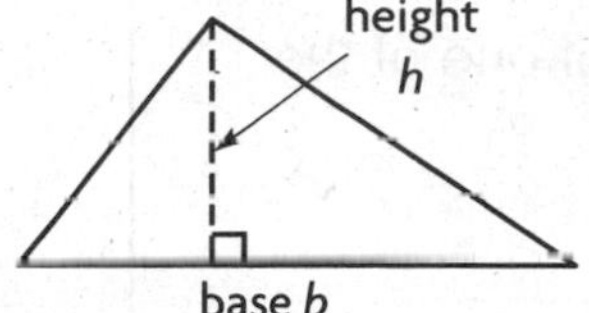

Find the area of the triangle.

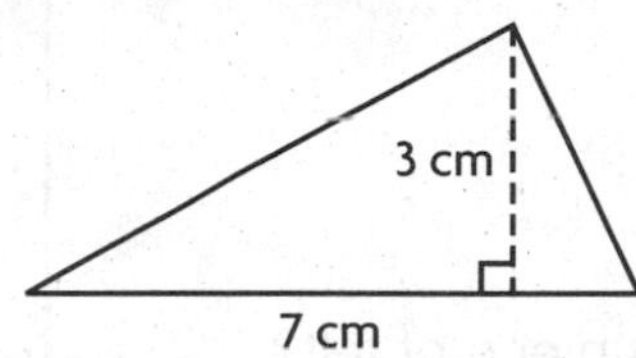

Step 1 Write the formula. $A = \frac{1}{2}bh$

Step 2 Rewrite the formula. Substitute the base and height measurements for b and h. $A = \frac{1}{2} \times 7 \times 3$

Step 3 Simplify by multiplying. $A = \frac{1}{2} \times 21$

$A = 10.5$

Step 4 Use the appropriate units. $A = 10.5 \text{ cm}^2$

Find the area of the triangle.

1. 

Write the formula. $A = \frac{1}{2} \times$ ______

Substitute for b and h. $A = \frac{1}{2} \times$ ______ $\times$ ______

Simplify. $A = \frac{1}{2} \times$ ______

$A =$ ______ ft^2

2. 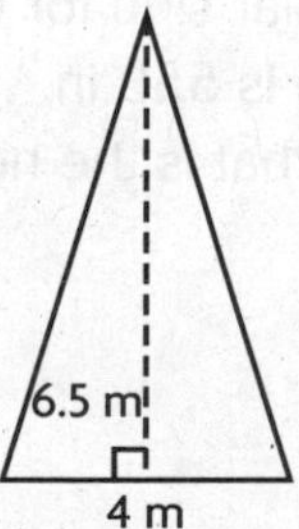

$A =$ ______________

3. 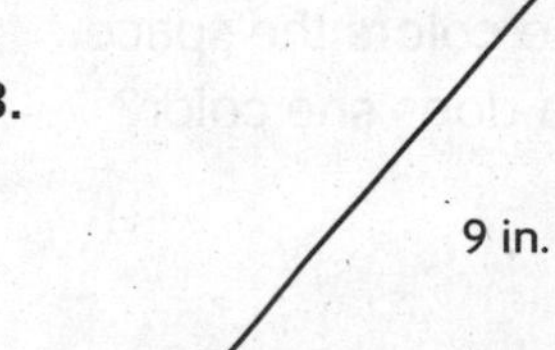

$A =$ ______________

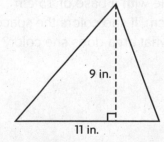

Name ______________________

1. Farah cut triangular pieces of felt to use in her art project. The size of one of the triangular pieces is shown.

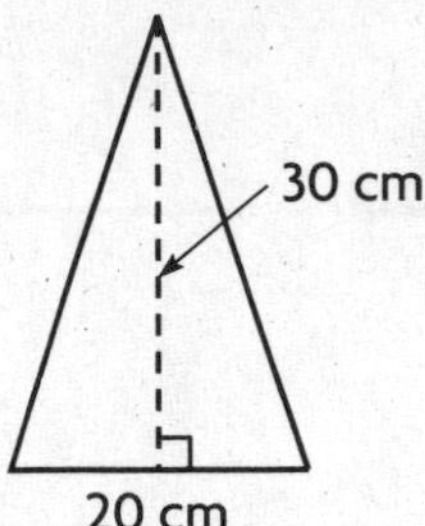

What is the area of this piece of felt?

Ⓐ 600 square centimeters
Ⓑ 300 square centimeters
Ⓒ 50 square centimeters
Ⓓ 25 square centimeters

2. Liang used 75 square inches of fabric to make a triangular pennant to take to a football game. The base of the pennant was 6 inches. What was the height of the pennant?

Ⓐ 3 inches
Ⓑ 12.5 inches
Ⓒ 25 inches
Ⓓ 37.5 inches

3. Marta drew this diagram of a triangular window at the art museum.

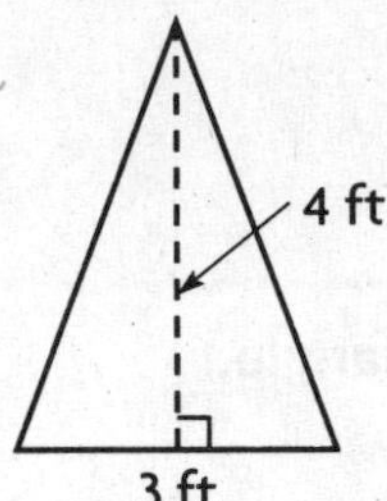

What is the area of the window?

Ⓐ 14 square feet
Ⓑ 12 square feet
Ⓒ 7 square feet
Ⓓ 6 square feet

4. Hiro used 60 square inches of fabric to make a triangular sail for his model sailboat. The base of the sail was 8 inches. What was the height of the sail?

Ⓐ 15 inches
Ⓑ 7.5 inches
Ⓒ 5 inches
Ⓓ 2.5 inches

Problem Solving REAL WORLD

5. Bayla draws a triangle with a base of 15 cm and a height of 8.5 cm. If she colors the space inside the triangle, what area does she color?

____

6. Alicia is making a triangular sign for the school play. The area of the sign is 558 in.^{2}. The base of the triangle is 36 in. What is the height of the triangle?

____

Name ______________________________

Lesson 76

COMMON CORE STANDARD CC.6.G.1

Lesson Objective: Investigate the relationship between the areas of trapezoids and parallelograms.

Explore Area of Trapezoids

Show the relationship between the areas of trapezoids and parallelograms.

Step 1 On grid paper, draw two copies of the trapezoid. Count the grid squares to make your trapezoid match this one.

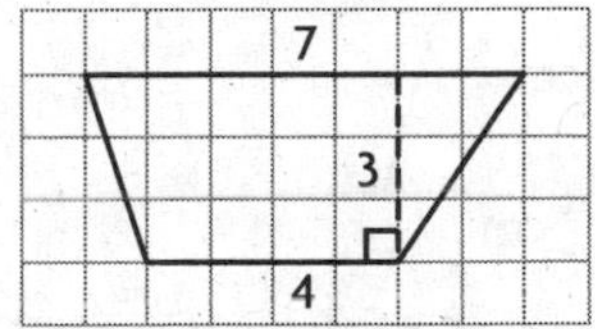

Step 2 Cut out the trapezoids.

Step 3 Turn one trapezoid until the two trapezoids form a parallelogram.

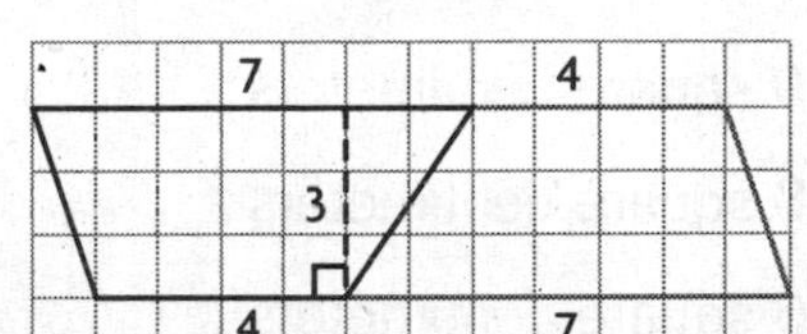

Step 4 Find the length of the base of the parallelogram. Add the lengths of one shorter trapezoid base and one longer trapezoid base.

$4 + 7 = 11$ units

Step 5 Find the area of the parallelogram. Use the formula $A = bh$.

$A = 11 \times 3 = 33$ square units

Step 6 The parallelogram is made of two congruent trapezoids. So, divide by 2 to find the area of one trapezoid.

$33 \div 2 = 16.5$ square units

Find the area of the trapezoid.

1. Trace and cut out two copies of the trapezoid. Arrange them to form a parallelogram.

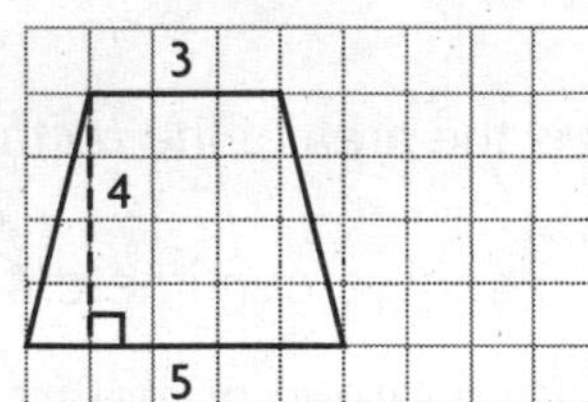

   a. Find the base of the parallelogram. 3 + ______ = ______

   b. Find the area of the parallelogram, using $A = bh$.

   $A =$ ______ $\times$ ______ $=$ ______ square units

   c. Find the area of the trapezoid.

   ______ $\div 2 =$ ______ square units

2.

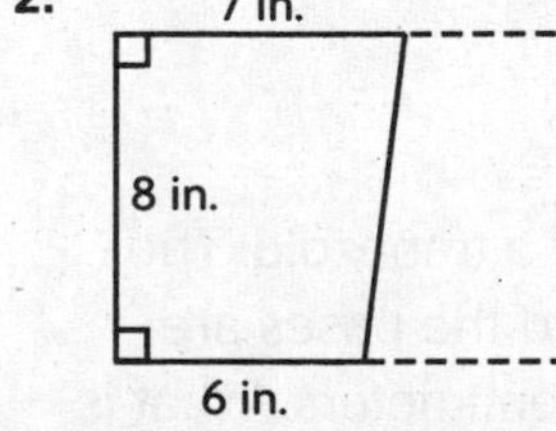

______ in.^{2}

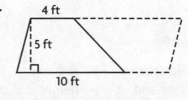

3.

4 ft
5 ft
10 ft

______ ft^2

4.

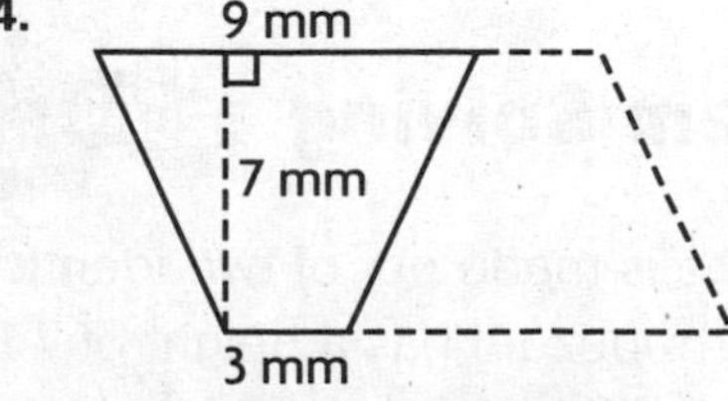

______ mm^2

Name ______________________________

Lesson 76
CC.6.G.1

1. Tamara made a copy of a trapezoid to make a design in the shape of a parallelogram.

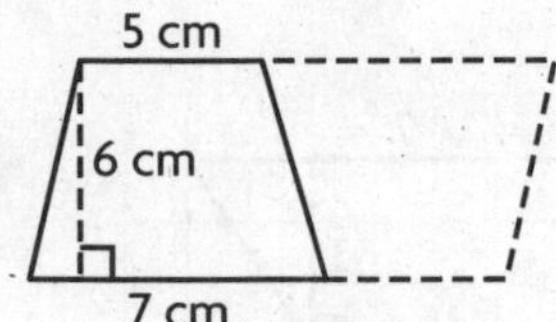

What is the area of each trapezoid?

Ⓐ 9 square centimeters
Ⓑ 18 square centimeters
Ⓒ 36 square centimeters
Ⓓ 72 square centimeters

2. Leon makes a rectangular logo for his skateboarding club. He cuts from fabric two copies of the trapezoid shown and joins them to form a rectangle.

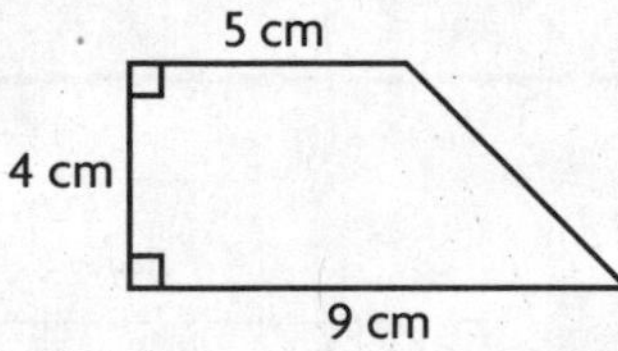

What is the area of the rectangular logo?

Ⓐ 56 square centimeters
Ⓑ 28 square centimeters
Ⓒ 18 square centimeters
Ⓓ 9 square centimeters

3. Josh constructs a banner in the shape of a parallelogram by making a copy of a trapezoid.

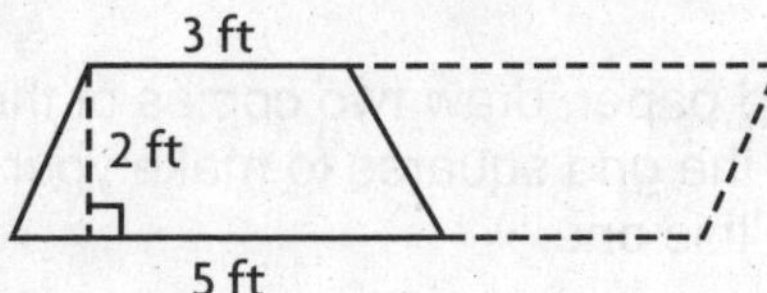

What is the area of each trapezoid?

Ⓐ 8 square feet
Ⓑ 10 square feet
Ⓒ 16 square feet
Ⓓ 20 square feet

4. Glenda cuts a trapezoid with the shown dimensions from construction paper. She uses a copy of the trapezoid to create a rectangular design.

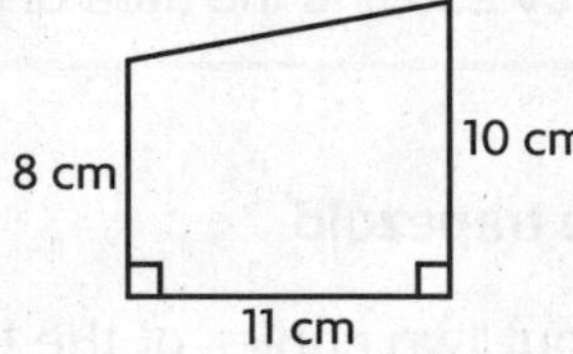

What is the area of the rectangular design?

Ⓐ 29 square centimeters
Ⓑ 40 square centimeters
Ⓒ 99 square centimeters
Ⓓ 198 square centimeters

Problem Solving REAL WORLD

5. A cake is made out of two identical trapezoids. Each trapezoid has a height of *11* inches and bases of *9* inches and *14* inches. What is the area of one of the trapezoid pieces?

____

6. A sticker is in the shape of a trapezoid. The height is *3* centimeters, and the bases are *2.5* centimeters and *5.5* centimeters. What is the area of the sticker?

____

Name ______________________________

Lesson 77

COMMON CORE STANDARD CC.6.G.1

Lesson Objective: Find the area of trapezoids.

Algebra • Area of Trapezoids

To find the area of a trapezoid, use the formula
Area $= \frac{1}{2} \times (\text{base}_1 + \text{base}_2) \times \text{height}$.

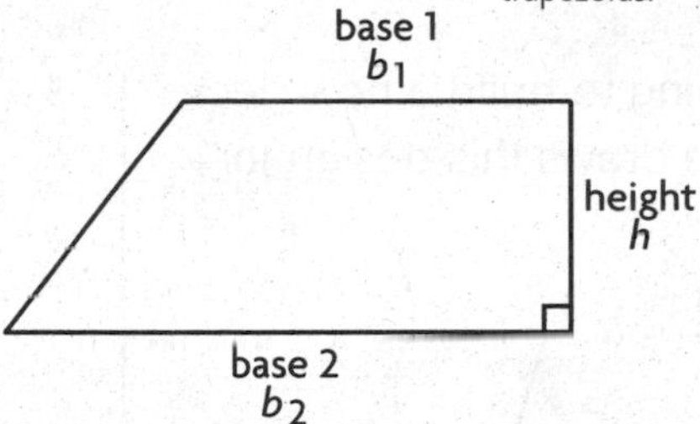

Find the area of the trapezoid.

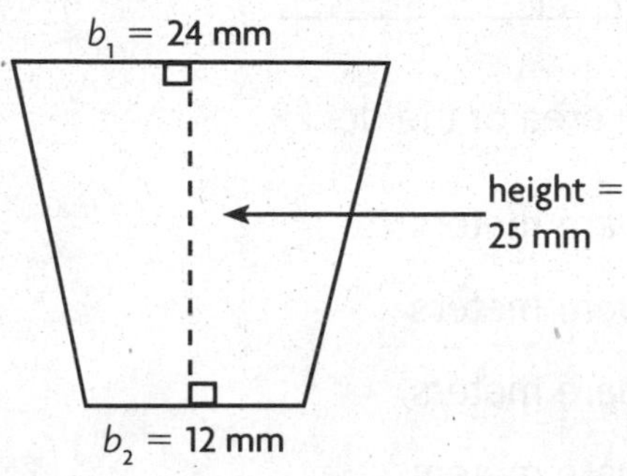

Step 1 Write the formula to find the area. $A = \frac{1}{2}(b_1 + b_2)h$

Step 2 Replace the variable b_1 with 24, b_2 with 12, and h with 25. $A = \frac{1}{2} \times (24 + 12) \times 25$

Step 3 Use the order of operations to simplify. $A = \frac{1}{2} \times 36 \times 25$

$A = 18 \times 25$

$A = 450$

Step 4 Use the appropriate units. $A = 450 \text{ mm}^2$

Find the area.

1.

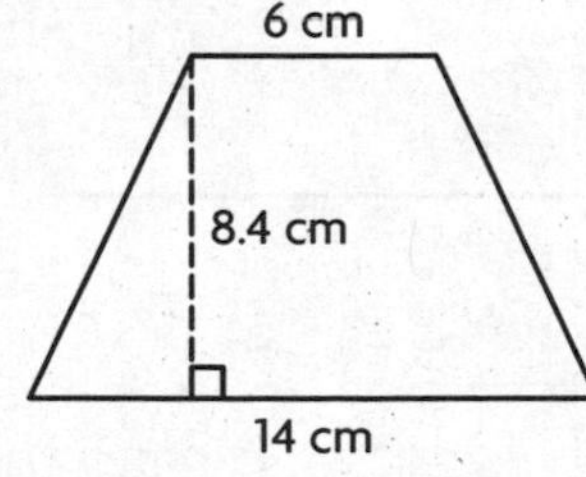

Write the formula. $A =$ ______________

Replace the variables. $A = \frac{1}{2} \times ($______ + ______$) \times$ ______

Simplify. $A = \frac{1}{2} \times$ ______ $\times$ ______

$A =$ ______________

2.

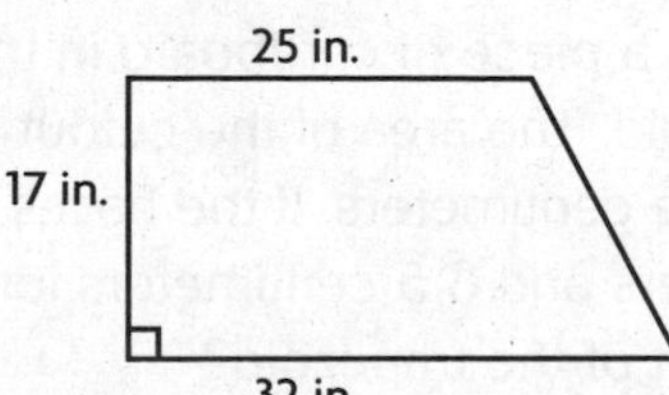

____

3.

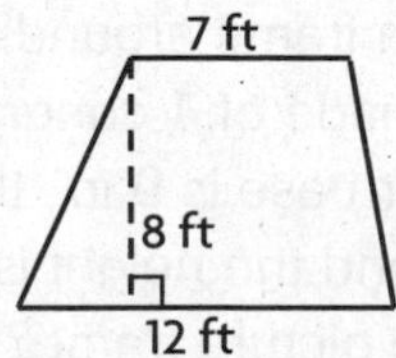

____

Name ______________________________

1. Olivia's father is going to build a new deck in the backyard. He draws this design for the deck.

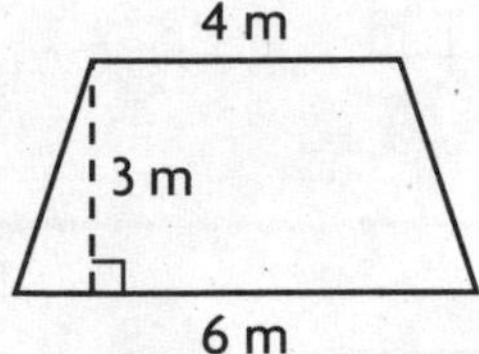

What is the area of the deck?

Ⓐ 72 square meters

Ⓑ 36 square meters

Ⓒ 30 square meters

Ⓓ 15 square meters

2. The lid on a ceramic box is in the shape of a trapezoid. The area of the lid is 36 square inches. The bases of the lid are 5 inches and 7 inches. What is the height of the lid?

Ⓐ 48 inches

Ⓑ 24 inches

Ⓒ 6 inches

Ⓓ 1 inch

3. Mr. Wen has a desk that is shaped like a trapezoid. The diagram shows the dimensions of the desk.

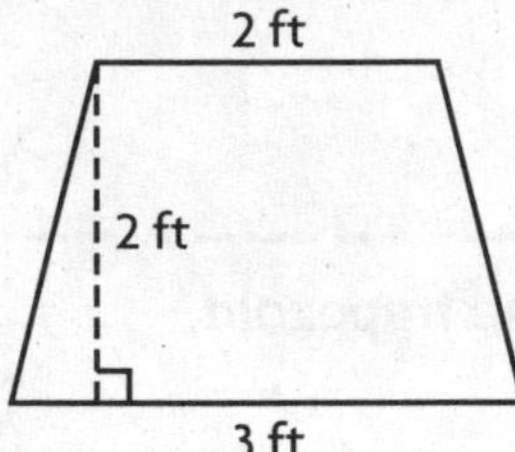

What is the area of the desk?

Ⓐ 5 square feet Ⓒ 10 square feet

Ⓑ 7 square feet Ⓓ 12 square feet

4. Rita is making a large poster for an art project. The shape and dimensions of her poster are shown.

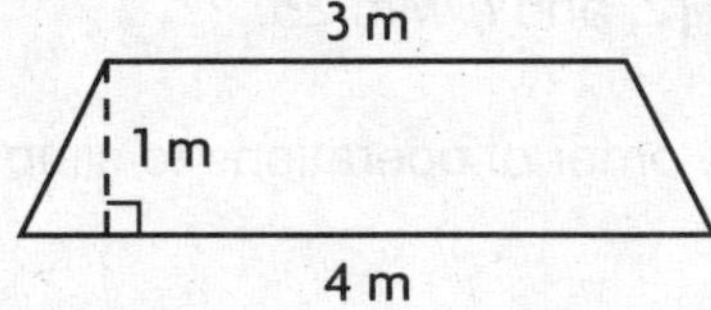

What is the area of the poster?

Ⓐ 3.5 square meters

Ⓑ 7 square meters

Ⓒ 8 square meters

Ⓓ 12 square meters

Problem Solving REAL WORLD

5. Sonia makes a wooden frame around a square picture. The frame is made of 4 congruent trapezoids. The shorter base is 9 in., the longer base is 12 in., and the height is 1.5 in. What is the area of the picture frame?

____

6. Bryan cuts a piece of cardboard in the shape of a trapezoid. The area of the cutout is 43.5 square centimeters. If the bases are 6 centimeters and 8.5 centimeters long, what is the height of the trapezoid?

____

Name ______________________________

Lesson 78

COMMON CORE STANDARD CC.6.G.1

Lesson Objective: Find the area of regular polygons.

Area of Regular Polygons

In a regular polygon, all sides have the same length and all angles have the same measure. To find the area of a regular polygon, divide it into triangles.

Step 1 Draw line segments from each vertex to the center of the regular polygon.

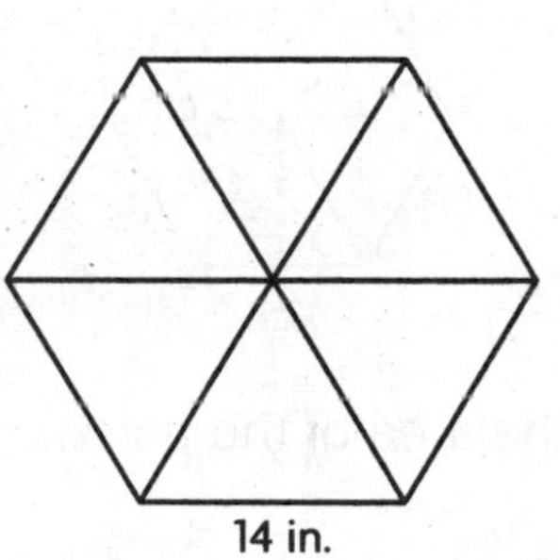

Step 2 Examine the figure.

The line segments divide the polygon into congruent triangles. This polygon is a hexagon. A hexagon has 6 sides, so there are 6 triangles.

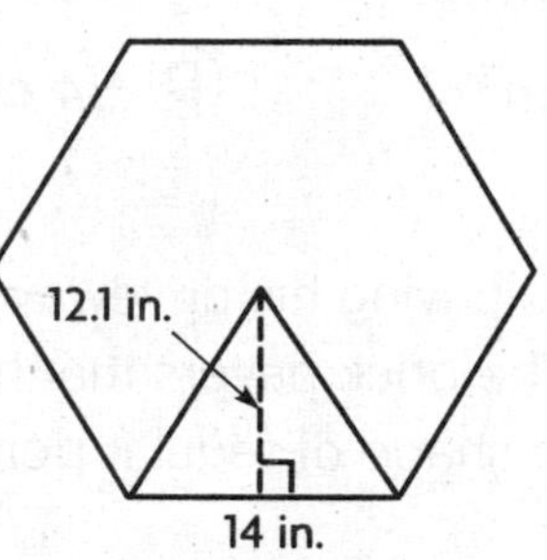

Step 3 Find the area of one triangle. Use the formula $A = \frac{1}{2}bh$.

The base of the triangle (or one side of the hexagon) is 14 in. The height of the triangle is 12.1 in.

$A = \frac{1}{2} \times 14 \times 12.1 = \frac{1}{2} \times 169.4 = 84.7 \text{ in.}^2$

Step 4 Multiply by 6, because there are 6 triangles. $84.7 \times 6 = 508.2$

So, the area of the regular hexagon is 508.2 square inches.

Find the area of the regular polygon.

1. Number of congruent triangles inside the pentagon: ______

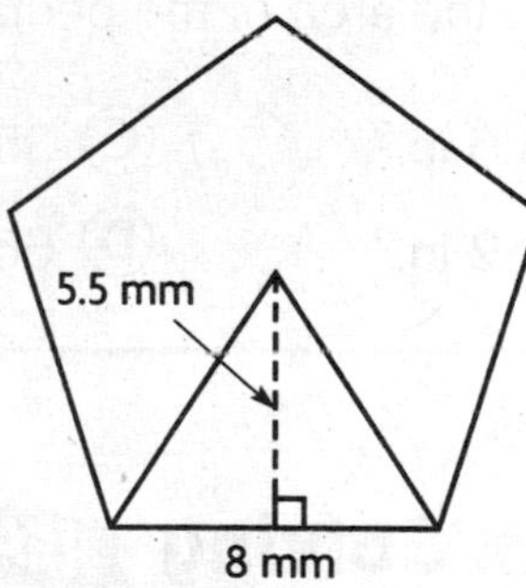

Area of each triangle:

$A = \frac{1}{2} \times$ ______ $\times 5.5 = \frac{1}{2} \times$ ______ $=$ ______ mm^2

Area of the pentagon: ______ $\times$ ______ $=$ ______ mm^2

2. 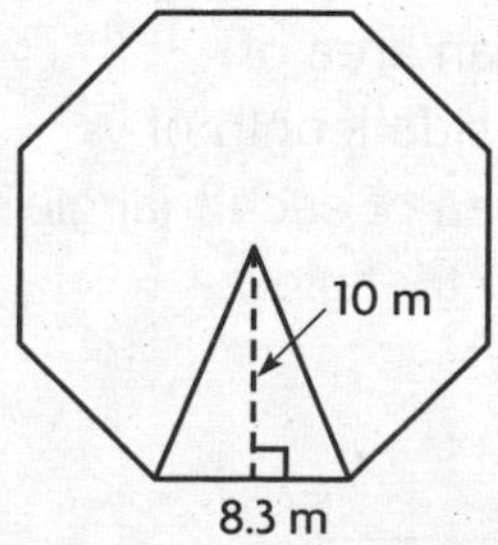

______________ m^2

3. 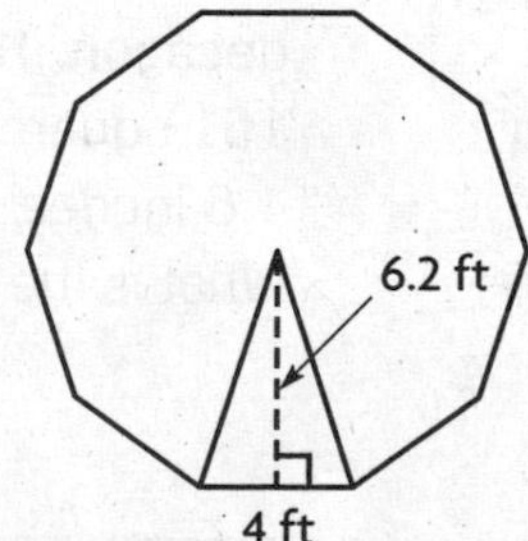

______________ ft^2

4. 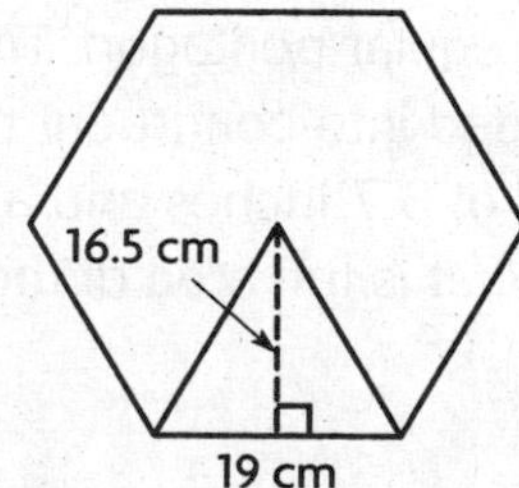

______________ cm^2

Name ______________________

Lesson 78
CC.6.G.1

1. Marcia has a regular hexagonal patch on her backpack. A diagram of the patch is shown.

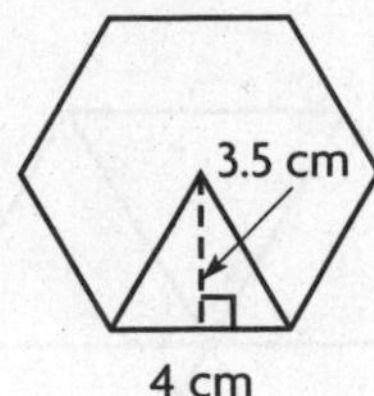

What is the area of the patch?

Ⓐ 7 cm^2
Ⓑ 14 cm^2
Ⓒ 42 cm^2
Ⓓ 84 cm^2

2. Radimir is paving his driveway using brick pavers. The brick pavers that he is using are in the shape of regular pentagons as shown.

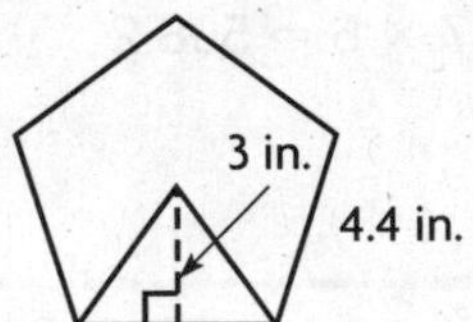

What is the area of the pentagon shown?

Ⓐ 6.6 in.^{2}
Ⓑ 13.2 in.^{2}
Ⓒ 33 in.^{2}
Ⓓ 66 in.^{2}

3. Giselle has a pendant on her necklace that is shaped like a regular hexagon. On the pendant, there are lines from the center to each vertex that divide it into congruent triangles. Each triangle has an area of 2 square centimeters. What is the area of the pendant?

Ⓐ 10 cm^2
Ⓑ 12 cm^2
Ⓒ 20 cm^2
Ⓓ 24 cm^2

4. Amira's bathroom floor is made of regular octagon tiles and square tiles. A diagram of one of the octagon tiles is shown.

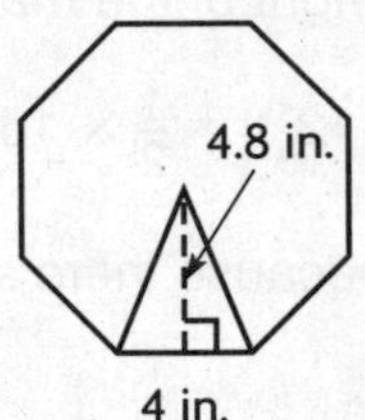

What is the area of one of the octagon tiles?

Ⓐ 9.6 in.^{2}
Ⓑ 19.2 in.^{2}
Ⓒ 38.4 in.^{2}
Ⓓ 76.8 in.^{2}

Problem Solving REAL WORLD

5. Stu is making a stained glass window in the shape of a regular pentagon. The pentagon can be divided into congruent triangles, each with a base of 8.7 inches and a height of 6 inches. What is the area of the window?

____

6. A dinner platter is in the shape of a regular decagon. The platter has an area of 161 square inches and a side length of 4.6 inches. What is the area of each triangle? What is the height of each triangle?

____

Name ___________________________

Lesson 79

COMMON CORE STANDARD CC.6.G.1

Lesson Objective: Find the area of composite figures.

Composite Figures

A **composite figure** is made up of two or more simpler figures, such as triangles and quadrilaterals.

The composite figure shows the front view of a bird house. Complete Steps 1–4 to find the area of the shaded region.

8 cm
20 cm
10 cm
10 cm
16 cm

Step 1 Find the area of the rectangle.

$A = lw = 16 \times$ ________ $=$ ________ cm^2

Step 2 Find the area of the triangle.

$A = \frac{1}{2}bh = \frac{1}{2} \times$ ________ $\times$ ________

$= \frac{1}{\cancel{2}_1} \times \frac{\cancel{16}^{8}}{1} \times$ ________ $=$ ________ cm^2

Step 3 Find the area of the square.

$A = s^2 = ($________$)^2$

$=$ ________ cm^2

Step 4 Add the areas of the rectangle and triangle. Then subtract the area of the square.

Shaded area $=$ ________ $+$ ________ $-$ ________ $=$ ________ cm^2

So, the area of the shaded region is ________ cm^2.

Find the area of the shaded region.

1.

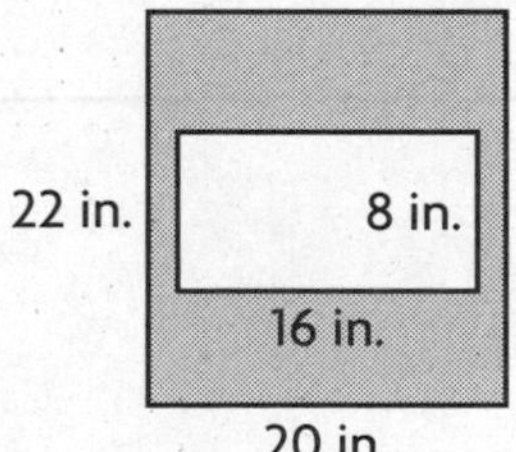

____

2.

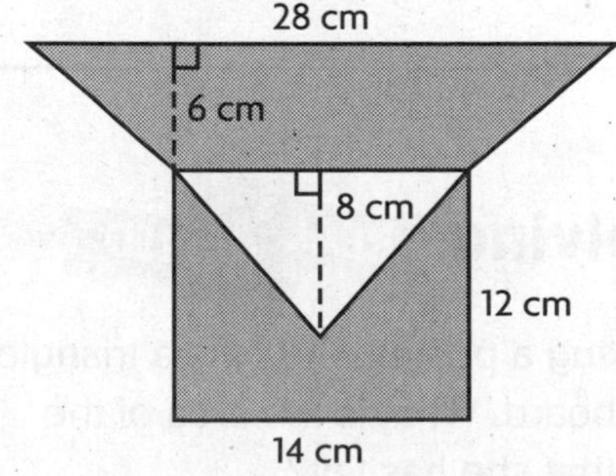

____

Name ___________________________________

1. Melvin wants to install new carpet in his basement. He needs to know the area of the basement to determine how much carpet he will need to purchase. The figure shows the dimensions of Melvin's basement.

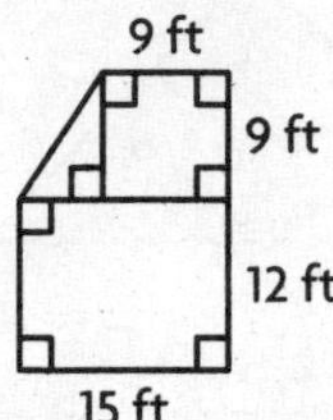

What is the area of his basement?

Ⓐ 315 ft²   Ⓒ 189 ft²
Ⓑ 288 ft²   Ⓓ 180 ft²

2. Jacob is constructing a model of a spacecraft for his science project. The design of the wing of the spacecraft is shown.

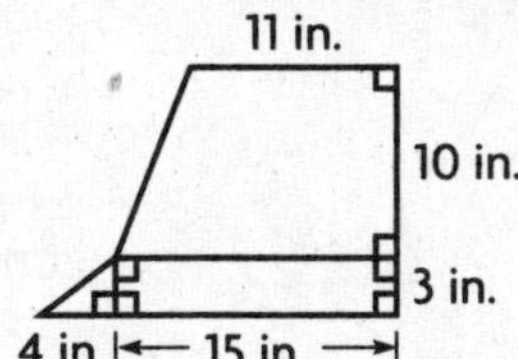

What is the area of the wing?

Ⓐ 70 in.²   Ⓒ 150 in.²
Ⓑ 130 in.²   Ⓓ 181 in.²

3. Mrs. Webster cut a triangle with a height of 4 inches and a base of 6 inches out of a sheet of paper measuring 10 inches by 12 inches. She recycled the unused paper. What is the area of the paper she recycled?

Ⓐ 12 in.²
Ⓑ 24 in.²
Ⓒ 108 in.²
Ⓓ 120 in.²

4. Sofia wants to remodel some rooms in her home. She needs to know the total area of the rooms before she can begin. The figure shows the dimensions of the rooms she wants to remodel.

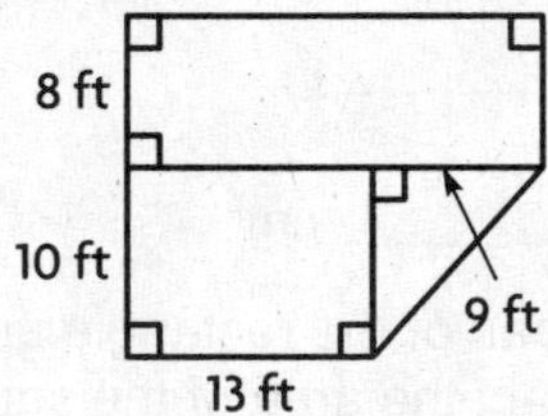

What is the total area of the rooms she is going to remodel?

Ⓐ 130 ft²   Ⓒ 351 ft²
Ⓑ 279 ft²   Ⓓ 396 ft²

Problem Solving REAL WORLD

5. Janelle is making a poster. She cuts a triangle out of poster board. What is the area of the poster board that she has left?

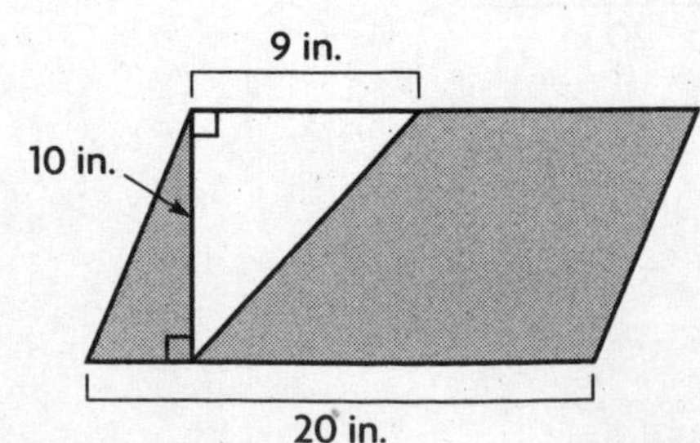

____

Name ______________________________

Lesson 80

COMMON CORE STANDARD CC.6.G.1

Lesson Objective: Determine the effect of changing dimensions on the area of a polygon by using the strategy *find a pattern.*

Problem Solving • Changing Dimensions

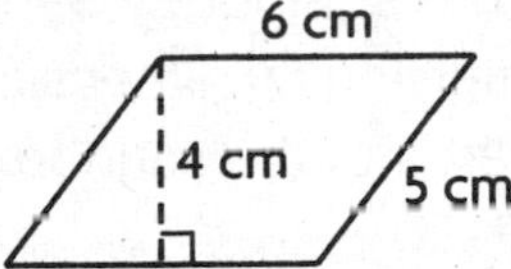

Amy is sewing a quilt out of fabric pieces shaped like parallelograms. The smallest of the parallelograms is shown at the right. The dimensions of another parallelogram she is using can be found by multiplying the dimensions of the smallest parallelogram by 3. How do the areas of the parallelograms compare?

Read the Problem		
What do I need to find?	**What information do I need to use?**	**How will I use the information?**
I need to find ______________ ______________ ______________ ______________ ______________.	I need to use ______________ ______________ ______________ ______________ ______________.	I can draw a sketch of each ______ and calculate the ______________. Then I can ______ ______________.

Solve the Problem		
Sketch	**Multiplier**	**Area**
	none	$A = 6 \times$ ____ $=$ ____ cm^2
	3	$A =$ ____ $\times$ ____ $=$ ______ cm^2

When the dimensions are multiplied by 3, the area is multiplied by ____.

1. Sunni drew a parallelogram with area 20 in.^{2}. If she doubles the dimensions, what is the area of the new parallelogram?

____

2. Abe drew a square with side length 20 mm. If he draws a new square with dimensions that are half that of the previous square, what is the area of the new square?

____

Name ____________________

Lesson 80
CC.6.G.1

1. Jeremy wants to enlarge his younger brother's 5-foot by 5-foot sandbox by multiplying its dimensions by 3. How will the area of the sandbox be affected?

   (A) It will be multiplied by 9.

   (B) It will be multiplied by 3.

   (C) It will be multiplied by $\frac{1}{3}$.

   (D) It will be multiplied by $\frac{1}{9}$.

2. Malcolm wants to enlarge a 2-inch by 3-inch photograph by multiplying its dimensions by 5. How will the area of the photograph be affected?

   (A) It will be multiplied by $\frac{1}{25}$.

   (B) It will be multiplied by $\frac{1}{5}$.

   (C) It will be multiplied by 5.

   (D) It will be multiplied by 25.

3. Katie wants to shrink this triangle by multiplying its dimensions by $\frac{1}{2}$.

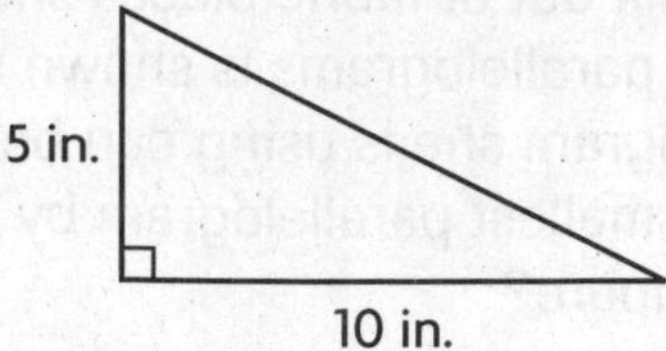

   How will the area of the triangle be affected?

   (A) It will be multiplied by $\frac{1}{16}$.

   (B) It will be multiplied by $\frac{1}{8}$.

   (C) It will be multiplied by $\frac{1}{4}$.

   (D) It will be multiplied by $\frac{1}{2}$.

Problem Solving REAL WORLD

4. Kimberly wants to enlarge her 5-foot by 10-foot rectangular patio by multiplying its dimensions by 2. How will the area of the patio be affected? Explain how you know.

____

____

____

____

____

____

Name ______________________________

Lesson 81

COMMON CORE STANDARD CC.6.G.2

Lesson Objective: Investigate the volume of rectangular prisms with fractional edge lengths.

Fractions and Volume

Find the volume of a rectangular prism that is $2\frac{1}{2}$ units long, 2 units wide, and $1\frac{1}{2}$ units high.

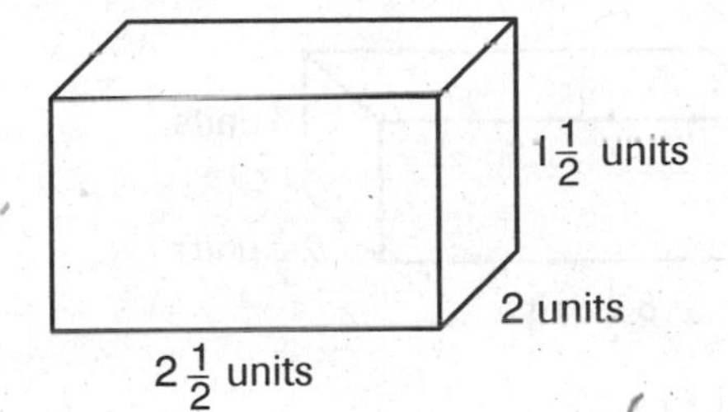

Step 1 Stack cubes with $\frac{1}{2}$-unit side length to form a rectangular prism.

Length: 5 cubes $= \frac{1}{2} + \frac{1}{2} + \frac{1}{2} + \frac{1}{2} + \frac{1}{2} = 2\frac{1}{2}$ units

Width: 4 cubes $= \frac{1}{2} + \frac{1}{2} + \frac{1}{2} + \frac{1}{2} = 2$ units

Height: 3 cubes $= \frac{1}{2} + \frac{1}{2} + \frac{1}{2} = 1\frac{1}{2}$ units

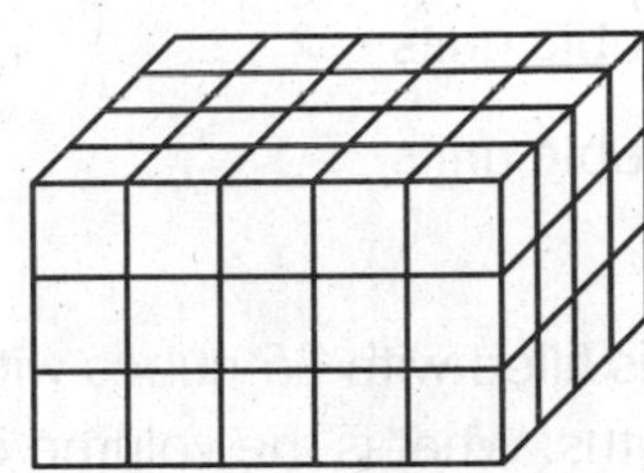

Step 2 Count the total number of cubes.

60 cubes

Step 3 It takes 8 cubes with $\frac{1}{2}$-unit side lengths to make 1 unit cube. So, each smaller cube has $\frac{1}{8}$ the volume of a unit cube.

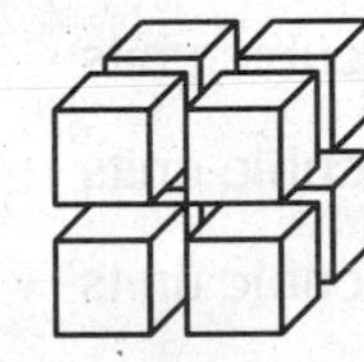

Divide 60 by 8 to find how many unit cubes it would take to form the prism. Write the remainder as a fraction and simplify.

$60 \div 8 = 7\frac{4}{8}$ $\quad 7\frac{4}{8} = 7\frac{1}{2}$

So, the volume of the prism is $7\frac{1}{2}$ cubic units.

1. Find the volume of the rectangular prism.

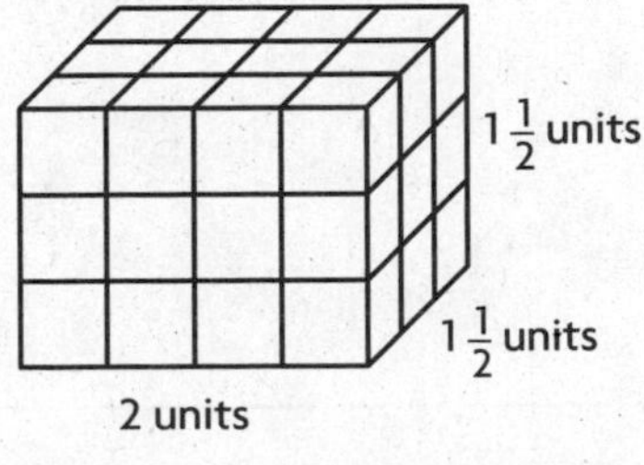

a. Stack cubes with $\frac{1}{2}$-unit side lengths to form the prism.

b. Count the cubes. ________

c. Divide by 8. ________ $\div 8 =$ ________

d. The prism has a volume of ________ cubic units.

Name ______________________________

Lesson 81
CC.6.G.2

1. What is the volume of the rectangular prism shown?

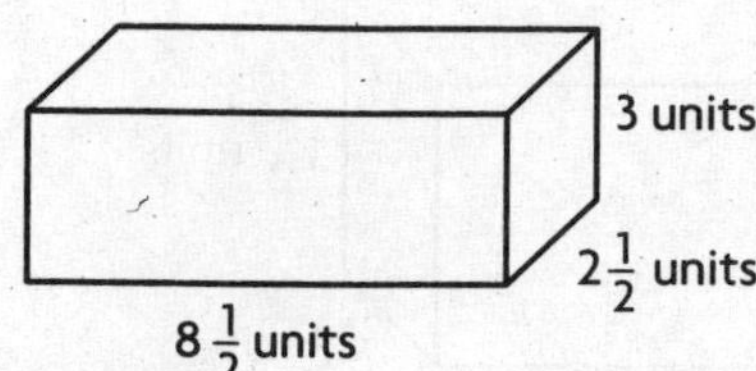

Ⓐ $63\frac{3}{4}$ cubic units
Ⓑ $42\frac{1}{2}$ cubic units
Ⓒ 28 cubic units
Ⓓ 14 cubic units

2. A prism is filled with 25 cubes with $\frac{1}{2}$-unit side lengths. What is the volume of the prism in cubic units?

Ⓐ $3\frac{1}{8}$ cubic units
Ⓑ $3\frac{1}{3}$ cubic units
Ⓒ $12\frac{1}{8}$ cubic units
Ⓓ $12\frac{1}{2}$ cubic units

3. A box measures 4 units by $2\frac{1}{2}$ units by $1\frac{1}{2}$ units. What is the greatest number of cubes with a side length of $\frac{1}{2}$ unit that can be packed inside the box?

Ⓐ 16 Ⓒ 64
Ⓓ 30 Ⓓ 120

4. What is the volume of the box shown?

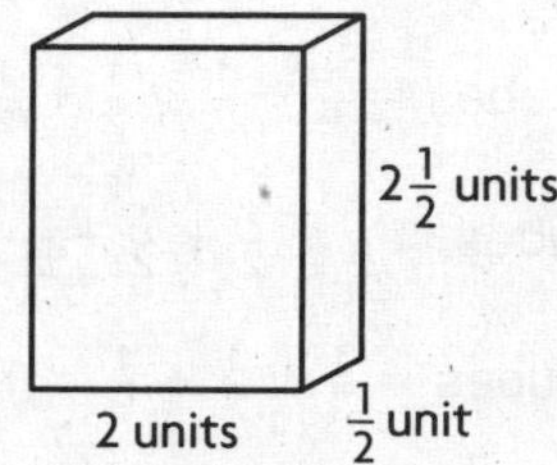

Ⓐ $6\frac{1}{2}$ cubic units
Ⓑ 5 cubic units
Ⓒ $2\frac{1}{2}$ cubic units
Ⓓ 1 cubic unit

Problem Solving REAL WORLD

5. Miguel is pouring liquid into a container that is $4\frac{1}{2}$ inches long by $3\frac{1}{2}$ inches wide by 2 inches high. How many cubic inches of liquid will fit in the container?

____

6. A shipping crate is shaped like a rectangular prism. It is $5\frac{1}{2}$ feet long by 3 feet wide by 3 feet high. What is the volume of the crate?

____

Name ______________________________

Lesson 82

COMMON CORE STANDARD CC.6.G.2

Lesson Objective: Use formulas to find the volume of rectangular prisms with fractional edge lengths.

Algebra • Volume of Rectangular Prisms

You can find the volume of a prism by using the formula $V = Bh$. V stands for volume, B stands for the area of the base, and h stands for the height.

For a rectangular prism, any face can be the base, since all faces are rectangles.

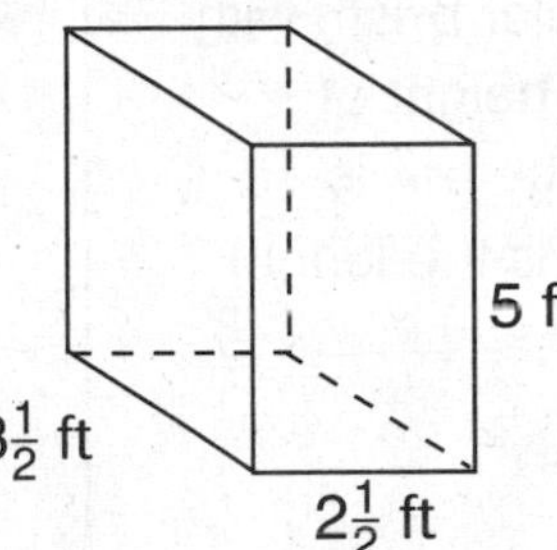

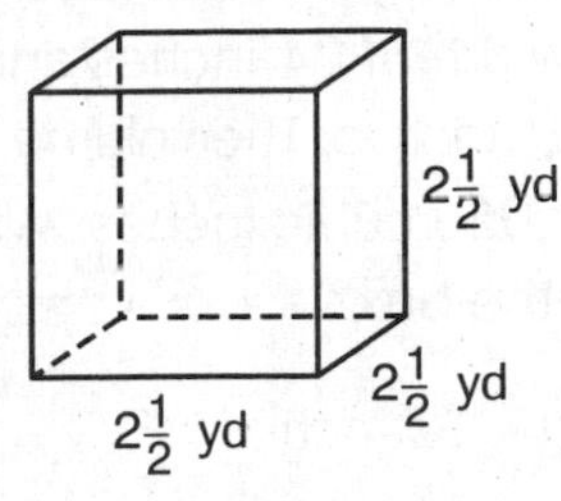

Find the volume of the rectangular prism.

Step 1 Find the area of the base.
The base is $2\frac{1}{2}$ ft by $3\frac{1}{2}$ ft.

$A = l \times w$

$A = 2\frac{1}{2}\text{ ft} \times 3\frac{1}{2}\text{ ft} = 8\frac{3}{4}\text{ ft}^2$

Step 2 Multiply the area of the base by the height.

$V = Bh$

$V = 8\frac{3}{4}\text{ ft}^2 \times 5\text{ ft} = 43\frac{3}{4}\text{ ft}^3$

So, the volume of the rectangular prism is $43\frac{3}{4}\text{ ft}^3$.

Find the volume of the cube.

Step 1 Because the length, width, and height are all equal, you can use a special formula.

$V = Bh = l \times w \times h$

$V = s^3$

Step 2 Substitute $2\frac{1}{2}$ for s.

$V = s^3 = \left(2\frac{1}{2}\right)^3 = \left(\frac{5}{2}\right)^3$

$V = \frac{5}{2}\text{ yd} \times \frac{5}{2}\text{ yd} \times \frac{5}{2}\text{ yd} = \frac{125}{8}\text{ yd}^3$

$= 15\frac{5}{8}\text{ yd}^3$

So, the volume of the cube is $15\frac{5}{8}\text{ yd}^3$.

Find the volume.

1.

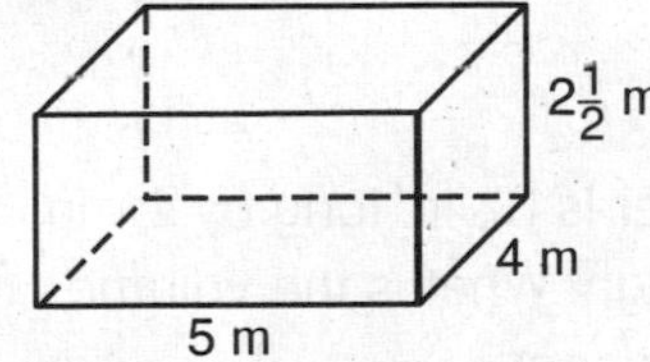

____

2.

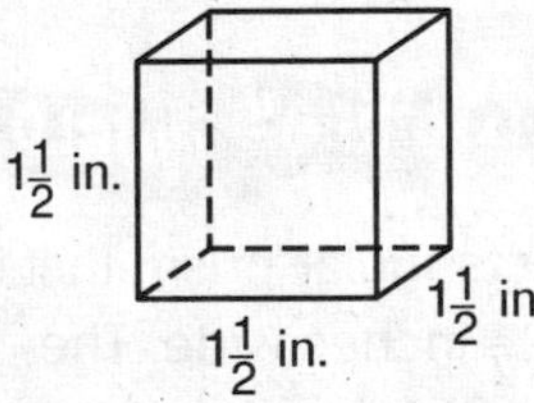

____

3.

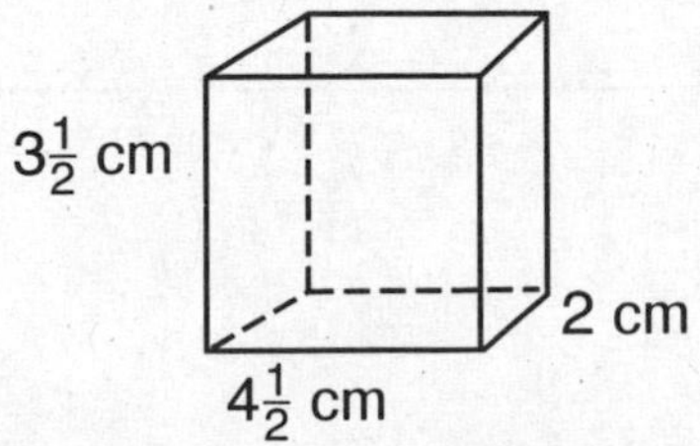

____

4.

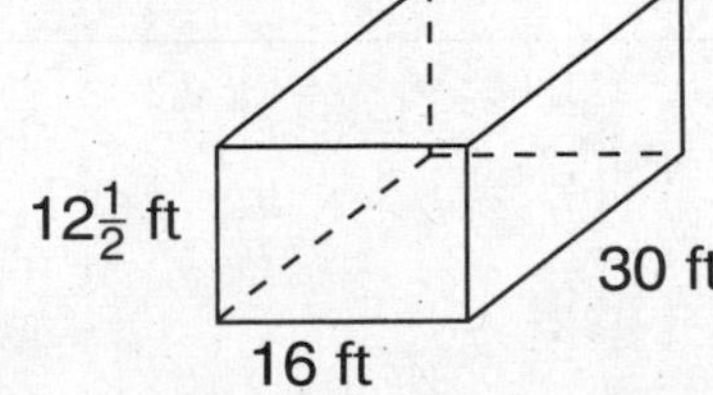

____

Name ________________________

Lesson 82
CC.6.G.2

1. A moving box is a rectangular prism with a width of 24 inches and a height of $18\frac{1}{2}$ inches. The volume of the box is 10,656 cubic inches. What is the length of the box?

   Ⓐ 12 inches
   Ⓑ 24 inches
   Ⓒ 42 inches
   Ⓓ 432 inches

2. Marci bought a box of energy-efficient light bulbs. The box had dimensions of 10 inches by $5\frac{1}{2}$ inches by 6 inches. What is the volume of this box?

   Ⓐ 330 cubic inches
   Ⓑ $300\frac{1}{2}$ cubic inches
   Ⓒ 296 cubic inches
   Ⓓ $21\frac{1}{2}$ cubic inches

3. Mr. Jackson rented a storage unit in the shape of a rectangular prism. The volume of the unit is 230 cubic yards. The storage unit is $5\frac{3}{4}$ yards wide and 10 yards long. What is the height of the storage unit?

   Ⓐ 2 yards
   Ⓑ 4 yards
   Ⓒ 14 yards
   Ⓓ 50 yards

4. A rectangular box is 20 inches long, $18\frac{1}{2}$ inches wide, and $24\frac{1}{2}$ inches high. What is the volume of the box?

   Ⓐ $1,086\frac{1}{8}$ cubic inches
   Ⓑ $2,173\frac{1}{4}$ cubic inches
   Ⓒ $4,532\frac{1}{2}$ cubic inches
   Ⓓ 9,065 cubic inches

Problem Solving REAL WORLD

5. A cereal box is a rectangular prism that is 8 inches long and $2\frac{1}{2}$ inches wide. The volume of the box is 200 in.^{3}. What is the height of the box?

   ____

6. A stack of paper is $8\frac{1}{2}$ in. long by 11 in. wide by 4 in. high. What is the volume of the stack of paper?

   ____

Lesson Objective: Plot polygons on a coordinate plane, and use coordinates to find side lengths.

Name ______________________

Figures on the Coordinate Plane

The vertices of a parallelogram are $A(^-2, 2)$, $B(^-3, 5)$, $C(4, 5)$, and $D(5, 2)$. Graph the parallelogram and find the length of side AD.

Step 1 Draw the parallelogram on the coordinate plane. Plot the points and then connect the points with straight lines.

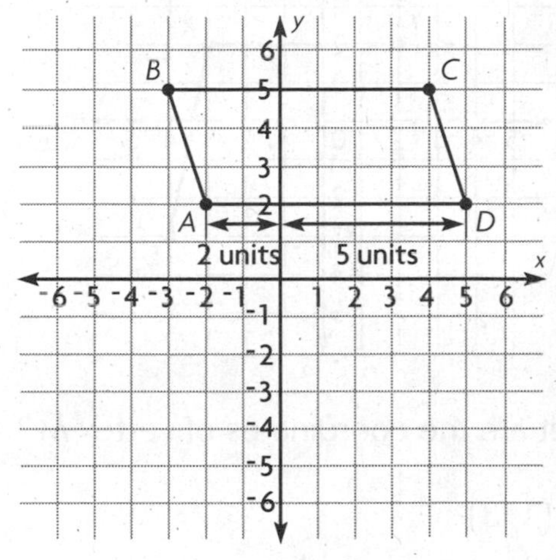

Step 2 Find the length of side *AD*.

Horizontal distance of *A* from 0: $|^-2| = 2$
Horizontal distance of *D* from 0: $|5| = 5$

Points *A* and *D* are in different quadrants, so add to find the distance from *A* to *D*.
$2 + 5 = 7$ units

So, the length of side *AD* is 7 units.

Graph the figure and find the length of the given side.

1. Triangle *JKL*
$J(^-3, ^-3)$, $K(^-3, 5)$, $L(5, 2)$

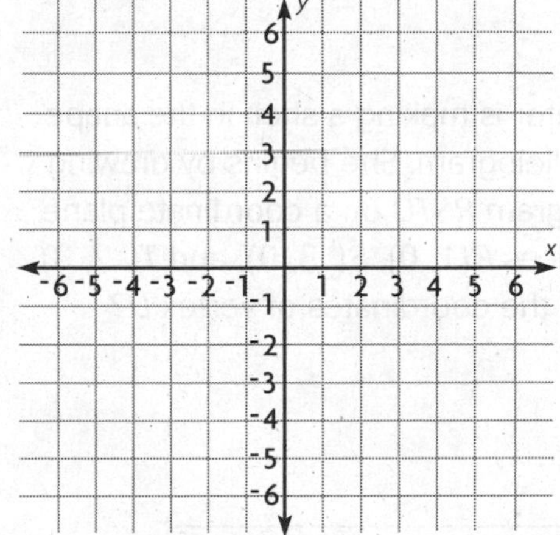

length of $\overline{JK}$ = ______

2. Trapezoid *WXYZ*
$W(^-2, ^-3)$, $X(^-2, 3)$, $Y(3, 5)$, $Z(3, ^-3)$

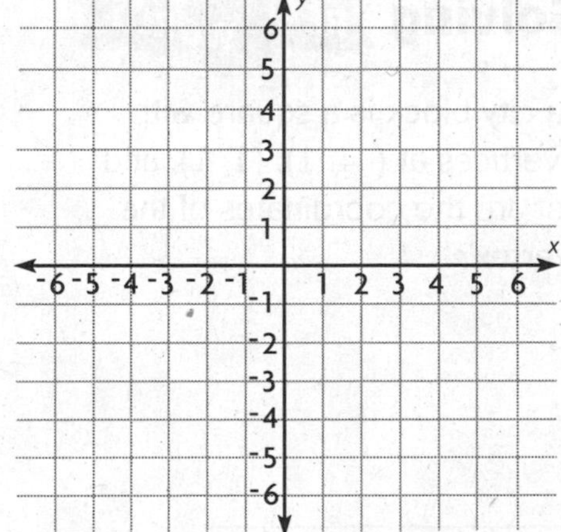

length of $\overline{WZ}$ = ______

Name ___________________________

Lesson 83
CC.6.G.3

1. Andrew is drawing a sketch of the garden he is going to plant. Line segments *JK* and *KL* are two sides of parallelogram *JKLM*.

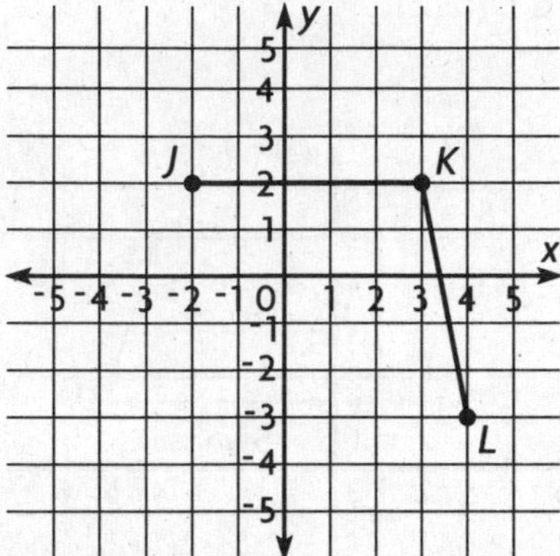

What are the coordinates of vertex *M*?

Ⓐ (1, 3)
Ⓑ (⁻1, 3)
Ⓒ (1, ⁻3)
Ⓓ (⁻1, ⁻3)

2. Mrs. Moy is building a rectangular garden in her yard. She already has placed stakes to mark 3 of the corners of the garden. She needs to place the final stake. The map shows the location of the 3 stakes she has already placed.

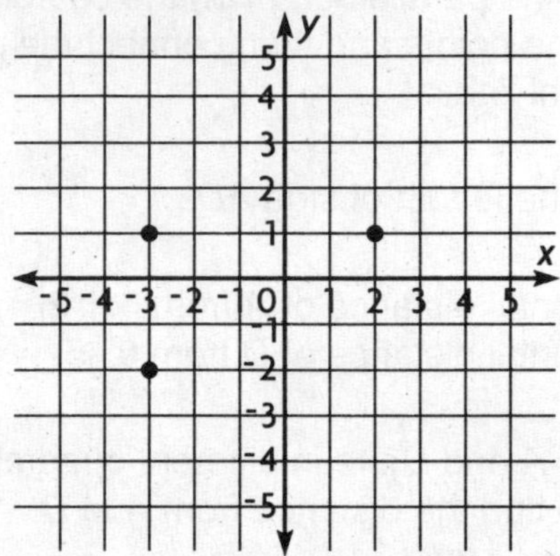

What are the coordinates for the final stake?

Ⓐ (2, ⁻2)
Ⓑ (⁻1, ⁻2)
Ⓒ (⁻2, ⁻1)
Ⓓ (2, 2)

Problem Solving REAL WORLD

3. On a map, a city block is a square with three of its vertices at (⁻4, 1), (1, 1), and (1, ⁻4). What are the coordinates of the remaining vertex?

____

4. A carpenter is making a shelf in the shape of a parallelogram. She begins by drawing parallelogram *RSTU* on a coordinate plane with vertices *R*(1, 0), *S*(⁻3, 0), and *T*(⁻2, 3). What are the coordinates of vertex *U*?

____

Name ______________________________

Lesson 84

COMMON CORE STANDARD CC.6.G.4

Lesson Objective: Use nets to represent three-dimensional figures.

Three-Dimensional Figures and Nets

Solid figures have three dimensions–length, width, and height. They can be named by the shapes of their bases, the number of bases, and the shapes of their lateral faces.

Identify and draw a net for the solid figure.

Step 1 Describe the base of the figure.
The base is a square.

Step 2 Describe the lateral surfaces.
The lateral surfaces are triangles.

So, the figure is a square pyramid.

Step 3 Name the shapes to be used in the net. Then make a sketch. Draw a square for the base, and four triangles for the lateral faces.

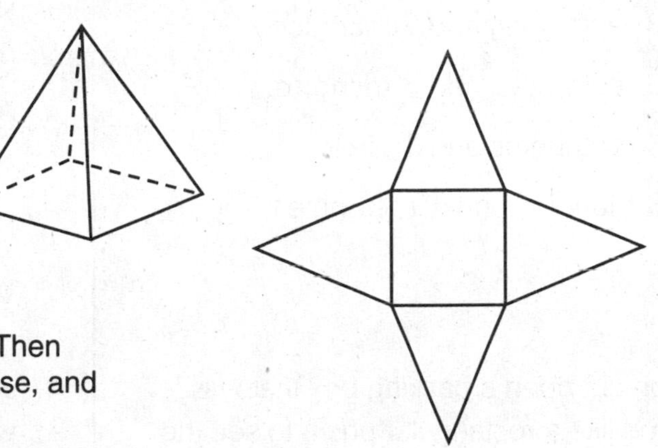

Identify and draw a net for the solid figure.

1.

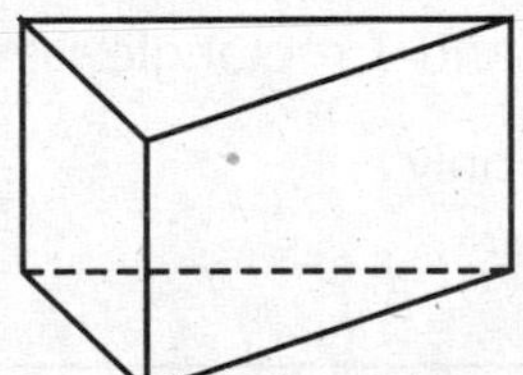

figure: ______________________________

2.

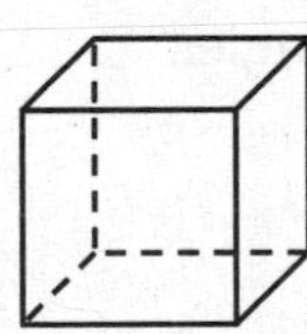

figure: ______________________________

Name ______________________________

1. An employee at a tent manufacturer is sewing together tents. Each tent is shaped like a triangular prism (including the floor). What shapes can the employee use for each tent?

Ⓐ 3 rectangles and 2 triangles

Ⓑ 2 rectangles and 3 triangles

Ⓒ 4 rectangles and 1 circle

Ⓓ 3 triangles and 1 rectangle

2. Wilson cut open a packing box that was shaped like a rectangular prism to see the net. What shapes did Wilson see?

Ⓐ 1 triangle and 2 rectangles

Ⓑ 1 square and 3 rectangles

Ⓒ 6 rectangles only

Ⓓ 6 triangles only

3. Georgette's computer came in a box shaped like a cube. How many square faces does the box have?

Ⓐ 2

Ⓑ 4

Ⓒ 6

Ⓓ 8

4. Julio made a triangular pyramid out of wood. What shapes did he use?

Ⓐ 3 triangles only

Ⓑ 4 rectangles only

Ⓒ 3 triangles and 1 rectangle

Ⓓ 4 triangles only

Problem Solving REAL WORLD

5. Hobie's Candies are sold in triangular-pyramid-shaped boxes. How many triangles are needed to make one box?

____

6. Nina used plastic rectangles to make 6 rectangular prisms. How many rectangles did she use?

____

Name ______________________________

Lesson 85

COMMON CORE STANDARD CC.6.G.4

Lesson Objective: Use nets to recognize that the surface area of a prism is equal to the sum of the areas of its faces.

Explore Surface Area Using Nets

The net of a solid figure shows you all of the faces or surfaces of the figure. A net can help you find the **surface area** of a figure.

Find the surface area of the rectangular prism.

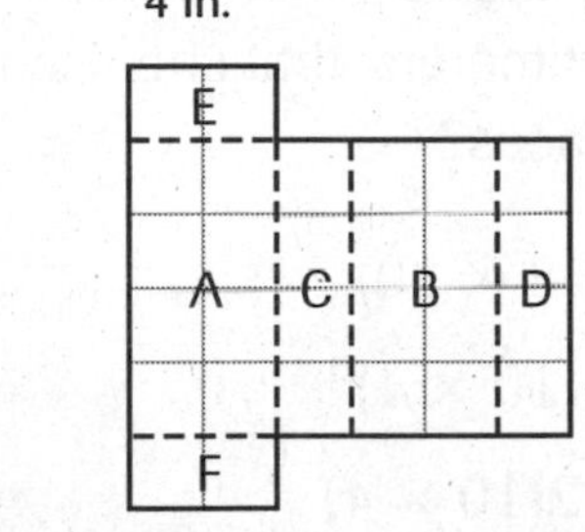

Step 1 Make a net of the rectangular prism. The prism has 6 rectangular faces, so the net has 6 rectangles.

Step 2 Find the area of each face of the prism.

First Way: Count the grid squares on each rectangle to find its area.

Second Way: Calculate the area of each rectangle by multiplying *length* × *width*.

A: 8 squares	$4 \times 2 = 8$
B: 8 squares	$4 \times 2 = 8$
C: 4 squares	$4 \times 1 = 4$
D: 4 squares	$4 \times 1 = 4$
E: 2 squares	$2 \times 1 = 2$
F: 2 squares	$2 \times 1 = 2$

Step 3 Add the areas of all the rectangular faces. 28 squares 28 square inches

So, the surface area of the rectangular prism is 28 square inches (in.^{2}).

Use the net to find the surface area of the prism.

1.

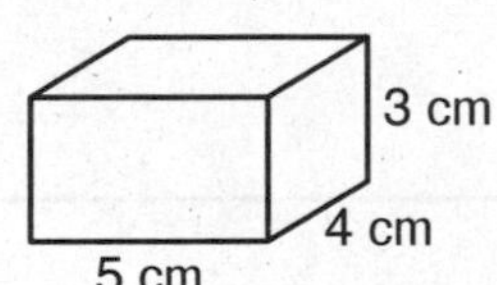

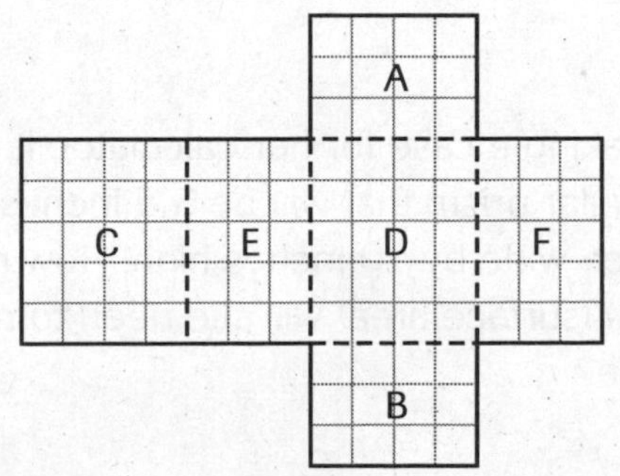

a. Find the area of each face.

A: ________ B: ________

C: ________ D: ________

E: ________ F: ________

b. Add: A + B + C + D + E + F = ________

c. The surface area is ________ cm^2.

Name ______________________________

1. Jami covered the lateral faces of the wooden box shown with felt.

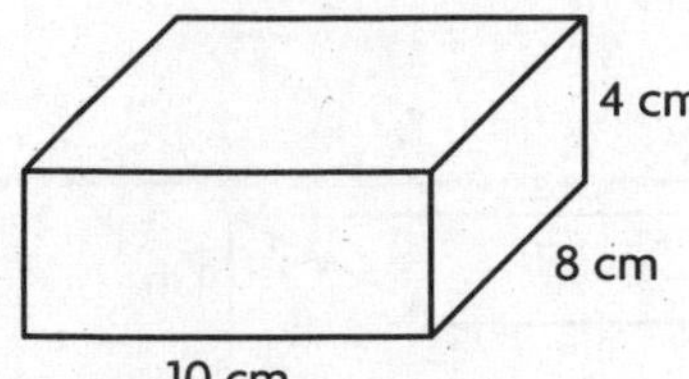

Which expression shows the amount of felt, in square centimeters, that she used to cover the lateral faces?

Ⓐ $2(8 \times 4) + 2(8 \times 10)$
Ⓑ $2(8 \times 4) + 2(10 \times 4)$
Ⓒ $2(10 \times 8) + 2(10 \times 4)$
Ⓓ $2(10 \times 8) + 2(10 \times 4) + 2(8 \times 4)$

2. The net of a rectangular prism is shown.

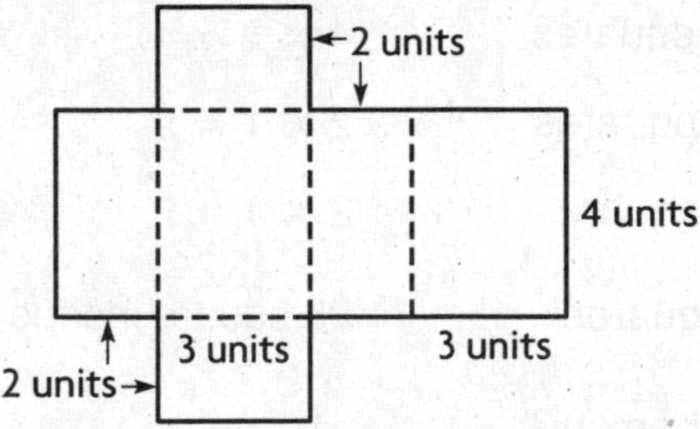

What is the surface area of this prism?

Ⓐ 24 square units
Ⓑ 26 square units
Ⓒ 52 square units
Ⓓ 58 square units

3. Darrell is decorating the top and lateral faces of this box with collages made of pictures from his favorite magazines.

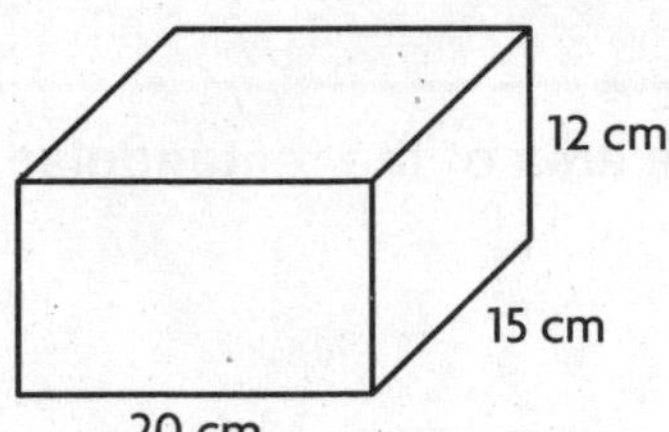

Which expression shows the amount of surface area, in square centimeters, that Darrell will cover with collages?

Ⓐ $2(20 \times 15) + 2(15 \times 12) + (20 \times 12)$
Ⓑ $2(20 \times 12) + 2(15 \times 12) + (20 \times 15)$
Ⓒ $2(20 \times 12) + 2(20 \times 15) + (12 \times 15)$
Ⓓ $2(20 \times 12) + 2(20 \times 15) + 2(12 \times 15)$

Problem Solving REAL WORLD

4. Jeremiah is covering a cereal box with fabric for a school project. If the box is 6 inches long by 2 inches wide by 14 inches high, how much surface area does Jeremiah have to cover?

____

5. Tia is making a case for her calculator. It is a rectangular prism that will be 3.5 inches long by 1 inch wide by 10 inches high. How much material (surface area) will she need to make the case?

____

Name ______________________________

Lesson 86

COMMON CORE STANDARD CC.6.G.4

Lesson Objective: Find the surface area of prisms.

Algebra • Surface Area of Prisms

You can find the surface area of a figure by adding the lateral surface area to the sum of the areas of the bases.

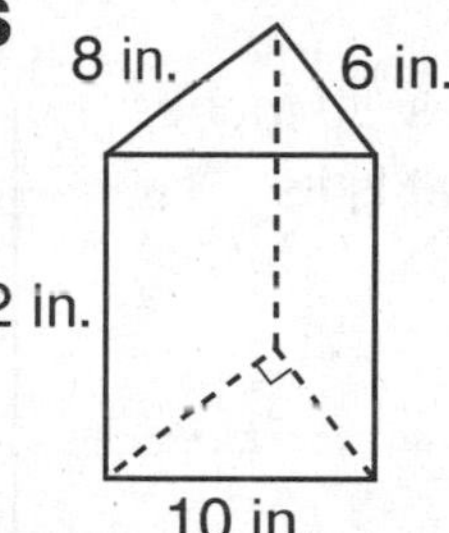

Use a net to find the surface area.

Step 1 Draw a net.

Note any faces that have equal areas.

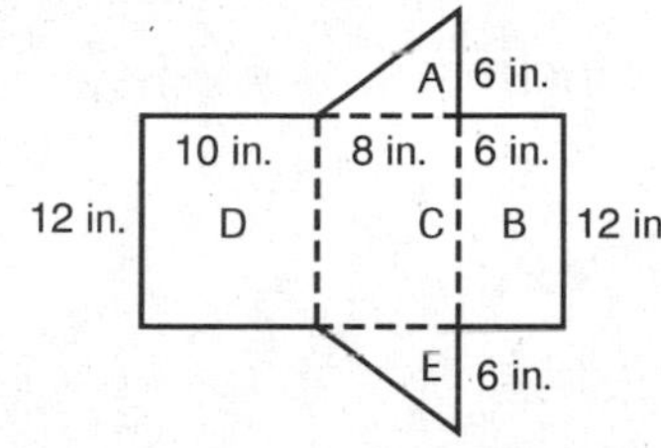

Step 2 Both triangular bases have the same area.

Base A: $A = \frac{1}{2}bh = \frac{1}{2} \times 6 \times 8 = 24 \text{ in.}^2$

Base E: $A = 24 \text{ in.}^2$

Step 3 Find the areas of the rectangular faces.

Face B: $A = lw = 6 \times 12 = 72 \text{ in.}^2$

Face C: $A = lw = 8 \times 12 = 96 \text{ in.}^2$

Face D: $A = lw = 10 \times 12 = 120 \text{ in.}^2$

Step 4 Add the areas: A + B + C + D + E

$24 + 72 + 96 + 120 + 24 = 336 \text{ in.}^2$

So, the surface area of the triangular prism is 336 square inches (in.^2).

Use a net to find the surface area.

1.

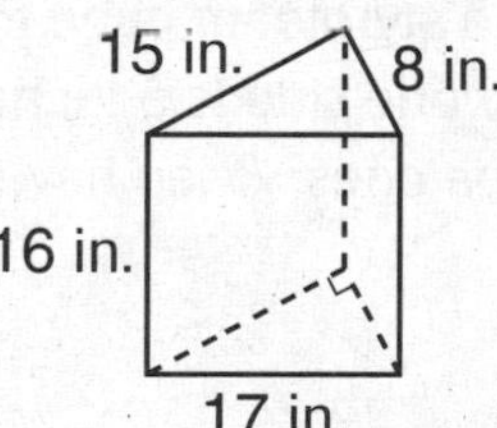

____

2.

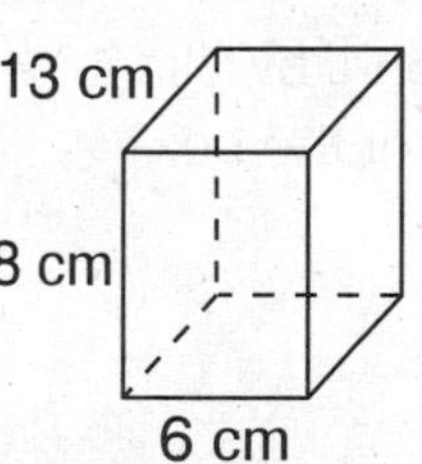

____

3.

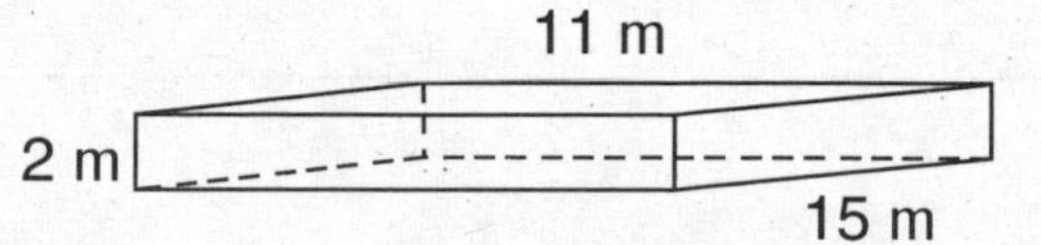

____

4.

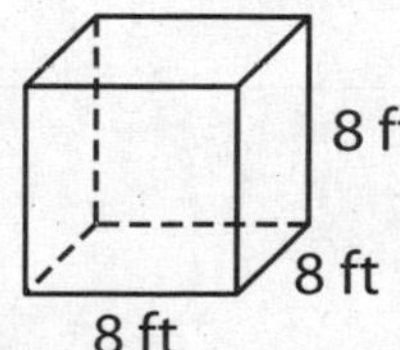

____

Name ______________________________

Lesson 86

CC.6.G.4

1. A rectangular prism measures 10 inches by 6 inches by 6 inches. What is its surface area?

   Ⓐ 360 square inches

   Ⓑ 312 square inches

   Ⓒ 240 square inches

   Ⓓ 192 square inches

2. A rectangular gift box measures 8 inches by 10 inches by 3 inches. What is its surface area?

   Ⓐ 184 square inches

   Ⓑ 214 square inches

   Ⓒ 240 square inches

   Ⓓ 268 square inches

3. Liam made a music box. The box is a rectangular prism that measures 12 centimeters by 8 centimeters by 5 centimeters. What is the surface area of the box?

   Ⓐ 196 square centimeters

   Ⓑ 240 square centimeters

   Ⓒ 392 square centimeters

   Ⓓ 480 square centimeters

4. Emily's decorative box is shaped like a cube and measures 5 inches by 5 inches by 5 inches. What is its surface area?

   Ⓐ 75 square inches

   Ⓑ 100 square inches

   Ⓒ 125 square inches

   Ⓓ 150 square inches

Problem Solving REAL WORLD

5. A shoe box measures 15 in. by 7 in. by $4\frac{1}{2}$ in. What is the surface area of the box?

   ____

6. Vivian is working with a styrofoam cube for art class. The length of one side is 5 inches. How much surface area does Vivian have to work with?

   ____

Name ___________________________

Lesson 87

COMMON CORE STANDARD CC.6.G.4

Lesson Objective: Find the surface area of pyramids.

Algebra • Surface Area of Pyramids

To find the surface area of a pyramid, add the area of the base to the **lateral area**. The lateral area is the combined area of the triangular faces.

Find the surface area of the square pyramid.

Step 1 The base is a square with side length of 6 in. Use the formula $A = s^2$ to find the area. Substitute 6 for the variable s.

$A = 6^2 = 36 \text{ in.}^2$

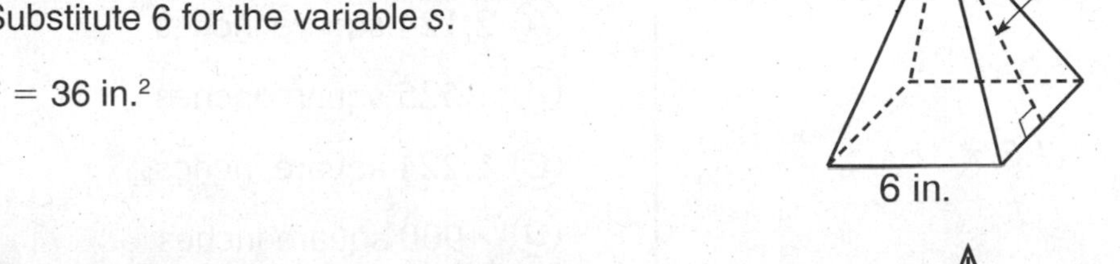

Step 2 The lateral faces are four triangles with base of 6 in. and height of 8 in. Find the area of one triangular lateral face using the formula $A = \frac{1}{2}bh$. Substitute 6 for b and 8 for h.

$A = \frac{1}{2}(6)(8) = 24 \text{ in.}^2$

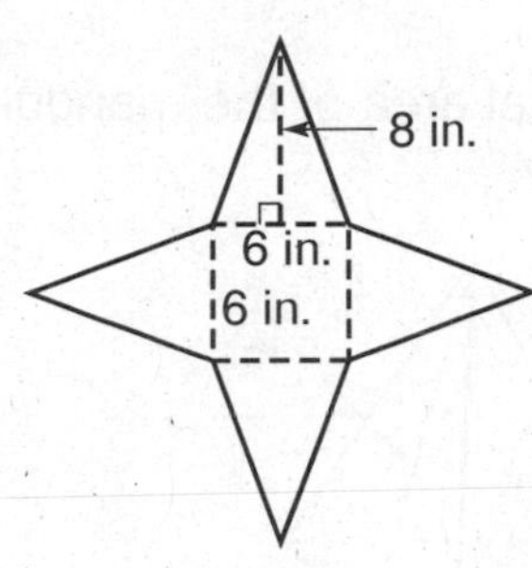

Step 3 Multiply by 4 to find the total lateral area. $L = 24 \times 4 = 96 \text{ in.}^2$

Step 4 Add the area of the base and the lateral area. $S = 36 \text{ in.}^2 + 96 \text{ in.}^2 = 132 \text{ in.}^2$

So, the surface area of the square pyramid is 132 square inches (in.^{2}).

Use a net to find the surface area of the square pyramid.

1.

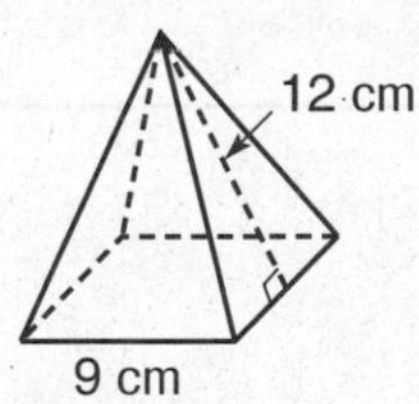

a. Area of the base: ______________

b. Area of one triangular lateral face: ______________

c. Total lateral area: ______________

d. Total surface area: ______________

2.

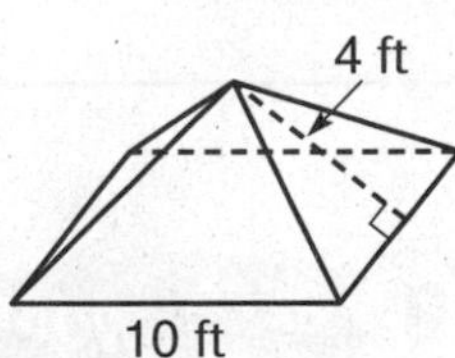

a. Area of the base: ______________

b. Area of one triangular lateral face: ______________

c. Total lateral area: ______________

d. Total surface area: ______________

Name ______________________________

1. A square pyramid has a base with a side length of 7.5 feet and lateral faces with heights of 16 feet. Which expression could be used to find the surface area, in square feet, of the pyramid?

   Ⓐ $7.5^2 \times \frac{1}{2} \times 7.5 \times 16$

   Ⓑ $7.5^2 + \frac{1}{2} \times 7.5 \times 16$

   Ⓒ $7.5 \times 4 \times \frac{1}{2} \times 7.5 \times 16$

   Ⓓ $7.5^2 + 4 \times \frac{1}{2} \times 7.5 \times 16$

2. What is the lateral area of the triangular pyramid shown?

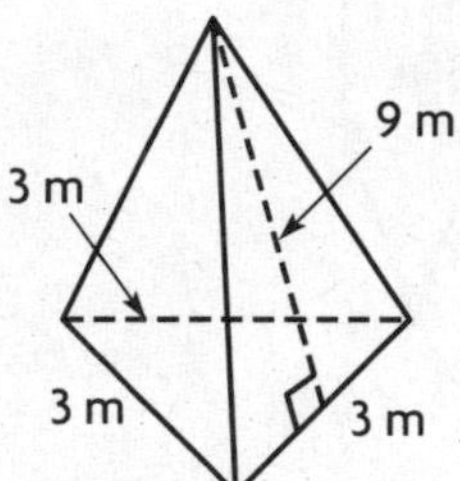

   Ⓐ 40.5 square meters

   Ⓑ 49.5 square meters

   Ⓒ 81.0 square meters

   Ⓓ 85.5 square meters

3. What is the lateral area of the square pyramid shown?

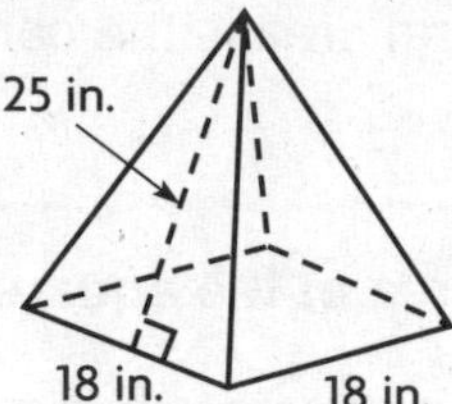

   Ⓐ 2,124 square inches

   Ⓑ 1,525 square inches

   Ⓒ 1,224 square inches

   Ⓓ 900 square inches

4. A triangular pyramid has a base with an area of 7 square centimeters and lateral faces with bases of 4 centimeters and heights of 12 centimeters. What is the surface area of the pyramid?

   Ⓐ 72 square centimeters

   Ⓑ 79 square centimeters

   Ⓒ 103 square centimeters

   Ⓓ 151 square centimeters

Problem Solving REAL WORLD

5. Cho is building a sandcastle in the shape of a triangular pyramid. The area of the base is 7 square feet. Each side of the base has a length of 4 feet and the height of each face is 2 feet. What is the surface area of the pyramid?

____

6. The top of a skyscraper is shaped like a square pyramid. Each side of the base has a length of 60 meters and the height of each triangle is 20 meters. What is the lateral area of the pyramid?

____

Name ______________________________

Lesson 88

COMMON CORE STANDARD CC.6.G.4

Lesson Objective: Solve problems involving area, surface area, and volume by applying the strategy *use a formula.*

Problem Solving • Geometric Measurements

Leslie stores gardening supplies in this shed shaped like a rectangular prism. What is the area of the ground covered by the shed?

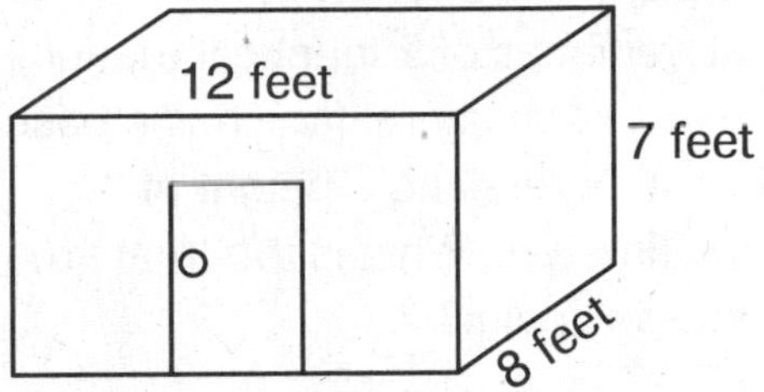

Read the Problem	Solve the Problem
What do I need to find? I need to find ____________________ ______________________________ ______________________________.	Choose the measure—area, surface area, or volume—that gives the area of the ground covered by the barrel. Explain. ______________________________ ______________________________ ______________________________ ______________________________.
What information do I need to use? I need to use ____________________ ______________________________.	Choose an appropriate formula. ______________________________
How will I use the information? First, I will decide ______________ __________. Then I will choose a ______________ I can use to calculate this measure. Finally, I will ______________ ______________________________ ______________________________.	Replace the variables *l* and *w* in the area formula with their values in the dimensions of the shed. l = ________ ft w = ________ ft Evaluate the formula. A = ________ × ________ = ________ ft^2

Solve.

1. Leslie is covering bricks with paint. Each brick is 8 in. long, 4 in. wide, and 2 in. high. How many square inches will Leslie paint on each brick?

   ____

2. Leslie's planting box is shaped like a rectangular prism. It is 60 cm long, 35 cm wide, and 40 cm high. How many cubic cm of soil will Leslie need to fill the box?

   ____

Name ______________________________

Lesson 88
CC.6.G.4

1. As part of her art project, Sarah is painting the lateral faces of 2 identical triangular pyramids. Each lateral face has a base of 6 centimeters and a height of 8.5 centimeters. What is the total area that she will paint?

   Ⓐ 25.5 square centimeters
   Ⓑ 51 square centimeters
   Ⓒ 76.5 square centimeters
   Ⓓ 153 square centimeters

2. Albert wants to know how much water a fish tank shaped like a rectangular prism can hold. What geometric measure does Albert need to find?

   Ⓐ the volume of the fish tank
   Ⓑ the surface area of the fish tank
   Ⓒ the area of the base of the fish tank
   Ⓓ the perimeter of the base of the fish tank

3. Miguel is painting a cabinet shaped like a rectangular prism. He is going to paint all of the exterior sides except the top and the bottom. The cabinet is 6 feet tall, 4 feet wide, and 2 feet deep. What is the surface area of the portion of the cabinet that Miguel is going to paint?

   Ⓐ 36 square feet
   Ⓑ 48 square feet
   Ⓒ 72 square feet
   Ⓓ 88 square feet

4. Ms. Jessup is planning to lay new sod on her front yard. Her rectangular front yard is 85 feet long by 32 feet wide. What is the area of Ms. Jessup's front yard?

   Ⓐ 117 square feet
   Ⓑ 234 square feet
   Ⓒ 1,360 square feet
   Ⓓ 2,720 square feet

Problem Solving REAL WORLD

5. Lourdes is decorating a toy box for her sister. She will use self-adhesive paper to cover all of the exterior sides except the bottom of the box. The toy box is 4 feet long, 3 feet wide, and 2 feet high. What is the surface area of the portion of the box Lourdes is going to cover with self-adhesive paper? Explain how you found your answer.

____

____

____

____

Name ______________________

COMMON CORE STANDARD CC.6.SP.1

Lesson Objective: Recognize statistical questions.

Recognize Statistical Questions

A **statistical question** is a question about a set of **data** that can vary. To answer a statistical question, you need to collect or look at a set of data.

Identify the statistical questions about Jack's homework time.

A. How many times did Jack spend longer than an hour on homework this week?
Statistical question. Jack is unlikely to do homework for the same amount of time each day, so the question asks about a set of data that can vary. You could answer it with data about Jack's homework time for a week.

B. How long did Jack do homework today?
Not a statistical question. It asks about Jack's homework time on one day. It does not refer to a set of data that varies.

Write a statistical question about your school's cafeteria.

Think of what kind of data could vary in the situation. In this situation, it might be menu items, students, or activities.

These are both statistical questions:

A. How many students were in the cafeteria during fourth period each day for the past two weeks?

B. What was the greatest number of entrees served in one day in the cafeteria last month?

Identify the statistical question. Circle the letter of the question.

1. **A.** How many people flew from New York to San Francisco yesterday?
   B. How many people flew from New York to San Francisco each day this month?

2. **A.** How many siblings does each of your classmates have?
   B. How many siblings does your best friend have?

Write a statistical question you could ask in the situation.

3. Hannah recorded the temperature in her yard every day for a week.

   ____

4. Ian knows his scores for each time he has bowled this year.

   ____

Name ____________________

Lesson 89
CC.6.SP.1

1. The number of points a basketball player scored each game for one week is recorded. Which is a **not** a statistical question for the situation?

   Ⓐ What is the greatest number of points the basketball player scored?

   Ⓑ What is the least number of points the basketball player scored?

   Ⓒ How many points did the basketball player score in the first game of the week?

   Ⓓ How many total points did the basketball player score during the week?

2. Which is a statistical question that could be asked about the data shown in the table?

Trail Lengths

Trail	Length (miles)
Pinkney	1.75
Armstead	2.34
Oak	1.69

   Ⓐ What is the length of the longest trail?

   Ⓑ In what state is the shortest trail?

   Ⓒ Who uses the trails?

   Ⓓ How are the trails used?

3. The length of each movie in a DVD collection is recorded. Which is a **not** a statistical question for the situation?

   Ⓐ What is the length of the shortest movie?

   Ⓑ What is the length of the longest movie?

   Ⓒ What movie is more than 2 hours long?

   Ⓓ What actors star in the longest movie?

4. Students at Meghann's school participate in a recycling program for one month. The amount of paper that is recycled each day as well as the number of students who participated each day is recorded. Which is a **not** a statistical question for the situation?

   Ⓐ On what day did the recycling program begin?

   Ⓑ What is the least amount of paper recycled per day?

   Ⓒ What is the average number of students who participated each day?

   Ⓓ What is the greatest amount of paper recycled per day?

Problem Solving REAL WORLD

5. The city tracked the amount of waste that was recycled from 2000 to 2007. Write a statistical question about the situation.

   ____

   ____

6. The daily low temperature is recorded for a week. Write a statistical question about the situation.

   ____

   ____

Name ___________________________

Lesson 90

COMMON CORE STANDARD CC.6.SP.2

Lesson Objective: Describe the distribution of a data set collected to answer a statistical question.

Describe Distributions

When interpreting data, it helps to make a graph and then analyze the distribution of data.

Mr. Chen asked all of his students how long it takes them to clean their rooms. He displayed the information in a histogram. Describe the data distribution.

Step 1
Look for clusters.

There are no groups of data that are separated from the rest, so there are no clusters of data.

Step 2
Look for gaps.

There are no intervals that contain no data, so there are no gaps in the data.

Step 3
Look for peaks.

There is one peak, at the interval 41–60.

Step 4
Look for symmetry.

Imagine folding the graph in half vertically, along the interval 41–60. The halves are not identical, but they are close. The graph has symmetry.

1. Sally has a restaurant. She recorded the cost of each person's dinner on Friday. Describe the distribution.

____

____

____

____

____

8 9 10 11 12 13 14 15 16

Cost (in dollars) of Dinners Ordered Friday

Name ______________________________

Lesson 90
CC.6.SP.2

1. The ages of people at a movie theater were recorded and displayed in a histogram.

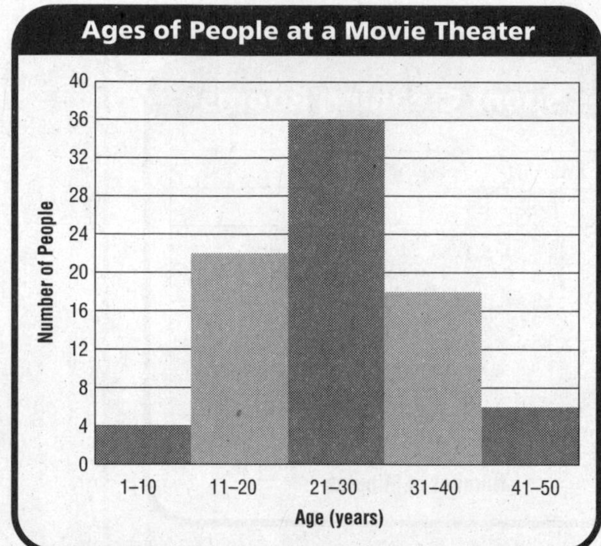

Which interval represents a peak in the data?

Ⓐ 1–10
Ⓑ 11–20
Ⓒ 21–30
Ⓓ 31–40

2. Mr. Cruz used a dot plot to display the number of questions that each student answered correctly on the math quiz.

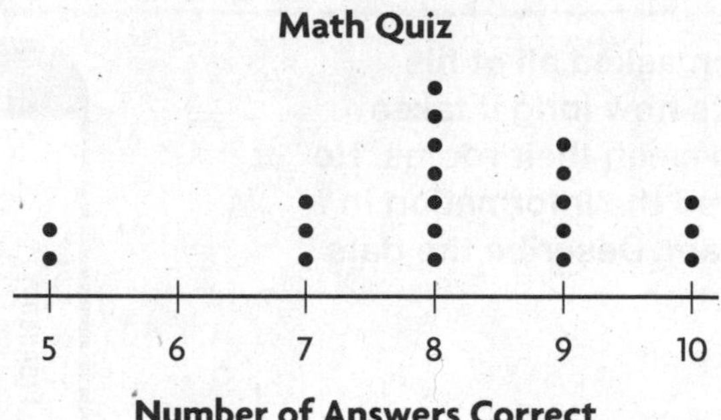

Which statement correctly describes the data?

Ⓐ There is a cluster from 5 to 7.
Ⓑ The median of the data is 7.5
Ⓒ The mode of the data is 9.
Ⓓ There is a gap at 6.

Problem Solving REAL WORLD

3. Mr. Carpenter teaches five classes each day. For several days in a row, he kept track of the number of students who were late to class and displayed the results in a dot plot. Describe the data.

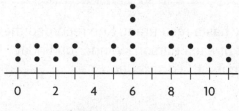

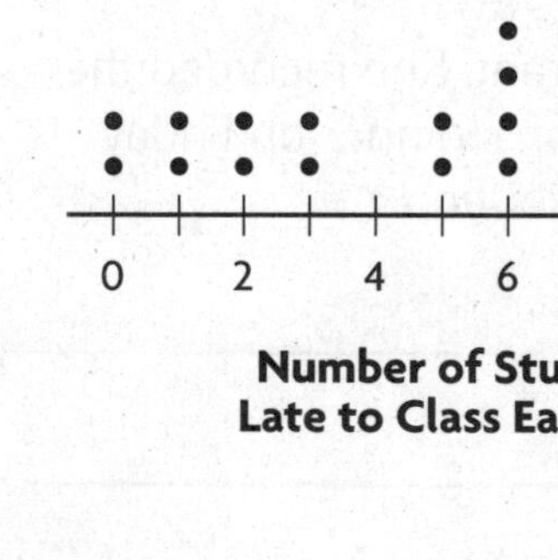

____

____

____

____

____

Name ______________________________

Lesson 91

COMMON CORE STANDARD CC.6.SP.2

Lesson Objective: Draw conclusions about the distribution of a data set by using the strategy *work backward.*

Problem Solving • Misleading Statistics

Zaire wants to move to a town where the annual snowfall is no more than 5 inches. A real estate agent tells her that the mean annual snowfall in a certain town is 4.5 inches. Other statistics about the town are given in the table. Does this location match what Zaire wants? Why or why not?

Town Statistics for Annual Snowfall (in.)	
Minimum	0.5
Maximum	12
Median	8
Mean	4.5

Read the Problem

What do I need to find?	What information do I need to use?	How will I use the information?
I need to decide if the annual snowfall in the town is ______________ ______________.	I need the ______________ in the table.	I will work backward from the statistics to draw conclusions about the ______________ ______________.

Solve the Problem

The minimum annual snowfall is __________

The maximum annual snowfall is __________

The median annual snowfall is __________

The mean annual snowfall is __________

Think: The median is __________, which means that half of the data is equal to or greater than __________.

So, the annual snowfall is usually __________ than 5 inches because at least half of the annual snowfall values are __________ than 5 inches. This location does not match what Zaire wants.

1. Mack says he typically spends 4 hours per week practicing his piano. For the past 6 weeks, he has practiced for 1, 1, 1, 2, 10, and 9 hours. Do you agree with Mack? Explain.

____

____

____

____

1. Mrs. Cho recorded statistics about her students' scores on the history exam in the table shown.

Scores on History Exam	
Minimum	70
Maximum	98
Median	92
Mean	85
Lower Quartile	88
Upper Quartile	95

Which statement is **not** true?

Ⓐ Most students scored 85 on the exam.

Ⓑ The range of the scores is 28.

Ⓒ The interquartile range of the scores is 7.

Ⓓ Half of the students scored 92 or higher on the exam.

2. The box plot shows statistics for the daytime temperatures in a city for two weeks.

Daytime Temperatures

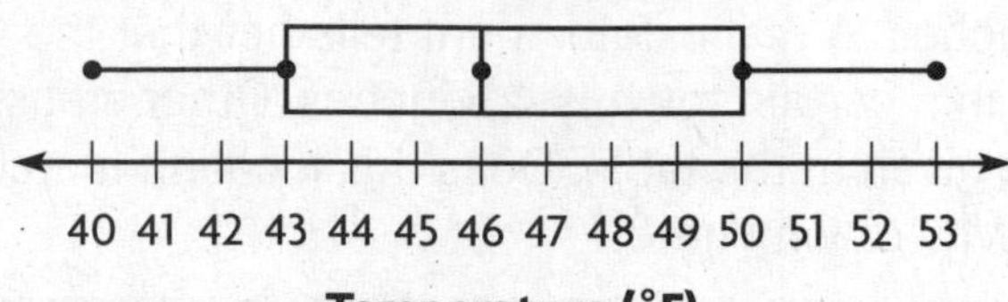

Temperature (°F)

Which conclusion can be drawn using the statistics?

Ⓐ The daytime temperature in the city is usually around 46°F.

Ⓑ On half of the days during the two weeks, the temperature was at least 46°F.

Ⓒ The range of the daytime temperatures is 10°F.

Ⓓ The interquartile range of the data is 4°F.

Problem Solving REAL WORLD

3. Cynthia has 5 books with heights of 5 inches, 6 inches, 7 inches, 11 inches, and 11 inches. She says that her books are about 8 inches high. Do you agree or disagree with Cynthia's claim? Explain your answer.

____

____

____

____

____

____

Name ____________________

Lesson 92

COMMON CORE STANDARD CC.6.SP.3

Lesson Objective: Recognize what measures of center and variability indicate about a data set.

Apply Measures of Center and Variability

You can use measures of center and variability to compare sets of data.

Two math groups were given the same test.

Test Scores		
	Mean	Interquartile range
Group A	76.9	30
Group B	81.1	8

Compare the data.

Step 1 Compare the means. Group B's scores are higher on average than Group A's scores because it has a greater mean.

Step 2 Compare the interquartile ranges. Group B has a smaller interquartile range, which means their scores do not vary as much as Group A's scores.

Compare the data.

1.

Bowling Scores		
	Median	Range
Team X	66	11
Team Y	70	19

____

____

____

____

____

____

____

2.

Cantaloupes Weights in Pounds		
	Mean	Range
Farm 1	4	1.5
Farm 2	7	3

____

____

____

____

____

____

____

Name ______________________________

1. The prices of MP3 players at Electronic City and Best Electronics are shown in the table.

Prices of MP3 Players	
Electronic City	$24, $108, $30, $44, $62, $80
Best Electronics	$69, $42, $120, $59, $66, $76

Which statement is true?

Ⓐ The variation between the prices at each store is the same.

Ⓑ The mean price at Electronic City is greater than the mean price at Best Electronics.

Ⓒ The interquartile range of the prices at Electronic City is greater than the interquartile range of the prices at Best Electronics.

Ⓓ The median price at Electronic City is greater than the median price at Best Electronics.

2. The table shows the number of Jimmy and Darnell's shot attempts in 7 basketball games.

Number of Shot Attempts	
Jimmy	5, 3, 2, 4, 0, 1, 6
Darnell	4, 6, 3, 4, 7, 5, 6

Which statement is true?

Ⓐ The mean of Jimmy's shot attempts is the same as the mean of Darnell's shot attempts.

Ⓑ The number of Jimmy's shot attempts varied more from game to game than the number of Darnell's shot attempts.

Ⓒ The mean of Jimmy's shot attempts is greater than the mean of Darnell's shot attempts.

Ⓓ The range of Jimmy's shot attempts is the same as the range of Darnell's shot attempts.

Problem Solving REAL WORLD

3. Mrs. Mack measured the heights of her students in two classes. Class 1 has a median height of 130 cm and an interquartile range of 5 cm. Class 2 has a median height of 134 cm and an interquartile range of 8 cm. Write a statement that compares the data.

____

____

____

____

4. Richard's science test scores are 76, 80, 78, 84, and 80. His math test scores are 100, 80, 73, 94, and 71. Compare the medians and interquartile ranges.

____

____

____

____

____

Name ___________________________

Lesson 93

COMMON CORE STANDARD CC.6.SP.4

Lesson Objective: Display data in dot plots and frequency tables.

Dot Plots and Frequency Tables

A **dot plot** displays data by placing dots above a number line. Each dot represents one data value.

Paloma sells produce at the farmers' market. The chart shows the number of pounds she sells each day. What was the most common number of pounds that Paloma sold?

Produce Sold (pounds)			
15	19	15	16
20	16	17	20
11	12	15	20
15	13	11	15

Step 1 Draw a number line with an appropriate scale. The chart contains numbers from 11 to 20, so use a scale from 10 to 20.

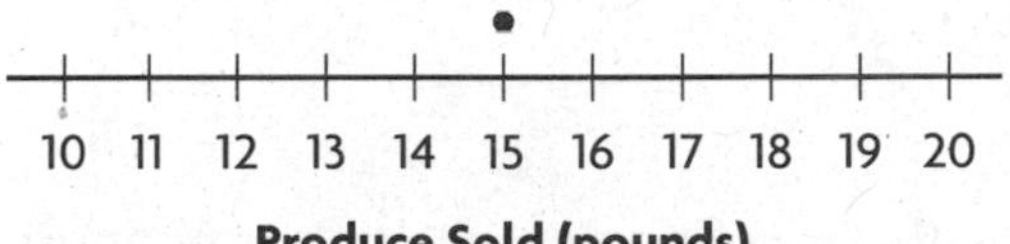

Step 2 For each data value in the chart, plot a dot above the number on the number line. The first data value in the chart is 15, so the dot is placed above 15 on the number line.

Complete the dot plot for the other values in the table. Since there are 16 data values, there should be 16 dots in all.

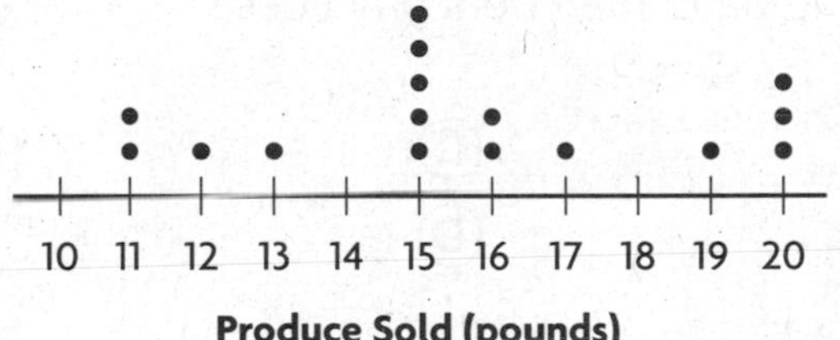

Step 3 The number of pounds Paloma sells most often is the value with the most dots. The stack with the most dots is at 15 pounds.

So, Paloma most often sells 15 pounds of produce.

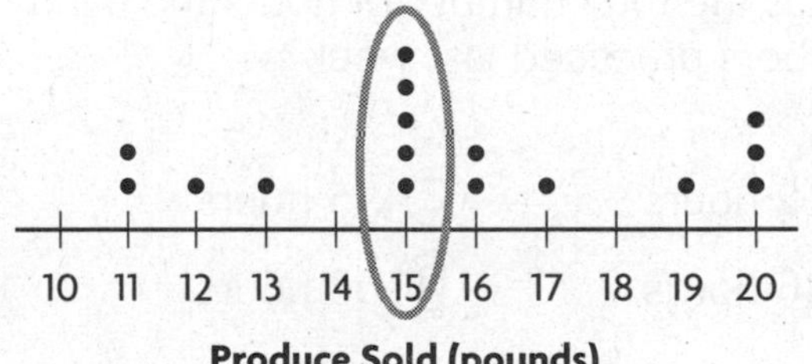

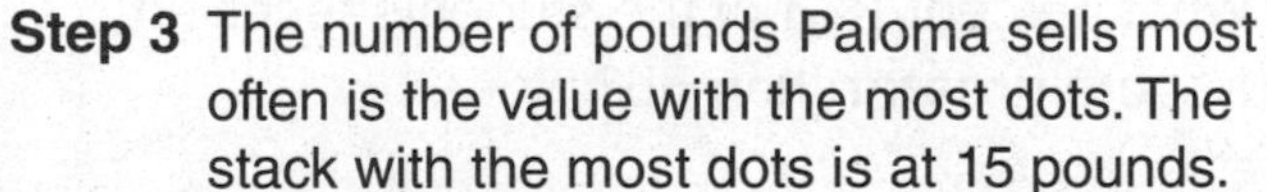

Use the data in the chart at right.

Number of Cars Sold per Month					
26	32	35	29	30	26
25	29	28	31	29	26
35	26	26	28	26	30

1. Complete the dot plot.

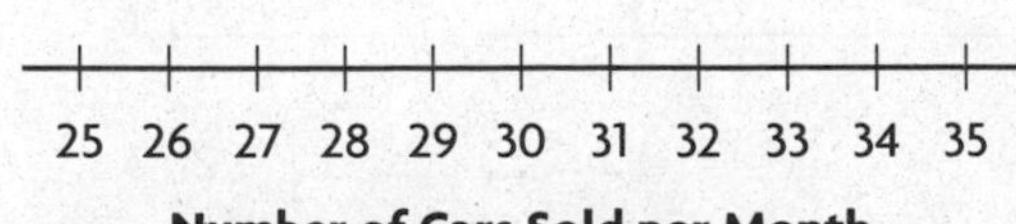

2. What is the most common number of cars sold per month?

____

Name ________________________________

Lesson 93
CC.6.SP.4

The dot plot shows how many hours members of the band practiced last week. Use the dot plot for 1–2.

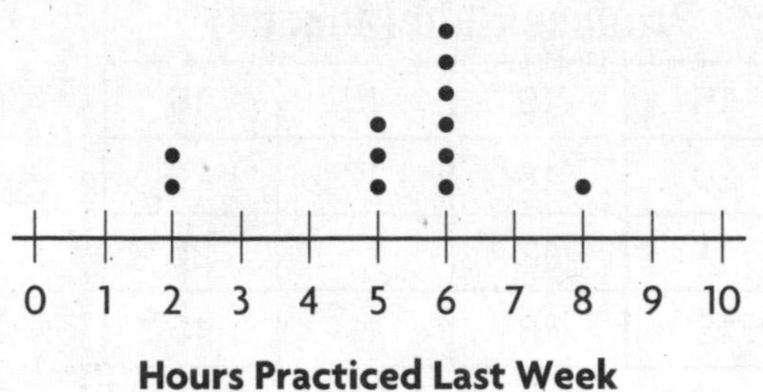

1. What is the most common number of hours that the band members practiced?

   (A) 2
   (B) 5
   (C) 6
   (D) 8

2. What is the total number of hours the band members practiced last week?

   (A) 12 hours
   (B) 36 hours
   (C) 55 hours
   (D) 63 hours

The frequency table shows Mrs. Cho's students' scores on a recent English test. Use the frequency table for 3–4.

English Test Scores

Score	Frequency
41–50	1
51–60	2
61–70	8
71–80	12
81–90	20
91–100	7

3. What percent (%) of the students received a score of 71–80?

   (A) 36%
   (B) 24%
   (C) 12%
   (D) 8%

4. What percent (%) of the students received a score **greater** than 80?

   (A) 27%
   (B) 39%
   (C) 54%
   (D) 78%

Problem Solving REAL WORLD

5. The frequency table shows the ages of the actors in a youth theater group. What percent of the actors are 10 to 12 years old?

   ____

Actors in a Youth Theater Group	
Age	**Frequency**
7–9	8
10–12	22
13–15	10

Name ______________________________

Lesson 94

COMMON CORE STANDARD CC.6.SP.4

Lesson Objective: Display data in histograms.

Histograms

A **histogram** looks like a bar graph without spaces between bars. When you have data to organize, it is helpful to group the data into intervals and let each bar show the frequency, or number of data, in that interval.

Complete the frequency table below, using the data to the right. Then make a histogram.

Number of Hours of TV Watching per Week				
4	14	24	17	10
21	21	15	20	23
5	22	19	18	8
24	19	20	22	24

Step 1 Sort the data into each interval.
Only the 4 (1 item) is in the interval 1–4.
8 and 5 (2 items) are in 5–9.
10 and 14 (2 items) are in 10–14.
17, 15, 19, 18, 19 (5 items) are in 15–19.
24, 21, 21, 20, 23, 22, 24, 20, 22, 24
(10 items) are in 20–24.

Hours of TV/week	1–4	5–9	10–14	15–19	20–24
Frequency	1	2	2	5	10

Step 2 Check that all 20 items in the table are in the frequency table by adding.
$1 + 2 + 2 + 5 + 10 = 20$

Step 3 Make the histogram of the data.
Use a vertical scale from 0 to 12.
Title and label the histogram.
Draw a bar for each interval.
Draw bars the same width.
Draw the bar as high as the frequency.

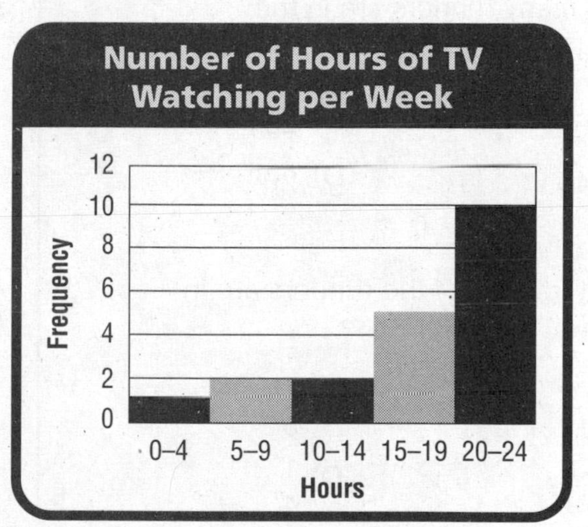

For 1–2, use the table shown.

Minutes on Treadmill Each Day				
28	28	24	52	35
43	29	34	55	21
38	60	71	59	62
19	64	39	70	55

1. Complete the frequency table of the data.

Number of Minutes	0–19	20–39	40–59	60–79
Frequency				

2. Make a histogram of the data.

Name ______________________________

Lesson 94
CC.6.SP.4

The histogram shows the ages of the runners who participated in a marathon. Use the histogram for 1–2.

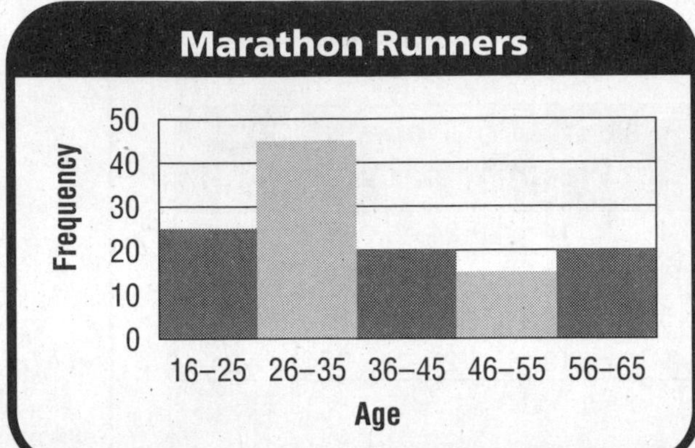

1. How many runners are in the 26–45 age group?

   Ⓐ 65 Ⓒ 25
   Ⓑ 45 Ⓓ 20

2. What fraction of the runners are in the 16–25 age group?

   Ⓐ $\frac{1}{10}$ Ⓒ $\frac{1}{5}$
   Ⓑ $\frac{1}{8}$ Ⓓ $\frac{1}{4}$

The school nurse recorded the heights, in inches, of the sixth-grade students. The histogram shows the results. Use the histogram for 3–4.

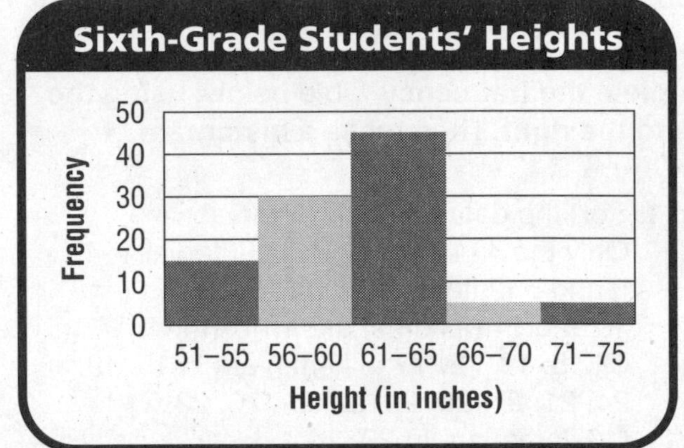

3. How many students are in the 56–60 inch group?

   Ⓐ 5 Ⓒ 30
   Ⓑ 15 Ⓓ 45

4. What fraction of the students are in the 61–65 inch group?

   Ⓐ $\frac{9}{10}$ Ⓒ $\frac{13}{40}$
   Ⓑ $\frac{9}{20}$ Ⓓ $\frac{3}{20}$

Problem Solving REAL WORLD

For 5–6, use the histogram.

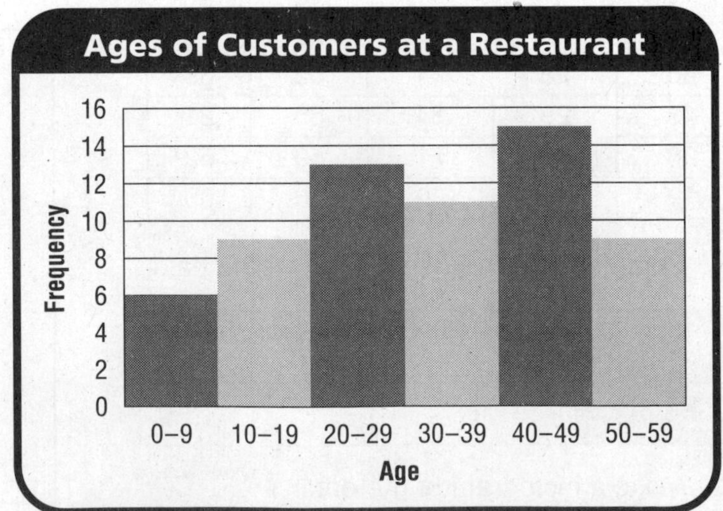

5. For which two age groups are there the same number of customers?

   ____

6. How many customers are in the restaurant? How do you know?

   ____

   ____

Name ______________________________

Lesson 95

COMMON CORE STANDARD CC.6.SP.4

Lesson Objective: Solve problems involving data by using the strategy *draw a diagram.*

Problem Solving • Data Displays

The table shows the highest state populations in 2007, rounded to the nearest million. What percent of the states had at least 15 million residents?

2007 State Populations (in millions)					
18	10	6	9	6	9
6	37	13	12	6	11
24	8	6	6	19	6
10	6				

Read the Problem

What do I need to find?	What information do I need to use?	How will I use the information?
I need to find the ______________ that had at least _____ million people.	I will use the ______________ ______________.	I will pick ______________ for the data, find the ______________ for each interval and use the frequencies to make a ______________. I will use the information from the histogram to find a ______________.

Solve the Problem

Make a frequency table.

Millions	5–9	10–14	15–19	20–24	25–29	30–34	35–40
Frequency			2			0	

Use the frequency table to make a ______________.

States with at least 15 million: 2 + ___ + ___ = ___

Total states: 20

Percent with at least 15 million: $\frac{\square}{20}$ = ____ = ____%

So, _____ of the states have populations over 15 million.

2007 Population of States

Frequency: 0, 2, 4, 6, 8, 10, 12

5–9, 10–14, 15–19, 20–24, 25–29, 30–34, 35–40

Population (in millions)

Use the data in the histogram above.

1. What percent of the states had between 5 million and 14 million residents?

   States with 5–14 million: ______

   Percent with 5–14 million: ______ %

2. What percent of the states had less than 10 million residents?

   States with less than 10 million: ______

   Percent with less than 10 million: ______ %

Name ______________________________

Lesson 95
CC.6.SP.4

1. The data shows the number of siblings for each student in a class. What is the most common number of siblings among the students in the class?

Number of Siblings				
4	0	5	3	1
4	3	2	2	0
1	2	1	6	1
1	5	2	2	2

Ⓐ 0 Ⓒ 2
Ⓑ 1 Ⓓ 3

2. Tabitha records the number of books she reads each month.

Books Read Each Month					
4	2	2	1	3	3
3	5	1	3	5	3

For what percent (%) of months does she read **more** than 3 books?

Ⓐ 15% Ⓒ 33%
Ⓑ 25% Ⓓ 66%

3. The manager at a clothing store recorded the number of customers each hour for one day.

Number of Customers Each Hour					
10	12	2	13	6	4
4	15	11	4	8	10

What is the most common number of customers per hour?

Ⓐ 4 Ⓒ 11
Ⓑ 10 Ⓓ 12

4. Shantelle works in a music store. She records the number of CDs purchased by each customer in one day.

Number of CDs Purchased				
1	3	1	2	1
3	4	2	2	2
1	3	4	2	2

What is the most common number of CDs purchased by each customer?

Ⓐ 1 Ⓒ 3
Ⓑ 2 Ⓓ 4

Problem Solving REAL WORLD

5. The ages of the players on a baseball team are recorded in the table.

What percent (%) of the players are younger than 10 years old? Explain how you know.

Ages of Players (years)				
8	11	13	12	14
12	10	11	9	11

____

____

Name ______________________________

Lesson 96

COMMON CORE STANDARD CC.6.SP.4

Lesson Objective: Display data in box plots.

Box Plots

The weights in ounces of 12 kittens are 20, 18, 22, 15, 17, 25, 25, 23, 13, 18, 16, and 22.

A **box plot** for the data would show how the values are spread out.

Make a box plot for the data.

Step 1 Write the numbers in order from least to greatest. Find the median and the least and greatest values.

13 15 16 17 18 (18 20) 22 22 23 25 25

Since there is an even number of values, the median is the mean of the two middle values. The median is 19. The least value is 13, and the greatest value is 25.

Step 2 Find the lower and upper quartiles.

The **lower quartile** is the median of the lower half of the data.

The **upper quartile** is the median of the upper half of the data.

(13 15 16 17 18 18) | (20 22 22 23 25 25)

lower quartile — upper quartile

Draw a line where the median should be. Now the data set has been split into halves. (If there were an odd number of values in the data set, the median would be one of the data values, but you would not include it in the upper or lower half.) The lower quartile is 16.5, and the upper quartile is 22.5.

Step 3 Plot the five points on a number line, and construct the box and whiskers. Use an appropriate scale.

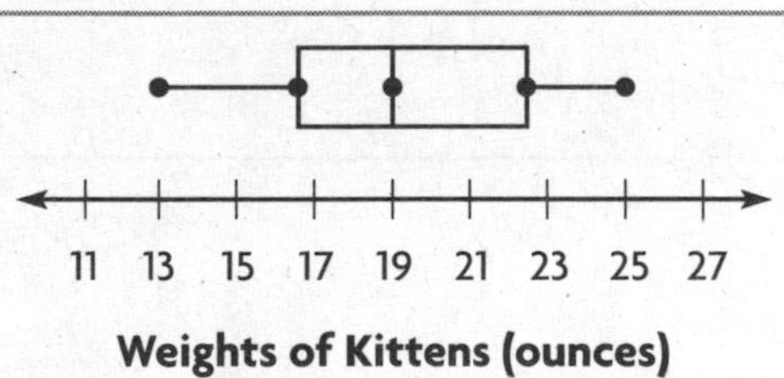

The numbers of laps completed on a track are 4, 5, 2, 7, 6, 8, 9, 8, and 6. Use the data for 1–4.

1. What is the median? ______

2. What is the lower quartile? ______

3. What is the upper quartile? ______

4. Make a box plot for the data.

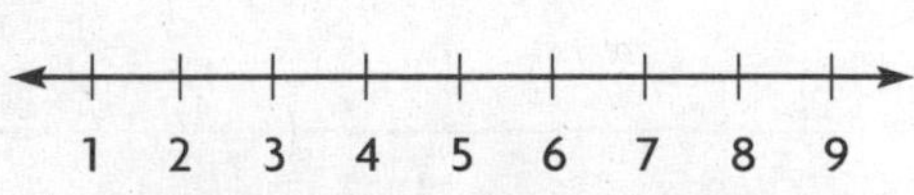

1. The chart shows the number of items purchased by customers in an express check-out line at the grocery store.

Number of Items
15, 1, 9, 7, 11, 12, 13, 13, 3

What is the lower quartile of the data?

Ⓐ 5
Ⓑ 7
Ⓒ 11
Ⓓ 13

2. The box plot displays data for the ages of students in a dance class.

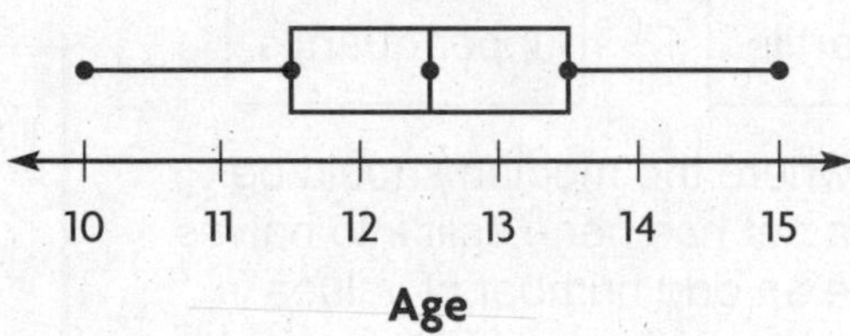

What is the median of the data?

Ⓐ 10
Ⓑ 11.5
Ⓒ 12.5
Ⓓ 13.5

3. The chart shows points scored by a basketball team in their last several games.

Points Scored
76, 62, 75, 88, 84, 89, 71

What is the upper quartile of the data?

Ⓐ 71
Ⓑ 76
Ⓒ 88
Ⓓ 89

4. The prices of a football jersey at several different stores are shown.

Football Jersey Prices
$55, $78, $63, $82, $70

What is the median price?

Ⓐ $80
Ⓑ $70
Ⓒ $59
Ⓓ $21

Problem Solving REAL WORLD

5. The amounts spent at a gift shop today are $19, $30, $28, $22, $20, $26, and $26. What is the median? What is the lower quartile?

____

6. The weights of six puppies in ounces are 8, 5, 7, 5, 6, and 9. What is the upper quartile of the data?

____

Name ___________________________

Lesson 97

COMMON CORE STANDARDS CC.6.SP.5a, CC.6.SP.5b

Lesson Objective: Describe a data set by stating what quantity was measured and how it was measured.

Describe Data Collection

To describe a set of data, describe these features:

Attribute: the characteristic being recorded or measured
Unit: the unit of measurement, such as inches or grams
Means: the tool used for the observations or measurements
Observations: the number of observations or measurements

Describe the data set shown in the chart.

Step 1 What attribute is measured?
The attribute is *length of time* spent walking a dog.

Step 2 What unit of measurement is used?
The time is shown in *minutes.*

Step 3 What means was likely used to obtain the measurements?
To measure time, you use a *clock*, *timer*, or *stopwatch.*

Step 4 How many observations were made?
Count the number or observations: 8

Daily Dog Walks

Day	Time (min)	Day	Time (min)
1	35	5	60
2	40	6	25
3	25	7	90
4	55	8	20

Describe the data set by listing the attribute measured, the unit of measure, the likely means of measurement, and the number of observations.

1. Attribute: ___________________

Unit of measurement: ___________

Means: ___________________

Number of observations: ___________

Pet Weights (lb)

5.2	8	9.5	48.4	0.9
4.7	10.5	32	18	12

2. Attribute: ___________________

Unit of measurement: ___________

Means: ___________________

Number of observations: ___________

Serving Volume (cups)

Lettuce	2	Soup	1.5
Cheese	0.25	Ice Cream	0.75
Sauce	0.5		

Name ___________________________________

Lesson 97

CC.6.SP.5a, CC.6.SP.5b

1. The table shows data collected by an electricity supplier.

Monthly Electricity Usage (kilowatt-hours)		
917 kWh	1,129 kWh	1,007 kWh
837 kWh	983 kWh	924 kWh

What is the attribute being measured?

(A) monthly electricity usage
(B) kilowatt-hours
(C) electricity meter
(D) electricity

2. How many observations are in the data set shown?

Heights of Television Towers (meters)			
457	502	498	526
678	619	564	642

(A) 2
(B) 4
(C) 6
(D) 8

3. What is the unit of measure for the data set shown?

Heights of Plants (inches)				
10.1	7.3	8.6	6.4	7.7
7.9	8.4	9.3	7.9	8.1
6.5	7.5	8.2	8.8	9.8

(A) heights of plants
(B) inches
(C) plants
(D) ruler

4. What was the likely means of measurement for the data set shown?

Distance Driven Daily for a Week (miles)						
22	103	47	31	56	124	45

(A) measuring tape
(B) odometer
(C) yardstick
(D) ruler

Problem Solving REAL WORLD

5. The table below gives the amount of time Preston spends on homework. Name the likely means of measurement.

Amount of Time Spent on Homework (hours)							
5	3	1	2	4	1	3	2

____

6. The table below shows the speed of cars on a highway. Name the unit of measure.

Speeds of Cars (miles per hour)							
71	55	53	65	68	61	59	62
70	69	57	50	56	66	67	63

____

Name ______________________________

Lesson 98

COMMON CORE STANDARD CC.6.SP.5c

Lesson Objective: Understand the mean as a fair share and as a balance point.

Mean as Fair Share and Balance Point

Five students brought 3, 4, 5, 3, and 5 cups of flour to the cooking club. They divided it evenly so that each student got the same amount for cooking. Use counters to show how many cups each student got.

Step 1 Make 5 stacks of counters: one stack for each student.

Use one counter for each cup of flour.

Step 2 Take counters from taller stacks and put them on shorter stacks. Move counters until all the stacks are the same height.

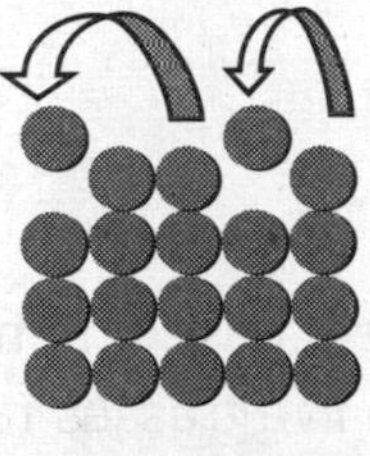

Step 3 Count the counters in each stack. There are **4** counters in each stack.

So, 4 is the mean of the data. When you divide the flour equally, each student gets 4 cups.

Use counters to find the mean of the data set.

1. 3, 5, 7, 5

Draw 4 stacks to show the data set.

Make the stacks the same height.

____ counters in each stack.

Mean: ____

2. 5, 7, 4, 3, 4, 1

Draw 6 stacks to show the data set.

Make the stacks the same height.

____ counters in each stack.

Mean: ____

Name ______________________________

Lesson 98
CC.6.SP.5c

1. Khalifa has a bookcase with 5 shelves. There are 11, 12, 9, 11, and 7 books on each of the 5 shelves. If she rearranges the books so that each shelf has the same number of books, how many books will be on each shelf?

   Ⓐ 10
   Ⓑ 11
   Ⓒ 12
   Ⓓ 13

2. The sixth graders raised money to fund a field trip. The five classes raised $42, $51, $38, $49, and $40. The classes decided to combine their money so that each class would have the same amount. What is the fair share, in dollars ($), raised by each class?

   Ⓐ $12
   Ⓑ $42
   Ⓒ $44
   Ⓓ $51

3. The desks in a classroom are arranged in 3 rows. There are 6 desks in the first row, 3 desks in the second row, and 6 desks in the third row. If the desks are rearranged so that each row has the same number of desks, how many desks will be in each row?

   Ⓐ 2
   Ⓑ 3
   Ⓒ 5
   Ⓓ 6

4. Alivia goes to lunch with 3 of her friends. The costs of their meals are $8, $4, $7, and $5. If they split the bill evenly, how much should each person pay?

   Ⓐ $3
   Ⓑ $6
   Ⓒ $9
   Ⓓ $15

Problem Solving REAL WORLD

5. Three baskets contain 8, 8, and 11 soaps. Can the soaps be rearranged so that there is an equal whole number of soaps in each basket? Explain why or why not.

   ____
   ____
   ____

6. Five pages contain 6, 6, 9, 10, and 11 stickers. Can the stickers be rearranged so that there is an equal whole number of stickers on each page? Explain why or why not.

   ____
   ____
   ____

Name ______________________________

Measures of Center

Lesson 99

COMMON CORE STANDARD CC.6.SP.5c

Lesson Objective: Summarize a data set by using mean, median, and mode.

A **measure of center** is a single value that describes the middle of a data set.

The **mean** is the sum of all items in a set of data divided by the number of items in the set.

The **median** is the middle number or the mean of the middle two numbers when the items in the data set are listed in order.

The **mode** is the data value that is repeated more than other values. A data set can have more than one mode, or no mode.

Find the mean, median, and mode for the set of data.
80, 74, 82, 77, 86, 75

Find the mean.

Step 1 Find the sum of the data.
$80 + 74 + 82 + 77 + 86 + 75 = 474$

Step 2 Count the number of data items.
There are 6 items.

Step 3 Divide.

$$\frac{\text{sum}}{\text{number of items}} = \frac{474}{6} = 79$$

So, the mean is 79.

Find the median.

Step 1 Order the data.
74, 75, 77, 80, 82, 86

Step 2 Find the middle number.
There are two middle numbers: 77 and 80.

Step 3 Find their mean.

$$\frac{77 + 80}{2} = 78.5$$

So, the median is 78.5.

Find the mode.

Use the ordered list and look for numbers that repeat.
No numbers repeat. So, there is no mode.

Find the mean, median, and mode.

1. 31, 3, 14, 31, 11

   mean: ________ median: ________

   mode: ________

2. 95, 18, 51, 1, 22, 5

   mean: ________ median: ________

   mode: ________

3. 14, 22, 15, 7, 14, 0, 12

   mean: ________ median: ________

   mode: ________

4. 67, 103, 94, 65, 18, 114, 94, 63, 94, 27

   mean: ________ median: ________

   mode: ________

Name ______________________

1. Every day for one week, Keller recorded the number of customers who bought blueberry muffins at his cafe. The customer counts are 13, 8, 12, 15, 11, 20, and 19. What is the mean of the data?

Ⓐ 11
Ⓑ 12
Ⓒ 13
Ⓓ 14

2. Carmen is training for a swim meet. The table shows the number of laps she swims each day.

Carmen's Training Log

Day	Number of Laps
Monday	40
Tuesday	45
Wednesday	55
Thursday	45
Friday	40
Saturday	50

Which shows the mode(s) of the data?

Ⓐ 40 and 45
Ⓑ 45 and 50
Ⓒ 45
Ⓓ 40

3. Todd and his friends collect coins. The numbers of coins in their collections are 45, 73, 86, 24, 57, 100, 58, 86, 68, and 74. What is the median of the data?

Ⓐ 67.1
Ⓑ 70.5
Ⓒ 76
Ⓓ 86

4. Michelle recorded the number of customers who bought plain bagels at her bakery each day for one week. The customer counts are 15, 7, 6, 9, 10, 12, and 11. What is the mean of the data?

Ⓐ 6
Ⓑ 9
Ⓒ 10
Ⓓ 15

Problem Solving REAL WORLD

5. An auto manufacturer wants their line of cars to have a median gas mileage of 25 miles per gallon or higher. The gas mileage for their five models are 23, 25, 26, 29, and 19. Do their cars meet their goal? Explain.

____

____

____

6. A sporting goods store is featuring several new bicycles, priced at $300, $250, $325, $780, and $350. They advertise that the average price of their bicycles is under $400. Is their ad correct? Explain.

____

____

____

Name ____________________

Lesson 100

COMMON CORE STANDARD CC.6.SP.5c

Lesson Objective: Describe overall patterns in data, including clusters, peaks, gaps, and symmetry.

Patterns in Data

The histogram shows the number of minutes a caller had to be placed on hold before talking to a representative.

According to the graph, there were 10 people who were on hold for 0 to 4 minutes.

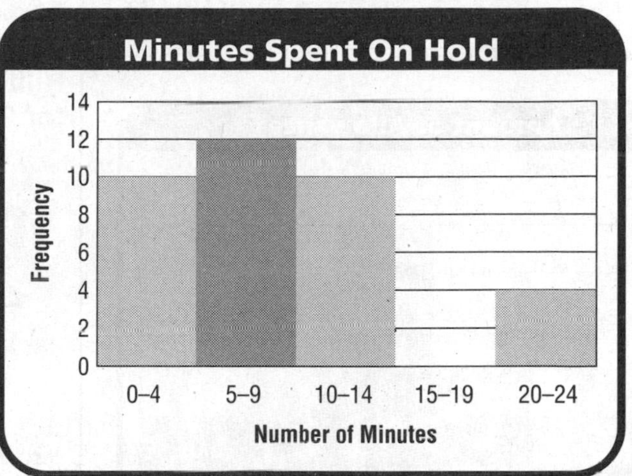

Does the graph contain any clusters or gaps? If so, where? Does the graph have symmetry?

Step 1 Look for a group of data points that lie within a small interval. These are clusters.	The bars for 0–4, 5–9, and 10–14 are in a group. This is a cluster of data.
Step 2 Look for an interval that contains no data. These are gaps.	There is no bar above the interval 15–19. This is a gap in the data. This means there were no people who were on hold for 15 to 19 minutes.
Step 3 Look for symmetry. If you draw a vertical line in the graph, the bars on the left and right sides will match if the graph has symmetry.	A line cannot be drawn anywhere on the graph and have the bars on either side match. There is no symmetry.

Use the dot plot to answer the questions.

1. Are there any clusters? If so, where?

____

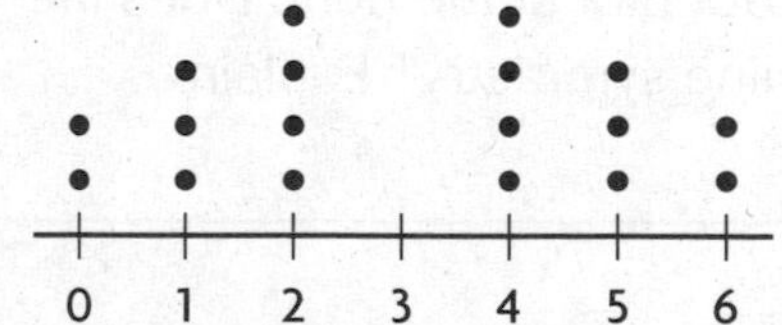

2. Are there any gaps? If so, where?

____

3. Is there symmetry? If so, where can the line of symmetry be drawn?

____

Name ______________________________

Lesson 100
CC.6.SP.5c

1. The histogram shows the amount of monthly allowance for the students in Linda's class.

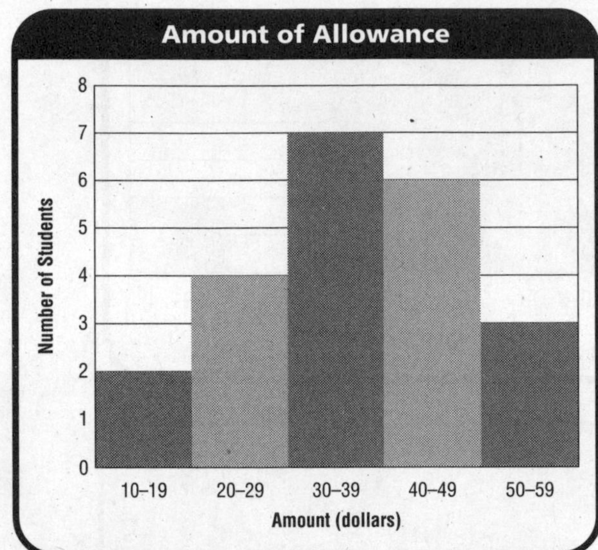

Which interval of dollar amounts represents the peak of the histogram?

Ⓐ 10–19
Ⓑ 20–29
Ⓒ 30–39
Ⓓ 40–49

The dot plot shows the number of students in each sixth-grade class at Hilltop Middle School. Use the dot plot for 2–3.

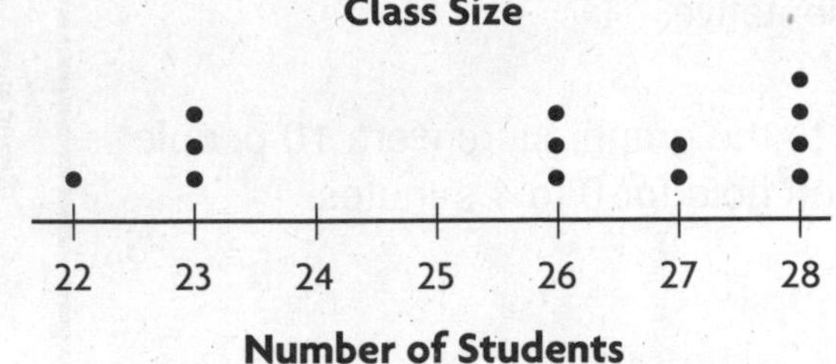

2. For which interval is there a gap in the data?

Ⓐ 26 to 28
Ⓑ 24 to 25
Ⓒ 23 to 26
Ⓓ 22 to 23

3. Which interval names a cluster in the data?

Ⓐ 23 to 25
Ⓑ 24 to 25
Ⓒ 24 to 28
Ⓓ 26 to 28

Problem Solving REAL WORLD

4. Look at the dot plot at the right. Does the graph have line symmetry? Explain.

____

____

____

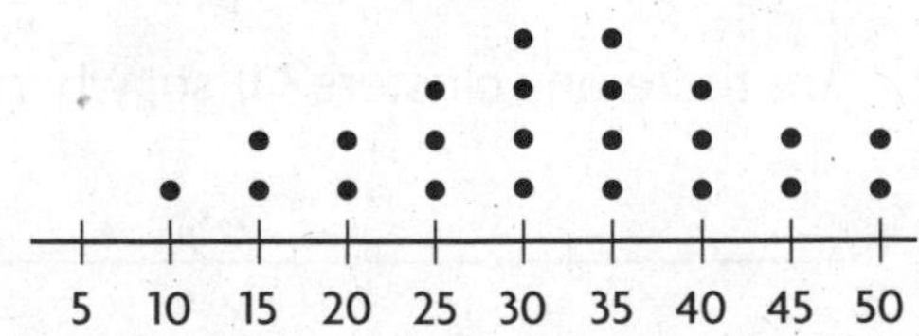

Name ________________________________

Lesson 101

COMMON CORE STANDARD CC.6.SP.5c

Lesson Objective: Understand mean absolute deviation as a measure of variability from the mean.

Mean Absolute Deviation

The **mean absolute deviation** tells how far away the data values are from the mean. A small mean absolute deviation means that most values are close to the mean. A large mean absolute deviation means that the data values are more spread out.

The prices of 8 lunches are $10, $8, $3, $5, $9, $6, $7, and $8. The mean is $7. Find the mean absolute deviation.

Step 1 Determine how far each data value is from the mean. You can use a number line.

Plot a value on the number line. Then count how many spaces you must move to reach the mean, 7.

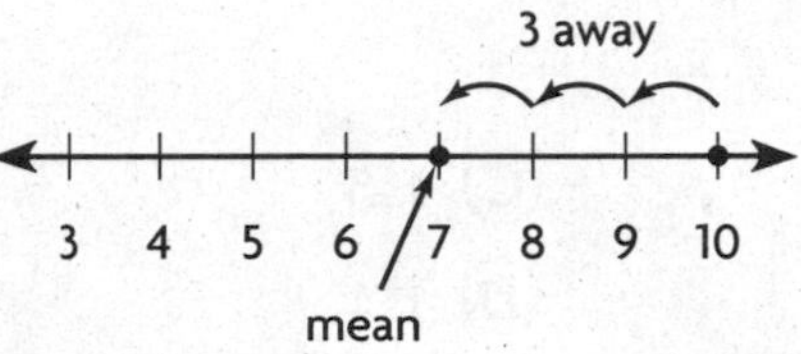

Step 2 Make a list of all of the distances.

Data values:	10	8	3	5	9	6	7	8
Distance from mean:	3	1	4	2	2	1	0	1

Step 3 Find the mean of the distances by finding the sum and dividing by 8. The quotient is the mean absolute deviation.

$$\frac{3+1+4+2+2+1+0+1}{8} = \frac{14}{8} = 1.75$$

So, on average, each data value is 1.75 away from the mean.

Use counters or a number line to find the mean absolute deviation.

1. ages of people on a team in years:
9, 12, 10, 8, 11
mean = 10 years

distances from mean = ______________

mean absolute deviation = ______

2. Sam's test scores:
86, 71, 92, 84, 76, 95
mean = 84

mean absolute deviation = ______

3. prices of dinner menu items:
$15, $10, $13, $19, $20, $12, $9, $14
mean = $14

mean absolute deviation = ______

4. daily low temperatures, °F, in a city:
45, 39, 40, 52, 44
mean = 44°F

mean absolute deviation = ______

Name ______________________________

Lesson 101
CC.6.SP.5c

1. The dot plot shows the number of history books borrowed from the library each day during a 10-day period. The mean of the number of books borrowed each day is 8.

History Books Borrowed

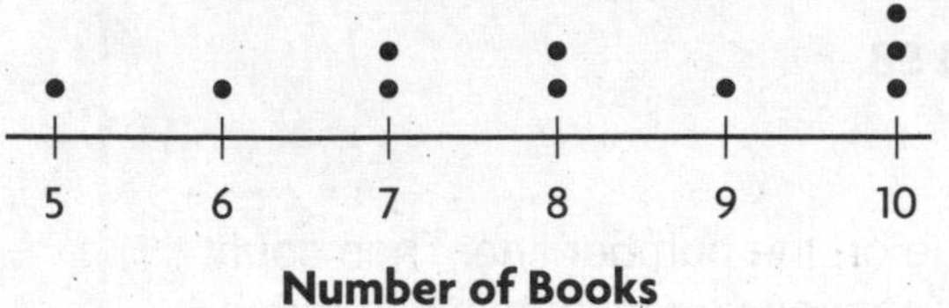

Number of Books

What is the mean absolute deviation of the data?

Ⓐ 14 Ⓒ 1.5
Ⓑ 10 Ⓓ 1.4

2. Angie plays the violin. The number of hours she practiced each week for 5 weeks are 2, 3, 5, 7, and 8. The mean number of hours per week she practiced is 5. What is the mean absolute deviation of the data?

Ⓐ 2 Ⓒ 10
Ⓑ 5 Ⓓ 25

3. The table shows the mean absolute deviation of the number of canned goods collected per person for a food drive by 4 sixth-grade classes.

Number of Canned Goods

Class	Mean Absolute Deviation
Mr. Williams	2.5
Mrs. Chung	3.6
Mrs. Singh	4.2
Mr. Scott	1.3

In which class did the number of canned goods that were collected per student vary the **most**?

Ⓐ Mr. Williams
Ⓑ Mrs. Chung
Ⓒ Mrs. Singh
Ⓓ Mr. Scott

Problem Solving

4. In science class, Troy found the mass, in grams, of 6 samples to be 10, 12, 7, 8, 5, and 6. What is the mean absolute deviation?

____

5. Five recorded temperatures are 71°F, 64°F, 72°F, 81°F, and 67°F. What is the mean absolute deviation?

____

Name ____________________

Lesson 102

COMMON CORE STANDARD CC.6.SP.5c

Lesson Objective: Summarize a data set by using range, interquartile range, and mean absolute deviation.

Measures of Variability

A **measure of variability** is a single number that describes how far apart the numbers are in a data set. **Range, interquartile range**, and mean absolute deviation are all measures of variability.

The box plot shows the cost of various concert tickets. Find the range and interquartile range of the data in the box plot.

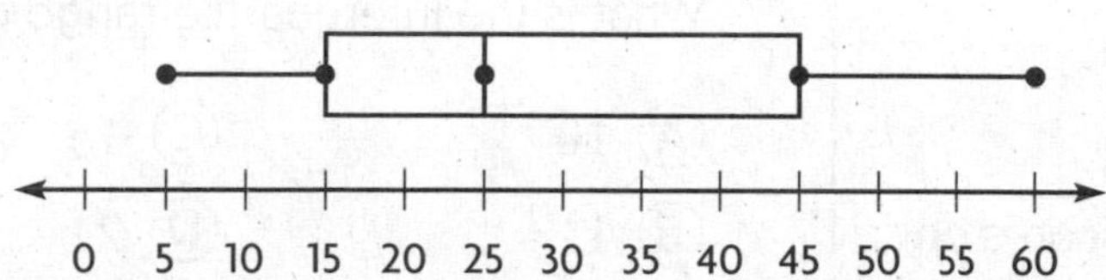

Step 1 To find the range, subtract the least value from the greatest value.

60 − 5 = 55
greatest, least, range

Step 2 To find the interquartile range, subtract the lower quartile from the upper quartile.

45 − 15 = 30
upper quartile, lower quartile, interquartile range

Make a box plot for the data. Then find the range and interquartile range.

1. number of free throws made:
   8, 13, 9, 4, 1, 6, 2, 2, 14, 6, 9, 11

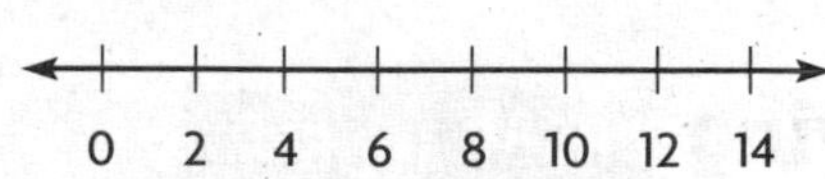

   range = ______

   interquartile range = ______

2. minutes spent cooking dinner:
   45, 38, 52, 29, 28, 31, 44, 40, 25

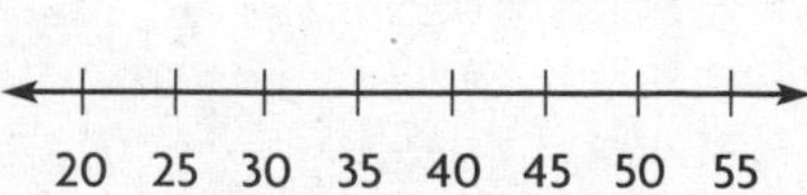

   range = ______

   interquartile range = ______

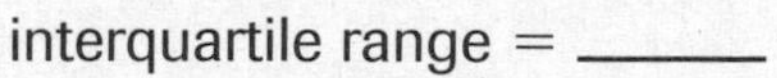

Name ______________________________

Lesson 102
CC.6.SP.5c

1. The chart shows the toll rates to drive across several different bridges.

Toll Rates ($)
1.00, 6.50, 4.50, 3.25, 2.25, 1.50, 2.00

What is the mean absolute deviation of the data?

Ⓐ $1.50 Ⓒ $5.50
Ⓑ $3.00 Ⓓ $10.50

2. Mrs. Gupta displayed the highest scores on the history quiz in the box plot shown.

Highest Scores on History Quiz

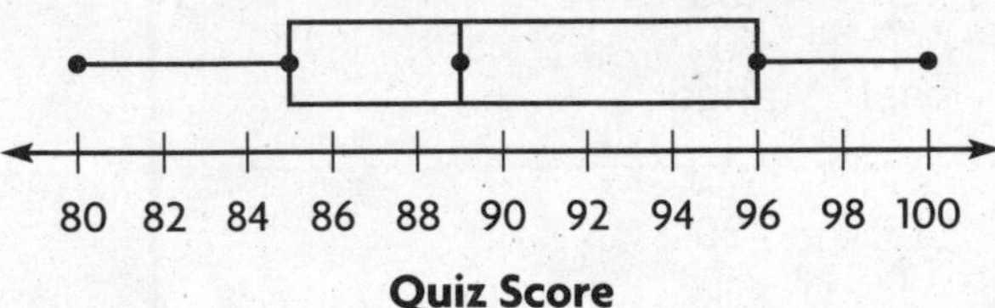

What is the range of the data?

Ⓐ 11 Ⓒ 89
Ⓑ 20 Ⓓ 100

3. The box plot displays data for the number of shoe brands sold by several department stores.

Shoe Brands Sold

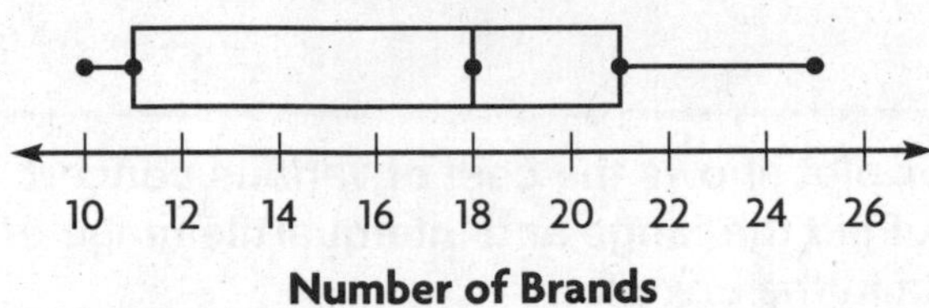

What is the interquartile range of the data?

Ⓐ 10 Ⓒ 15
Ⓑ 11 Ⓓ 21

4. The chart shows the prices of cell phone plans that a company offers.

Cell Phone Plan Prices
$49, $70, $55, $100, $85, $35

What is the interquartile range of the prices?

Ⓐ $85 Ⓒ $49
Ⓑ $65 Ⓓ $36

Problem Solving REAL WORLD

5. The following data set gives the amount of time, in minutes, it took five people to cook a recipe. What is the mean absolute deviation for the data?

33, 38, 31, 36, 37

____

6. The prices of six food processors are $63, $59, $72, $68, $61, and $67. What is the mean absolute deviation for the data?

____

Name ______________________________

Lesson 103

COMMON CORE STANDARD CC.6.SP.5d

Lesson Objective: Determine the effects of outliers on measures of center and variability.

Effects of Outliers

Sometimes a data set contains a number that is much less or much greater than the rest. This number is called an **outlier.** Taking note of outliers can help you understand a data set.

Use a dot plot to find the outlier for the quiz scores. Then tell how the outlier affects the mean and median.

Scores on 20-question Quiz				
15	16	17	13	18
12	5	14	14	16

Mean: 14 Median: 14.5

Step 1 Plot the data on the number line.

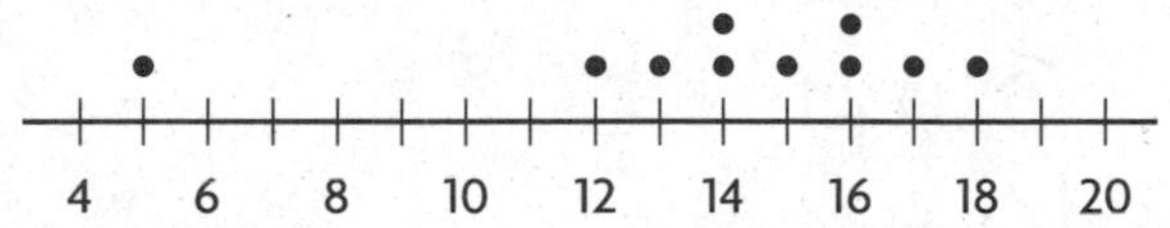

Step 2 Find the outlier.

Most of the points are between 12 and 18.
5 is much less than the rest, so it is an outlier.

Step 3 Find the median and mean without the outlier.

Median: Make an ordered list and find the middle value.

12, 13, 14, 14, (15) 16, 16, 17, 18
The new median is 15.

Mean: One value has been removed. Add the new list of values and divide by 9.

$$\frac{12 + 13 + 14 + 14 + 15 + 16 + 16 + 17 + 18}{9} = 15$$

The new mean is 15.

Step 4 Describe the effect of the outlier.
Without the outlier, the mean went up from 14 to 15.
The median went up from 14.5 to 15.

Use the table for Problems 1–3.

Shirt Prices ($)				
29	33	24	14	29
31	31	33		

Mean: $28 Median: $30

1. Find the outlier by drawing a dot plot of the data.

15 18 21 24 27 30 33

Outlier: ________

2. Find the mean and median without the outlier.

Median: $ ________ Mean: $ ________

3. Without the outlier, the mean ______________________________.

The median ______________________________.

Name ____________________

Lesson 103
CC.6.SP.5d

1. The prices of karaoke machines at 6 different stores are $77, $85, $78, $72, $80, and $118. What is the outlier in the data set?

   Ⓐ $74
   Ⓑ $79
   Ⓒ $85
   Ⓓ $118

2. The amounts of money Gillian earned each week from babysitting are $5, $10, $20, $10, $15, $5, $42, and $5. How is the mean of the data set affected when the outlier is removed?

   Ⓐ The mean is unchanged.
   Ⓑ The mean increases by $4.
   Ⓒ The mean decreases by $4.
   Ⓓ The mean increases by $1.

3. The low temperatures for the week in Carrollton, in degrees Fahrenheit (°F), were 17, 41, 11, 14, 11, 13, and 15. What is the mean of the temperatures **without** the outlier?

   Ⓐ 11.6°F
   Ⓑ 13.5°F
   Ⓒ 14.5°F
   Ⓓ 17.4°F

4. The number of points scored by a football team in 6 different games are 26, 38, 33, 20, 3, and 28. What is the outlier in the data set?

   Ⓐ 3
   Ⓑ 25
   Ⓒ 27
   Ⓓ 38

Problem Solving REAL WORLD

5. Duke's science quiz scores are 99, 91, 60, 94, and 95. Describe the effect of the outlier on the mean and median.

   ____
   ____
   ____
   ____

6. The number of people who attended an art conference for five days was 42, 27, 35, 39, and 96. Describe the effect of the outlier on the mean and median.

   ____
   ____
   ____

Name ______________________________

Lesson 104

COMMON CORE STANDARD CC.6.SP.5d

Lesson Objective: Choose appropriate measures of center and variability to describe data, and justify the choice.

Choose Appropriate Measures of Center and Variability

Sometimes one measure of center or variability represents the data better than another measure of variability. For example, the median might be a better representation than the mean.

Cheeseburger prices at several different restaurants are $5, $3, $2, $6, $4, and $14. Should the mean, median, or mode be used to describe the data? Should the range or interquartile range be used?

Measure of Center	Measure of Variability
Step 1 Find the mean, median, and mode. Mean: $\frac{5 + 3 + 2 + 6 + 4 + 14}{6} \approx \$5.67$ Median: 2 3 4 | 5 6 14 $\frac{4 + 5}{2} = \$4.50$ Mode = none	**Step 1** Find the range and interquartile range. Range: $14 - 2 = \$12$ Interquartile range: $6 - 3 = \$3$ 2 (3) 4 | 5 (6) 14
Step 2 Compare. There are six data values, and the mean is greater than four of them. The outlier of $14 is causing this. So, the median is a better measure of center.	**Step 2** Compare. All of the data values except one are between $2 and $6. The interquartile range is a better measure.

1. The times, in minutes, spent cleaning a room are 60, 50, 33, 28, and 44. Decide which measure(s) of center best describes the data set. Explain your reasoning.

____

____

____

____

2. The amounts of snowfall, in inches, are 4, 3, 20, 6, 8, and 2. Decide which measure(s) of variability best describes the data set. Explain your reasoning.

____

____

____

____

Name ___________________________

1. Brianna received pledge amounts of $89, $35, $22, $36, $32, $31, and $28 for her participation in a walkathon. Which measure of center **best** describes the pledge amounts?

   Ⓐ median

   Ⓑ mode

   Ⓒ mean

   Ⓓ range

2. The number of lunch specials on the menus of several different restaurants are 11, 14, 2, 10, 14, 10, and 12. What measure **best** describes the variation in the data?

   Ⓐ lower quartile

   Ⓑ interquartile range

   Ⓒ range

   Ⓓ upper quartile

3. The hockey team's scores for several games were 4, 2, 3, 0, 0, 1, and 10. What measure **best** describes the variation of the data?

   Ⓐ lower quartile

   Ⓑ upper quartile

   Ⓒ interquartile range

   Ⓓ range

4. Vishal compared the prices of a video game at several different stores. The prices are $43, $64, $38, $36, $37, $34, and $28. Which measure of center **best** describes the prices?

   Ⓐ median

   Ⓑ mode

   Ⓒ mean

   Ⓓ range

Problem Solving REAL WORLD

5. Brett's history quiz scores are 84, 78, 92, 90, 85, 91, and 0. Decide which measure(s) of center best describes the data set. Explain your reasoning.

   mean = ___________ median = ___________

   mode = ___________

   ____

   ____

   ____

6. Eight students were absent the following number of days in a year: 4, 8, 0, 1, 7, 2, 6, and 3. Decide if the range or interquartile range better describes the data set, and explain your reasoning.

   range = ______ interquartile range = ______

   ____

   ____

Name

Lesson 1

COMMON CORE STANDARD CC.6.RP.1
Lesson Objective: Model ratios.

Model Ratios

Daniel is growing tulips and daffodils in a pot. For every 3 tulips he plants, he plants 1 daffodil. How many daffodils will he plant if he plants 12 tulips?

Step 1 Make a model and write the ratio. The ratio of tulips to daffodils is 3:1.

= 1 tulip
= 1 daffodil

Step 2 Model the number of daffodils Daniel will plant if he plants 6 tulips.

Step 3 Use the model and ratio to make a table. The table shows that for every 3 tulips, there is 1 daffodil.

Tulips	3	6	9	12
Daffodils	1	2	3	4

Step 4 Find 12 tulips on the table. The number of daffodils is 4.

Step 5 Write the new ratio. The new ratio is 12:4.

So, if Daniel plants 12 tulips, he will plant 4 daffodils.

Write the ratio of triangles to squares.

1. 2 : 3
2. 4 : 7

Draw a model of the ratio. Possible models are shown.

3. 5:1
4. 3:4

Complete the table.

5. 1 table for every 5 students

Students	5	10	15	20
Tables	1	2	3	4

6. 7 pencils for every 1 student

Students	1	2	3	4
Pencils	7	14	21	28

Name

Lesson 1

CC.6.RP.1

1. For every team competing in a robotics competition, there are 4 students. How many students are on 3 teams?
   - Ⓐ 1
   - Ⓑ 3
   - Ⓒ 7
   - Ⓓ 12 (answer)

2. Jillian uses 3 tablespoons of whipped cream for each bowl of dessert that she prepares. Which model could be used to describe the ratio of tablespoons of whipped cream to the number of bowls of dessert?
   - Ⓐ 3 red counters and 1 yellow counter (answer)
   - Ⓑ 2 red counters and 1 yellow counter
   - Ⓒ 4 red counters and 1 yellow counter
   - Ⓓ 2 red counters and 4 red counters

3. John has 2 comic books. Leroy has 3 comic books. What model shows the ratio of the number of John's comic books to the number of Leroy's comic books?
   - Ⓐ ●●●●○
   - Ⓑ ●●●●●
   - Ⓒ ●●○○○ (answer)
   - Ⓓ ○○○○○○

4. In every classroom in Millview Middle School, there are 2 computers. How many computers are in 4 classrooms?
   - Ⓐ 2
   - Ⓑ 4
   - Ⓒ 6
   - Ⓓ 8 (answer)

Problem Solving REAL WORLD

5. There are 4 quarts in 1 gallon. How many quarts are in 3 gallons?

   12 quarts

6. Martin mixes 1 cup lemonade with 4 cups cranberry juice to make his favorite drink. How much cranberry juice does he need if he uses 5 cups of lemonade?

   20 cups

Name

Lesson 2

COMMON CORE STANDARD CC.6.RP.1
Lesson Objective: Write ratios and rates.

Ratios and Rates

A **ratio** is a comparison of two numbers by division. Ratios can compare parts of a whole or compare one part to the whole. A **rate** is a ratio that compares two numbers that have different units.

The picture shows a group of school supplies. One part is pencils. The other part is notebooks. Write the ratio of pencils to notebooks. Write the ratio using words, as a fraction, and with a colon.

Write the number of pencils first, and then write the number of notebooks.

12 to 4	$\frac{12}{4}$	12:4
number of pencils to number of notebooks	$\frac{\text{number of pencils}}{\text{number of notebooks}}$	number of pencils : number of notebooks

You could also write a ratio comparing part to whole. Write the ratio of notebooks to school supplies, three ways.

4 to 16	$\frac{4}{16}$	4:16
number of notebooks to number of school supplies	$\frac{\text{number of notebooks}}{\text{number of school supplies}}$	number of notebooks : number of school supplies

Write each ratio three ways.

1. Write the ratio of circles to squares.

   5 to 7 $\frac{5}{7}$ 5 : 7

2. Write the ratio of squares to shapes.

   7 to 12 $\frac{7}{12}$ 7 : 12

Name

Lesson 2

CC.6.RP.1

1. At Fabric World, ribbon is sold at a rate of $2 for 1 yard. What rate gives the cost for 8 yards of fabric?
   - Ⓐ $2:1 yard
   - Ⓑ $8:4 yards
   - Ⓒ $10:1 yard
   - Ⓓ $16:8 yards (answer)

2. Brenda planted 8 daisies, 3 pansies, 5 zinnias, and 6 marigolds in her garden. What is the ratio of zinnias to daisies?
   - Ⓐ 5:22
   - Ⓑ 5:8 (answer)
   - Ⓒ 6:5
   - Ⓓ 8:3

3. Ashley has 4 pairs of low-top sneakers, 7 pairs of high-top sneakers, 3 pairs of sandals, and 1 pair of boots. What is the ratio of the pairs of low-top sneakers to the total number of pairs of shoes?
   - Ⓐ 4 to 15 (answer)
   - Ⓑ 7 to 15
   - Ⓒ 4 to 3
   - Ⓓ 1 to 3

4. Andre purchased 1 quart of lemonade from a concession stand for $1.50. Which shows the rate for 6 quarts of lemonade?
   - Ⓐ $\frac{\$0.25}{\text{6 quarts}}$
   - Ⓑ $\frac{\$1.50}{\text{1 quart}}$
   - Ⓒ $\frac{\$7.50}{\text{1 quart}}$
   - Ⓓ $\frac{\$9.00}{\text{6 quarts}}$ (answer)

Problem Solving REAL WORLD

5. Gemma spends 4 hours each week playing soccer and 3 hours each week practicing her clarinet. Write the ratio of hours spent practicing clarinet to hours spent playing soccer three different ways.

   $\frac{3}{4}$; 3 to 4, 3:4

6. Randall bought 2 game controllers at Electronics Plus for $36. What is the unit rate for a game controller at Electronics Plus?

   $\frac{\$18}{\text{1 controller}}$

Answer Key

Name ______________________

Lesson 3
COMMON CORE STANDARD CC.6.RP.2
Lesson Objective: Use unit rates to make comparisons.

Find Unit Rates

When comparing prices of items, the better buy is the item with a lower unit price.

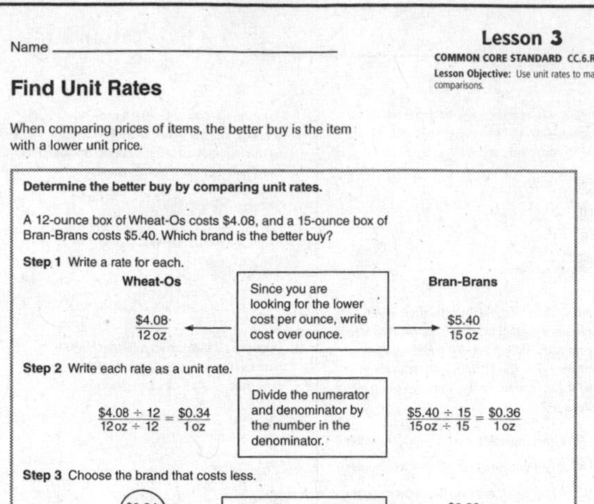

Determine the better buy by comparing unit rates.

A 12-ounce box of Wheat-Os costs $4.08, and a 15-ounce box of Bran-Brans costs $5.40. Which brand is the better buy?

Step 1 Write a rate for each.

Wheat-Os $\frac{\$4.08}{12 \text{ oz}}$ ← Since you are looking for the lower cost per ounce, write cost over ounce. → **Bran-Brans** $\frac{\$5.40}{15 \text{ oz}}$

Step 2 Write each rate as a unit rate.

$\frac{\$4.08 \div 12}{12 \text{ oz} \div 12} = \frac{\$0.34}{1 \text{ oz}}$ Divide the numerator and denominator by the number in the denominator. $\frac{\$5.40 \div 15}{15 \text{ oz} \div 15} = \frac{\$0.36}{1 \text{ oz}}$

Step 3 Choose the brand that costs less.

$\frac{\$0.34}{1 \text{ oz}}$ (circled) $0.34 is less than $0.36. $\frac{\$0.36}{1 \text{ oz}}$

So, Wheat-Os are the better buy.

Determine the better buy by comparing unit rates.

1. 20 pens for $1.60 or 25 pens for $2.25
   a. Write a rate for each. $\frac{\$1.60}{20 \text{ pens}}$ and $\frac{\$2.25}{25 \text{ pens}}$
   b. Write each rate as a unit rate. $\frac{\$0.08}{1 \text{ pen}}$ and $\frac{\$0.09}{1 \text{ pen}}$
   c. Which is the better buy? 20 pens for $1.60

2. 13 berries for $2.60 or 17 berries for $3.06
   a. Write a rate for each. $\frac{\$2.60}{13 \text{ berries}}$ and $\frac{\$3.06}{17 \text{ berries}}$
   b. Write each rate as a unit rate. $\frac{\$0.20}{1 \text{ berry}}$ and $\frac{\$0.18}{1 \text{ berry}}$
   c. Which is the better buy? 17 berries for $3.06

Name ______________________

Lesson 3
CC.6.RP.2

1. Juan paid $2.52 for 12 ounces of peanuts. What is the unit rate?
   Ⓐ $\frac{\$0.21}{1 \text{ ounce}}$ (shaded) Ⓒ $\frac{\$4.76}{1 \text{ ounce}}$
   Ⓑ $\frac{\$2.52}{12 \text{ ounces}}$ Ⓓ $\frac{\$30.24}{12 \text{ ounces}}$

2. Dora used the grocery ads to list apple prices at four stores.
   Gordon's: 4 pounds for $3.32
   Greenwise: 2 pounds for $1.62
   PJ's: 3 pounds for $2.37
   Tosko: 5 pounds for $4.50
   Which store charges the **least** amount per pound?
   Ⓐ Gordon's
   Ⓑ Greenwise
   Ⓒ PJ's (shaded)
   Ⓓ Tosko

3. Robert compared the cost of popcorn at 4 movies theaters.
   Cinema World: 33 ounces for $5.61
   Tons of Movies: 27 ounces for $5.13
   Parkside Theater: 28 ounces for $5.04
   Landview Cinema: 32 ounces for $4.80
   Which movie theater charges the **least** amount per ounce?
   Ⓐ Cinema World
   Ⓑ Tons of Movies
   Ⓒ Parkside Theater
   Ⓓ Landview Cinema (shaded)

4. Dmitri bought 28 ounces of trail mix for $3.92. What is the unit rate?
   Ⓐ $\frac{\$0.14}{1 \text{ ounce}}$ (shaded) Ⓒ $\frac{\$7.14}{1 \text{ ounce}}$
   Ⓑ $\frac{\$3.92}{28 \text{ ounces}}$ Ⓓ $\frac{\$109.76}{28 \text{ ounces}}$

Problem Solving REAL WORLD

5. Sylvio's flight is scheduled to travel 1,792 miles in 3.5 hours. At what average rate will the plane have to travel to complete the trip on time?
   512 miles per hour

6. Rachel bought 2 pounds of apples and 3 pounds of peaches for a total of $10.45. The apples and peaches cost the same amount per pound. What was the unit rate?
   $2.09 per pound

Name ______________________

Lesson 4
COMMON CORE STANDARD CC.6.RP.3a
Lesson Objective: Use a multiplication table to find equivalent ratios.

Equivalent Ratios and Multiplication Tables

To find equivalent ratios, you can use a multiplication table or multiply by a form of 1.

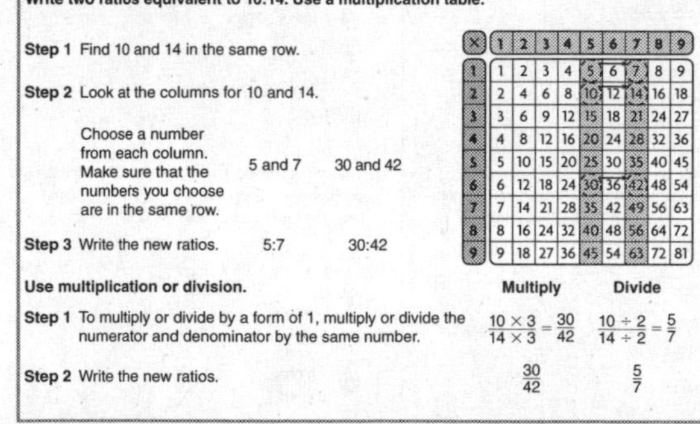

Write two ratios equivalent to 10:14. Use a multiplication table.

Step 1 Find 10 and 14 in the same row.

Step 2 Look at the columns for 10 and 14.
Choose a number from each column. Make sure that the numbers you choose are in the same row. 5 and 7 30 and 42

Step 3 Write the new ratios. 5:7 30:42

×	1	2	3	4	5	6	7	8	9
1	1	2	3	4	5	6	7	8	9
2	2	4	6	8	10	12	14	16	18
3	3	6	9	12	15	18	21	24	27
4	4	8	12	16	20	24	28	32	36
5	5	10	15	20	25	30	35	40	45
6	6	12	18	24	30	36	42	48	54
7	7	14	21	28	35	42	49	56	63
8	8	16	24	32	40	48	56	64	72
9	9	18	27	36	45	54	63	72	81

Use multiplication or division.

Step 1 To multiply or divide by a form of 1, multiply or divide the numerator and denominator by the same number.
Multiply: $\frac{10 \times 3}{14 \times 3} = \frac{30}{42}$ Divide: $\frac{10 \div 2}{14 \div 2} = \frac{5}{7}$

Step 2 Write the new ratios. $\frac{30}{42}$ $\frac{5}{7}$

Solve. Possible answers are given.

1. Write a ratio that is equivalent to 6:16.
   a. Find 6 and 16 in the same row.
   b. Choose a pair of numbers from a different row, in the same columns as 6 and 16. 15 and 40
   c. Write the equivalent ratio. 6:16 = 15:40

×	1	2	3	4	5	6	7	8	9
1	1	2	3	4	5	6	7	8	9
2	2	4	6	8	10	12	14	16	18
3	3	6	9	12	15	18	21	24	27
4	4	8	12	16	20	24	28	32	36
5	5	10	15	20	25	30	35	40	45
6	6	12	18	24	30	36	42	48	54
7	7	14	21	28	35	42	49	56	63
8	8	16	24	32	40	48	56	64	72
9	9	18	27	36	45	54	63	72	81

2. Write two ratios equivalent to $\frac{5}{9}$.
   $\frac{10}{18}, \frac{15}{27}$

3. Write two ratios equivalent to $\frac{8}{6}$.
   $\frac{4}{3}, \frac{16}{12}$

Name ______________________

Lesson 4
CC.6.RP.3a

1. In Natalia's class, there are 10 boys and 14 girls. Which ratio is equivalent to $\frac{10}{14}$?
   Ⓐ $\frac{10}{21}$
   Ⓑ $\frac{5}{7}$ (shaded)
   Ⓒ $\frac{5}{6}$
   Ⓓ $\frac{17}{14}$

2. In Abraham's last basketball game of the season, the ratio of free throws he made to the free throws he attempted was $\frac{12}{18}$. Which is an equivalent ratio?
   Ⓐ $\frac{2}{18}$
   Ⓑ $\frac{6}{12}$
   Ⓒ $\frac{4}{6}$ (shaded)
   Ⓓ $\frac{12}{9}$

3. Of the 24 students in a class, 8 said they have at least two siblings. Which ratio is equivalent to $\frac{8}{24}$?
   Ⓐ $\frac{4}{24}$
   Ⓑ $\frac{6}{24}$
   Ⓒ $\frac{4}{12}$ (shaded)
   Ⓓ $\frac{12}{28}$

4. There are 21 sedans and 12 sports utility vehicles on the lot of a car dealership. Which ratio is equivalent to $\frac{21}{12}$?
   Ⓐ $\frac{7}{4}$ (shaded)
   Ⓑ $\frac{24}{12}$
   Ⓒ $\frac{21}{9}$
   Ⓓ $\frac{7}{2}$

Problem Solving REAL WORLD

5. Tristan uses 7 stars and 9 diamonds to make a design. Write two ratios that are equivalent to $\frac{7}{9}$.
   $\frac{14}{18}, \frac{21}{27}$

6. There are 12 girls and 16 boys in Javier's math class. There are 26 girls and 14 boys in Javier's choir class. Is the ratio of girls to boys in the two classes equivalent? Explain.
   No; the ratio $\frac{26}{14}$ is not equivalent to the ratio $\frac{12}{16}$.

Answer Key

Name ______________

Lesson 5
COMMON CORE STANDARD CC.6.RP.3a
Lesson Objective: Solve problems involving ratios by using the strategy *find a pattern.*

Problem Solving • Use Tables to Compare Ratios

Use tables of equivalent ratios to solve the problem.

Kevin's cookie recipe uses a ratio of 4 parts flour to 2 parts sugar. Anna's recipe uses 5 parts flour to 3 parts sugar. Could their recipes make the same cookies?

Read the Problem	Solve the Problem
What do I need to find? I need to find out if the ratio of flour to sugar in Kevin's recipe is equivalent to the ratio in Anna's recipe	Make a table of equivalent ratios for each recipe.
What information do I need to use? I will use the ratios of flour to sugar	Find an amount of flour that is in both tables. 20
How will I use the information? I will make tables to compare the ratios	Write the ratio for Kevin's recipe. $\frac{20}{10}$ Write the ratio for Anna's recipe. $\frac{20}{12}$ Are the ratios the same? no So, their recipes could not make the same cookies.

Kevin's Recipe					
Flour	4	8	12	16	20
Sugar	2	4	6	8	10

Anna's Recipe					
Flour	5	10	15	20	25
Sugar	3	6	9	12	15

1. Sherona takes a 6-minute break after every 24 minutes of study. Benedict takes an 8-minute break after every 32 minutes of study. Are their ratios of study time to break time equivalent?

   yes

2. Micah buys 10 pens for every 2 pencils. Rachel buys 12 pens for every 3 pencils. Are their ratios of pens to pencils bought equivalent?

   no

Name ______________

Lesson 5
CC.6.RP.3a

1. The table shows the basketball standings for teams in an intramural league.

Basketball Standings

Team	Wins	Losses
Bears	15	10
Stars	12	9
Wildcats	6	5
Knights	8	6

Which basketball teams have equivalent ratios of wins to losses?

Ⓐ Stars and Knights (answer)
Ⓑ Wildcats and Stars
Ⓒ Knights and Wildcats
Ⓓ Bears and Stars

2. The number of comedy and action films that 4 friends have in their DVD collections is recorded in the table.

DVD Collections

Friend	Comedy	Action
Winston	12	5
Chang	10	15
Ricardo	3	11
Shaneka	8	12

Which 2 people have equivalent ratios of comedy films to action films?

Ⓐ Winston and Chang
Ⓑ Winston and Ricardo
Ⓒ Ricardo and Shaneka
Ⓓ Chang and Shaneka (answer)

Problem Solving REAL WORLD

3. Out of the people who called in during a radio station poll, 9 out of 25 chose pop as their favorite type of music, 1 out of 5 callers chose rock, 6 out of 75 callers chose classical, and 18 out of 50 callers chose R&B. Which pair of ratios are equivalent? Explain how you know.

The ratio of callers who chose pop and the ratio of callers who chose R&B; Possible explanation: The ratios for each type of music are $\frac{9}{25}, \frac{1}{5}, \frac{6}{75}$, and $\frac{18}{50}$. Since $\frac{9 \times 2}{25 \times 2} = \frac{18}{50}$, the ratio of callers who chose pop as their favorite type of music and the ratio of callers who chose R&B as their favorite type of music are equivalent.

Name ______________

Lesson 6
COMMON CORE STANDARD CC.6.RP.3a
Lesson Objective: Use tables to solve problems involving equivalent ratios.

Algebra • Use Equivalent Ratios

You can find equivalent ratios by using a table or by multiplying or dividing the numerator and denominator by the same number.

Kate reads 5 chapters in 2 hours. At this rate, how many chapters will she read in 6 hours?

Step 1 Make a table of equivalent ratios.

		5 · 2	5 · 3
Chapters read	5	10	15
Time (hours)	2	4	6
		2 · 2	2 · 3

Step 2 Find 6 hours in the table. Find the number of chapters that goes with 6 hours: 15

Step 3 Write the new ratio: $\frac{15}{6}$

The ratios $\frac{5}{2}$ and $\frac{15}{6}$ are equivalent ratios. So, Kate will read 15 chapters in 6 hours.

Julian runs 10 kilometers in 60 minutes. At this pace, how many kilometers can he run in 30 minutes?

Step 1 Write equivalent ratios with a missing value. $\frac{10}{60} = \frac{■}{30}$

Step 2 Divide the numerator and denominator by 2 to write the ratios using a common denominator. $\frac{10 \div 2}{60 \div 2} = \frac{■}{30}$

The denominators are the same, so the numerators are equal to each other. $\frac{5}{30} = \frac{■}{30} \rightarrow ■ = 5$

So, Julian can run 5 kilometers in 30 minutes.

Use equivalent ratios to find the unknown value.

1. $\frac{4}{5} = \frac{16}{20}$

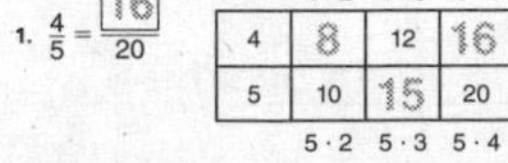

	4 · 2	4 · 3	4 · 4
4	8	12	16
5	10	15	20
	5 · 2	5 · 3	5 · 4

2. $\frac{8}{12} = \frac{2}{3}$

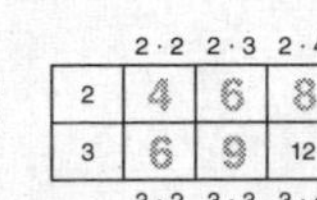

	2 · 2	2 · 3	2 · 4
2	4	6	8
3	6	9	12
	3 · 2	3 · 3	3 · 4

3. $\frac{24}{27} = \frac{8}{9}$

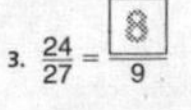

4. $\frac{3}{7} = \frac{9}{21}$

5. $\frac{8}{10} = \frac{4}{5}$

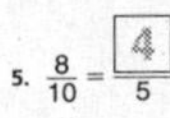

6. $\frac{30}{45} = \frac{6}{9}$

Name ______________

Lesson 6
CC.6.RP.3a

1. Kelsey can make 3 loaves of bread with 7 cups of flour. How many loaves of bread can she make with 21 cups of flour?

Ⓐ 7
Ⓑ 9 (answer)
Ⓒ 63
Ⓓ 147

2. Antonio burns 75 calories for every 15 minutes he rides his bicycle. At that rate, how many calories will Antonio burn if he rides his bicycle for 60 minutes?

Ⓐ 4 calories
Ⓑ 150 calories
Ⓒ 225 calories
Ⓓ 300 calories (answer)

3. Jung-Su reads 35 pages of a novel in 2 hours. At that rate, how many pages will he read in 6 hours?

Ⓐ 70
Ⓑ 105 (answer)
Ⓒ 210
Ⓓ 420

4. Dwayne hikes 60 miles in 3 days. At that rate, how many days does it take him to hike a total of 240 miles?

Ⓐ 12 (answer)
Ⓑ 14
Ⓒ 15
Ⓓ 19

Problem Solving REAL WORLD

5. Honeybees produce 7 pounds of honey for every 1 pound of beeswax they produce. Use equivalent ratios to find how many pounds of honey are produced when 25 pounds of beeswax are produced.

   $\frac{7}{1} = \frac{■}{25}$; 175 pounds of honey

6. A 3-ounce serving of tuna provides 21 grams of protein. Use equivalent ratios to find how many grams of protein are in 9 ounces of tuna.

   $\frac{3}{21} = \frac{9}{■}$; 63 grams of protein

Answer Key

Name ______________________

Lesson 7

COMMON CORE STANDARD CC.6.RP.3a

Lesson Objective: Use a graph to represent equivalent ratios.

Algebra • Equivalent Ratios and Graphs

Jake collects 12 new coins each year. Use equivalent ratios to graph the growth of his coin collection over time.

Step 1 Write an ordered pair for the first year. Let the x-coordinate represent the number of years: 1. Let the y-coordinate represent the number of coins: 12.

Ordered pair: (1, 12)

Step 2 Make a table of equivalent ratios.

Coins	12	24	36	48	60
Year	1	2	3	4	5

Step 3 Write ordered pairs for the values in the table.

(1, 12), (2, 24), (3, 36), (4, 48), (5, 60)

Step 4 Label the x-axis and y-axis.

Step 5 Graph the ordered pairs as points.

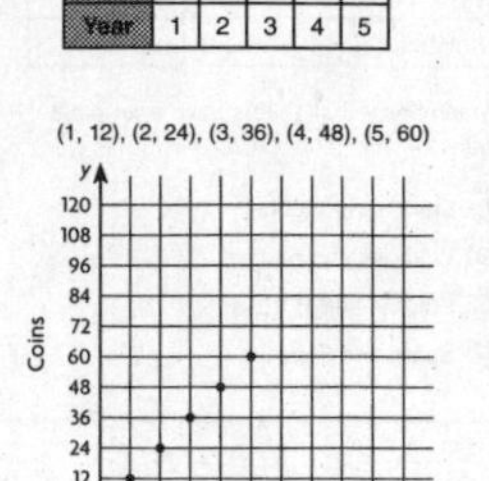

The point (1, 12) represents the year Jake started his collection. It shows that he had 12 coins after 1 year.

Use the graph for 1–5.

1. Helen walks at a rate of 3 miles in 1 hour. Write an ordered pair. Let the y-coordinate represent miles and the x-coordinate represent hours. (1, 3)
2. Complete the table of equivalent ratios.

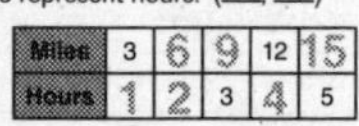

Miles	3	6	9	12	15
Hours	1	2	3	4	5

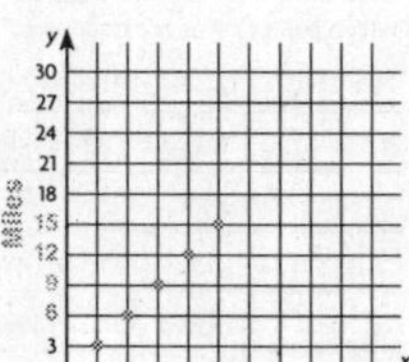

3. Write ordered pairs for the values in the table. (1, 3), (2, 6), (3, 9), (4, 12), (5, 15)
4. Label the graph. Graph the ordered pairs.
5. What does the point (2, 6) represent on the graph?

Helen walks 6 miles in 2 hours.

www.harcourtschoolsupply.com
© Houghton Mifflin Harcourt Publishing Company 13 Core Standards for Math, Grade 6

Name ______________________

Lesson 7

CC.6.RP.3a

1. The graph shows the amount of money Timothy earns from his tutoring job.

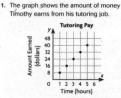

Tutoring Pay (Amount Earned (dollars) vs. Time (hours))

How much does Timothy earn for 4 hours of tutoring?

Ⓐ $32 (marked) Ⓒ $16
Ⓑ $24 Ⓓ $8

2. Shawn takes a trip on a train that travels at a rate of 95 miles per hour. Which set of ordered pairs represents the train's distance over time?

Ⓐ (1, 95), (2, 96), (3, 97), (4, 98)
Ⓑ (1, 95), (1, 190), (1, 285), (1, 380)
Ⓒ (1, 95), (2, 95), (3, 95), (4, 95)
Ⓓ (1, 95), (2, 190), (3, 285), (4, 380) (marked)

3. The graph shows the rate at which a helicopter travels over time.

Helicopter Travel (Distance (miles) vs. Time (hours))

How far does the helicopter travel in 7 hours?

Ⓐ 1,080 miles Ⓒ 143 miles
Ⓑ 945 miles (marked) Ⓓ 135 miles

4. Mrs. Carter is charged $0.50 per minute for international phone calls. Which set of ordered pairs represents the cost of an international phone call for different numbers of minutes?

Ⓐ (1, 0.5), (1, 1), (1, 1.5), (1, 2), (1, 2.5)
Ⓑ (1, 0.5), (3, 1), (5, 1.5), (7, 2), (9, 2.5)
Ⓒ (2, 2), (4, 4), (8, 8), (16, 16), (32, 32)
Ⓓ (1, 0.5), (10, 5), (50, 25), (100, 50) (marked)

Problem Solving REAL WORLD

5. A tree absorbs water at a rate of 140 liters per day. Use a table to list a set of 5 ordered pairs that represents the amount of water absorption of the tree over time. Explain how you know your answer is correct.

Possible answer: (1, 140), (2, 280), (3, 420), (4, 560), and (5, 700). I used the unit rate (140 liters/1 day) to complete a table of equivalent ratios and write ordered pairs: (number of days, liters of water).

Number of Days	1	2	3	4	5
Amount of Water of Absorbed (liters)	140	280	420	560	700

www.harcourtschoolsupply.com
© Houghton Mifflin Harcourt Publishing Company 14 Core Standards for Math, Grade 6

Name ______________________

Lesson 8

COMMON CORE STANDARD CC.6.RP.3b

Lesson Objective: Solve problems using unit rates.

Algebra • Use Unit Rates

You can find equivalent ratios by first finding a unit rate.

Marcia makes bracelets to sell at craft fairs. She sold 14 bracelets for $154. How much could she expect to earn if she sells 25 bracelets?

Step 1 Write equivalent ratios.

$\frac{\text{money}}{\text{bracelets}} \rightarrow \frac{\$154}{14} = \frac{■}{25} \leftarrow \frac{\text{money}}{\text{bracelets}}$

Step 2 Since 25 is not a multiple of 14, use the known ratio to find a unit rate.

$\frac{\$154 \div 14}{14 \div 14} = \frac{■}{25}$

$\frac{\$11}{1} = \frac{■}{25}$

Marcia earns $11 per bracelet.

Step 3 Write an equivalent ratio by multiplying the unit rate's numerator and denominator by the same value. Since $1 \cdot 25 = 25$, multiply by 25 over 25.

$\frac{\$11 \cdot 25}{1 \cdot 25} = \frac{■}{25}$

Step 4 Since the denominators are equal, the numerators are also equal.

$\frac{\$275}{25} = \frac{■}{25}$

So, Marcia would earn $275 if she sells 25 bracelets.

Use a unit rate to find the unknown value.

1. $\frac{120}{20} = \frac{300}{■}$

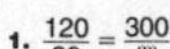

a. Find the unit rate: $\frac{120 \div 20}{20 \div 20} = \frac{300}{■}$

b. $\frac{6}{1} = \frac{300}{■}$

c. $\frac{6 \cdot 50}{1 \cdot 50} = \frac{300}{■}$

d. ■ = 50

2. $\frac{■}{100} = \frac{90}{15}$

■ = 600

3. $\frac{90}{■} = \frac{44}{22}$

■ = 45

4. $\frac{45}{10} = \frac{■}{54}$

■ = 243

www.harcourtschoolsupply.com
© Houghton Mifflin Harcourt Publishing Company 15 Core Standards for Math, Grade 6

Name ______________________

Lesson 8

CC.6.RP.3b

1. If 5 bags of oranges weigh 35 pounds, how many pounds do 2 bags of oranges weigh?

Ⓐ 7 pounds Ⓒ 14 pounds (marked)
Ⓑ 10 pounds Ⓓ 70 pounds

2. The table shows the numbers of calories in 4 ounces of several types of fruit juice.

Calories in 4 Ounces of Juice

Type of Juice	Calories
Apple	60
Grape	76
Orange	56

How many calories are there in 5 ounces of apple juice?

Ⓐ 300 calories Ⓒ 15 calories
Ⓑ 75 calories (marked) Ⓓ 12 calories

3. On a map of Arizona, 2 inches represent 54 miles. The map distance from Yuma to Sentinel is 3 inches. What is the actual distance, in miles, between the cities?

Ⓐ 81 miles (marked)
Ⓑ 45 miles
Ⓒ 27 miles
Ⓓ 9 miles

4. If 7 bags of empty aluminum cans weigh 21 pounds, how many pounds do 15 bags of empty aluminum cans weigh?

Ⓐ 3 pounds
Ⓑ 5 pounds
Ⓒ 45 pounds (marked)
Ⓓ 105 pounds

Problem Solving REAL WORLD

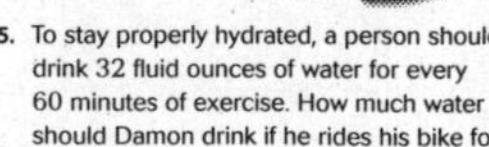

5. To stay properly hydrated, a person should drink 32 fluid ounces of water for every 60 minutes of exercise. How much water should Damon drink if he rides his bike for 135 minutes?

72 fluid ounces

6. Lillianne made 6 out of every 10 baskets she attempted during basketball practice. If she attempted to make 25 baskets, how many did she make?

15 baskets

www.harcourtschoolsupply.com
© Houghton Mifflin Harcourt Publishing Company 16 Core Standards for Math, Grade 6

Answer Key

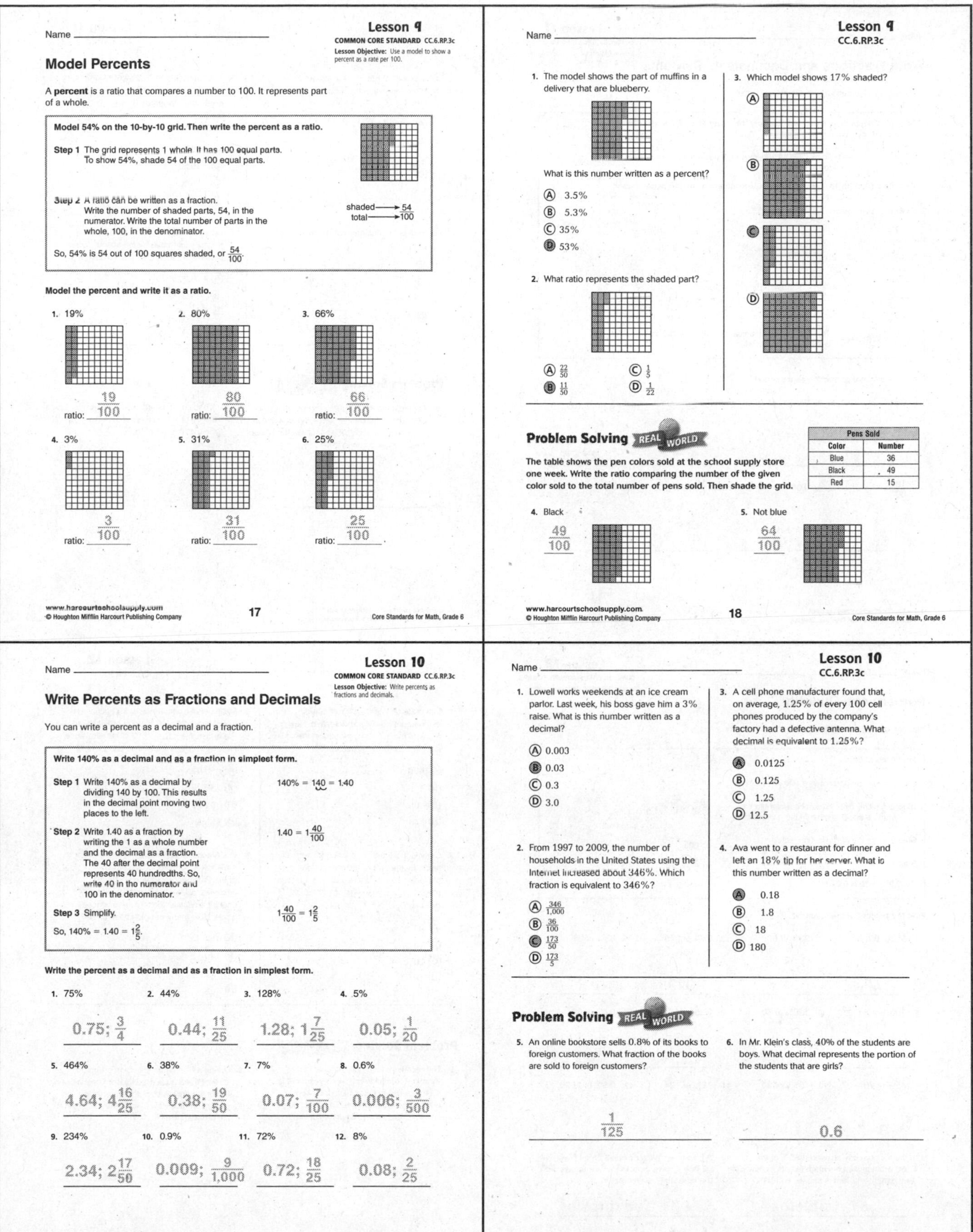

Name ______________________

Lesson 9

COMMON CORE STANDARD CC.6.RP.3c

Lesson Objective: Use a model to show a percent as a rate per 100.

Model Percents

A **percent** is a ratio that compares a number to 100. It represents part of a whole.

Model 54% on the 10-by-10 grid. Then write the percent as a ratio.

Step 1 The grid represents 1 whole. It has 100 equal parts. To show 54%, shade 54 of the 100 equal parts.

Step 2 A ratio can be written as a fraction. Write the number of shaded parts, 54, in the numerator. Write the total number of parts in the whole, 100, in the denominator.

shaded → 54
total → 100

So, 54% is 54 out of 100 squares shaded, or $\frac{54}{100}$.

Model the percent and write it as a ratio.

1. 19% ratio: $\frac{19}{100}$
2. 80% ratio: $\frac{80}{100}$
3. 66% ratio: $\frac{66}{100}$
4. 3% ratio: $\frac{3}{100}$
5. 31% ratio: $\frac{31}{100}$
6. 25% ratio: $\frac{25}{100}$

www.harcourtschoolsupply.com
© Houghton Mifflin Harcourt Publishing Company 17 Core Standards for Math, Grade 6

Name ______________________

Lesson 9

CC.6.RP.3c

1. The model shows the part of muffins in a delivery that are blueberry.

What is this number written as a percent?

Ⓐ 3.5%
Ⓑ 5.3%
Ⓒ 35%
Ⓓ 53% (answer)

2. What ratio represents the shaded part?

Ⓐ $\frac{22}{50}$
Ⓑ $\frac{11}{50}$ (answer)
Ⓒ $\frac{1}{5}$
Ⓓ $\frac{1}{22}$

3. Which model shows 17% shaded?

Ⓐ Ⓑ Ⓒ (answer) Ⓓ

Problem Solving REAL WORLD

The table shows the pen colors sold at the school supply store one week. Write the ratio comparing the number of the given color sold to the total number of pens sold. Then shade the grid.

Pens Sold	
Color	Number
Blue	36
Black	49
Red	15

4. Black $\frac{49}{100}$
5. Not blue $\frac{64}{100}$

www.harcourtschoolsupply.com
© Houghton Mifflin Harcourt Publishing Company 18 Core Standards for Math, Grade 6

Name ______________________

Lesson 10

COMMON CORE STANDARD CC.6.RP.3c

Lesson Objective: Write percents as fractions and decimals.

Write Percents as Fractions and Decimals

You can write a percent as a decimal and a fraction.

Write 140% as a decimal and as a fraction in simplest form.

Step 1 Write 140% as a decimal by dividing 140 by 100. This results in the decimal point moving two places to the left. $140\% = 140 = 1.40$

Step 2 Write 1.40 as a fraction by writing the 1 as a whole number and the decimal as a fraction. The 40 after the decimal point represents 40 hundredths. So, write 40 in the numerator and 100 in the denominator. $1.40 = 1\frac{40}{100}$

Step 3 Simplify. $1\frac{40}{100} = 1\frac{2}{5}$

So, $140\% = 1.40 = 1\frac{2}{5}$.

Write the percent as a decimal and as a fraction in simplest form.

1. 75% $0.75; \frac{3}{4}$
2. 44% $0.44; \frac{11}{25}$
3. 128% $1.28; 1\frac{7}{25}$
4. 5% $0.05; \frac{1}{20}$
5. 464% $4.64; 4\frac{16}{25}$
6. 38% $0.38; \frac{19}{50}$
7. 7% $0.07; \frac{7}{100}$
8. 0.6% $0.006; \frac{3}{500}$
9. 234% $2.34; 2\frac{17}{50}$
10. 0.9% $0.009; \frac{9}{1,000}$
11. 72% $0.72; \frac{18}{25}$
12. 8% $0.08; \frac{2}{25}$

www.harcourtschoolsupply.com
© Houghton Mifflin Harcourt Publishing Company 19 Core Standards for Math, Grade 6

Name ______________________

Lesson 10

CC.6.RP.3c

1. Lowell works weekends at an ice cream parlor. Last week, his boss gave him a 3% raise. What is this number written as a decimal?

Ⓐ 0.003
Ⓑ 0.03 (answer)
Ⓒ 0.3
Ⓓ 3.0

2. From 1997 to 2009, the number of households in the United States using the Internet increased about 346%. Which fraction is equivalent to 346%?

Ⓐ $\frac{346}{1,000}$
Ⓑ $\frac{36}{100}$
Ⓒ $\frac{173}{50}$ (answer)
Ⓓ $\frac{173}{5}$

3. A cell phone manufacturer found that, on average, 1.25% of every 100 cell phones produced by the company's factory had a defective antenna. What decimal is equivalent to 1.25%?

Ⓐ 0.0125 (answer)
Ⓑ 0.125
Ⓒ 1.25
Ⓓ 12.5

4. Ava went to a restaurant for dinner and left an 18% tip for her server. What is this number written as a decimal?

Ⓐ 0.18 (answer)
Ⓑ 1.8
Ⓒ 18
Ⓓ 180

Problem Solving REAL WORLD

5. An online bookstore sells 0.8% of its books to foreign customers. What fraction of the books are sold to foreign customers? $\frac{1}{125}$

6. In Mr. Klein's class, 40% of the students are boys. What decimal represents the portion of the students that are girls? 0.6

www.harcourtschoolsupply.com
© Houghton Mifflin Harcourt Publishing Company 20 Core Standards for Math, Grade 6

Answer Key

Name ______________________

Lesson 11

COMMON CORE STANDARD CC.6.RP.3c

Lesson Objective: Write fractions and decimals as percents.

Write Fractions and Decimals as Percents

You can write fractions and decimals as percents.

To write a decimal as a percent, multiply the decimal by 100 and write the percent symbol.

0.073 = 7.3% ← To multiply by 100, move the decimal point two places to the right.

To write a fraction as a percent, divide the numerator by the denominator. Then write the decimal as a percent.

To write $\frac{3}{8}$ as a percent, first divide 3 by 8.

$$\begin{array}{r} 0.375 \\ 8\overline{)3.000} \\ -24 \\ 60 \\ -56 \\ 40 \\ -40 \\ 0 \end{array}$$

So, $\frac{3}{8}$ = 0.375.

0.375 = 37.5% ← To write 0.375 as a percent, multiply by 100 and write the percent symbol.

Write the decimal or fraction as a percent.

1. 0.45 — 45%
2. 0.6 — 60%
3. 2.34 — 234%
4. $\frac{7}{8}$ — 87.5%
5. $\frac{19}{50}$ — 38%
6. 0.03 — 3%
7. $1\frac{11}{16}$ — 168.75%
8. $\frac{51}{10}$ — 510%

Name ______________________

Lesson 11

CC.6.RP.3c

1. In a litter, 2 out of 8 kittens are male. What percent of the kittens in the litter are female?
   - (A) 25%
   - (B) 28%
   - **(C) 75%**
   - (D) 82%

2. How is the decimal 1.7 expressed as a percent?
   - (A) 0.17%
   - (B) 1.7%
   - (C) 17%
   - **(D) 170%**

3. The Totally Clean Toothpaste Company advertises that $\frac{9}{10}$ of all people surveyed prefer their toothpaste. What percent of the people surveyed prefer Totally Clean Toothpaste?
   - (A) 900%
   - **(B) 90%**
   - (C) 9%
   - (D) 0.9%

4. On Friday, 0.325 of the students in Keisha's math class were absent. What percent of the students were absent?
   - (A) 0.325%
   - (B) 3.25%
   - **(C) 32.5%**
   - (D) 325%

Problem Solving REAL WORLD

5. According to the U.S. Census Bureau, $\frac{3}{25}$ of all adults in the United States visited a zoo in 2007. What percent of all adults in the United States visited a zoo in 2007?

   12%

6. A bag contains red and blue marbles. Given that $\frac{17}{20}$ of the marbles are red, what percent of the marbles are blue?

   15%

Name ______________________

Lesson 12

COMMON CORE STANDARD CC.6.RP.3c

Lesson Objective: Find a percent of a quantity.

Percent of a Quantity

You can use ratios to write a percent of a quantity.

Find 0.9% of 30.

Step 1 Write the percent as a rate per 100. $0.9\% = \frac{0.9}{100}$

Step 2 Multiply by a fraction equivalent to 1 to get a whole number in the numerator. $\frac{0.9}{100} \times \frac{10}{10} = \frac{9}{1{,}000}$

Step 3 Write the multiplication problem. $\frac{9}{1{,}000} \times 30$

Step 4 Multiply. $\frac{9}{1{,}000} \times 30 = \frac{27}{100} = 0.27$

So, 0.9% of 30 is 0.27.

Find the percent of the quantity.

1. 8% of 90 — 7.2
2. 20% of 80 — 16
3. 95% of 340 — 323
4. 33% of 28 — 9.24
5. 200% of 8.5 — 17
6. 125% of 70 — 87.5
7. 0.25% of 120 — 0.3
8. 0.4% of 50 — 0.2
9. 45% of 70 — 31.5
10. 155% of 30 — 46.5
11. 75% of 124 — 93
12. 0.8% of 1,000 — 8

13. James correctly answered 85% of the 60 problems on his math test. How many questions did James answer correctly?

    51 problems

14. A basketball player missed 25% of her 52 free throws. How many free throws did the basketball player make?

    39 free throws

Name ______________________

Lesson 12

CC.6.RP.3c

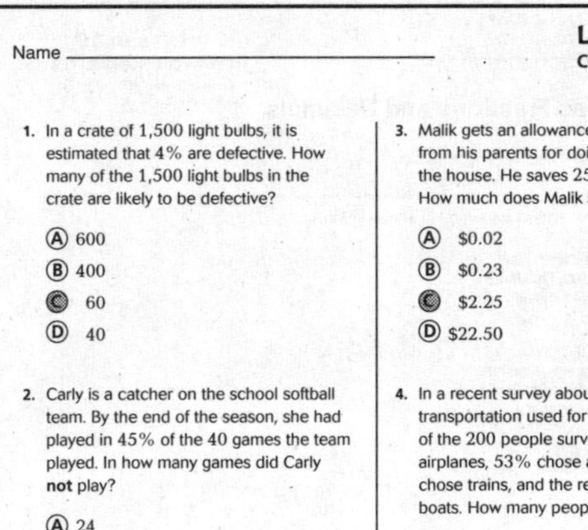

1. In a crate of 1,500 light bulbs, it is estimated that 4% are defective. How many of the 1,500 light bulbs in the crate are likely to be defective?
   - (A) 600
   - (B) 400
   - **(C) 60**
   - (D) 40

2. Carly is a catcher on the school softball team. By the end of the season, she had played in 45% of the 40 games the team played. In how many games did Carly **not** play?
   - (A) 24
   - **(B) 22**
   - (C) 20
   - (D) 18

3. Malik gets an allowance of $9 each week from his parents for doing chores around the house. He saves 25% of his allowance. How much does Malik save each week?
   - (A) $0.02
   - (B) $0.23
   - **(C) $2.25**
   - (D) $22.50

4. In a recent survey about the types of transportation used for vacation, 36% of the 200 people surveyed chose airplanes, 53% chose automobiles, 2% chose trains, and the remainder chose boats. How many people chose boats?
   - (A) 182
   - (B) 140
   - (C) 72
   - **(D) 18**

Problem Solving REAL WORLD

5. The recommended daily amount of vitamin C for children 9 to 13 years old is 45 mg. A serving of a juice drink contains 60% of the recommended amount. How much vitamin C does the juice drink contain?

   27 mg

6. During a 60-minute television program, 25% of the time is used for commercials and 5% of the time is used for the opening and closing credits. How many minutes remain for the program itself?

   42 minutes

Name ______________________

Lesson 13
COMMON CORE STANDARD CC.6.RP.3c
Lesson Objective: Solve percent problems by applying the strategy *use a model.*

Problem Solving • Percents

Use a model to solve the percent problem.

Lucia is driving to visit her parents, who live 240 miles away from her house. She has already driven 15% of the distance. How many miles does she still have to drive?

Read the Problem	Solve the Problem
What do I need to find? I need to find the difference between the total distance and the distance already driven.	Use a bar model to help. Draw a bar to represent the total distance. Then draw a bar that represents the distance driven plus the distance left. 100% total distance 240 miles; distance driven ? 15%
What information do I need to use? The total distance is 240 miles and she has already driven 15% of the total distance.	The model shows that 100% = 240 miles, so 1% of 240 = $\frac{240}{100}$ = 2.4 miles.
How will I use the information? I will draw a model to find the number of miles already driven and subtract that amount from the total distance.	15% of 240 = 15 × 2.4 = 36. So, Lucia has already driven 36 miles. She still has to drive 240 − 36 = 204 miles.

1. At a deli, 56 sandwiches were sold during lunchtime. Twenty-five percent of the sandwiches sold were tuna salad sandwiches. How many of the sandwiches sold were not tuna salad?
   42 sandwiches

2. Mr. Brown bought a TV for $450. He has already paid 60% of the purchase price. How much has he already paid and how much does he have left to pay?
   $270; $180

Name ______________________

Lesson 13
CC.6.RP.3c

1. Ricardo has saved 83% of the money he needs to buy a new skateboard that costs $150. How much **more** does he need to save to buy the skateboard?
   - **(A) $25.50** (shaded)
   - (B) $67
   - (C) $83
   - (D) $124.50

2. Deanna has 80 books in her collection. If 60% of the books are fiction, how many of the books are nonfiction?
   - (A) 60
   - (B) 48
   - **(C) 32** (shaded)
   - (D) 20

3. Michele has visited 30 lighthouses in Virginia and Maryland. Twenty percent of the lighthouses were in Virginia. How many **more** lighthouses did she visit in Maryland than in Virginia?
   - (A) 6
   - **(B) 18** (shaded)
   - (C) 20
   - (D) 24

4. Quincy is using 320 pieces of stone tile to make a red, white, and blue mosaic. If 20% of the pieces are blue and 35% are white, how many pieces are red?
   - (A) 64
   - (B) 112
   - **(C) 144** (shaded)
   - (D) 176

Problem Solving REAL WORLD

5. Of 450 lunches sold at school on Thursday, 40% were hamburgers and the rest were pizza. How many **more** pizza lunches were sold than hamburgers? Explain how you found your answer.
   90; Since 40% of the lunches were hamburgers, 60% were pizza. I found 40% of 450 (180) to find the number of hamburger lunches sold, and 60% of 450 (270) to find the number of pizza lunches sold. Then I subtracted 270 − 180 to find that 90 more pizza lunches were sold.

Name ______________________

Lesson 14
COMMON CORE STANDARD CC.6.RP.3c
Lesson Objective: Find the whole given a part and the percent.

Find the Whole From a Percent

You can use equivalent ratios to find the whole, given a part and the percent.

54 is 60% of what number?

Step 1 Write the relationship among the percent, part, and whole. The percent is 60%. The part is 54. The whole is unknown.
$$\text{percent} = \frac{\text{part}}{\text{whole}} \qquad 60\% = \frac{54}{■}$$

Step 2 Write the percent as a ratio.
$$\frac{60}{100} = \frac{54}{■}$$

Step 3 Simplify the known ratio.

- Find the greatest common factor (GCF) of the numerator and denominator.
  60 = **2** × **2** × 3 × **5**
  100 = **2** × **2** × **5** × 5 → GCF = **2** × **2** × **5** = 20
- Divide both the numerator and denominator by the GCF.
$$\frac{60 \div 20}{100 \div 20} = \frac{54}{■} \qquad \frac{3}{5} = \frac{54}{■}$$

Step 4 Write an equivalent ratio.

- Look at the numerators. *Think:* 3 × 18 = 54
- Multiply the denominator by 18 to find the whole.
$$\frac{3 \times 18}{5 \times 18} = \frac{54}{■}$$

So, 54 is 60% of 90. $\frac{54}{90} = \frac{54}{■}$

Find the unknown value.

1. 12 is 40% of 30
2. 15 is 25% of 60
3. 24 is 20% of 120
4. 36 is 50% of 72
5. 4 is 80% of 5
6. 12 is 15% of 80
7. 36 is 90% of 40
8. 12 is 75% of 16
9. 27 is 30% of 90

Name ______________________

Lesson 14
CC.6.RP.3c

1. 9 is 15% of what number?
   - (A) 24
   - **(B) 60** (shaded)
   - (C) 85
   - (D) 135

2. A train is traveling from Orlando, Florida to Atlanta, Georgia. So far, it has traveled 75% of the distance, or 330 miles. How far is the train ride from Orlando to Atlanta?
   - (A) 247 miles
   - (B) 255 miles
   - (C) 405 miles
   - **(D) 440 miles** (shaded)

3. Carmen has saved 80% of the money she needs to buy a new video game. If she has saved $36, how much does the video game cost?
   - (A) $28.80
   - **(B) $45** (shaded)
   - (C) $63.80
   - (D) $80

4. The sixth graders at Amir's school voted for the location of their class trip. The table shows the results.

Class Trip Votes

Location	Percent
History museum	25%
Art museum	35%
Aquarium	40%

If 126 students voted for going to the art museum, how many sixth graders are at Amir's school?
   - (A) 161
   - (B) 315
   - **(C) 360** (shaded)
   - (D) 504

Problem Solving REAL WORLD

5. Michaela is hiking on a weekend camping trip. She has walked 6 miles so far. This is 30% of the total distance. What is the total number of miles she will walk?
   20 miles

6. A customer placed an order with a bakery for cupcakes. The baker has completed 37.5% of the order after baking 81 cupcakes. How many cupcakes did the customer order?
   216 cupcakes

Name ______

Lesson 15
COMMON CORE STANDARD CC.6.RP.3d
Lesson Objective: Use ratio reasoning to convert from one unit of length to another.

Convert Units of Length

To convert a unit of measure, multiply by a conversion factor. A **conversion factor** is a rate in which the two quantities are equal, but are expressed in different units.

Convert to the given unit. 2,112 ft = ______ mi

Customary Units of Length
1 foot (ft) = 12 inches (in.)
1 yard (yd) = 36 inches
1 yard = 3 feet
1 mile (mi) = 5,280 feet
1 mile = 1,760 yards

Step 1 Choose a conversion factor.

1 mile = 5,280 feet, so use the conversion factor $\frac{1 \text{ mile}}{5{,}280 \text{ feet}}$.

Step 2 Multiply by the conversion factor.

$2{,}112 \text{ ft} \times \frac{1 \text{ mi}}{5{,}280 \text{ ft}} = \frac{2{,}112 \text{ ft}}{1} \times \frac{1 \text{ mi}}{5{,}280 \text{ ft}} = \frac{2{,}112}{5{,}280} \text{ mi} = \frac{2}{5} \text{ mi}$

So, 2,112 ft = $\frac{2}{5}$ mi.

When converting metric units, move the decimal point to multiply or divide by a power of ten.

14 dm = ______ hm

× 10 × 10 × 10 × 10 × 10 × 10

kilo-	hecto-	deka-	meter	deci-	centi-	milli-

÷ 10 ÷ 10 ÷ 10 ÷ 10 ÷ 10 ÷ 10

Step 1 Start at the given unit.

Step 2 Move to the unit you are converting to.

Step 3 Move the decimal point that same number of spaces in the same direction. Fill any empty place-value positions with zeros.

So, 14 dm = 0.014 hm.

Convert to the given unit.

1. 4.5 miles = 7,920 yards
2. 0.8 hectometers = 80,000 millimeters
3. 48 inches = 4 feet
4. 45 centimeters = 0.045 dekameters

Name ______

Lesson 15
CC.6.RP.3d

1. April is making necklaces using beads that are 6 millimeters in diameter. What is the diameter of each bead in centimeters?
   - (A) 0.6 centimeter
   - (B) 0.06 centimeter
   - (C) 0.006 centimeter
   - (D) 0.0006 centimeter

2. Adam's porch is 8 yards long. What is the length of his porch in inches?
   - (A) 24 inches
   - (B) 96 inches
   - (C) 288 inches
   - (D) 384 inches

3. Cho ran a race that was 5 kilometers long. What was the length of the race in meters?
   - (A) 0.005 meter
   - (B) 50 meters
   - (C) 500 meters
   - (D) 5,000 meters

4. The distance from Caleb's house to his school is 1.5 miles. What is the distance in feet?
   - (A) 1,760 feet
   - (B) 2,640 feet
   - (C) 5,280 feet
   - (D) 7,920 feet

Problem Solving REAL WORLD

5. The giant swallowtail is the largest butterfly in the United States. Its wingspan can be as large as 16 centimeters. What is the maximum wingspan in millimeters?

   160 mm

6. The 102nd floor of the Sears Tower in Chicago is the highest occupied floor. It is 1,431 feet above the ground. How many yards above the ground is the 102nd floor?

   477 yd

Name ______

Lesson 16
COMMON CORE STANDARD CC.6.RP.3d
Lesson Objective: Use ratio reasoning to convert from one unit of capacity to another.

Convert Units of Capacity

Capacity is the measure of the amount that a container can hold. When converting customary units, multiply the initial measurement by a conversion factor.

Convert to the given unit. 35 c = ______ qt

Customary Units of Capacity
8 fluid ounces (fl oz) = 1 cup (c)
2 cups = 1 pint (pt)
2 pints = 1 quart (qt)
4 cups = 1 quart
4 quarts = 1 gallon (gal)

Step 1 Choose a conversion factor.

1 quart = 4 cups, so use the conversion factor $\frac{1 \text{ quart}}{4 \text{ cups}}$.

Step 2 Multiply by the conversion factor.

$35 \text{ c} \times \frac{1 \text{ qt}}{4 \text{ c}} = \frac{35 \text{ c}}{1} \times \frac{1 \text{ qt}}{4 \text{ c}} = \frac{35}{4} \text{ qt} = 8\frac{3}{4} \text{ qt}$

You can rename the fractional part using the smaller unit.

$8\frac{3}{4}$ quarts = 8 quarts, 3 cups

So, 35 c = $8\frac{3}{4}$ qt, or 8 qt, 3 c.

When converting metric units, move the decimal point to multiply or divide by a power of ten.

26 cL = ______ hL

× 10 × 10 × 10 × 10 × 10 × 10

kilo-	hecto-	deka-	liter	deci-	centi-	milli-

÷ 10 ÷ 10 ÷ 10 ÷ 10 ÷ 10 ÷ 10

Step 1 Start at the given unit.

Step 2 Move to the unit you are converting to.

Step 3 Move the decimal point that same number of spaces in the same direction. Fill any empty place-value positions with zeros.

So, 26 cL = 0.0026 hL.

Convert to the given unit.

1. 0.72 kiloliters = 7,200 deciliters
2. 78 qt = 19 gal, 2 qt
3. 52 liters = 0.52 hectoliters
4. 5 pints = 10 cups

Name ______

Lesson 16
CC.6.RP.3d

1. Jason made 36 pints of lemonade for the class picnic. How many gallons of lemonade did he make?
   - (A) 9 gallons
   - (B) 6 gallons
   - (C) $4\frac{1}{2}$ gallons
   - (D) $2\frac{1}{2}$ gallons

2. Chandelle filled her bathtub with 15 gallons of water. How many pints of water did she put in the tub?
   - (A) 30 pints
   - (B) 60 pints
   - (C) 90 pints
   - (D) 120 pints

3. Edmund has a pitcher that holds 2 quarts of liquid. How many cups can the pitcher hold?
   - (A) 4 cups
   - (B) 8 cups
   - (C) 16 cups
   - (D) 32 cups

4. Mrs. Ruiz bought **six** 2-liter bottles of juice. How many dekaliters of juice did she buy?
   - (A) 0.012 dekaliter
   - (B) 0.12 dekaliter
   - (C) 1.2 dekaliters
   - (D) 120 dekaliters

Problem Solving REAL WORLD

5. A bottle contains 3.5 liters of water. A second bottle contains 3,750 milliliters of water. How many more milliliters are in the larger bottle than in the smaller bottle?

   250 mL

6. Arnie's car used 100 cups of gasoline during a drive. He paid $3.12 per gallon for gas. How much did the gas cost?

   $19.50

Answer Key

Name ______________________

Lesson 17

COMMON CORE STANDARD CC.6.RP.3d

Lesson Objective: Use ratio reasoning to convert from one unit of weight or mass to another.

Convert Units of Weight and Mass

In the customary system, weight is the measure of the heaviness of an object. When converting customary units, multiply the initial measurement by a conversion factor.

Convert to the given unit. 19 lb = ______ oz

Customary Units of Weight
1 pound (lb) = 16 ounces (oz)
1 ton (T) = 2,000 pounds

Step 1 Choose a conversion factor.

16 ounces = 1 pound, so use the conversion factor $\frac{16 \text{ ounces}}{1 \text{ pound}}$.

Step 2 Multiply by the conversion factor.

$19 \text{ lb} \times \frac{16 \text{ oz}}{1 \text{ lb}} = \frac{19 \cancel{\text{lb}}}{1} \times \frac{16 \text{ oz}}{1 \cancel{\text{lb}}} = \frac{304}{1} \text{ oz} = 304 \text{ oz}$

So, 19 lb = 304 oz.

In the metric system, mass is the measure of the amount of matter in an object. When converting metric units, move the decimal point to multiply or divide by a power of ten.

3.1 dag = ______ mg

× 10	× 10	× 10	× 10	× 10	× 10	
kilo-	hecto-	deka-	gram	deci-	centi-	milli-
÷ 10	÷ 10	÷ 10	÷ 10	÷ 10	÷ 10	

Step 1 Start at the given unit.

Step 2 Move to the unit you are converting to.

Step 3 Move the decimal point that same number of spaces in the same direction. Fill any empty place-value positions with zeros.

So, 3.1 dag = 31,000 mg.

Convert to the given unit.

1. 43.2 dg = 0.0432 hg
2. 4,500 pounds = $2\frac{1}{4}$ tons
3. 3.5 grams = 3,500 milligrams
4. 3 pounds = 48 ounces

Name ______________________

Lesson 17

CC.6.RP.3d

1. Mr. Connell's car weighs 1.5 tons. What is the weight of his car in pounds?
   - Ⓐ 2,000 pounds
   - Ⓑ 2,500 pounds
   - Ⓒ 3,000 pounds (filled)
   - Ⓓ 4,000 pounds
2. How many grams are equivalent to 102 milligrams?
   - Ⓐ 10.2 grams
   - Ⓑ 1.02 grams
   - Ⓒ 0.102 gram (filled)
   - Ⓓ 0.0102 gram
3. Lonnie has a box of cereal with a mass of 347 grams. What is the mass in centigrams?
   - Ⓐ 3.47 centigrams
   - Ⓑ 34.7 centigrams
   - Ⓒ 3,470 centigrams
   - Ⓓ 34,700 centigrams (filled)
4. Li Mei is mailing a package. The package weighs 35 ounces. What is the weight of the package in pounds and ounces?
   - Ⓐ 2 pounds
   - Ⓑ 2 pounds, 3 ounces (filled)
   - Ⓒ 3 pounds, 5 ounces
   - Ⓓ 4 pounds, 3 ounces

Problem Solving REAL WORLD

5. Maggie bought 52 ounces of swordfish selling for $6.92 per pound. What was the total cost?

   $22.49

6. Three bunches of grapes have masses of 1,000 centigrams, 1,000 decigrams, and 1,000 grams, respectively. What is the total combined mass of the grapes in kilograms?

   1.11 kg

Name ______________________

Lesson 18

COMMON CORE STANDARD CC.6.RP.3d

Lesson Objective: Transform units to solve problems.

Transform Units

To solve problems involving different units, use the relationship among units to help you set up a multiplication problem.

Green peppers are on sale for $1.80 per pound. How much would 2.5 pounds of green peppers cost?

Step 1 Identify the units.

You know two quantities: pounds of peppers and total cost per pound. You want to know the cost of 2.5 pounds.

$1.80 per lb = $\frac{\$1.80}{1 \text{ lb}}$

Step 2 Determine the relationship among the units.

The answer needs to be in dollars. Set up the multiplication problem so that pounds will divide out.

$\frac{\$1.80}{1 \text{ lb}} \times 2.5 \text{ lb} = \frac{\$1.80}{1 \cancel{\text{lb}}} \times \frac{2.5 \cancel{\text{lb}}}{1} = \$4.50$

Step 3 Use the relationship.

So, 2.5 pounds of peppers will cost $4.50.

Solve.

1. If 2 bags of cherries cost $5.50, how much do 7 bags cost?
   a. What are you trying to find? cost of 7 bags
   b. Set up the problem. $\frac{\$5.50}{2 \text{ bags}} \times \frac{7 \text{ bags}}{1}$
   c. What is the cost of 7 bags? $19.25
2. The area of a living room is 24 square yards. If the width is 12 feet, what is the length of the living room in yards?
   a. What is the width in yards? $12 \text{ ft} \times \frac{1 \text{ yd}}{3 \text{ ft}} = 4 \text{ yd}$
   b. Set up the problem. $\frac{24 \text{ yd} \times \text{yd}}{4 \text{ yd}}$
   c. What is the length in yards? 6 yd

Name ______________________

Lesson 18

CC.6.RP.3d

1. Sofia knitted a rectangular afghan that has an area of 24 square feet. If the length of the afghan is 2 yards, what is the width in feet?
   - Ⓐ 12 feet
   - Ⓑ 8 feet
   - Ⓒ 6 feet
   - Ⓓ 4 feet (filled)
2. A house painter uses 6 gallons of paint per day. How many gallons does the painter use in a 5-day workweek?
   - Ⓐ 11 gallons
   - Ⓑ 16 gallons
   - Ⓒ 24 gallons
   - Ⓓ 30 gallons (filled)
3. A rectangular football field, including both end zones, is 120 yards long. The field has an area of 57,600 square feet. What is the width of the field in feet?
   - Ⓐ 480 feet
   - Ⓑ 360 feet
   - Ⓒ 160 feet (filled)
   - Ⓓ 53 feet
4. Lucy's car gets 32 miles per gallon of gasoline. How many miles can she drive on 4 gallons of gas?
   - Ⓐ 256 miles
   - Ⓑ 128 miles (filled)
   - Ⓒ 24 miles
   - Ⓓ 8 miles

Problem Solving REAL WORLD

5. Green grapes are on sale for $2.50 a pound. How much will 9 pounds cost?

   $22.50

6. A car travels 32 miles for each gallon of gas. How many gallons of gas does it need to travel 192 miles?

   6 gal

Answer Key

Name ________________

Lesson 19
COMMON CORE STANDARD CC.6.RP.3d
Lesson Objective: Solve problems involving distance, rate, and time by applying the strategy *use a formula.*

Problem Solving • Distance, Rate, and Time Formulas

Use a formula to solve the problem.

A bug crawls at a rate of 2 feet per minute. How long will it take the bug to crawl 25 feet?

Read the Problem	Solve the Problem
What do I need to find? I need to find the amount of time it will take the bug to crawl 25 feet	Write the appropriate formula. $t = d \div r$
What information do I need to use? I need to use the distance the bug crawls and the rate at which the bug crawls.	Substitute the values for *d* and *r*. $t = 25 \text{ ft} \div \frac{2 \text{ ft}}{1 \text{ min}}$
How will I use the information? First I will choose the formula $t = d \div r$ because I need to find time. Next I will substitute 25 ft for *d* and $\frac{25 \text{ ft}}{1 \text{ min}}$ for *r*. Then I will divide to find the time.	Rewrite the division as multiplication by the reciprocal. $t = \frac{25 \text{ ft}}{1} \times \frac{1 \text{ min}}{2 \text{ ft}} = 12.5$ min

1. A family drives for 3 hours at an average rate of 57 miles per hour. How far does the family travel?

171 miles

2. A train traveled 283.5 miles in 3.5 hours. What was the train's average rate of speed?

81 miles per hour

Name ________________

Lesson 19
CC.6.RP.3d

1. Sunni is riding a raft down a stream that is moving at a rate of 75 feet per minute. How far downstream does she travel in 5 minutes?

Ⓐ 750 feet
Ⓑ 375 feet (filled)
Ⓒ 225 feet
Ⓓ 15 feet

2. A sprinting cheetah covered a distance of 518 meters in 18.5 seconds. How fast was the cheetah running?

Ⓐ 30 meters per second
Ⓑ 28 meters per second (filled)
Ⓒ 25 meters per second
Ⓓ 22 meters per second

3. Tamika drove $142\frac{1}{2}$ miles at a rate of 57 miles per hour. For how long was Tamika driving?

Ⓐ 1 hour
Ⓑ $1\frac{1}{2}$ hours
Ⓒ 2 hours
Ⓓ $2\frac{1}{2}$ hours (filled)

4. The table shows data from four cyclists during a training session.

Training Session

Cyclist	Distance (in miles)	Start Time	End Time
Alisha	$35\frac{3}{4}$	2:30 P.M.	5:15 P.M.
Jose	$38\frac{1}{4}$	1:30 P.M.	4:30 P.M.
Raul	$31\frac{1}{4}$	1:50 P.M.	4:20 P.M.
Ruthie	$21\frac{3}{4}$	4:45 P.M.	6:15 P.M.

How fast did Raul travel in miles per hour?

Ⓐ $12\frac{1}{2}$ miles per hour (filled)
Ⓑ $12\frac{3}{4}$ miles per hour
Ⓒ 13 miles per hour
Ⓓ $14\frac{1}{2}$ miles per hour

Problem Solving REAL WORLD

5. The table shows data from a school exercise program. If Malinda jogs at the target rate, how far will she travel? Explain how you know.

Exercise Program Information

Type	Target Rate (kilometers per hour)	Start Time	End Time
Walking	3.5	8:30 A.M.	10:00 A.M.
Jogging	8.5	7:15 A.M.	8:30 A.M.
Biking	19.5	11:50 A.M.	2:05 P.M.

10.625 kilometers; First, I found the elapsed time from 7:15 to 8:30, which is 1.25 hours. I know the rate and the time, so I needed to use the formula $d = r \times t$. I substituted the values for the rate (8.5 km/h) and time (1.25 h) into the formula, to find that $d = 10.625$ km.

Name ________________

Lesson 20
COMMON CORE STANDARD CC.6.NS.1
Lesson Objective: Use a model to show division of fractions.

Model Fraction Division

Use fraction strips to find $\frac{1}{2} \div 3$.

Step 1 $\frac{1}{2} \div 3$ can mean divide $\frac{1}{2}$ into 3 equal parts and find how much is in each part. Find a fraction strip such that 3 of that strip make the same length as a single $\frac{1}{2}$-strip.

Step 2 There are three $\frac{1}{6}$-strips in $\frac{1}{2}$, so $\frac{1}{2} \div 3 = \frac{1}{6}$.

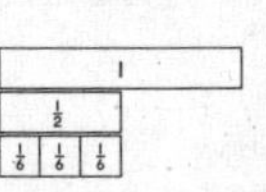

Use the model to find the quotient.

1. $\frac{2}{3} \div 6 = \frac{1}{9}$

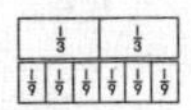

2. $\frac{1}{4} \div 2 = \frac{1}{8}$

Draw a model with fraction strips. Then find the quotient.

3. $\frac{3}{4} \div 6$

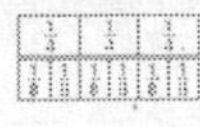

$\frac{3}{4} \div 6 = \frac{1}{8}$

4. $\frac{2}{3} \div 4$

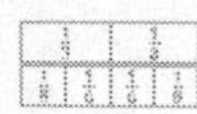

$\frac{2}{3} \div 4 = \frac{1}{6}$

Name ________________

Lesson 20
CC.6.NS.1

1. Monique made $\frac{5}{8}$ pound of trail mix and divided the mix into 4 equal portions. What is the weight of each portion?

Ⓐ $\frac{1}{8}$ pound
Ⓑ $\frac{5}{32}$ pound (filled)
Ⓒ $1\frac{1}{4}$ pounds
Ⓓ $2\frac{1}{2}$ pounds

2. Sung Lee studied for 4 hours. If he studies $\frac{2}{3}$ of an hour for each class, how many classes does he have?

Ⓐ 2
Ⓑ 3
Ⓒ 6 (filled)
Ⓓ 8

3. Joanne has $\frac{9}{10}$ yard of fabric that she wants to divide into 3 equal pieces. How long should each piece be?

Ⓐ $\frac{3}{10}$ yard (filled)
Ⓑ $\frac{10}{27}$ yard
Ⓒ $\frac{3}{5}$ yard
Ⓓ $\frac{10}{13}$ yard

4. Jayson takes a total of 5 hours of swimming lessons per week. If each lesson is $\frac{5}{6}$ of an hour, how many lessons does he take per week?

Ⓐ 5
Ⓑ 6 (filled)
Ⓒ 10
Ⓓ 11

Problem Solving REAL WORLD

5. Mrs. Jennings has $\frac{3}{4}$ gallon of paint for an art project. She plans to divide the paint equally into jars. If she puts $\frac{1}{8}$ gallon of paint into each jar, how many jars will she use?

6

6. If one jar of glue weighs $\frac{1}{12}$ pound, how many jars can Rickie get from $\frac{2}{3}$ pound of glue?

8

Name ____________

Lesson 21
COMMON CORE STANDARD CC.6.NS.1
Lesson Objective: Use compatible numbers to estimate quotients of fractions and mixed numbers.

Estimate Quotients

You can use compatible numbers to help you estimate the quotient of fractions and mixed numbers.

Example 1: Estimate $19\frac{5}{7} \div 3\frac{4}{5}$ using compatible numbers.

Step 1 Find whole numbers that are close to $19\frac{5}{7}$ and $3\frac{4}{5}$ that are easy to divide mentally.

Think: $19\frac{5}{7}$ is close to 20, and $3\frac{4}{5}$ is close to 4.

Step 2 Rewrite the problem and then divide: $20 \div 4 = 5$

So, the estimated quotient is 5.

Example 2: Estimate $6\frac{1}{5} \div \frac{3}{8}$ using compatible numbers.

Step 1 Rewrite the problem using compatible numbers. $6 \div \frac{1}{2}$

Step 2 Divide. Think: How many halves are in 6 wholes? 12

So, the estimated quotient is 12.

Estimate using compatible numbers.

1. $8\frac{1}{6} \div 1\frac{7}{8}$
   a. Rewrite the problem using compatible numbers. $8 \div 2$
   b. What is the estimated quotient? 4

2. $11\frac{7}{9} \div \frac{4}{10}$
   a. Rewrite the problem using compatible numbers. $12 \div \frac{1}{2}$
   b. What is the estimated quotient? 24

Name ____________

Lesson 21
CC.6.NS.1

1. Shing estimates that it takes him $\frac{4}{5}$ hour to mow a yard. Which is the **best** estimate of the number of yards he can mow in $4\frac{1}{4}$ hours?
   (A) 8
   (B) 6
   (C) 4 ●
   (D) 3

2. Melinda has $24\frac{1}{3}$ feet of rope to cut into jump ropes that are each $8\frac{1}{6}$ feet long. Which is the **best** estimate of the number of jump ropes she can cut?
   (A) 3 ●
   (B) 5
   (C) 10
   (D) 16

3. A car travels $83\frac{7}{10}$ miles on $2\frac{1}{4}$ gallons of fuel. Which is the **best** estimate of the number of miles the car travels on one gallon of fuel?
   (A) 38 miles
   (B) 42 miles ●
   (C) 62 miles
   (D) 84 miles

4. Rama has $14\frac{4}{5}$ pounds of birdseed to fill bird feeders. Each feeder holds $2\frac{7}{8}$ pounds of birdseed. About how many bird feeders can she fill?
   (A) 3
   (B) 4
   (C) 5 ●
   (D) 6

Problem Solving REAL WORLD

5. Estimate the number of pieces Sharon will have if she divides $15\frac{1}{3}$ yards of fabric into $4\frac{4}{5}$-yard lengths.
   about 3

6. Estimate the number of $\frac{1}{2}$-quart containers Ethan can fill from a container with $8\frac{7}{8}$ quarts of water.
   about 18

Name ____________

Lesson 22
COMMON CORE STANDARD CC.6.NS.1
Lesson Objective: Divide fractions.

Divide Fractions

You can multiply by reciprocals to divide fractions.

Write the reciprocal of $\frac{1}{7}$.

To find the reciprocal of a number, switch the numerator and the denominator. $\frac{1}{7} \to \frac{7}{1}$

Since $\frac{1}{7} \times \frac{7}{1} = 1$, the reciprocal of $\frac{1}{7}$ is $\frac{7}{1}$.

Find the quotient of $\frac{4}{5} \div \frac{1}{4}$. Write it in simplest form.

Step 1 Find the reciprocal of the second fraction. Think: $\frac{1}{4} \times \frac{4}{1} = 1$. The reciprocal of $\frac{1}{4}$ is $\frac{4}{1}$.

Step 2 Write a multiplication problem using the reciprocal of the second fraction. $\frac{4}{5} \div \frac{1}{4} = \frac{4}{5} \times \frac{4}{1}$

Step 3 Multiply. $\frac{4}{5} \times \frac{4}{1} = \frac{16}{5}$

Step 4 Simplify. $\frac{16}{5} = 3\frac{1}{5}$

So, $\frac{4}{5} \div \frac{1}{4} = 3\frac{1}{5}$.

Find the quotient. Write it in simplest form.

1. $\frac{5}{6} \div \frac{2}{3}$ — $1\frac{1}{4}$
2. $\frac{3}{8} \div \frac{1}{6}$ — $2\frac{1}{4}$
3. $\frac{2}{3} \div \frac{1}{2}$ — $1\frac{1}{3}$
4. $6 \div \frac{2}{3}$ — 9
5. $12 \div \frac{3}{4}$ — 16
6. $\frac{5}{8} \div \frac{1}{2}$ — $1\frac{1}{4}$
7. $\frac{7}{10} \div \frac{2}{5}$ — $1\frac{3}{4}$
8. $\frac{5}{6} \div \frac{1}{6}$ — 5

Name ____________

Lesson 22
CC.6.NS.1

1. Rupali has a piece of string that is $\frac{5}{8}$ yard long. She wants to cut the string into 4 equal pieces. How long should each piece be?
   (A) $\frac{2}{5}$ yard
   (B) $\frac{5}{32}$ yard ●
   (C) $\frac{1}{8}$ yard
   (D) $\frac{9}{12}$ yard

2. Anna has $\frac{4}{5}$ pound of cookies. She places the cookies into bags that hold $\frac{1}{10}$ pound each. How many bags does she fill?
   (A) 2
   (B) 3
   (C) 8 ●
   (D) 12

3. Robert bought $\frac{3}{4}$ pound of grapes and divided them into 6 equal portions. What is the weight of each portion?
   (A) 8 pounds
   (B) $4\frac{1}{2}$ pounds
   (C) $\frac{2}{5}$ pound
   (D) $\frac{1}{8}$ pound ●

4. Mrs. Ruiz has $\frac{11}{12}$ yard of string to hang 3 banners. She uses the same length of string to hang each banner. How much string does she use for each banner?
   (A) $\frac{11}{12}$ yard
   (B) $\frac{6}{11}$ yard
   (C) $\frac{4}{11}$ yard
   (D) $\frac{11}{36}$ yard ●

Problem Solving REAL WORLD

5. Rick knows that 1 cup of glue weighs $\frac{1}{16}$ pound. He has $\frac{3}{4}$ pound of glue. How many cups of glue does he have?
   12 cups

6. Mrs. Jennings had $\frac{5}{7}$ gallon of paint. She gave $\frac{1}{7}$ gallon each to some students. How many students received paint if Mrs. Jennings gave away all the paint?
   5 students

Answer Key

Name ______________________

Lesson 23

COMMON CORE STANDARD CC.6.NS.1

Lesson Objective: Use a model to show division of mixed numbers.

Model Mixed Number Division

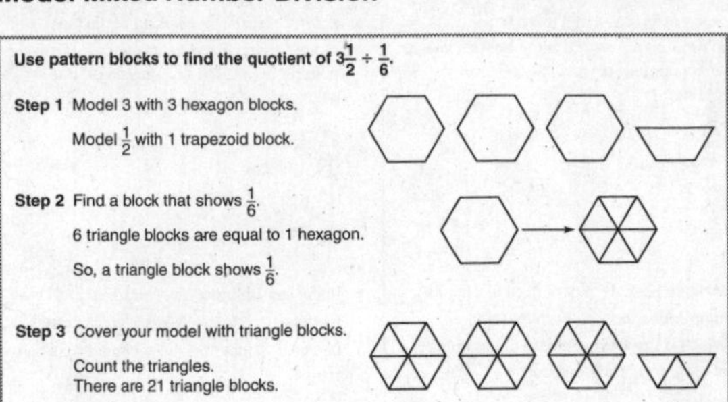

Use pattern blocks to find the quotient of $3\frac{1}{2} \div \frac{1}{6}$.

Step 1 Model 3 with 3 hexagon blocks.
Model $\frac{1}{2}$ with 1 trapezoid block.

Step 2 Find a block that shows $\frac{1}{6}$.
6 triangle blocks are equal to 1 hexagon.
So, a triangle block shows $\frac{1}{6}$.

Step 3 Cover your model with triangle blocks.
Count the triangles.
There are 21 triangle blocks.

So, $3\frac{1}{2} \div \frac{1}{6} = 21$.

Use the model to find the quotient.

1. $2\frac{1}{3} \div \frac{1}{6} =$ 14
2. $2\frac{1}{2} \div \frac{1}{2} =$ 5

Use pattern blocks to find the quotient. Then draw the model.

3. $1\frac{1}{2} \div \frac{1}{6} =$ 9
4. $1\frac{2}{3} \div \frac{1}{3} =$ 5

Name ______________________

Lesson 23

CC.6.NS.1

1. A box of energy bars contains 8 bars. The total weight of the bars is $10\frac{2}{3}$ ounces. If each bar has the same weight, what is the weight of one bar?
   - **Ⓐ $1\frac{1}{3}$ ounces**
   - Ⓑ $1\frac{2}{3}$ ounces
   - Ⓒ $2\frac{2}{3}$ ounces
   - Ⓓ $6\frac{2}{3}$ ounces

2. City workers are repaving a street that is $1\frac{1}{2}$ miles long. If they repave $\frac{1}{4}$ mile per day, how long will it take to repave the entire street?
   - **Ⓐ 6 days**
   - Ⓑ 4 days
   - Ⓒ 3 days
   - Ⓓ 2 days

3. Mr. Spencer has $7\frac{1}{5}$ liters of juice. He wants to pour equal amounts of juice into 3 punch bowls. How many liters of juice should he pour into each bowl?
   - Ⓐ $1\frac{4}{5}$ liters
   - **Ⓑ $2\frac{2}{5}$ liters**
   - Ⓒ $2\frac{4}{5}$ liters
   - Ⓓ $3\frac{1}{5}$ liters

4. Clemente has $5\frac{1}{3}$ yards of wood to construct shelves. He will use a $\frac{2}{3}$-yard piece of wood for each shelf. How many shelves can he make?
   - Ⓐ 12
   - Ⓑ 10
   - **Ⓒ 8**
   - Ⓓ 6

Problem Solving

5. Marty has $2\frac{4}{5}$ quarts of juice. He pours the same amount of juice into 2 bottles. How much does he pour into each bottle?

   $1\frac{2}{5}$ quarts

6. How many $\frac{1}{3}$-pound servings are in $4\frac{2}{3}$ pounds of cheese?

   14

Name ______________________

Lesson 24

COMMON CORE STANDARD CC.6.NS.1

Lesson Objective: Divide mixed numbers.

Divide Mixed Numbers

To divide mixed numbers, first rewrite the mixed numbers as fractions greater than 1. Then multiply the dividend by the reciprocal of the divisor.

Find the quotient of $7\frac{1}{2} \div 2\frac{1}{2}$. Write it in simplest form.

Step 1 Write the mixed numbers as fractions. $7\frac{1}{2} \div 2\frac{1}{2} = \frac{15}{2} \div \frac{5}{2}$

Step 2 Use the reciprocal of the divisor to write a multiplication problem. $= \frac{15}{2} \times \frac{2}{5}$

Step 3 Simplify. Look for common factors in the numerators and denominators. Divide out the common factors. $= \frac{\cancel{15}^{3}}{\cancel{2}_{1}} \times \frac{\cancel{2}^{1}}{\cancel{5}_{1}}$

Step 4 Multiply and simplify the product. $= \frac{3}{1} = 3$

So, $7\frac{1}{2} \div 2\frac{1}{2} = 3$.

Find the quotient. Write it in simplest form.

1. $\frac{3}{4} \div 1\frac{1}{2}$ — $\frac{1}{2}$
2. $4\frac{1}{2} \div 1\frac{3}{4}$ — $2\frac{4}{7}$
3. $8 \div 2\frac{3}{4}$ — $2\frac{10}{11}$
4. $5\frac{5}{8} \div 1\frac{1}{2}$ — $3\frac{3}{4}$
5. $2\frac{5}{8} \div \frac{5}{6}$ — $3\frac{3}{20}$
6. $\frac{4}{7} \div 1\frac{2}{3}$ — $\frac{12}{35}$
7. $4\frac{7}{10} \div \frac{4}{5}$ — $5\frac{7}{8}$
8. $4\frac{2}{5} \div \frac{8}{15}$ — $8\frac{1}{4}$
9. $24 \div 2\frac{2}{3}$ — 9
10. $8\frac{3}{4} \div 2\frac{1}{3}$ — $3\frac{3}{4}$
11. $3\frac{7}{8} \div 4$ — $\frac{31}{32}$
12. $2\frac{5}{8} \div 3\frac{1}{2}$ — $\frac{3}{4}$

Name ______________________

Lesson 24

CC.6.NS.1

1. Yoon Ki drove from Phoenix to Tucson in $1\frac{1}{2}$ hours. Then she drove from Tucson to El Paso in $4\frac{3}{4}$ hours. The second part of her trip was how many times as long as the first part?
   - Ⓐ $7\frac{1}{8}$
   - Ⓑ $6\frac{1}{4}$
   - Ⓒ $3\frac{1}{4}$
   - **Ⓓ $3\frac{1}{6}$**

2. Tina wants to run $12\frac{3}{5}$ miles over 7 days. She wants to run the same distance each day. How far must she run each day?
   - **Ⓐ $1\frac{4}{5}$ miles**
   - Ⓑ $5\frac{3}{5}$ miles
   - Ⓒ $12\frac{16}{35}$ miles
   - Ⓓ $19\frac{3}{5}$ miles

3. A bookstore packs 6 books in a box. The total weight of the books is $14\frac{1}{4}$ pounds. If each book has the same weight, what is the weight of one book?
   - Ⓐ $\frac{5}{8}$ pound
   - **Ⓑ $2\frac{3}{8}$ pounds**
   - Ⓒ $8\frac{1}{4}$ pounds
   - Ⓓ $85\frac{1}{2}$ pounds

4. Pela has $5\frac{3}{4}$ feet of string to make necklaces. She wants to make 4 necklaces that are the same length. How long should each necklace be?
   - Ⓐ $1\frac{1}{4}$ feet
   - **Ⓑ $1\frac{7}{16}$ feet**
   - Ⓒ $1\frac{3}{4}$ feet
   - Ⓓ $1\frac{15}{16}$ feet

Problem Solving

REAL WORLD

5. It takes Nim $2\frac{2}{3}$ hours to weave a basket. He worked Monday through Friday, 8 hours a day. How many baskets did he make?

   15

6. A tree grows $1\frac{3}{4}$ feet per year. How long will it take the tree to grow from a height of $21\frac{1}{4}$ feet to a height of 37 feet?

   9 years

Answer Key

Name ____________________

Lesson 25

COMMON CORE STANDARD CC.6.NS.1

Lesson Objective: Solve problems with fractions and mixed numbers by applying the strategy *use a model.*

Problem Solving • Fraction Operations

Draw a model to solve the problem.

Naomi cuts a $\frac{3}{4}$-foot paper roll into sections, each $\frac{1}{16}$ foot long. If she discards $\frac{1}{8}$ foot of the roll, how many sections does she still have?

Read the Problem	Solve the Problem
What do I need to find? The number of sections Naomi has	Draw a model to solve the problem.
What information do I need to use? Naomi starts with a $\frac{3}{4}$-foot paper roll. Each section is $\frac{1}{16}$ foot. She discards $\frac{1}{8}$ foot.	Show $\frac{3}{4}$. Divide $\frac{3}{4}$ into eighths. She discarded $\frac{1}{8}$, so cross out 1 eighth. $\frac{3}{4} - \frac{1}{8} = \frac{5}{8}$
How will I use the information? I will draw a model to find how many sections Naomi has	Divide $\frac{5}{8}$ into sixteenths. There are 10 sixteenths in $\frac{5}{8}$, so she has 10 sections left.

1. Jeff has $\frac{2}{3}$ gallon of sherbet. He gives each of his friends one $\frac{1}{12}$-gallon scoop. There is $\frac{1}{6}$ gallon left in the carton. How many friends got sherbet?

   6 friends

2. A branch measuring $8\frac{7}{8}$ feet was cut from a tree. Crystal made $2\frac{3}{16}$ feet walking sticks from the branch. She discarded $\frac{1}{8}$ foot of the branch. How many walking sticks did she make from the branch?

   4 walking sticks

Name ____________________

Lesson 25

CC.6.NS.1

1. Marianna divided 16 yards of fabric into $3\frac{1}{3}$-yard pieces. She has $2\frac{2}{3}$ yards of fabric left over. How many $3\frac{1}{3}$-yard pieces did Marianna make?

   Ⓐ 51
   Ⓑ 10
   Ⓒ 4
   Ⓓ 3

2. There were $12\frac{3}{4}$ cups of orange juice in a carton. Each day, Alberto drank $1\frac{1}{4}$ cups of orange juice. Today, there is $\frac{1}{4}$ cup of orange juice left. For how many days has Alberto drunk orange juice?

   Ⓐ 20
   Ⓑ 16
   Ⓒ 11
   Ⓓ 10

3. Gordon had $5\frac{5}{8}$ cups of milk. He used $\frac{3}{4}$ cup of milk for each batch of biscuits he made. After making biscuits, he had $\frac{3}{8}$ cup of milk left over. How many batches of biscuits did Gordon make?

   Ⓐ 4
   Ⓑ 5
   Ⓒ 6
   Ⓓ 7

4. It will take Mr. Warner $15\frac{1}{2}$ hours to install a fence. Each day, he works $1\frac{1}{3}$ hours on the fence. After he finished working on the fence yesterday, he had $3\frac{1}{2}$ hours of work left to do. For how many days has Mr. Warner worked on the fence?

   Ⓐ 4
   Ⓑ 9
   Ⓒ 14
   Ⓓ 15

Problem Solving REAL WORLD

5. A concession stand sells ice cream in large ice cream cones, placing $\frac{1}{16}$ gallon in each cone. One day, the stand has $\frac{3}{4}$ gallon of vanilla ice cream. At the end of the day, there is $\frac{3}{16}$ gallon of vanilla remaining. How many people ordered vanilla ice cream cones that day? Explain how you know.

   9 people; Possible explantion: I used bar models to help find the answer. I made one model to show the amount of vanilla ice cream to start, $\frac{3}{4}$ gallon. Then I made another model to show that there is $\frac{3}{16}$ gallon remaining, and counted the number of sixteenths in $\frac{3}{4} - \frac{3}{16} = \frac{9}{16}$ to find that 9 people ordered vanilla ice cream.

Name ____________________

Lesson 26

COMMON CORE STANDARD CC.6.NS.2

Lesson Objective: Fluently divide multi-digit numbers.

Divide Multi-Digit Numbers

When you divide multi-digit whole numbers, you can estimate to check if the quotient is reasonable.

Divide 399 ÷ 42.

Step 1 Estimate, using compatible numbers. 400 and 40 are compatible numbers because 40 divides evenly into 400.	$400 \div 40 = 10$
Step 2 Divide the original numbers.	$42\overline{)399}$ = 9 r21; -378; 21
Step 3 You can write the remainder as a fraction. Use the remainder for the numerator, and the divisor for the denominator. Simplify if possible.	$\frac{21 \div 21}{42 \div 21} = \frac{1}{2}$; $399 \div 42 = 9\frac{1}{2}$
Step 4 Compare the quotient with your estimate.	Since $9\frac{1}{2}$ is close to 10, the quotient is reasonable.

Estimate. Then find the quotient. Write the remainder, if any, with an r.

Possible estimates are given.

1. $17\overline{)965}$ — 50; 56 r13
2. $29\overline{)4,380}$ — 150; 151 r1
3. $62\overline{)1,178}$ — 20; 19

Estimate. Then find the quotient. Write the remainder, if any, as a fraction.

Possible estimates are given.

4. $836 \div 32$ — 30; $26\frac{1}{8}$
5. $1,392 \div 18$ — 70; $77\frac{1}{3}$
6. $2,518 \div 48$ — 50; $52\frac{11}{24}$

Name ____________________

Lesson 26

CC.6.NS.2

1. A total of 3,570 people attended 14 performances of a play. The same number of tickets were sold for each performance. How many tickets were sold for each performance?

   Ⓐ 255
   Ⓑ 266
   Ⓒ 277
   Ⓓ 288

2. Melba saved $13,992 over an 11-year period. She saved the same amount each year. How much did she save each year?

   Ⓐ $1,400
   Ⓑ $1,399
   Ⓒ $1,300
   Ⓓ $1,272

3. Tabitha's parents deposited a total amount of $7,920 into her college fund during a 36-month period. They deposited the same amount each month. What was their monthly contribution to Tabitha's college fund?

   Ⓐ $200
   Ⓑ $217
   Ⓒ $220
   Ⓓ $264

4. Factory workers packaged 2,128 books into 19 cartons. Each carton contains the same number of books. How many books are in each carton?

   Ⓐ 100
   Ⓑ 112
   Ⓒ 124
   Ⓓ 136

Problem Solving REAL WORLD

5. A plane flew a total of 2,220 miles. Its average speed was 555 miles per hour. How many hours did the plane fly?

   4 hours

6. A van is carrying 486 pounds. There are 27 boxes in the van. What is the average weight of each box in the van?

   18 pounds

Answer Key

Name ____________________

Lesson 27

COMMON CORE STANDARD CC.6.NS.3

Lesson Objective: Fluently add and subtract multi-digit decimals.

Add and Subtract Decimals

Estimate 84.9 + 0.463. Then find the sum.

84.9 → 85
+ 0.463 → + 0
85

Round each number to the nearest whole number. So, a good estimate is 85.

Now line up the decimal points. Then add.

84.9 + 0.463 → Write zeros as placeholders. → 84.900 + 0.463 → Regroup. → 84.900 + 0.463 = 85.363

The answer is close to the estimate. So, the answer is reasonable.

Evaluate 45.2 − (27.93 − 10.84) using the order of operations.

Perform the operations in parentheses.
27.93 − 10.84 = 17.09

Subtract.
45.20 − 17.09 = 28.11

So, 45.2 − (27.93 − 10.84) is 28.11.

Estimate. Then find the sum or difference. For 1–7, possible estimates are given.

1. 62.38 + 26.92 — 90; 89.3
2. 48.28 − 9.41 — 40; 38.87
3. 81.04 + 52 + 16.44 — 150; 149.48
4. 27.29 − 19.39 — 10; 7.90
5. 743.5 − 462.87 — 200; 280.63
6. 98.01 + 52.003 — 150; 150.013
7. 74.9 − 16.227 — 50; 58.673

Evaluate using the order of operations.

8. (235.152 + 77.12) − 46.326 — 265.946
9. 11.024 − (1.518 + 1.7) — 7.806

www.harcourtschoolsupply.com
© Houghton Mifflin Harcourt Publishing Company
53
Core Standards for Math, Grade 6

Name ____________________

Lesson 27

CC.6.NS.3

1. A building is 52 meters tall. The building next to it is 50.36 meters tall. What is the difference between the heights of the buildings?
   - **(A) 1.64 meters**
   - (B) 2.36 meters
   - (C) 16.4 meters
   - (D) 164 meters

2. There are 4.14 grams of salt in a solution. If 1.8 grams of salt are added to the solution, how many grams of salt will be in the solution?
   - **(A) 5.94 grams**
   - (B) 4.94 grams
   - (C) 4.32 grams
   - (D) 2.34 grams

3. A scientist is comparing the sizes of two insects. One insect is 1.33 centimeters long, and the other insect is 2.01 centimeters long. What is the difference in size between the two insects?
   - (A) 3.34 centimeters
   - (B) 1.877 centimeters
   - (C) 1.72 centimeters
   - **(D) 0.68 centimeter**

4. Jen's arm is 51 centimeters long. Madeline's arm is 49.2 centimeters long. What is the difference in their arm lengths?
   - (A) 0.18 centimeter
   - **(B) 1.8 centimeters**
   - (C) 2.2 centimeters
   - (D) 18 centimeters

Problem Solving REAL WORLD

5. The average annual rainfall in Clearview is 38 inches. This year, 29.777 inches fell. How much less rain fell this year than falls in an average year?

   8.223 inches

6. At the theater, the Worth family spent $18.00 on adult tickets, $16.50 on children's tickets, and $11.75 on refreshments. How much did they spend in all?

   $46.25

www.harcourtschoolsupply.com
© Houghton Mifflin Harcourt Publishing Company
54
Core Standards for Math, Grade 6

Name ____________________

Lesson 28

COMMON CORE STANDARD CC.6.NS.3

Lesson Objective: Fluently multiply multi-digit decimals.

Multiply Decimals

When multiplying decimals, you can estimate to help you place the decimal point in the product.

Estimate $32.05 × 7.4. Then find the product.

Step 1 Estimate. Round each factor to the nearest ten or the nearest whole number.

32.05 × 7.4 → 30 × 7 = 210

$32.05 is about $30, and 7.4 is close to 7.

So, the product should be close to $210.

Step 2 Multiply.

32.05
× 7.4
12820
224350
237170

Step 3 Place the decimal point. Remember, the product is estimated to be 210. Place the decimal point so that the product is close in value to 210.

237.17

So, the product is $237.17.

Estimate. Then find the product. Possible estimates are given.

1. 8.6 × 4.1 — 36; 35.26
2. 12.8 × 2.21 — 20; 28.288
3. $8.65 × 9.2 — $81; $79.58

Evaluate using the order of operations.

4. 19.5 × (21.04 − 18.7) — 45.63
5. 11.7 + (7.92 × 8.5) — 79.02

www.harcourtschoolsupply.com
© Houghton Mifflin Harcourt Publishing Company
55
Core Standards for Math, Grade 6

Name ____________________

Lesson 28

CC.6.NS.3

1. Maria works 24.5 hours each week at a bookstore. She earns $8.76 per hour. How much does Maria earn each week?
   - (A) $2,146.20
   - **(B) $214.62**
   - (C) $15.74
   - (D) $11.21

2. Shawna is taking violin lessons. Her violin instructor charges $33.50 per hour. If Shawna has violin lessons for 3.5 hours each week, what is the weekly cost of her lessons?
   - (A) $11.72
   - (B) $116.75
   - **(C) $117.25**
   - (D) $1,172.50

3. The expression 0.005 × 0.85 represents the number of grams of iron in a liquid. How many grams of iron are in the liquid?
   - (A) 4.25 grams
   - (B) 0.425 gram
   - (C) 0.0425 gram
   - **(D) 0.00425 gram**

4. Michael works 15.5 hours each week at a music store. He earns $9.48 per hour. How much does Michael earn each week?
   - (A) $1,469.40
   - **(B) $146.94**
   - (C) $24.98
   - (D) $6.02

Problem Solving REAL WORLD

5. Blaine exchanges $100 for yen before going to Japan. If each U.S. dollar is worth 88.353 yen, how many yen should Blaine receive?

   8,835.3 yen

6. A camera costs 115 Canadian dollars. If each Canadian dollar is worth 0.952 U.S. dollars, how much will the camera cost in U.S. dollars?

   $109.48 U.S.

www.harcourtschoolsupply.com
© Houghton Mifflin Harcourt Publishing Company
56
Core Standards for Math, Grade 6

Answer Key

Name ______________________

Lesson 29

COMMON CORE STANDARD CC.6.NS.3

Lesson Objective: Fluently divide decimals by whole numbers.

Divide Decimals by Whole Numbers

When you divide a decimal by a whole number, place the decimal point in the quotient directly above the decimal point in the dividend.

Estimate 12)60.84. Then find the quotient.

Step 1 Estimate the quotient, using compatible numbers.

60 and 12 are compatible numbers because 12 divides evenly into 60.

60 ÷ 12 = 5

Step 2 Use long division to divide.

```
   5.07
12)60.84
  -60
     8
    -0
     84
    -84
      0
```

Place the decimal point in the quotient directly above the decimal point in the dividend.

Since 8 tenths cannot be shared among 12 groups, write 0 as a placeholder in the tenths place.

So, 60.84 ÷ 12 = 5.07.

Estimate. Then find the quotient. Possible estimates are given.

1. 16.48 ÷ 8 — 2; 2.06
2. 191.7 ÷ 9 — 20; 21.3
3. 4)21.64 — 5; 5.41
4. 14)41.44 — 3; 2.96
5. 21)49.14 — 2; 2.34
6. 6)3.78 — 0.5; 0.63
7. 92.8 ÷ 16 — 5; 5.8
8. 5)1.725 — 0.3; 0.345
9. 11)135.3 — 10; 12.3
10. 9)7.29 — 0.8; 0.81

Name ______________________

Lesson 29

CC.6.NS.3

1. Chester walked his neighbors' dogs to earn money. He earned $89.49 during a 3-month period. What was the average amount Chester earned each month?
   - Ⓐ $298.30
   - **Ⓑ $29.83**
   - Ⓒ $28.95
   - Ⓓ $27.84

2. Keyshawn's kitchen sink has leaked 36.054 liters of water during the past 6 months. What is the average amount of water leaked each month?
   - Ⓐ 6 liters
   - **Ⓑ 6.009 liters**
   - Ⓒ 6.9 liters
   - Ⓓ 60.09 liters

3. A piece of land measuring 112.815 square kilometers was divided and then sold in equal parts to 9 different people. How many square kilometers did each person buy?
   - Ⓐ 0.12535 square kilometer
   - Ⓑ 1.2535 square kilometers
   - **Ⓒ 12.535 square kilometers**
   - Ⓓ 125.35 square kilometers

4. Kai's father pays him to work in the family store. Kai earned $75.72 during a 4-week period. What was the average amount Kai earned each week?
   - Ⓐ $189.30
   - Ⓑ $71.72
   - Ⓒ $19.43
   - **Ⓓ $18.93**

Problem Solving REAL WORLD

5. Jake earned $10.44 interest on his savings account for an 18-month period. What was the average amount of interest Jake earned on his savings account per month?

   $0.58

6. Gloria worked for 6 hours a day for 2 days at the bank and earned $114.24. How much did she earn per hour?

   $9.52

Name ______________________

Lesson 30

COMMON CORE STANDARD CC.6.NS.3

Lesson Objective: Fluently divide whole numbers and decimals by decimals.

Divide with Decimals

When dividing a decimal by a decimal, rewrite the divisor as a whole number. To keep an equivalent problem, move the decimal point in the dividend the same direction and number of places.

Rewrite the problem so that the divisor is a whole number.

300.7 ÷ 1.24 — 300.7 is the dividend and 1.24 is the divisor.

Change the Divisor

1.24 × 100 = 124 — Multiply 1.24 by 100 because 1.24 has two decimal places.

Change the Dividend

300.7 × 100 = 30,070 — To keep an equivalent problem, multiply the dividend by the same number, 100.

So, 300.7 ÷ 1.24 is the same problem as 30,070 ÷ 124.

Find the quotient.

0.55)24.2

Step 1

Rewrite the problem so that the divisor is a whole number.

Divisor 0.55 × 100 = 55

Dividend 24.2 × 100 = 2,420

Step 2

Divide.

```
   44
55)2420
  -220
    220
   -220
      0
```

So, 24.2 ÷ 0.55 = 44.

Rewrite the problem so that the divisor is a whole number.

1. 8.9 ÷ 0.62 — 890 ÷ 62
2. 21.05 ÷ 0.2 — 210.5 ÷ 2
3. 512.3 ÷ 2.71 — 51,230 ÷ 271
4. 18.62 ÷ 0.02 — 1,862 ÷ 2

Find the quotient.

5. 8.75 ÷ 0.7 — 12.5
6. 72.24 ÷ 5.6 — 12.9
7. 0.21)1.3545 — 6.45
8. 2.17)18.228 — 8.4

Name ______________________

Lesson 30

CC.6.NS.3

1. Amir wants to buy a new MP3 player that costs $76.50. If he saves $8.50 each week, how many weeks will it take Amir to save enough money to buy the MP3 player?
   - Ⓐ 0.09
   - Ⓑ 0.9
   - **Ⓒ 9**
   - Ⓓ 90

2. Christopher drove 199.5 miles in 3.5 hours. If he drove at a constant speed, how far did he drive in one hour?
   - Ⓐ 5.7 miles
   - **Ⓑ 57 miles**
   - Ⓒ 500 miles
   - Ⓓ 570 miles

3. Michael earned $50.43 in 6.15 hours. How much did he earn each hour?
   - Ⓐ $0.82
   - Ⓑ $3.10
   - Ⓒ $4.43
   - **Ⓓ $8.20**

4. Darby wants to buy a new pair of sneakers that costs $66.50. If she saves $9.50 each week, how many weeks will it take Darby to save enough money to buy the sneakers?
   - Ⓐ 0.07
   - Ⓑ 0.7
   - **Ⓒ 7**
   - Ⓓ 70

Problem Solving REAL WORLD

5. If Amanda walks at an average speed of 2.72 miles per hour, how long will it take her to walk 6.8 miles?

   2.5 hours

6. Chad cycled 62.3 miles in 3.5 hours. If he cycled at a constant speed, how far did he cycle in 1 hour?

   17.8 miles

Answer Key

Name ____________________

Lesson 31
COMMON CORE STANDARD CC.6.NS.4
Lesson Objective: Write the prime factorization of numbers.

Prime Factorization

A number written as the product of prime numbers is called the **prime factorization** of that number. To break a number down into its prime factors, divide it by prime numbers. The first eight prime numbers are listed below.

2, 3, 5, 7, 11, 13, 17, 19

You can use a factor tree to find the prime factorization of a number.

165 → ③ 55 → ⑤ ⑪

Divide the number by the least prime factor possible. Try 2, 3, 5, and so on.

Break 55 down because it is not a prime number.

The numbers at the bottom of the branches are all prime.

You can use a ladder diagram to find the prime factorization of a number.

⑤ 165
③ 33
⑪ 11
1

165 ends in 5, so it is divisible by 5. Divide 165 by 5.

Write the quotient below 165.

The sum of the digits in 33 is divisible by 3, so divide 33 by 3.

11 is prime. Divide 11 by itself.

The bottom number is 1 and all the numbers to the left are prime.

Write the number as a product of prime factors. The factors should be in order from least to greatest.

So, the prime factorization of 165 is 3 × 5 × 11.

Find the prime factorization of the number.

1. 21 — 3 × 7
2. 130 — 2 × 5 × 13
3. 84 — 2 × 2 × 3 × 7

Name ____________________

Lesson 31
CC.6.NS.4

1. The combination for the lock on Santiago's suitcase is based on the prime factorization of 315. What is the prime factorization of 315?
   - Ⓐ 5 × 7 × 9
   - Ⓑ 3 × 7 × 15
   - **Ⓒ 3 × 3 × 5 × 7**
   - Ⓓ 2 × 3 × 3 × 5 × 7

2. The combination for Mr. Tao's briefcase is based on the prime factorization of 45. What is the prime factorization of 45?
   - Ⓐ 3 × 15
   - Ⓑ 5 × 9
   - **Ⓒ 3 × 3 × 5**
   - Ⓓ 2 × 3 × 3 × 5

3. Manuel left out one prime factor when he wrote this prime factorization for 168.

   2 × 2 × 2 × 3 × ■

   What is the missing prime factor?
   - Ⓐ 2
   - Ⓑ 3
   - Ⓒ 5
   - **Ⓓ 7**

4. Bethaney left out one prime factor when she wrote this prime factorization for 1,092.

   2 × 2 × ■ × 7 × 13

   What is the missing prime factor?
   - Ⓐ 2
   - **Ⓑ 3**
   - Ⓒ 7
   - Ⓓ 13

Problem Solving REAL WORLD

5. A computer code is based on the prime factorization of 160. Find the prime factorization of 160.

   2 × 2 × 2 × 2 × 2 × 5

6. The combination for a lock is a 3-digit number. The digits are the prime factors of 42 listed from least to greatest. What is the combination for the lock?

   237

Name ____________________

Lesson 32
COMMON CORE STANDARD CC.6.NS.4
Lesson Objective: Find the least common multiple of two whole numbers.

Least Common Multiple

The **least common multiple**, or **LCM**, is the least number that two or more numbers have in common in their list of nonzero multiples.

Find the LCM of 3 and 9.

List the first ten nonzero multiples of each number:

Multiples of 3: 3, 6, 9, 12, 15, 18, 21, 24, 27, 30

Multiples of 9: 9, 18, 27, 36, 45, 54, 63, 72, 81, 90

The first three nonzero multiples that 3 and 9 have in common are 9, 18, and 27.

So, the LCM of 3 and 9 is 9.

Find the LCM.

1. 4, 10

   List the first ten multiples for each number.

   Multiples of 4: 4, 8, 12, 16, 20, 24, 28, 32, 36, 40

   Multiples of 10: 10, 20, 30, 40, 50, 60, 70, 80, 90, 100

   List the numbers that appear in both lists.

   Common multiples: 20 and 40

   The LCM of 4 and 10 is 20.

2. 6, 8

   List the first ten multiples for each number.

   Multiples of 6: 6, 12, 18, 24, 30, 36, 42, 48, 54, 60

   Multiples of 8: 8, 16, 24, 32, 40, 48, 56, 64, 72, 80

   List the numbers that appear in both lists.

   Common multiples: 24 and 48

   The LCM of 6 and 8 is 24.

3. 5, 20 — 20
4. 6, 15 — 30
5. 12, 30 — 60
6. 7, 14 — 14
7. 10, 15 — 30
8. 6, 18 — 18

Name ____________________

Lesson 32
CC.6.NS.4

1. Gina purchases materials to make watches for a jewelry show. There are 6 watch faces in a pack and 9 watch bands in a pack. What is the **least** number of watches Gina can make without having any supplies left over?
   - Ⓐ 12
   - Ⓑ 16
   - **Ⓒ 18**
   - Ⓓ 24

2. Stefani makes team shirts to sell at the basketball games. She puts one patch in the middle of each shirt. There are 3 patches in a pack and 5 shirts in a pack. What is the **least** number of team shirts Stefani can make without having any supplies left over?
   - Ⓐ 3
   - Ⓑ 5
   - Ⓒ 8
   - **Ⓓ 15**

3. Max purchases materials to make dog collars for a pet show. There are 6 buckles in a pack and 8 straps in a pack. What is the **least** number of dog collars Max can make without having any supplies left over?
   - Ⓐ 12
   - Ⓑ 16
   - Ⓒ 18
   - **Ⓓ 24**

4. Sarah makes necklaces to sell at the craft festival. She uses one pendant for each necklace. There are 4 ribbons in a pack and 6 pendants in a pack. What is the **least** number of necklaces Sarah can make without having any supplies left over?
   - Ⓐ 8
   - **Ⓑ 12**
   - Ⓒ 18
   - Ⓓ 24

Problem Solving REAL WORLD

5. Juanita is making necklaces to give as presents. She plans to put 15 beads on each necklace. Beads are sold in packages of 20. What is the least number of packages she can buy to make necklaces and have no beads left over?

   3 packs

6. Pencils are sold in packages of 10, and erasers are sold in packages of 6. What is the least number of pencils and erasers you can buy so that there is one pencil for each eraser with none left over?

   30 pencils and 30 erasers

Answer Key

Name ______________________

Lesson 33
COMMON CORE STANDARD CC.6.NS.4
Lesson Objective: Find the greatest common factor of two whole numbers.

Greatest Common Factor

A **common factor** is a number that is a factor of two or more numbers. The **greatest common factor**, or **GCF**, is the greatest factor that two or more numbers have in common.

Find the common factors of 9 and 27. Then find the GCF.

Step 1
List the factors of each number.
Factors of 9: 1, 3, 9
Factors of 27: 1, 3, 9, 27

Step 2
Identify the common factors.
Common factors of 9 and 27:
1, 3, 9

The greatest of the common factors is 9.
So, the GCF of 9 and 27 is 9.

You can use the GCF and the Distributive Property to express the sum of two numbers as a product.

Write 9 + 27 as a product.

Step 1
Write each number as the product of the GCF and another factor.

$9 = 9 \times 1 \quad 27 = 9 \times 3$

Step 2
Write an expression multiplying the GCF and the sum of the two factors from Step 1.

$9 \times (1 + 3)$

The product $9 \times (1 + 3)$ has the same value as 9 + 27.

So, $9 + 27 = 9 \times (1 + 3)$.

Find the GCF.

1. 18, 45 — 9

2. 33, 66 — 33

3. 72, 96 — 24

4. 50, 80 — 10

Use the GCF and the Distributive Property to express the sum as a product.

5. 18 + 24 — $6 \times (3 + 4)$

6. 15 + 75 — $15 \times (1 + 5)$

7. 36 + 54 — $18 \times (2 + 3)$

8. 16 + 20 — $4 \times (4 + 5)$

Name ______________________

Lesson 33
CC.6.NS.4

1. Madison has 56 roses and 42 daisies to use in floral centerpieces for a party. Each centerpiece will have the same number of flowers and will contain only roses or only daisies. What is the **greatest** number of flowers that Madison can use in each centerpiece?

Ⓐ 14 (filled)
Ⓑ 8
Ⓒ 7
Ⓓ 6

2. Manny wants to make necklaces from two pieces of jewelry wire that measure 60 inches and 36 inches. He will cut both lengths of jewelry wire into equal pieces that are as long as possible. Into what lengths should he cut the pieces of wire?

Ⓐ 20 inches
Ⓑ 12 inches (filled)
Ⓒ 4 inches
Ⓓ 3 inches

3. Mr. Gentry teaches two science classes. There are 28 students in his biology class and 21 students in his environmental science class. He divides both classes into equal-sized lab groups. Each science class has their own lab groups. What is the **greatest** number of students in each lab group?

Ⓐ 4
Ⓑ 5
Ⓒ 6
Ⓓ 7 (filled)

4. Chauncey has two pieces of rope that measure 8 feet and 12 feet. He wants to cut the rope into equal pieces that are as long as possible. Into what lengths should Chauncey cut the pieces of rope?

Ⓐ 8 feet
Ⓑ 6 feet
Ⓒ 4 feet (filled)
Ⓓ 2 feet

Problem Solving REAL WORLD

5. Jerome is making prizes for a game at the school fair. He has two bags of different candies, one with 15 pieces of candy and one with 20 pieces. Every prize will have one kind of candy, the same number of pieces, and the greatest number of pieces possible. How many candies should be in each prize?

5 candies

6. There are 24 sixth graders and 40 seventh graders. Mr. Chan wants to divide both grades into groups of equal size, with the greatest possible number of students in each group. How many students should be in each group?

8 students

Name ______________________

Lesson 34
COMMON CORE STANDARD CC.6.NS.4
Lesson Objective: Solve problems involving greatest common factor by using the strategy *draw a diagram.*

Problem Solving • Apply the Greatest Common Factor

Use the Distributive Property and a diagram to solve.

Bethany is packing cookies for her drama club's bake sale. She has 28 oatmeal cookies and 36 peanut butter cookies to pack. Each bag will contain only one kind of cookie, and every bag will have the same number of cookies. What is the greatest number of cookies she can pack in each bag? How many bags of each kind will there be?

Read the Problem	Solve the Problem
What do I need to find? I need to find the greatest number of cookies for each bag and the number of bags for each kind of cookie.	**Step 1** Find the GCF of 28 and 36. Use prime factorization. $28 = 2 \times 2 \times 7 \quad 36 = 2 \times 2 \times 3 \times 3$ Multiply common prime factors: $2 \times 2 =$ 4 GCF: 4
What information do I need to use? I need to use the number of oatmeal cookies and the number of peanut butter cookies.	**Step 2** Write 28 as a product of the GCF and another factor. $28 = 4 \times$ 7 Write 36 as a product of the GCF and another factor. $36 = 4 \times$ 9
How will I use the information? First, I can find the GCF of 28 and 36. Then I can draw a diagram showing the bags of cookies.	**Step 3** Use the Distributive Property to write 28 + 36 as a product. $28 + 36 = 4 \times (7 + 9)$ **Step 4** Use the product to draw a diagram of the bags of cookies. Write O for each oatmeal cookie and P for each peanut butter cookie.

O	O	O	O	O	O	O	P	P	P	P	P	P	P	P	P
O	O	O	O	O	O	O	P	P	P	P	P	P	P	P	P
O	O	O	O	O	O	O	P	P	P	P	P	P	P	P	P
O	O	O	O	O	O	O	P	P	P	P	P	P	P	P	P

So, each bag will have 4 cookies. There will be 7 bags of oatmeal cookies and 9 bags of peanut butter cookies.

1. Jacob is putting 18 nonfiction and 30 fiction books on bookshelves. Each shelf will have only fiction or only nonfiction, and every shelf will have the same number of books. What is the greatest number of books for each shelf, and how many shelves will there be for each type of book?

6; 3 shelves with non-fiction and 5 shelves with fiction

Name ______________________

Lesson 34
CC.6.NS.4

1. Kenya placed 21 apples and 28 oranges into different bowls. Each bowl held the same amount of fruit and contained only apples or only oranges. What is the **greatest** number of pieces of fruit that Kenya could have placed in each bowl?

Ⓐ 14
Ⓑ 7 (filled)
Ⓒ 4
Ⓓ 3

2. Mr. Hill has 27 students in his class, and Mr. Young has 24 students in his class. Both classes are divided into equal-sized teams, with the **greatest** possible number of students on each team. How many teams are there in all?

Ⓐ 3
Ⓑ 8
Ⓒ 9
Ⓓ 17 (filled)

3. Leslie baked 64 chocolate chip cookies and 88 peanut butter cookies. She wants to place the cookies in snack bags for a party. Each snack bag will contain the same number of cookies and contain only one type of cookie. If she places the **greatest** number of cookies in each snack bag, how many snack bags contain peanut butter cookies?

Ⓐ 2
Ⓑ 4
Ⓒ 8
Ⓓ 11 (filled)

4. Caleb's bookcase holds 16 nonfiction books and 12 fiction books. Each shelf holds the same number of books and contains only one type of book. Each shelf holds the **greatest** number of books possible. How many shelves does the bookcase have?

Ⓐ 7 (filled)
Ⓑ 4
Ⓒ 3
Ⓓ 2

Problem Solving REAL WORLD

5. Otis wants to place 75 green marbles and 60 red marbles in bags to give to his friends. Each bag should contain the same number of marbles, and all marbles in a bag should be the same color. If he places the **greatest** possible number of marbles in each bag, how many bags will have green marbles? Explain how you know.

5; Possible explanation: The number of marbles in each bag is the greatest common factor of 75 and 60. To find the greatest common factor, I used the prime factorization of the numbers to find the product of the common prime factors: $75 = 3 \times 5 \times 5$ and $60 = 2 \times 2 \times 3 \times 5$, so the GCF is $3 \times 5 = 15$. Since each bag conatins 15 marbles and there are 75 green marbles, there will be $75 \div 15 \times 5$ bags of green marbles.

Name ______________________

Lesson 35

COMMON CORE STANDARD CC.6.NS.4

Lesson Objective: Multiply fractions.

Multiply Fractions

To multiply fractions, you can multiply numerators and multiply denominators. Write the product in simplest form.

Find $\frac{3}{10} \times \frac{4}{5}$.

Step 1 Multiply numerators. Multiply denominators. $\frac{3}{10} \times \frac{4}{5} = \frac{3 \times 4}{10 \times 5} = \frac{12}{50}$

Step 2 Write the product in simplest form. $\frac{12}{50} = \frac{12 \div 2}{50 \div 2} = \frac{6}{25}$

So, $\frac{3}{10} \times \frac{4}{5} = \frac{6}{25}$.

To simplify an expression with fractions, follow the order of operations as you would with whole numbers.

Find $\left(\frac{5}{7} - \frac{3}{14}\right) \times \frac{1}{10}$.

Step 1 Perform the operation in parentheses. To subtract, write an equivalent fraction using a common denominator.

Multiply the numerator and denominator of $\frac{5}{7}$ by 2 to get a common denominator of 14.

$$\left(\frac{5}{7} - \frac{3}{14}\right) \times \frac{1}{10} = \left(\frac{5 \times 2}{7 \times 2} - \frac{3}{14}\right) \times \frac{1}{10} = \left(\frac{10}{14} - \frac{3}{14}\right) \times \frac{1}{10} = \frac{7}{14} \times \frac{1}{10}$$

Step 2 Multiply numerators. Multiply denominators. $= \frac{7 \times 1}{14 \times 10} = \frac{7}{140}$

Step 3 Write the product in simplest form. Divide the numerator and the denominator by the GCF. $= \frac{7 \div 7}{140 \div 7} = \frac{1}{20}$

So, $\left(\frac{5}{7} - \frac{3}{14}\right) \times \frac{1}{10} = \frac{1}{20}$.

Find the product. Write the product in simplest form.

1. $\frac{3}{4} \times \frac{1}{5}$ — $\frac{3}{20}$
2. $\frac{4}{7} \times \frac{5}{12}$ — $\frac{5}{21}$
3. $\frac{3}{8} \times \frac{2}{9}$ — $\frac{1}{12}$
4. $\frac{4}{5} \times \frac{5}{8}$ — $\frac{1}{2}$

Evaluate using the order of operations.

5. $\frac{7}{8} - \frac{5}{6} \times \frac{1}{2}$ — $\frac{11}{24}$
6. $\left(\frac{4}{5} + \frac{1}{3}\right) \times \frac{5}{9}$ — $\frac{17}{27}$
7. $\frac{3}{4} \times \frac{2}{5} + \frac{1}{4}$ — $\frac{11}{20}$
8. $\frac{3}{10} \times \left(\frac{2}{3} - \frac{1}{6}\right)$ — $\frac{3}{20}$

Name ______________________

Lesson 35

CC.6.NS.4

1. Mr. Bryon had a gas can with $4\frac{1}{4}$ gallons of gasoline in it. He used $\frac{1}{4}$ of the amount in the can to mow his lawn. How many gallons did Mr. Bryon use to mow his lawn?
   - Ⓐ $\frac{15}{16}$ gallon
   - **Ⓑ $1\frac{1}{16}$ gallons**
   - Ⓒ $4\frac{1}{16}$ gallons
   - Ⓓ $4\frac{1}{2}$ gallons

2. Alana bought $2\frac{5}{8}$ pounds of mixed nuts for the school picnic. Her classmates ate $\frac{3}{4}$ of the mixed nuts. How much of the mixed nuts did her classmates eat?
   - **Ⓐ $1\frac{31}{32}$ pounds**
   - Ⓑ 2 pounds
   - Ⓒ $2\frac{15}{32}$ pounds
   - Ⓓ $3\frac{1}{2}$ pounds

3. Kelly feeds her cat $\frac{7}{8}$ cup of food per day. How much food does she feed her cat in one week, including the weekend?
   - Ⓐ $1\frac{3}{4}$ cups
   - Ⓑ $4\frac{3}{8}$ cups
   - Ⓒ $5\frac{5}{6}$ cups
   - **Ⓓ $6\frac{1}{8}$ cups**

4. The table shows how many hours some of the part-time employees at the Pizza Shop worked last week.

Pizza Shop

Name	Hours Worked
Conrad	$6\frac{2}{3}$
Giovanni	$9\frac{1}{2}$
Sally	$10\frac{3}{4}$

Louisa worked $1\frac{1}{3}$ times as many hours as Giovanni worked. How many hours did Louisa work last week?

- Ⓐ $3\frac{5}{6}$ hours
- Ⓑ $10\frac{5}{6}$ hours
- **Ⓒ $12\frac{2}{3}$ hours**
- Ⓓ $14\frac{1}{3}$ hours

Problem Solving REAL WORLD

5. Jason ran $\frac{5}{7}$ of the distance around the school track. Sara ran $\frac{4}{5}$ of Jason's distance. What fraction of the total distance around the track did Sara run?

   $\frac{4}{7}$

6. A group of students attend a math club. Half of the students are boys and $\frac{4}{9}$ of the boys have brown eyes. What fraction of the group are boys with brown eyes?

   $\frac{2}{9}$

Name ______________________

Lesson 36

COMMON CORE STANDARD CC.6.NS.4

Lesson Objective: Simplify fractional factors by using the greatest common factor.

Simplify Factors

Sometimes you can simplify before you multiply fractions.

Find the product of $\frac{5}{6} \times \frac{4}{15}$. Simplify before multiplying.

Step 1 Rewrite as a single fraction. $\frac{5 \times 4}{6 \times 15}$

Step 2 Look for numbers in the numerator that have common factors with numbers in the denominator. Find the GCF. $\frac{⑤ \times \boxed{4}}{\boxed{6} \times ⑮}$

The GCF of 5 and 15 is 5.
The GCF of 6 and 4 is 2.

Step 3 Divide.

5 ÷ 5 = 1　　6 ÷ 2 = 3
15 ÷ 5 = 3　　4 ÷ 2 = 2

$\frac{\cancel{5}^{1} \times \cancel{4}^{2}}{\cancel{6}_{3} \times \cancel{15}_{3}}$

Step 4 Rewrite the fraction with the new numbers. Multiply the numerators. Multiply the denominators. $\frac{1 \times 2}{3 \times 3} = \frac{2}{9}$

So, $\frac{5}{6} \times \frac{4}{15} = \frac{2}{9}$.

Find the product. Simplify before multiplying.

1. $\frac{4}{9} \times \frac{3}{14}$ — $\frac{2}{21}$
2. $\frac{3}{4} \times \frac{2}{5}$ — $\frac{3}{10}$
3. $\frac{3}{20} \times \frac{5}{6}$ — $\frac{1}{8}$
4. $\frac{7}{10} \times \frac{4}{5}$ — $\frac{14}{25}$
5. $\frac{3}{16} \times \frac{8}{27}$ — $\frac{1}{18}$
6. $\frac{1}{8} \times \frac{2}{7}$ — $\frac{1}{28}$

Name ______________________

Lesson 36

CC.6.NS.4

1. India has a $\frac{3}{5}$-pound bag of nuts. She uses $\frac{5}{6}$ of the bag to bake brownies. How many pounds of nuts did India use to make the brownies?
   - Ⓐ $\frac{7}{8}$ pound
   - **Ⓑ $\frac{1}{2}$ pound**
   - Ⓒ $\frac{1}{6}$ pound
   - Ⓓ $\frac{2}{15}$ pound

2. Otis bought a total of $\frac{7}{10}$ pound of grapes and cherries. The weight of the grapes is $\frac{2}{3}$ of the total weight. What is the weight of the grapes?
   - Ⓐ $\frac{20}{21}$ pound
   - Ⓑ $\frac{9}{13}$ pound
   - **Ⓒ $\frac{7}{15}$ pound**
   - Ⓓ $\frac{3}{10}$ pound

3. In a class, $\frac{2}{5}$ of the students said their favorite food is pizza. Of those students, $\frac{5}{12}$ said their favorite pizza topping is pepperoni. What fraction of the students in the class said their favorite pizza topping is pepperoni?
   - Ⓐ $\frac{1}{10}$
   - **Ⓑ $\frac{1}{6}$**
   - Ⓒ $\frac{10}{17}$
   - Ⓓ $\frac{2}{3}$

4. Aubrey has $\frac{3}{4}$ gallon of milk to use for two recipes. She uses $\frac{1}{12}$ of the milk for one of the recipes. How much milk does she use?
   - Ⓐ $\frac{1}{4}$ gallon
   - Ⓑ $\frac{1}{8}$ gallon
   - Ⓒ $\frac{1}{12}$ gallon
   - **Ⓓ $\frac{1}{16}$ gallon**

Problem Solving REAL WORLD

5. Amber has a $\frac{4}{5}$-pound bag of colored sand. She uses $\frac{1}{2}$ of the bag for an art project. How much sand does she use for the project?

   $\frac{2}{5}$ pound

6. Tyler has $\frac{3}{4}$ month to write a book report. He finished the report in $\frac{2}{3}$ that time. How much time did it take Tyler to write the report?

   $\frac{1}{2}$ month

Answer Key

Name ____________

Lesson 37
COMMON CORE STANDARD CC.6.NS.5
Lesson Objective: Understand positive and negative numbers, and use them to represent real-world quantities.

Understand Positive and Negative Numbers

Positive integers are to the right of 0 on the number line.
Negative integers are to the left of 0 on the number line.
Opposites are the same distance from 0, on opposite sides.

What is the opposite of ⁻3?

Step 1 Graph the integer.

⁻5 ⁻4 ⁻3 ⁻2 ⁻1 0 1 2 3 4 5

⁻3 is a negative integer. Graph it to the left of 0.

Step 2 Graph the integer and its opposite on a number line.

⁻5 ⁻4 ⁻3 ⁻2 ⁻1 0 1 2 3 4 5

The opposite of ⁻3 is 3 places to the right of 0.

So, the opposite of ⁻3 is 3.

Graph the integer and its opposite on the number line.

1. 2 opposite: ⁻2
2. ⁻4 opposite: 4

⁻5 ⁻4 ⁻3 ⁻2 ⁻1 0 1 2 3 4 5

3. ⁻1 opposite: 1
4. 7 opposite: ⁻7

⁻10 ⁻8 ⁻6 ⁻4 ⁻2 0 2 4 6 8 10

Write the opposite of the opposite of the integer.

5. ⁻18 ⁻18
6. 90 90
7. ⁻31 ⁻31

Name ____________

Lesson 37
CC.6.NS.5

1. Which situation could be represented by the integer ⁺6?
   - Ⓐ A football team loses 6 yards on a play.
   - Ⓑ A golfer's score is 6 over par. (shaded)
   - Ⓒ A town is 6 feet below sea level.
   - Ⓓ A video game player loses 6 points.

2. Which situation could be represented by the integer ⁻2?
   - Ⓐ A football team gains 2 yards on a play.
   - Ⓑ A golfer's score is 2 over par.
   - Ⓒ A city is 2 feet below sea level. (shaded)
   - Ⓓ A student earns 2 bonus points on a quiz.

3. Which situation could be represented by the integer ⁺15?
   - Ⓐ A football team gains 15 yards on a play. (shaded)
   - Ⓑ A $15 withdrawal is made from a bank account
   - Ⓒ A town is 15 feet below sea level.
   - Ⓓ A video game player loses 15 points.

4. Maria withdrew $20 from her checking account. What integer represents the withdrawal?
   - Ⓐ ⁻20 (shaded)
   - Ⓑ 0
   - Ⓒ 20
   - Ⓓ ⁻40

Problem Solving REAL WORLD

5. Dakshesh won a game by scoring 25 points. Randy scored the opposite number of points as Dakshesh. What is Randy's score?

   ⁻25 points

6. When Dakshesh and Randy played the game again, Dakshesh scored the opposite of the opposite of his first score. What is his score?

   25 points

Name ____________

Lesson 38
COMMON CORE STANDARD CC.6.NS.6a
Lesson Objective: Plot rational numbers on a number line, and use a number line to identify opposites.

Rational Numbers and the Number Line

Graph ⁻0.8 and 1.3 on the number line.

Step 1 Use positive and negative integers to help you locate the decimals. 0.8 is between 0 and 1, so ⁻0.8 is between 0 and ⁻1. 1.3 is between 1 and 2.

Step 2 The number line is marked in tenths. There is a tick mark every 0.1. Count 8 tick marks to the left of 0 for ⁻0.8. Count 3 tickmarks to the right of 1 for 1.3.

⁻0.8 1.3
⁻2 ⁻1 0 1 2

Graph $\frac{3}{5}$ and $^-1\frac{1}{2}$ on the number line.

Step 1 Use positive and negative integers to help you locate the fractions. $\frac{3}{5}$ is between 0 and 1. $1\frac{1}{2}$ is between 1 and 2, so $^-1\frac{1}{2}$ is between ⁻1 and ⁻2.

Step 2 The number line is marked in tenths. There is a tick mark every $\frac{1}{10}$. Use equivalent fractions to help you graph the points.
$^-1\frac{1}{2} = {}^-1\frac{5}{10}$ Count 5 tick marks to the left of ⁻1.
$\frac{3}{5} = \frac{6}{10}$ Count 6 tick marks to the right of 0.

$^-1\frac{1}{2}$ $\frac{3}{5}$
⁻2 ⁻1 0 1 2

Graph the number on the horizontal number line.

1. $^-1\frac{2}{5}$
2. 0.6
3. ⁻1.2
4. $1\frac{8}{10}$

$^-1\frac{2}{5}$ ⁻1.2 0.6 $1\frac{8}{10}$
⁻2 ⁻1 0 1 2

Name ____________

Lesson 38
CC.6.NS.6a

1. The normal low temperature during January for a town in Alaska is ⁻8.6°F. Between which two integers does this temperature lie?
   - Ⓐ ⁻10 and ⁻9
   - Ⓑ ⁻9 and ⁻8 (shaded)
   - Ⓒ ⁻8 and ⁻7
   - Ⓓ ⁻7 and ⁻6

2. A city's elevation is 140.2 feet **below** sea level. Between which two integers does this elevation lie?
   - Ⓐ ⁻141 and ⁻140 (shaded)
   - Ⓑ ⁻140 and 0
   - Ⓒ 0 and 140
   - Ⓓ 140 and 141

3. The integer ⁻3.5 represents a fee that was charged to Carl's bank account. Between which two integers does this number lie?
   - Ⓐ 3 and 4
   - Ⓑ 3 and 8
   - Ⓒ ⁻3 and 8
   - Ⓓ ⁻4 and ⁻3 (shaded)

4. The freezing point of bromine is about ⁻7.2° Celsius. Between which two integers does this temperature lie?
   - Ⓐ ⁻10 and ⁻9
   - Ⓑ ⁻9 and ⁻8
   - Ⓒ ⁻8 and ⁻7 (shaded)
   - Ⓓ ⁻7 and ⁻6

Problem Solving REAL WORLD

5. The outdoor temperature yesterday reached a low of ⁻4.5°F. Between what two integers was the temperature?

   ⁻5 and ⁻4

6. Jacob needs to graph $^-6\frac{2}{3}$ on a horizontal number line. Should he graph it to the left or right of ⁻6?

   left

Answer Key

Name ______________________

Lesson 39
COMMON CORE STANDARD CC.6.NS.6b
Lesson Objective: Identify the relationship between points on a coordinate plane.

Ordered Pair Relationships

You can tell which quadrant to graph a point in by looking at whether the coordinates are positive or negative.

Find the quadrant for the point (4, ⁻5).

Step 1 The *x*-coordinate is 4, a positive number. So, the point must be in Quadrant I or IV.

Step 2 The *y*-coordinate is ⁻5, a negative number. So, the point must be in Quadrant III or IV.

Step 3 The only quadrant that the *x*- and *y*-coordinates have in common is Quadrant IV.

So, the point (4, ⁻5) is in Quadrant IV.

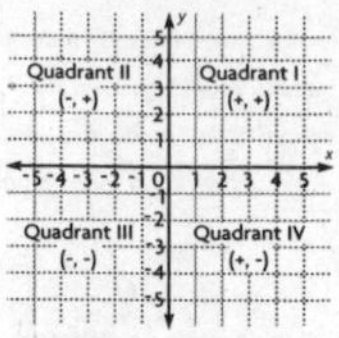

Quadrant II (−, +) Quadrant I (+, +) Quadrant III (−, −) Quadrant IV (+, −)

Two points are reflections of each other if the x-axis or y-axis forms a line of symmetry for the two points. This means that if you folded the graph along that axis, the two points would line up.

(⁻1, 3) and (⁻1, ⁻3) are reflected across the *x*-axis. The *x*-coordinates are the same. The *y*-coordinates are opposites.

(2, 4) and (⁻2, 4) are reflected across the *y*-axis. The *y*-coordinates are the same. The *x*-coordinates are opposites.

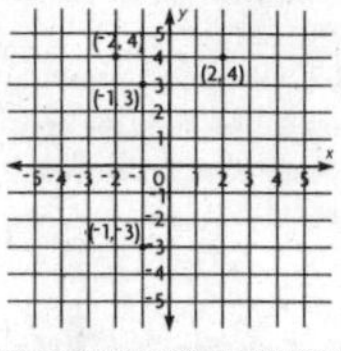

Identify the quadrant where the point is located.

1. (⁻1, 5)
   x-coordinate: ⁻1 Quadrant: II or III
   y-coordinate: 5 Quadrant: I or II
   The point is in Quadrant II.

2. (⁻3, ⁻2)
   x-coordinate: ⁻3 Quadrant: II or III
   y-coordinate: ⁻2 Quadrant: III or IV
   The point is in Quadrant III.

3. (2, 4) Quadrant: I
4. (⁻6, 7) Quadrant: II
5. (8, ⁻1) Quadrant: IV
6. (⁻7, ⁻5) Quadrant: III

The two points are reflections of each other across the x- or y-axis. Identify the axis.

7. (2, 7) and (⁻2, 7) axis: y
8. (⁻1, 4) and (⁻1, ⁻4) axis: x
9. (5, ⁻6) and (5, 6) axis: x
10. (8, ⁻3) and (⁻8, ⁻3) axis: y

Name ______________________

Lesson 39
CC.6.NS.6b

1. The city of Dellville is represented by the point (3, ⁻2) on a coordinate plane. In which quadrant does the point lie?
   Ⓐ Quadrant I
   Ⓑ Quadrant II
   Ⓒ Quadrant III
   Ⓓ Quadrant IV

2. The point (⁻7, 1) represents the location of a fountain on a map of a park. In which quadrant does the point lie?
   Ⓐ Quadrant I
   Ⓑ Quadrant II
   Ⓒ Quadrant III
   Ⓓ Quadrant IV

3. The town of Cedarcroft is represented by the point (11, 1) on a coordinate plane. In which quadrant does the point lie?
   Ⓐ Quadrant I
   Ⓑ Quadrant II
   Ⓒ Quadrant III
   Ⓓ Quadrant IV

4. A baseball stadium is represented by the point (⁻3, ⁻5) on a coordinate plane. In which quadrant does the point lie?
   Ⓐ Quadrant I
   Ⓑ Quadrant II
   Ⓒ Quadrant III
   Ⓓ Quadrant IV

Problem Solving REAL WORLD

5. A town's post office is located at the point (7, 5) on a coordinate plane. In which quadrant is the post office located?
   Quadrant I

6. The grocery store is located at a point on a coordinate plane with the same *y*-coordinate as the bank but with the opposite *x*-coordinate. The grocery store and bank are reflections of each other across which axis?
   y-axis

Name ______________________

Lesson 40
COMMON CORE STANDARD CC.6.NS.6c
Lesson Objective: Convert between fractions and decimals.

Fractions and Decimals

Terminating decimals end. **Repeating decimals** do not end but have repeating digits. One way to convert a terminating decimal to a fraction or mixed number is to read the number.

Look at the decimal 5.75. The right-hand digit is in the hundredths place. Read 5.75 as "five and seventy-five hundredths."

whole number → $5\frac{75}{100}$ ← fraction

As a mixed number, the whole number is 5. The numerator is 75. The denominator is 100.

Write the fraction in simplest form using the greatest common factor.

75: 1, 3, (5), 15, (25), 75
100: 1, 2, 4, (5), 10, 20, (25), 50, 100
GCF = 25

$5\frac{75}{100} = 5\frac{75 \div 25}{100 \div 25} = 5\frac{3}{4}$

So, 5.75 = $5\frac{3}{4}$ in simplest form.

Identify the decimal and the fraction in simplest form for point *E*.

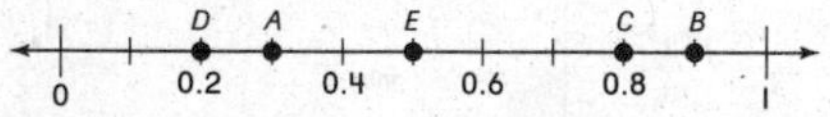

(Number line from 0 to 1 with points D, A, E, C, B; labels 0, 0.2, 0.4, 0.6, 0.8, 1)

Decimal
Between 0 and 1 there are 10 spaces. So, each space represents 0.1. Point *E* is one space to the right of 0.4. Point *E* is the next tenth, or 0.5.

Fraction
Read 0.5 as "five-tenths." Write $\frac{5}{10}$. Simplify by dividing the numerator and denominator by the GCF, 5.
$\frac{5 \div 5}{10 \div 5} = \frac{1}{2}$

So, Point *E* is at 0.5 = $\frac{1}{2}$.

Write as a fraction or mixed number in simplest form.

1. 0.48 $\frac{12}{25}$
2. 0.8 $\frac{4}{5}$
3. 0.004 $\frac{1}{250}$
4. 3.6 $3\frac{3}{5}$
5. 4.82 $4\frac{41}{50}$

Identify a decimal and a fraction or mixed number in simplest form for each point.

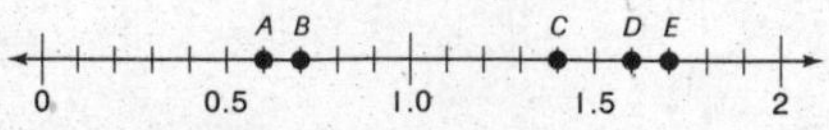

(Number line from 0 to 2 with points A, B, C, D, E; labels 0, 0.5, 1.0, 1.5, 2)

6. Point *A* 0.6; $\frac{3}{5}$
7. Point *B* 0.7; $\frac{7}{10}$
8. Point *C* 1.4; $1\frac{2}{5}$
9. Point *D* 1.6; $1\frac{3}{5}$
10. Point *E* 1.7; $1\frac{7}{10}$

Name ______________________

Lesson 40
CC.6.NS.6c

1. Calvin has a recipe that calls for $\frac{3}{8}$ pound of cheddar cheese. The packages he sees in the grocery store show the weights in decimal amounts. Which amount of cheese should Calvin buy?
   Ⓐ $0.\overline{3}$ pound
   Ⓑ 0.35 pound
   Ⓒ 0.375 pound
   Ⓓ $2.\overline{6}$ pounds

2. On Saturday morning, Briana and her friends walked 1.35 miles. What is this distance as a mixed number?
   Ⓐ $1\frac{1}{4}$ miles
   Ⓑ $1\frac{7}{20}$ miles
   Ⓒ $1\frac{2}{5}$ miles
   Ⓓ $1\frac{3}{5}$ miles

3. Josh's walking stick is 4.875 feet long. Which is the same length written as a mixed number?
   Ⓐ $4\frac{3}{8}$ feet
   Ⓑ $4\frac{3}{4}$ feet
   Ⓒ $4\frac{5}{6}$ feet
   Ⓓ $4\frac{7}{8}$ feet

4. Maria measured the distance between two pictures on her wall. The distance was $6\frac{3}{4}$ inches. Which is the same distance as a decimal?
   Ⓐ 5.25 inches
   Ⓑ 6.34 inches
   Ⓒ 6.75 inches
   Ⓓ 7.13 inches

Problem Solving REAL WORLD

5. Grace sold $\frac{5}{8}$ of her stamp collection. What is this amount as a decimal?
   0.625

6. What if you scored a 0.80 on a test? What fraction of the test, in simplest form, did you answer correctly?
   $\frac{4}{5}$

Answer Key

Name ______________________

Lesson 41

COMMON CORE STANDARD CC.6.NS.6c
Lesson Objective: Compare and order fractions and decimals.

Compare and Order Fractions and Decimals

You can compare fractions and decimals by rewriting them so all are fractions or decimals.

Use < or > to compare 0.77 and $\frac{7}{10}$.

Method 1

Write the fraction as a decimal. Then compare the decimals.

$\frac{7}{10} = 10\overline{)7.0} = 0.7$, -7.0, 0

$0.77 > 0.7$

So, $0.77 > \frac{7}{10}$.

Method 2

Write the decimal as a fraction. Rewrite $\frac{7}{10}$ with a denominator of 100. Then compare the fractions.

$0.77 = \frac{77}{100}$ $\quad \frac{7}{10} = \frac{7 \times 10}{10 \times 10} = \frac{70}{100}$

$77 > 70$

So, $\frac{77}{100} > \frac{70}{100}$ and $0.77 > \frac{7}{10}$.

Order 0.08, $\frac{1}{20}$, and 0.06 from least to greatest.

Write each number as a fraction.

$0.08 = \frac{8}{100}$ $\quad \frac{1}{20} = \frac{1}{20}$ $\quad 0.06 = \frac{6}{100}$

Compare the fractions.

Compare the fractions with the same denominator.

$8 > 6$

So, $\frac{8}{100} > \frac{6}{100}$.

Compare the fractions with different denominators using common denominators.

$\frac{1}{20} = \frac{1 \times 5}{20 \times 5} = \frac{5}{100}$, $5 < 6$, so $\frac{1}{20} < \frac{6}{100}$.

So, $\frac{1}{20} < \frac{6}{100} < \frac{8}{100}$.

So, the numbers from least to greatest are $\frac{1}{20}$, 0.06, and 0.08.

Compare. Write <, >, or = in each ◯.

1. $\frac{4}{11}$ (>) $\frac{2}{11}$
2. $\frac{5}{7}$ (<) $\frac{5}{6}$
3. 0.27 (<) 0.3
4. 0.9 (>) $\frac{4}{25}$

Order from least to greatest.

5. $\frac{3}{8}, \frac{5}{16}, \frac{1}{4}$ — $\frac{1}{4}, \frac{5}{16}, \frac{3}{8}$
6. $0.7, 0.82, \frac{4}{5}$ — $0.7, \frac{4}{5}, 0.82$
7. $2\frac{1}{6}, 1\frac{5}{12}, 2\frac{1}{4}$ — $1\frac{5}{12}, 2\frac{1}{6}, 2\frac{1}{4}$
8. $0.64, 0.6, \frac{5}{8}, 0.59$ — $0.59, 0.6, \frac{5}{8}, 0.64$

Name ______________________

Lesson 41

CC.6.NS.6c

1. In a survey about favorite breakfast foods, $\frac{3}{8}$ of those surveyed chose cereal, 0.125 chose yogurt, 0.1875 chose fruit, and $\frac{5}{16}$ chose toast. Which food got the **least** number of votes?

   Ⓐ cereal
   Ⓑ fruit
   Ⓒ toast
   Ⓓ yogurt

2. Sophia buys an apple that weighs 0.45 pound, a grapefruit that weighs $\frac{3}{4}$ pound, a navel orange that weighs $\frac{5}{8}$ pound, and a pear that weighs 0.5 pound. What is the order of the fruit from **least** weight to **greatest** weight?

   Ⓐ pear, apple, grapefruit, navel orange
   Ⓑ apple, pear, navel orange, grapefruit
   Ⓒ grapefruit, navel orange, pear, apple
   Ⓓ pear, navel orange, grapefruit, apple

3. The table shows the grades that four students received on their last math test.

   Math Test Grades

Student	Score
Alex	0.95
Octavia	$\frac{16}{20}$
Tonya	$\frac{9}{10}$
Wilson	0.87

   Which shows the students in order from **greatest** test score to **least** test score?

   Ⓐ Alex, Tonya, Wilson, Octavia
   Ⓑ Octavia, Wilson, Tonya, Alex
   Ⓒ Tonya, Octavia, Alex, Wilson
   Ⓓ Wilson, Alex, Octavia, Tonya

4. Sylvia walked 1.5 miles, Chase walked $1\frac{1}{5}$ miles, Anna walked 1.7 miles, and Anthony walked $1\frac{3}{4}$ miles. Who walked the farthest?

   Ⓐ Sylvia
   Ⓑ Chase
   Ⓒ Anna
   Ⓓ Anthony

Problem Solving REAL WORLD

5. One day it snowed $3\frac{3}{8}$ inches in Altoona and 3.45 inches in Bethlehem. Which city received less snow that day?

   Altoona

6. Malia and John each bought 2 pounds of sunflower seeds. Each ate some seeds. Malia has $1\frac{1}{3}$ pounds left, and John has $1\frac{2}{5}$ pounds left. Who ate more sunflower seeds?

   Malia

Name ______________________

Lesson 42

COMMON CORE STANDARD CC.6.NS.6c
Lesson Objective: Plot ordered pairs of rational numbers on a coordinate plane.

Rational Numbers and the Coordinate Plane

A **coordinate plane** is formed by two intersecting lines on a grid. The horizontal line is the *x*-axis. The vertical line is the *y*-axis. They intersect at the **origin**.

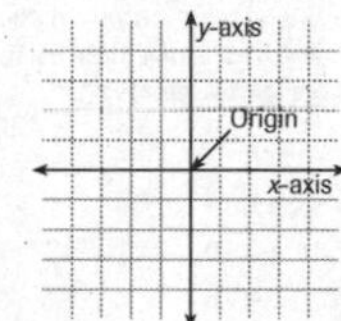

An **ordered pair** shows the horizontal and vertical distances a point is from the origin. Positive numbers in an ordered pair mean "right" for the first number and "up" for the second number. Negative numbers mean "left" for the first number and "down" for the second number.

Write the ordered pair for point *K*.

Step 1 Place your finger at point *K*. Place your pencil tip at the origin.

Step 2 With your pencil tip, count how many units to the right or left of the origin point *K* is. Record that number.

Point *K* is 2.5 units right of the origin, so the first number in the ordered pair is ⁺2.5, or 2.5.

Step 3 With your pencil tip, count how many units down from the origin point *K* is. Record that number.

Point *K* is 3.5 units down from the origin, so the second number in the ordered pair is ⁻3.5.

So, the ordered pair for point *K* is (2.5, ⁻3.5).

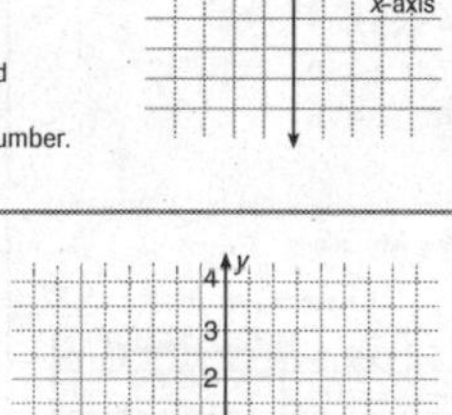
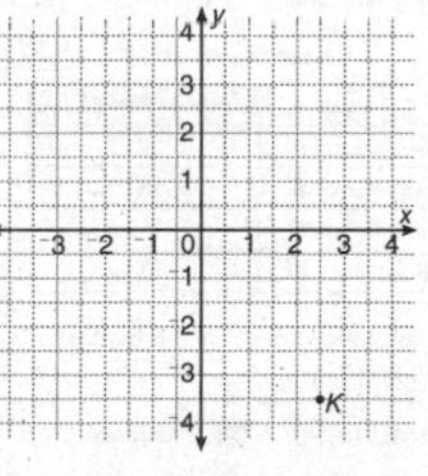

Write the ordered pair for each point.

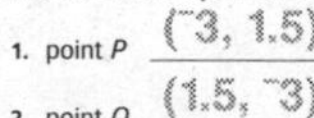

1. point *P* (⁻3, 1.5)
2. point *Q* (1.5, ⁻3)
3. point *R* (⁻1.5, 3)
4. point *S* (3, ⁻1.5)
5. point *T* (⁻1.5, ⁻3)
6. point *U* (2, 3.5)

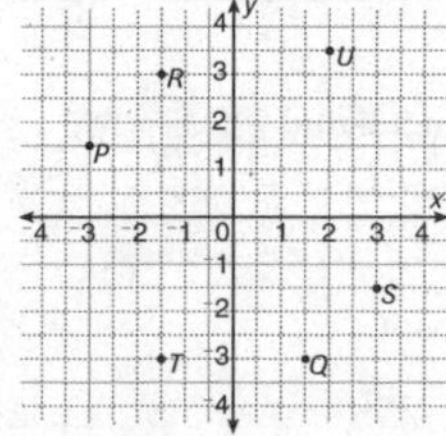

Name ______________________

Lesson 42

CC.6.NS.6c

Use the map for 1–2.

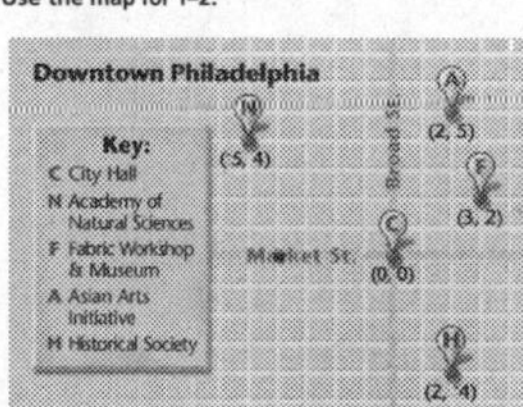

1. What ordered pair represents the Asian Arts Initiative?

   Ⓐ (2, 5)
   Ⓑ (5, 2)
   Ⓒ (⁻2, 5)
   Ⓓ (2, ⁻5)

2. What ordered pair represents the Fabric Workshop and Museum?

   Ⓐ (3, 2)
   Ⓑ (⁻5, 4)
   Ⓒ (2, 5)
   Ⓓ (2, ⁻4)

Use the coordinate plane for 3–4.

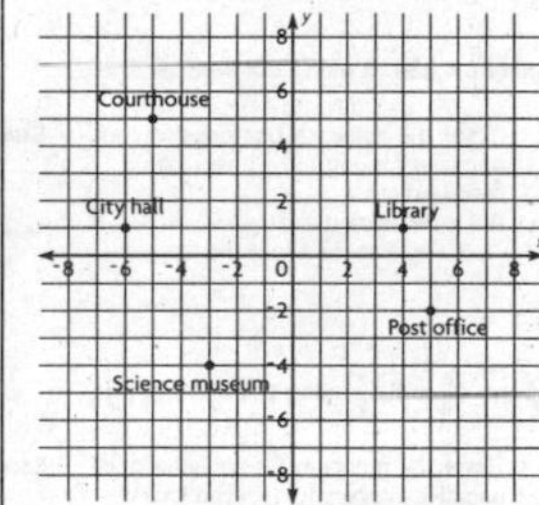

3. What ordered pair represents the library?

   Ⓐ (⁻6, 1)
   Ⓑ (⁻5, 5)
   Ⓒ (5, ⁻2)
   Ⓓ (4, 1)

4. What ordered pair represents the science museum?

   Ⓐ (⁻2, ⁻4)
   Ⓑ (⁻3, ⁻4)
   Ⓒ (⁻4, ⁻2)
   Ⓓ (5, ⁻2)

Problem Solving REAL WORLD

Use the map for 5–6.

Map of Elmwood

5. What is the ordered pair for the city hall?

   $(^{-}1, \frac{1}{2})$

6. The post office is located at $(^{-}\frac{1}{2}, 2)$. Graph and label a point on the map to represent the post office.

Answer Key

Name ____________________

Lesson 43

COMMON CORE STANDARD CC.6.NS.7a

Lesson Objective: Compare and order integers.

Compare and Order Integers

Use a number line to compare -2 and -4.

Step 1 Graph -2 and -4. Both numbers are negative integers. Graph them to the left of 0.

-5 -4 -3 -2 -1 0 1 2 3 4 5

Step 2 Decide which number is greater. Numbers become greater as you move to the right on a number line.

-2 is to the right of -4.

So, -2 is greater than -4. Write: -2 > -4.

Order these integers from least to greatest: 3, -7, 0, 4, -1.

Step 1 Graph the integers on a number line.

-10 -8 -6 -4 -2 0 2 4 6 8 10

Step 2 Write the numbers in order from left (least) to right (greatest). -7, -1, 0, 3, 4

Compare the numbers. Write < or >.

1. 3 (>) -6

-10 -8 -6 -4 -2 0 2 4 6 8 10

3 is to the **right** of -6 on the number line, so 3 is **greater** than -6.

2. -4 (<) 2
3. 1 (>) -5
4. -7 (<) -3

Order the numbers from least to greatest.

5. 4, -3, -5 — -5 < -3 < 4
6. -11, 2, 6 — -11 < 2 < 6
7. 8, -7, 4 — -7 < 4 < 8

Order the numbers from greatest to least.

8. 1, -2, 0 — 1 > 0 > -2
9. -6, 2, 5 — 5 > 2 > -6
10. -3, 3, -4 — 3 > -3 > -4

www.harcourtschoolsupply.com
© Houghton Mifflin Harcourt Publishing Company 85 Core Standards for Math, Grade 6

Name ____________________

Lesson 43

CC.6.NS.7a

1. The low temperatures in Harrisburg over 4 days were -1°C, -2°C, 4°C, and 0°C. Which list shows these temperatures written in order from **least** to **greatest**?

(A) -2°C, -1°C, 0°C, 4°C (answer)
(B) -2°C, 0°C, -1°C, 4°C
(C) -1°C, -2°C, 0°C, 4°C
(D) 4°C, 0°C, -1°C, -2°C

2. The table shows the elevation of four lakes.

Elevations of Bodies of Water

Lake	Elevation (ft)
Lake Clipson	-117
Lake Roney	66
Lake Harney	-81
Lake Campbell	97

Which lake has the **highest** elevation?

(A) Lake Clipson
(B) Lake Roney
(C) Lake Harney
(D) Lake Campbell (answer)

3. The table shows the average surface temperature of the planets in the solar system.

Average Surface Temperature of Planets

Planet	Temperature (°C)
Earth	15
Jupiter	-110
Mars	-65
Mercury	167
Neptune	-200
Saturn	-140
Uranus	-195
Venus	464

Which list shows the planets Mercury, Venus, Earth, and Mars written in order from **greatest** to **least** average surface temperature?

(A) Mercury, Venus, Earth, Mars
(B) Venus, Mercury, Earth, Mars (answer)
(C) Mars, Earth, Mercury, Venus
(D) Venus, Mercury, Mars, Earth

Problem Solving REAL WORLD

4. Meg and Derek played a game. Meg scored -11 points, and Derek scored 4 points. Write a comparison to show that Meg's score is less than Derek's score.

-11 < 4

5. Misha is thinking of a negative integer greater than -4. What number could she be thinking of?

Possible answers: -3, -2, -1

www.harcourtschoolsupply.com
© Houghton Mifflin Harcourt Publishing Company 86 Core Standards for Math, Grade 6

Name ____________________

Lesson 44

COMMON CORE STANDARDS CC.6.NS.7a, CC.6.NS.7b

Lesson Objective: Compare and order rational numbers.

Compare and Order Rational Numbers

Compare 0.5 and -3 using the number line.

Step 1 Graph the numbers. Use positive and negative integers to help you locate the decimals.
0.5 is between 0 and 1.
-3 is negative, so it is to the left of 0.

Step 2 As you move right on the number line, numbers become greater.

-3 -2 -1 0 1 2 3

So, 0.5 > -3.

Compare $-2\frac{1}{4}$ and $1\frac{1}{2}$ using the number line.

Step 1 Graph the numbers. Use positive and negative integers to help you locate the fractions.
$-2\frac{1}{4}$ is between -2 and -3. $1\frac{1}{2}$ is between 1 and 2.

Step 2 As you move left on the number line, numbers become less.

-3 -2 -1 0 1 2 3

So, $-2\frac{1}{4} < 1\frac{1}{2}$.

Compare the numbers. Write < or >.

1. -0.7 (>) $-1\frac{1}{8}$
2. 0.3 (>) -4.6
3. $-\frac{1}{4}$ (<) 3.2
4. $-\frac{5}{8}$ (>) $-2\frac{1}{2}$

Order the numbers from least to greatest.

5. 1.3, $-4\frac{1}{5}$, $-\frac{1}{2}$ — $-4\frac{1}{5} < -\frac{1}{2} < 1.3$
6. -2.5, -0.9, 1 — -2.5 < -0.9 < 1
7. 2, $2\frac{2}{3}$, -3.2 — $-3.2 < 2 < 2\frac{2}{3}$

www.harcourtschoolsupply.com
© Houghton Mifflin Harcourt Publishing Company 87 Core Standards for Math, Grade 6

Name ____________________

Lesson 44

CC.6.NS.7a, CC.6.NS.7b

1. The wind-chill temperatures on Sunday for four cities are -7.2°F, -6.7°F, -5.4°F, and -6.1°F. Which list shows these numbers in order from **least** to **greatest**?

(A) -7.2, -6.7, -5.4, -6.1
(B) -5.4, -6.1, -6.7, -7.2
(C) -7.2, -6.7, -6.1, -5.4 (answer)
(D) -6.1, -5.4, -6.7, -7.2

2. The table shows the freezing points of four different substances.

Freezing Points

Substance	Temperature (°C)
Substance A	-201.7
Substance B	-187.3
Substance C	-159.6
Substance D	-193.7

What substance freezes at the **highest** temperature?

(A) Substance A
(B) Substance B
(C) Substance C (answer)
(D) Substance D

3. The low temperatures during one week are shown in the table.

Low Temperatures

Day	Temperature (°F)
Sunday	-2.1
Monday	-3.8
Tuesday	-2.5
Wednesday	-0.4
Thursday	-1.7
Friday	-2.3
Saturday	-1.9

Which list shows the days arranged in order from **warmest** to **coldest** temperatures?

(A) Wednesday, Thursday, Saturday, Sunday, Friday, Tuesday, Monday (answer)
(B) Monday, Tuesday, Friday, Sunday, Saturday, Thursday, Wednesday
(C) Wednesday, Saturday, Thursday, Sunday, Tuesday, Friday, Monday
(D) Monday, Friday, Tuesday, Saturday, Thursday, Wednesday, Sunday

Problem Solving REAL WORLD

4. The temperature in Cold Town on Monday was 1°C. The temperature in Frosty Town on Monday was -2°C. Which town was colder on Monday?

Frosty Town

5. Stan's bank account balance is less than -$20.00 but greater than -$21.00. What could Stan's account balance be?

Possible answers are any amount from -$20.99 to -$20.01.

www.harcourtschoolsupply.com
© Houghton Mifflin Harcourt Publishing Company 88 Core Standards for Math, Grade 6

Answer Key

Name ______________________

Lesson 45

COMMON CORE STANDARD CC.6.NS.7c

Lesson Objective: Find and interpret the absolute value of rational numbers.

Absolute Value

Absolute value is a number's distance from 0 on a number line. Numbers and their opposites have the same absolute value.

Find the absolute value of ⁻3 and 4.

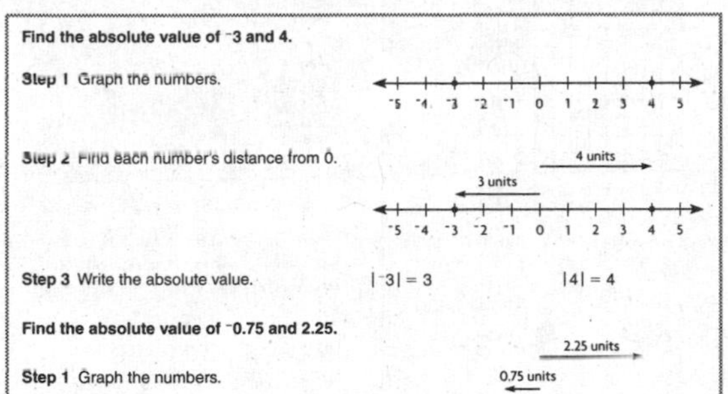

Step 1 Graph the numbers.

Step 2 Find each number's distance from 0.

Step 3 Write the absolute value. |⁻3| = 3 |4| = 4

Find the absolute value of ⁻0.75 and 2.25.

Step 1 Graph the numbers.

Step 2 Find each number's distance from 0.

Step 3 Write the absolute value. |⁻0.75| = 0.75 |2.25| = 2.25

Find the absolute value.

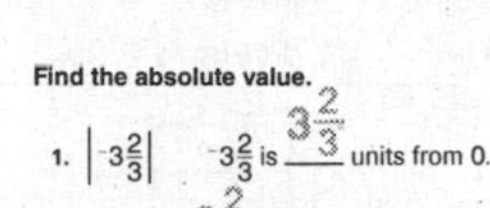

1. $\left|-3\frac{2}{3}\right|$ $-3\frac{2}{3}$ is $3\frac{2}{3}$ units from 0.

$\left|-3\frac{2}{3}\right| = 3\frac{2}{3}$

2. |⁻2.5| = 2.5
3. |7| = 7
4. $\left|\frac{4}{10}\right| = \frac{4}{10}$
5. |⁻1| = 1
6. $\left|-1\frac{4}{5}\right| = 1\frac{4}{5}$

Name ______________________

Lesson 45

CC.6.NS.7c

1. Which of the following has a value that is less than 0?
   - Ⓐ |⁻7|
   - Ⓑ |7|
   - Ⓒ ⁻7
   - Ⓓ 7

2. Which of the following does **not** have a value that is greater than 0?
   - Ⓐ |⁻11|
   - Ⓑ ⁻11
   - Ⓒ |11|
   - Ⓓ 11

3. The high temperature on Friday was ⁻3°C. What is the absolute value of ⁻3?
   - Ⓐ ⁻3
   - Ⓑ 0
   - Ⓒ 3
   - Ⓓ 6

4. During the first round of a board game, Alejandro lost 8 points. What does |⁻8| represent in this situation?
   - Ⓐ the decrease in Alejandro's score
   - Ⓑ the increase in Alejandro's score
   - Ⓒ the number of points Alejandro had at the end of the round
   - Ⓓ the number of points Alejandro had at the beginning of the round

Problem Solving REAL WORLD

5. Which two numbers are 7.5 units away from 0 on a number line?

   7.5 and ⁻7.5

6. Emilio is playing a game. He just answered a question incorrectly, so his score will change by ⁻10 points. Find the absolute value of ⁻10.

   10

Name ______________________

Lesson 46

COMMON CORE STANDARD CC.6.NS.7d

Lesson Objective: Interpret comparisons involving absolute values.

Compare Absolute Values

Use absolute value to express an elevation less than ⁻10 meters as a depth.

Step 1 Elevation indicates distance from sea level. A negative elevation means a distance below sea level. ⁻10 is 10 units below 0 on the vertical number line. This shows that the absolute value of ⁻10 is 10.

Step 2 Depth indicates distance below sea level. It is always expressed as a positive number. Use the absolute value of ⁻10 to find the depth: |⁻10| = 10

Step 3 List three elevations that are less than ⁻10 meters. Write the corresponding depths.

Elevation (m)	Depth (m)
⁻15	15
⁻20	20
⁻30	30

So, an elevation less than ⁻10 meters is a depth greater than 10 meters.

Complete the table.

1.

Elevations Greater than ⁻13	Depth
⁻12 feet	12 feet
⁻8 feet	8 feet
⁻2 feet	2 feet

2. Jordin's savings account balance is greater than ⁻$27. Use absolute value to describe the balance as a debt.

   Jordin's balance is a debt of less than $27.

3. The table shows the changes in the weights of 3 dogs. Which dog had the greatest decrease in weight? How much weight did the dog lose?

Dog	Weight Change (lb)
Duffy	1.3
Buddy	⁻1.1
Dinah	⁻1.4

Dinah; lost 1.4 lb

Name ______________________

Lesson 46

CC.6.NS.7d

1. On February 3, 1996, a record low temperature of ⁻47°F was reached in Iowa. The temperature the next day was a little warmer. Which could have been the temperature the next day?
   - Ⓐ ⁻51°F
   - Ⓑ ⁻49°F
   - Ⓒ ⁻47°F
   - Ⓓ ⁻45°F

2. While scuba diving, Amelia explored the ocean at an elevation of ⁻30 feet. Ricardo was closer to the surface of the water than Amelia. Which describes Ricardo's depth?
   - Ⓐ depth of greater than ⁻30 feet
   - Ⓑ depth of greater than 30 feet
   - Ⓒ depth of less than 30 feet
   - Ⓓ depth of less than ⁻30 feet

3. Cynthia and Antonio are hiking. Cynthia's elevation is ⁻17 feet. Antonio is a little lower than Cynthia. Which could be Antonio's elevation?
   - Ⓐ ⁻20 feet
   - Ⓑ ⁻15 feet
   - Ⓒ ⁻10 feet
   - Ⓓ ⁻5 feet

4. Last month, Margaret's puppy had a change in weight of ⁻9 ounces. Which does **not** show a greater change in weight?
   - Ⓐ loss of 10 ounces
   - Ⓑ loss of 8 ounces
   - Ⓒ gain of 14 ounces
   - Ⓓ gain of 12 ounces

Problem Solving

5. On Wednesday, Miguel's bank account balance was ⁻$55. On Thursday, his balance was less than that. Use absolute value to describe Miguel's balance on Thursday as a debt.

   In this situation, ⁻$55 represents a debt of $55. On Thursday, Miguel had a debt of more than $55.

6. During a game, Naomi lost points. She lost fewer than 3 points. Use an integer to describe her possible score.

   Possible answers: ⁻2, ⁻1

Answer Key

Name ____________________

Lesson 47

COMMON CORE STANDARD CC.6.NS.8

Lesson Objective: Find horizontal and vertical distances on the coordinate plane.

Distance on the Coordinate Plane

Find the distance between (4, ⁻2) and (4, 3).

Step 1 Graph the points. Points with the same *x*-coordinate are on the same vertical line. Think of the vertical line as a number line that shows the *y*-coordinates.

Step 2 Use absolute value to find the distances between the *y*-coordinates and 0.

|⁻2| shows the distance from ⁻2 to 0.
|⁻2| = 2 units
|3| shows the distance from 3 to 0.
|⁻3| = 3 units

Step 3 Since the points are in different quadrants, add to find the total distance between the *y*-coordinates.

So, the distance between (4, ⁻2) and (4, 3) is 5 units.

Use the same steps when two points have the same *y*-coordinates. Find the distance between the *x*-coordinates to find the distance between the points.

Graph the pair of points. Then find the distance between them.

1. (4, ⁻4) and (1, ⁻4)

The points are on the same horizontal line.

Distance from 4 to 0: |4| = 4

Distance from 1 to 0: |1| = 1

Subtract to find distance from (4, ⁻4) to (1, ⁻4):

4 − 1 = 3 units

2. (2, ⁻5) and (2, 3) 8 units
3. (⁻1, 3) and (5, 3) 6 units
4. (⁻6, 1) and (⁻6, ⁻2) 3 units

Name ____________________

Lesson 47

CC.6.NS.8

On the coordinate plane, each unit is 1 mile. Use the coordinate plane for 1–2.

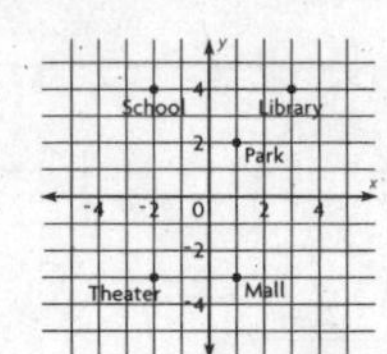

1. What is the distance from the school to the library?
   - Ⓐ 1 mile
   - Ⓑ 2 miles
   - Ⓒ 3 miles
   - Ⓓ 5 miles (answer)

2. What is the distance from the theater to the school?
   - Ⓐ 1 mile
   - Ⓑ 3 miles
   - Ⓒ 7 miles (answer)
   - Ⓓ 8 miles

Use the map for 3–4.

3. Lindsey is leaving the Asian Arts Initiative and wants to visit the Historical Society. How many blocks south does she need to walk?
   - Ⓐ 2 blocks
   - Ⓑ 4 blocks
   - Ⓒ 5 blocks
   - Ⓓ 9 blocks (answer)

4. Cesar leaves City Hall and goes to a store located at (⁻4, 0). How many blocks west does he walk?
   - Ⓐ 3 blocks
   - Ⓑ 4 blocks (answer)
   - Ⓒ 5 blocks
   - Ⓓ 6 blocks

Problem Solving REAL WORLD

The map shows the locations of several areas in an amusement park. Each unit represents 1 kilometer.

Amusement Park: Ferris Wheel, Bumper Cars, Rollercoaster, Water Slide, Restrooms

5. How far is the Ferris wheel from the rollercoaster?

4 kilometers

6. How far is the water slide from the restrooms?

7 kilometers

Name ____________________

Lesson 48

COMMON CORE STANDARD CC.6.NS.8

Lesson Objective: Solve problems on the coordinate plane by using the strategy *draw a diagram.*

Problem Solving • The Coordinate Plane

Zachary is drawing a coordinate map of his town. He has graphed the police station at the point (2, ⁻1). He is going to place the library 4 units up from the police station. What ordered pair shows where he will graph the library?

Read the Problem		
What do I need to find?	**What information do I need to use?**	**How will I use the information?**
I need to find the ordered pair for the library.	The ordered pair for the police station is (2, ⁻1). The library is 4 units up from the police station.	I can draw a diagram to graph the information on a coordinate plane.

Solve the Problem

Graph the point (2, ⁻1).
Label it Police Station.
From this point, count 4 units up.
Graph the new point, and label it Library.
So, the ordered pair for the library will be (2, 3).

Solve. Graph the pairs of points on the coordinate plane.

1. Zachary has graphed the middle school at (⁻6, 5). He has graphed the high school 3 units to the right of the middle school. What is the high school's ordered pair?

(⁻3, 5)

2. Zachary will graph the apartment building 2 units to the left and 5 units down from the grocery store. He has graphed the grocery store at (7, 8). Give the ordered pair for the apartment building.

(5, 3)

Name ____________________

Lesson 48

CC.6.NS.8

1. On a map of Geston County, the post office is located at (⁻6, 4). The fire station is located 3 units east of the post office. What ordered pair represents the location of the fire station?
   - Ⓐ (⁻3, 4) (answer)
   - Ⓑ (⁻6, 4)
   - Ⓒ (⁻6, 7)
   - Ⓓ (⁻6, 1)

2. On a map of a fair, the Ferris wheel is located at (3, 2). The carousel is located 5 units south of the Ferris wheel. What ordered pair represents the location of the carousel?
   - Ⓐ (⁻2, 2)
   - Ⓑ (3, ⁻3) (answer)
   - Ⓒ (8, 2)
   - Ⓓ (8, 7)

3. On a map of Braxton County, the library is located at (⁻3, ⁻7). The hospital is located 5 units west of the library. What ordered pair represents the location of the hospital?
   - Ⓐ (2, ⁻7)
   - Ⓑ (⁻3, ⁻2)
   - Ⓒ (⁻3, ⁻12)
   - Ⓓ (⁻8, ⁻7) (answer)

4. On a map of a sports facility, the tennis court is located at (⁻6, ⁻1). The basketball court is located 10 units north of the tennis court. What ordered pair represents the location of the basketball court?
   - Ⓐ (4, ⁻1)
   - Ⓑ (4, ⁻11)
   - Ⓒ (⁻6, 9) (answer)
   - Ⓓ (⁻16, 1)

Problem Solving REAL WORLD

5. A coordinate plane is used as a game board. The position of player 1 is at (⁻7, 3). The position of the player 2 is 3 units down from the position of the player 1. What are the coordinates of the position of player 2? Explain how you know.

(⁻7, 0); Possible explanation: I graphed and labeled a point at (⁻7, 3) and moved 3 units down. The coordinates of the point where I landed is (⁻7, 0). So, player 2 is at ordered pair (⁻7, 0).

Answer Key

Name ____________________

Lesson 49
COMMON CORE STANDARD CC.6.EE.1
Lesson Objective: Write and evaluate expressions involving exponents.

Exponents

An **exponent** tells how many times a number is used as a factor.

The **base** is the number being multiplied repeatedly.

For example, in 2^5, 5 is the exponent and 2 is the base.
$2^5 = 2 \times 2 \times 2 \times 2 \times 2 = 32$

Write the expression 4^5 using equal factors. Then find the value.

Step 1 Identify the base.	The base is 4.
Step 2 Identify the exponent.	The exponent is 5.
Step 3 Write the base as many times as the exponent tells you. Place a multiplication symbol between the bases.	$4 \times 4 \times 4 \times 4 \times 4$ You should have one less multiplication symbol than the value of the exponent.
Step 4 Multiply.	$4 \times 4 \times 4 \times 4 \times 4 = 1{,}024$

So, $4^5 = 1{,}024$.

Write as an expression using equal factors. Then find the value.

1. 3^4 — $3 \times 3 \times 3 \times 3$; 81
2. 2^6 — $2 \times 2 \times 2 \times 2 \times 2 \times 2$; 64
3. 4^3 — $4 \times 4 \times 4$; 64
4. 5^3 — $5 \times 5 \times 5$; 125
5. 10^4 — $10 \times 10 \times 10 \times 10$; 10,000
6. 8^5 — $8 \times 8 \times 8 \times 8 \times 8$; 32,768
7. 11^4 — $11 \times 11 \times 11 \times 11$; 14,641
8. 15^2 — 15×15; 225
9. 10^7 — $10 \times 10 \times 10 \times 10 \times 10 \times 10 \times 10$; 10,000,000
10. 25^4 — $25 \times 25 \times 25 \times 25$; 390,625

Name ____________________

Lesson 49
CC.6.EE.1

1. The bill with the greatest value ever printed in the United States had a value of 10^5 dollars. Which is another way to write that amount?
   - (A) $10,000
   - (B) $50,000
   - **(C) $100,000**
   - (D) $500,000

2. Carlos represented 729 with a base and an exponent. Which of the following is **not** possible?
   - (A) The base is less than the exponent.
   - **(B) The base and the exponent are equal.**
   - (C) The base and the exponent are multiples of 3.
   - (D) The base is an odd number and the exponent is an even number.

3. John is making a patio in his yard. He needs a total of 15^2 concrete blocks to cover the area. How many blocks does John need?
   - (A) 30
   - (B) 125
   - (C) 152
   - **(D) 225**

4. Which is a way to write $2 \times 2 \times 2 \times 5 \times 5$ with exponents and two bases?
   - **(A) $2^3 \times 5^2$**
   - (B) $3^2 \times 2^5$
   - (C) $2^5 \times 5^5$
   - (D) $2^5 \times 10 \times 5$

Problem Solving REAL WORLD

5. Each day Shelia doubles the number of push-ups she did the day before. On the fifth day, she does $2 \times 2 \times 2 \times 2 \times 2$ push-ups. Use an exponent to write the number of push-ups Shelia does on the fifth day.

   2^5

6. The city of Beijing has a population of more than 10^7 people. Write 10^7 without using an exponent.

   10,000,000

Name ____________________

Lesson 50
COMMON CORE STANDARD CC.6.EE.1
Lesson Objective: Use the order of operations to evaluate expressions involving exponents.

Evaluate Expressions Involving Exponents

A **numerical expression** is a mathematical phrase that includes only numbers and operation symbols.

You **evaluate** the expression when you perform all the computations.

To evaluate an expression, use the **order of operations.**

Order of Operations
1. Parentheses
2. Exponents
3. Multiply and Divide
4. Add and Subtract

Evaluate the expression $(10 + 6^2) - 4 \times 10$.

Step 1 Start with the *parentheses*. Use the order of operations for the computations inside the parentheses.	$10 + 6^2$ Find the value of the number with an *exponent*. Rewrite as multiplication: $10 + 6^2 = 10 + 6 \times 6$ *Multiply and divide* from left to right: $10 + 6 \times 6 = 10 + 36$ *Add and subtract* from left to right: $10 + 36 = 46$
Step 2 Rewrite the original expression, using the value from Step 1 for the part in parentheses.	$(10 + 6^2) - 4 \times 10 = 46 - 4 \times 10$
Step 3 Now that the parentheses are cleared, look for *exponents*.	There are no more *exponents*, so go on to the next step in the order of operations.
Step 4 *Multiply and divide* from left to right.	$46 - 4 \times 10 = 46 - 40$
Step 5 *Add and subtract* from left to right.	$46 - 40 = 6$

So, $(10 + 6^2) - 4 \times 10 = 6$.

Evaluate the expression.

1. $8^2 - (7^2 + 1)$ — 14
2. $5 - 2^2 + 12 \div 4$ — 4
3. $8 \times (16 - 2^4)$ — 0
4. $3^2 \times (28 - 20 \div 2)$ — 162
5. $(30 - 15 \div 3) \div 5^2$ — 1
6. $(6^2 - 3^2) - 9 \div 3$ — 24

Name ____________________

Lesson 50
CC.6.EE.1

1. Which expression has a value of 250?
   - (A) $1 + 6 \times 7 - 5^2$
   - (B) $1 + 7^2 - 6 \times 5$
   - (C) $(7 + 6) \times 5^2 - 1$
   - **(D) $(6^2 - 1) \times 7 + 5$**

2. An employee placed 2^4 books onto each of 5 shelves. How many books did she place on the shelves in all?
   - (A) 16
   - **(B) 80**
   - (C) 120
   - (D) 245

3. A scientist placed 8 one-celled organisms into a dish. Each cell split into 2 cells every hour. The expression 8×2^6 represents the number of cells after 6 hours. How many cells were in the dish after 6 hours?
   - (A) 64
   - (B) 208
   - **(C) 512**
   - (D) 826

4. Which expression has a value of 35?
   - (A) $7 + (2^2 - 3) + 4 \times 4$
   - (B) $3 \times (7^2 - 4) \times 4 + 2$
   - **(C) $4^2 + 3 \times (7 - 2) + 4$**
   - (D) $2^2 \times 7 - (4 + 4) \times 3$

Problem Solving REAL WORLD

5. Hugo is saving for a new baseball glove. He saves $10 the first week, and $6 each week for the next 6 weeks. The expression $10 + 6^2$ represents the total amount in dollars he has saved. What is the total amount Hugo has saved?

   $46

6. A scientist placed fish eggs in a tank. Each day, twice the number of eggs from the previous day hatch. The expression 5×2^6 represents the number of eggs that hatch on the sixth day. How many eggs hatch on the sixth day?

   320 eggs

Answer Key

Name ______________________

Lesson 51

COMMON CORE STANDARD CC.6.EE.2a

Lesson Objective: Write algebraic expressions.

Write Algebraic Expressions

Word problems use expressions that you can write with symbols. An **algebraic expression** has at least one variable. A **variable** is a letter or symbol that represents one or more numbers. Writing algebraic expressions for words helps you solve word problems.

These are a few common words that are used for operations.

add (+)	subtract (−)	multiply (×)	divide (÷)
sum increased by plus more than	difference minus decreased by less less than	product times	quotient divided by

17 more than *x*
$x + 17$

"More than" means add.
"17 more than *x*" means add 17 to *x*.

four times the sum of 7 and *n*
$4 \times (7 + n)$

"Times" means multiply.
"Sum" means add.
The words mean multiply 4 by $(7 + n)$.

A number next to a variable always shows multiplication.
For example, **5*n*** means the same as **5 × *n***.

Write an algebraic expression for the word expression.

1. *b* divided by 9 — $b \div 9$ or $\frac{b}{9}$
2. *c* more than 5 — $5 + c$
3. *d* decreased by 29 — $d - 29$
4. 8 times *g* — $8 \times g$ or $8g$
5. *p* increased by 12 — $p + 12$
6. the quotient of *k* and 14 — $k \div 14$ or $\frac{k}{14}$
7. 17 less than the product of 3 and *m* — $3 \times m - 17$ or $3m - 17$
8. 2 less than the quotient of *d* and 16 — $d \div 16 - 2$ or $\frac{d}{16} - 2$

Name ______________________

Lesson 51

CC.6.EE.2a

1. There are 16 ounces in 1 pound. Which expression gives the number of ounces in *p* pounds?

   Ⓐ $16 + p$
   Ⓑ $16 - p$
   Ⓒ $16p$
   Ⓓ $p \div 16$

2. The length of a swimming pool is 5 feet shorter than twice the width. Let *n* represent the width. Which expression gives the length of the swimming pool?

   Ⓐ $2n + 5$
   Ⓑ $2n - 5$
   Ⓒ $2(n - 5)$
   Ⓓ $2(n + 5)$

3. Carmen's family rents a boat at Big Lake at the rate described.

BIG LAKE BOAT
RENTAL
$200 each day
$4 for each gallon of gasoline used
19-ft

   Which expression gives the total cost of the day's rental if her family uses *n* gallons of gasoline?

   Ⓐ $200 - 4n$
   Ⓑ $200 + 4n$
   Ⓒ $(200 + 4) \times n$
   Ⓓ $200n + 4$

4. There are 5,280 feet in 1 mile. Which expression gives the number of feet in *m* miles?

   Ⓐ $5{,}280m$
   Ⓑ $5{,}280 \div m$
   Ⓒ $5{,}280 - m$
   Ⓓ $5{,}280 + m$

Problem Solving

5. Let *h* represent Mark's height in inches. Suzanne is 7 inches shorter than Mark. Write an algebraic expression that represents Suzanne's height in inches.

   $h - 7$

6. A company rents bicycles for a fee of $10 plus $4 per hour of use. Write an algebraic expression for the total cost in dollars for renting a bicycle for *h* hours.

   $10 + 4h$

Name ______________________

Lesson 52

COMMON CORE STANDARD CC.6.EE.2b

Lesson Objective: Identify and describe parts of expressions.

Identify Parts of Expressions

Each part of an expression between the operation signs + or − is a **term**. A **coefficient** is a number multiplied by a variable, or letter.

Describe the parts of the expression 6*b* − 7. Then write a word expression.

Step 1 Identify the terms.	There are two terms: 6*b* and 7.
Step 2 Describe the terms.	The first term shows multiplication: $6b = 6 \times b$. 6*b* is the product of 6 (the coefficient) and *b* (the variable). The second term is the number 7.
Step 3 Identify the operation separating the terms.	Subtraction gives the difference of the two terms in the expression.
Step 4 Write a word expression.	"the difference of 6 times *b* and 7" or "7 less than the product of 6 and *b*"

Identify the parts of the expression. Then write a word expression for the numerical or algebraic expression. 2–3. Possible answers given.

1. $5 \times (m - 2)$

   Identify the parts. 5; *m* − 2
   Describe the parts. the number 5; the difference of the variable *m* and the number 2
   Identify the operations. multiplication and subtraction
   Write a word expression. 5 times the difference of *m* and 2

2. $12 \div 2 + 7$

   The division is the quotient of 12 and 2. The addition is the sum of the quotient and 7. Word expression: the quotient of 12 and 2, plus 7

3. $8y + (2 \times 11)$

   The multiplications are the product of 8 and *y* and the product of 2 and 11. The addition is the sum of the products. Word expression: the product of 8 and *y* plus the product of 2 and 11

Name ______________________

Lesson 52

CC.6.EE.2b

1. The baker at Sweetie Pie Cafe baked 7 cherry pies and 8 apple pies yesterday. She cut each cherry pie into 6 slices and each apple pie into 8 slices. At the end of the day, there were 5 slices of pie left unsold. The expression $(7 \times 6) + (8 \times 8) - 5$ gives the number of slices that were sold. Which describes a part in this expression?

   Ⓐ the sum of 6 and 8
   Ⓑ the difference of 8 and 5
   Ⓒ the sum of 7 and 6
   Ⓓ the product of 8 and 8

2. The cost for a group of people to go to the movies is given by the expression $9a + 5b$, where *a* is the number of adults and *b* is the number of children. What are the coefficients of this expression?

   Ⓐ 9 and 5
   Ⓑ *a* and *b*
   Ⓒ 9*a* and 5*b*
   Ⓓ + and ×

3. Martin is making curtains. He buys 6 yards of fabric that cost *p* dollars per yard and 8 yards of fabric that cost *q* dollars per yard. The total amount of his purchase is given by the expression $6p + 8q$. What are the terms of this expression?

   Ⓐ 6 and 8
   Ⓑ *p* and *q*
   Ⓒ 6*p* and 8*q*
   Ⓓ + and ×

4. Heidi bought 5 pepperoni pizzas and 6 cheese pizzas for a party. Each pepperoni pizza was cut into 8 pieces and each cheese pizza was cut into 10 pieces. There were 9 pieces of pizza left. The expression $(5 \times 8) + (6 \times 10) - 9$ gives the number of pieces that were eaten. Which describes a part in this expression?

   Ⓐ the product of 5 and 8
   Ⓑ the sum of 8 and 6
   Ⓒ the difference between 10 and 9
   Ⓓ the sum of 6 and 10

Problem Solving

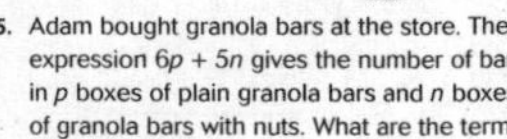

5. Adam bought granola bars at the store. The expression $6p + 5n$ gives the number of bars in *p* boxes of plain granola bars and *n* boxes of granola bars with nuts. What are the terms of the expression?

   6*p* and 5*n*

6. In the sixth grade, each student will get 4 new books. There is one class of 15 students and one class of 20 students. The expression $4 \times (15 + 20)$ gives the total number of new books. Write a word expression for the numerical expression.

   The product of 4 and the sum of 15 and 20.

Name ______________________

Lesson 53

COMMON CORE STANDARD CC.6.EE.2c

Lesson Objective: Evaluate algebraic expressions and formulas.

Evaluate Algebraic Expressions and Formulas

To evaluate an algebraic expression or formula, substitute the value for the variable. Then follow the order of operations.

Evaluate $5x + x^3$ for $x = 3, 2, 1$, and 0.

$5x + x^3$ for $x = 3$	$5x + x^3$ for $x = 2$	$5x + x^3$ for $x = 1$	$5x + x^3$ for $x = 0$
$5 \times 3 + 3^3$	$5 \times 2 + 2^3$	$5 \times 1 + 1^3$	$5 \times 0 + 0^3$
$5 \times 3 + 27$	$5 \times 2 + 8$	$5 \times 1 + 1$	$5 \times 0 + 0$
$15 + 27$	$10 + 8$	$5 + 1$	$0 + 0$
42	18	6	0

To evaluate an expression with more than one variable, substitute each variable's value. Then follow the order of operations.

Evaluate $4c - 7 + 2d$ for $c = 2$ and $d = 5$.

$4 \times 2 - 7 + 2 \times 5$

$8 - 7 + 10$

$1 + 10$

11

So, $4c - 7 + 2d = 11$ for $c = 2$ and $d = 5$.

Evaluate the expression for x = 3, 2, 1, and 0.

1. $13 + 6x$ — 31, 25, 19, 13
2. $5x + 2$ — 17, 12, 7, 2
3. $2x + 3 + x^2$ — 18, 11, 6, 3
4. $2x + x^2$ — 15, 8, 3, 0

Evaluate the expression for the given values of the variables.

5. $7x + y + 16$ for $x = 2, y = 3$ — 33
6. $8a + 11 - 2b$ for $a = 4, b = 2$ — 39
7. $12b - 2c + 3$ for $b = 5, c = 10$ — 43

Name ______________________

Lesson 53

CC.6.EE.2c

1. The expression $4c$ gives the science test score that a student receives for c correct problems. What is the score for 18 correct problems?

   Ⓐ 418
   Ⓑ 184
   Ⓒ 72
   Ⓓ 22

2. The expression $180 \times (n - 2)$ gives the sum of the measures of the angles, in degrees, of a polygon with n sides. What is the sum of the measures of the angles in a polygon with 10 sides?

   Ⓐ 1,080 degrees
   Ⓑ 1,440 degrees
   Ⓒ 1,880 degrees
   Ⓓ 2,160 degrees

3. The stock clerks at Mega Brands earn \$320 each week plus \$16 per hour for any overtime. They use the expression $320 + 16h$ to find their total earnings for a week in which they worked h hours of overtime. What are the total earnings of a stock clerk who worked 4 hours of overtime last week?

   Ⓐ \$324
   Ⓑ \$352
   Ⓒ \$384
   Ⓓ \$484

4. The expression $500v$ gives the number of points a player earns for completing v voyages in a video game. How many points are earned for completing 8 voyages?

   Ⓐ 508
   Ⓑ 1,800
   Ⓒ 2,500
   Ⓓ 4,000

Problem Solving REAL WORLD

5. The formula $P = 2\ell + 2w$ gives the perimeter P of a rectangular room with length ℓ and width w. A rectangular living room is 26 feet long and 21 feet wide. What is the perimeter of the room?

   94 feet

6. The formula $c = 5(f - 32) \div 9$ gives the Celsius temperature in c degrees for a Fahrenheit temperature of f degrees. What is the Celsius temperature for a Fahrenheit temperature of 122 degrees?

   50 degrees Celsius

Name ______________________

Lesson 54

COMMON CORE STANDARD CC.6.EE.3

Lesson Objective: Combine like terms by applying the strategy *use a model*.

Problem Solving • Combine Like Terms

Use a bar model to solve the problem.

Each hour a company assembles 10 bikes. It sends 6 of those bikes to stores and keeps the rest of the bikes to sell itself. The expression $10h - 6h$ represents the number of bikes the store keeps to sell itself for h hours of work. Simplify the expression by combining like terms.

Read the Problem		
What do I need to find?	**What information do I need to use?**	**How will I use the information?**
I need to simplify the expression $10h - 6h$	I need to use the like terms $10h$ and $6h$.	I can use a bar model to find the difference of the like terms.

Solve the Problem

Draw a bar model to subtract $6h$ from $10h$. Each square represents h, or $1h$.

10 h

h	h	h	h	h	h	h	h	h	h
h	h	h	h	h	h				

6 h   4 h

The model shows that $10h - 6h = 4h$.

So, a simplified expression for the number of bikes the store keeps is $4h$.

1. Bradley sells produce in boxes at a farmer's market. He put 6 ears of corn and 9 tomatoes in each box. The expression $6b + 9b$ represents the total pieces of produce in b boxes. Simplify the expression by combining like terms.

   $15b$

2. Andre bought pencils in packs of 8. He gave 2 pencils to his sister and 3 pencils from each pack to his friends. The expression $8p - 3p - 2$ represents the number of pencils Andre has left from p packs. Simplify the expression by combining like terms.

   $5p - 2$

Name ______________________

Lesson 54

CC.6.EE.3

1. Sandwiches cost \$5, french fries cost \$3, and drinks cost \$2. The expression $5n + 3n + 2n$ gives the total cost, in dollars for buying a sandwich, french fries, and a drink for n people. Which is another way to write this expression?

   Ⓐ $10n$
   Ⓑ $10n^3$
   Ⓒ $30n$
   Ⓓ $30n^3$

2. Jackets cost \$15 and a set of decorative buttons costs \$5. The delivery fee is \$5 per order. The expression $15n + 5n + 5$ gives the cost, in dollars, of buying jackets with buttons for n people. Which is another way to write this expression?

   Ⓐ $25n$
   Ⓑ $25n^2$
   Ⓒ $20n + 5$
   Ⓓ $20n^2 + 5$

3. Dana has n quarters. Ivan has 2 fewer than 3 times the number of quarters Dana has. The expression $n + 3n - 2$ gives the number of quarters they have altogether. Which is another way to write this expression?

   Ⓐ $2n^2$
   Ⓑ 2n
   Ⓒ $4n^2 - 2$
   Ⓓ $4n - 2$

4. Scarves cost \$12 and snowmen pins cost \$2. Shipping is \$3 per order. The expression $12n + 2n + 3$ gives the cost, in dollars, of buying scarves with pins for n people. Which is another way to write this expression?

   Ⓐ $14n^2 + 3$
   Ⓑ $14n + 3$
   Ⓒ $17n^2$
   Ⓓ $17n$

Problem Solving REAL WORLD

5. Debbie is n years old. Edna is 3 years older than Debbie, and Shawn is twice as old as Edna. The expression $n + n + 3 + 2 \times (n + 3)$ gives the sum of their ages. Simplify the expression by combining like terms. Explain how you found your answer.

   $4n + 9$; First, I used the Distributive Property to rewrite the expression as $n + n + 3 + (2 \times n) + (2 \times 3)$, or $n + n + 3 + 2n + 6$. Then I used the Commutative Property of Addition to switch the order of 3 and $2n$. Finally, I combined the like terms: $n + n + 2n + 3 + 6 = 4n + 9$.

Answer Key

Name ______________________

Lesson 55

COMMON CORE STANDARD CC.6.EE.3

Lesson Objective: Use the properties of operations to generate equivalent algebraic expressions.

Generate Equivalent Expressions

Equivalent expressions are two or more expressions that are equal for any value of the variable in the expressions. You can use the properties of operations to write equivalent expressions.

Write an equivalent expression for 4c + 2 + c.

Step 1 Identify like terms. — $4c$ and c

Step 2 Use properties of operations to combine like terms.
Commutative Property of Addition: switch 2 and c
Associative Property of Addition: group 4c and c
Add 4c and c.

$4c + 2 + c = 4c + c + 2$
$= (4c + c) + 2$
$= 5c + 2$

Use properties of operations to write an equivalent expression by combining like terms.

1. $7x + 2x + 5x$ — $14x$
2. $8a + 11 - 2a$ — $6a + 11$
3. $12b - 8b + 3$ — $4b + 3$
4. $9c - 6 + c$ — $10c - 6$
5. $4p + 1 - p$ — $3p + 1$
6. $8y - 2y + y$ — $7y$

Use the Distributive Property to write an equivalent expression.

7. $3(m + 7)$ — $3m + 21$
8. $4(2t + 3)$ — $8t + 12$
9. $5(9 + 6r)$ — $45 + 30r$
10. $8(4n - 2n)$ — $32n - 16n$

Name ______________________

Lesson 55

CC.6.EE.3

1. Chen bought a basketball for \$23, three baseball caps, and a pair of running shoes for \$37. To find the total cost in dollars, he wrote $23 + 3d + 37 = 23 + 37 + 3d$. Which property does the equation show?

   (A) Associative Property of Addition
   (B) Commutative Property of Addition
   (C) Distributive Property
   (D) Identity Property of 1

2. Tickets for the amusement park cost \$36 each. Which expression can be used to find the cost, in dollars, of k tickets for the amusement park?

   (A) $(k + 30) \times (k + 6)$
   (B) $(k + 30) + (k + 6)$
   (C) $(k \times 30) \times (k \times 6)$
   (D) $(k \times 30) + (k \times 6)$

3. A restaurant owner bought b large bags of flour for \$45 each and b large bags of sugar for \$25 each. The expression $b \times 45 + b \times 25$ gives the total cost, in dollars, of the flour and sugar. Which is another way to write this expression?

   (A) $b + (45 + 25)$
   (B) $b \times (45 + 25)$
   (C) $b + (45 \times b) + 25$
   (D) $b \times (45 + b) \times 25$

4. Ramon bought 6 packs of football cards, p packs of hockey cards, and $4p$ packs of baseball cards. Ramon wrote this number sentence to find the total number of cards he bought.

   $(6 + p) + 4p = 6 + (p + 4p)$

   Which property did Ramon use?

   (A) Associative Property of Addition
   (B) Commutative Property of Addition
   (C) Distributive Property
   (D) Identity Property of 1

Problem Solving REAL WORLD

5. The expression $15n + 12n + 100$ represents the total cost in dollars for skis, boots, and a lesson for n skiers. Simplify the expression $15n + 12n + 100$. Then find the total cost for 8 skiers.

   $27n + 100$; \$316

6. Casey has n nickels. Megan has 4 times as many nickels as Casey has. Write an expression for the total number of nickels Casey and Megan have. Then simplify the expression.

   $n + 4n$; $5n$

Name ______________________

Lesson 56

COMMON CORE STANDARD CC.6.EE.4

Lesson Objective: Identify equivalent algebraic expressions.

Identify Equivalent Expressions

Use properties to determine whether 5a + 7(3 + a) and 12a + 21 are equivalent.

Step 1 Rewrite the first expression using the Distributive Property. Multiply 7 and 3 and multiply 7 and a. — $5a + 7(3 + a) = 5a + 21 + 7a$

Step 2 Use the Commutative Property of Addition. Switch 21 and 7a. — $= 5a + 7a + 21$

Step 3 Use the Associative Property of Addition to group like terms. 5a and 7a are like terms. — $= (5a + 7a) + 21$

Step 4 Combine like terms. — $= 12a + 21$

Compare the expressions: $12a + 21$ and $12a + 21$. They are the same. So, the expressions $5a + 7(3 + a)$ and $12a + 21$ are equivalent.

Use properties to determine whether the expressions are equivalent.

1. $6(p + q)$ and $6p + q$ — not equivalent
2. $7y - 15 + 2y$ and $9y - 15$ — equivalent
3. $1 + (8r + 9)$ and $(2 + 8) + 8r$ — equivalent
4. $0 \times 11 + 5n$ and $5n$ — equivalent
5. $16s - 4 + s$ and $12s$ — not equivalent
6. $11d \times 2$ and $22d$ — equivalent
7. $10(e + 0.5g)$ and $10e + 5g$ — equivalent
8. $8m + (9m - 1)$ and $8m - 8$ — not equivalent
9. $7(1 \times 2h)$ and $21h$ — not equivalent

Name ______________________

Lesson 56

CC.6.EE.4

1. On Saturday, a farmer planted 10 rows of tomato plants with p plants in each row. On Sunday, she planted 6 rows of pepper plants with p plants in each row. Which expression gives the total number of plants the farmer planted this weekend?

   (A) $10(6 + p)$
   (B) $6(10 + p)$
   (C) $60p$
   (D) $16p$

2. Jacob made 8 pitchers of iced tea for the school picnic. Each pitcher filled g glasses. After the picnic, there were 2 glasses of iced tea left over. If no glasses were spilled, which expression gives the number of glasses that were drunk at the picnic?

   (A) $2(4g - 1)$
   (B) $4g(2 - 1)$
   (C) $2(1 - 4g)$
   (D) $4g(1 - 2)$

3. Jeremy's teacher buys 6 packs of thumbtacks. Each pack contains t thumbtacks. She uses 18 thumbtacks to display posters around her classroom. Which expression gives the number of thumbtacks she has left?

   (A) $3(6 - t)$
   (B) $3(t - 6)$
   (C) $6(t - 3)$
   (D) $6(3 - t)$

4. Jolene made 8 pink bracelets using b beads on each bracelet and 7 blue bracelets with b beads on each bracelet. Which expression gives the total number of beads she used?

   (A) $56b$
   (B) $15b$
   (C) $8(b + 7)$
   (D) $7(8 + b)$

Problem Solving 

5. Rachel needs to write 3 book reports with b pages and 3 science reports with s pages during the school year. Write an algebraic expression for the total number of pages Rachel will need to write.

   $3b + 3s$

6. Rachel's friend Yassi has to write $3(b + s)$ pages for reports. Use properties of operations to determine whether this expression is equivalent to the expression for the number of pages Rachel has to write.

   equivalent

Name ____________________

Lesson 57
COMMON CORE STANDARD CC.6.EE.5
Lesson Objective: Determine whether a number is a solution of an equation.

Solutions of Equations

An **equation** is a statement that two mathematical expressions are equal.

Some equations include only numbers, operation signs, and an equal sign. Example: $2 + 17 = 19$

Other equations also include variables, such as x. Example: $50 - x = 37$

For an equation with a variable, a **solution** is a value of the variable that makes the equation true.

Equation: $8.6 + m = 13$	Is $m = 5.3$ a solution?	Is $m = 4.4$ a solution?
Step 1 Write the equation.	$8.6 + m = 13$	$8.6 + m = 13$
Step 2 Substitute the given number for the variable m.	$8.6 + 5.3 \stackrel{?}{=} 13$	$8.6 + 4.4 \stackrel{?}{=} 13$
Step 3 Add.	$13.9 \neq 13$ ($\neq$ means *does not equal*)	$13 = 13$
Decide whether the equation is true.	The equation is not true. So, $m = 5.3$ is not a solution.	The equation is true. So, $m = 4.4$ is a solution.

Determine whether the given value of the variable is a solution of the equation.

1. $p - 4 = 6$; $p = 10$
   $10 - 4 \stackrel{?}{=} 6$
   $6 = 6$
   solution
2. $15.2 + y = 22$; $y = 6.8$
   solution
3. $n + 3 = 16$; $n = 12$
   not a solution
4. $7.4 - k = 5$; $k = 3.4$
   not a solution
5. $1\frac{1}{2} + t = 3\frac{1}{2}$; $t = 2$
   solution
6. $4x = 36$; $x = 8$
   not a solution

Name ____________________

Lesson 57
CC.6.EE.5

1. Sheila scored 87 points on her science quiz. She scored 2 more points than Felicia. The equation $p + 2 = 87$ gives the number of points p that Felicia scored on her science quiz. How many points did Felicia score on her quiz?
   Ⓐ 75
   Ⓑ 79
   Ⓒ 85 (answer)
   Ⓓ 89

2. After spending \$3.75 on a magazine, Lorraine has \$12.25 left. The equation $x - 3.75 = 12.25$ can be used to find the amount of money x Lorraine had before purchasing the magazine. Which is a solution of the equation?
   Ⓐ $x = \$16.00$ (answer)
   Ⓑ $x = \$12.25$
   Ⓒ $x = \$9.00$
   Ⓓ $x = \$8.25$

3. Luke is 14 years old. He is 2 years younger than his brother Frank. The equation $f - 2 = 14$ gives Frank's age f. How old is Frank?
   Ⓐ 16 (answer)
   Ⓑ 12
   Ⓒ 7
   Ⓓ 6

4. This month, Thelma's telephone bill is \$43.30. It is \$4.60 less than last month's bill. The equation $t - 4.60 = 43.30$ can be used to find the amount of last month's bill t. Which is a solution of the equation?
   Ⓐ $t = \$38.70$
   Ⓑ $t = \$39.60$
   Ⓒ $t = \$44.00$
   Ⓓ $t = \$47.90$ (answer)

Problem Solving REAL WORLD

5. Terrance needs to score 25 points to win a game. He has already scored 18 points. The equation $18 + p = 25$ gives the number of points p that Terrance still needs to score. Determine whether $p = 7$ or $p = 13$ is a solution of the equation, and tell what the solution means.
   $p = 7$ is a solution; $p = 13$ is not a solution; Terrance needs to score 7 points to win.

6. Madeline has used 50 sheets of a roll of paper towels, which is $\frac{5}{8}$ of the entire roll. The equation $\frac{5}{8}s = 50$ can be used to find the number of sheets s in a full roll. Determine whether $s = 32$ or $s = 80$ is a solution of the equation, and tell what the solution means.
   $s = 32$ is not a solution; $s = 80$ is a solution; There are 80 sheets in a full roll.

Name ____________________

Lesson 58
COMMON CORE STANDARD CC.6.EE.5
Lesson Objective: Determine whether a number is a solution of an inequality.

Solutions of Inequalities

An **inequality** is a mathematical sentence that compares expressions. A **solution of an inequality** is a value for a variable that makes the inequality true.

For the inequality $a < 3$ (a is less than 3), $a = 1$ is a solution because 1 is less than 3. $a = 3$ is *not* a solution because 3 is *not* less than 3.

Inequalities use these symbols: $<$ (less than), $>$ (greater than), $\leq$ (less than or equal to), and $\geq$ (greater than or equal to).

	For the inequality $x \leq 5$, is $x = 3$ a solution?	For the inequality $y > 8$, is $y = 3$ a solution?
Step 1 Understand the inequality.	$x \leq 5$ means "x is less than or equal to 5." Any value that is equal to 5 or less than 5 is a solution.	$y > 8$ means "y is greater than 8." Any value that is greater than 8 is a solution.
Step 2 Decide whether the value is a solution.	3 is less than 5, so $x = 3$ is a solution.	3 is not greater than 8, so $y = 3$ is not a solution.

Determine whether the given value of the variable is a solution of the inequality.

1. $m \geq 4$; $m = 2$
   $m \geq 4$ means "m is greater than or equal to 4."
   $m = 2$ is not a solution
2. $k < 7$; $k = 5$
   solution
3. $z \geq 12$; $z = 12$
   solution
4. $y \leq 3$; $y = 6$
   not a solution
5. $n > 13$; $n = 8$
   not a solution
6. $t < 7$; $t = 5$
   solution

Give two solutions of the inequality. Possible answers are given.

7. $x > 4$
   $x = 5$; $x = 6$
8. $p \leq 3$
   $p = 3$; $p = 2$
9. $v \geq 9$
   $v = 9$; $v = 10$

Name ____________________

Lesson 58
CC.6.EE.5

1. The inequality $w < 1,300$ represents the weight limit in pounds w of an elevator. Which is a solution of the inequality?
   Ⓐ $w = 1,239$ (answer)
   Ⓑ $w = 1,304$
   Ⓒ $w = 1,414$
   Ⓓ $w = 1,575$

2. A road sign shows that motorists must travel at a speed no more than 55 miles per hour. The inequality $s \leq 55$ represents the permitted speeds s. Which is **not** a solution of the inequality?
   Ⓐ $s = 50$
   Ⓑ $s = 52$
   Ⓒ $s = 55$
   Ⓓ $s = 60$ (answer)

3. Theodore must score at least 12 points to advance to the next level of a video game. The inequality $p \geq 12$ represents the possible number of points p that he can score to advance to the next level. Which is a solution of the inequality?
   Ⓐ $p = 4$
   Ⓑ $p = 0$
   Ⓒ $p = 13$ (answer)
   Ⓓ $p = 9$

4. A pitcher can hold no more than 64 ounces. The inequality $p \leq 64$ represents the possible number of ounces p the pitcher can hold. Which is a solution of the inequality?
   Ⓐ $p = 61$ (answer)
   Ⓑ $p = 66$
   Ⓒ $p = 68$
   Ⓓ $p = 70$

Problem Solving REAL WORLD

5. The inequality $s \geq 92$ represents the score s that Jared must earn on his next test to get an A on his report card. Give two possible scores that Jared could earn to get the A.
   92; 95

6. The inequality $m \leq \$20$ represents the amount of money that Sheila is allowed to spend on a new hat. Give two possible money amounts that Sheila could spend on the hat.
   \$20; \$19

Name ______________________

Lesson 59
COMMON CORE STANDARD CC.6.EE.6
Lesson Objective: Use algebraic expressions to solve problems.

Use Algebraic Expressions

You can use an algebraic expression to help solve a word problem. Use a variable to represent the unknown number.

Ina wants to serve salad at her party. She will need one head of lettuce for every 6 guests who attend. Write an expression she could use for deciding how much lettuce she needs.

Step 1 Decide what operation the problem uses. — Each head of lettuce will serve 6 people. Divide the number of guests by 6.

Step 2 Identify the unknown number. — The problem does not state how many guests will attend. Use the variable g for the number of guests.

Step 3 Write a word expression. Then use the word expression to write an algebraic expression. — "the number of guests divided by 6" $g \div 6$ or $\frac{g}{6}$

Ina finds out that 18 guests will attend. Evaluate the expression for this number of guests.

Step 1 Substitute 18 for g. $\frac{18}{6}$ — **Step 2** Divide. $\frac{18}{6} = 3$

So, Ina will need 3 heads of lettuce.

At her last party, Ina decorated with window stickers. For this party, she wants to use 4 times as many stickers.

1. Write an expression for the number of stickers Ina will use. (Use the variable s to represent the number of stickers she used at her last party.)
   $s \times 4$ or $4s$
2. Use the expression to find the new number of stickers if she used 14 stickers for her last party.
   $14 \times 4 = 56$
3. Ina wants to put an equal number of stickers on each of the windows. Write an expression to show how many stickers will go on each window. (Use the variable w to represent the number of windows.)
   $56 \div w$ or $\frac{56}{w}$
4. Use the expression to find the number of stickers for each window if there are 8 windows.
   $56 \div 8 = 7$

Name ______________________

Lesson 59
CC.6.EE.6

1. A builder needs 2 hinges to install each door. The expression $2d$ gives the number of hinges needed to install d doors. Which **best** describes the value of the variable d?
   - **(A) any positive whole number**
   - (B) a single unknown number
   - (C) any positive number
   - (D) any integer
2. Don wrote the expression 8 less than the product of m and 10. What algebraic expression did he write? What is the value of the expression for $m = 7$?
   - (A) $10m + 8$; 78
   - (B) $8m + 10$; 66
   - **(C) $10m - 8$; 62**
   - (D) $8m - 10$; 46
3. There were 3.5 inches of snow on the ground. New snow was reported to be falling at the rate of 2.5 inches per hour. What expression represents the number of inches of snow that should be on the ground after h hours? How many inches of snow should be on the ground after 8 hours?
   - (A) $8 + 3.5h$; 16.75 inches
   - **(B) $3.5 + 2.5h$; 23.5 inches**
   - (C) $2.5 + 8h$; 30.5 inches
   - (D) $(2.5 + 3.5) \times h$; 48 inches
4. A bicyclist travels $15h$ miles in h hours. Which **best** describes the value of h?
   - (A) a single unknown number
   - **(B) any nonnegative number**
   - (C) any whole number
   - (D) any integer

Problem Solving REAL WORLD

5. In the town of Pleasant Hill, there is an average of 16 sunny days each month. Write an expression to represent the approximate number of sunny days for any number of months. Tell what the variable represents.
   $16s$; s is the number of months
6. How many sunny days can a resident of Pleasant Hill expect to have in 9 months?
   144 days

Name ______________________

Lesson 60
COMMON CORE STANDARD CC.6.EE.7
Lesson Objective: Write algebraic equations.

Write Equations

To write an equation for a word sentence, write the words as mathematical expressions and write = for "equals" or "is."

Write an equation for the word sentence.

Example 1 6 fewer than a number is $12\frac{2}{3}$.

Step 1 Choose a variable.
6 fewer than a number is $12\frac{2}{3}$.
Let n represent a number.

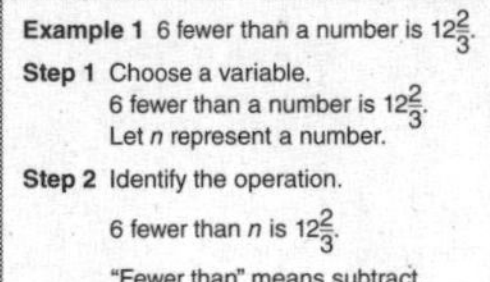

Step 2 Identify the operation.
6 fewer than n is $12\frac{2}{3}$.
"Fewer than" means subtract.

Step 3 Write an equation.

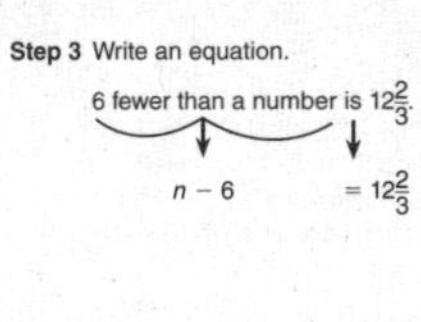

So, the equation is $n - 6 = 12\frac{2}{3}$.

Example 2

The quotient of 20.7 gallons and a number is 9 gallons.

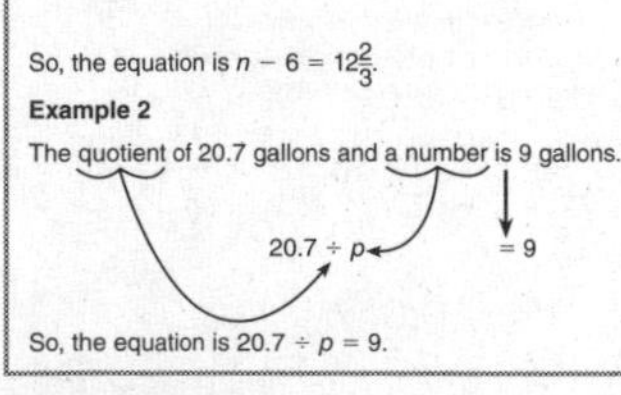

So, the equation is $20.7 \div p = 9$.

Write an equation for the word sentence.

1. 18 more than a number is 29.
   $n + 18 = 29$
2. 5.2 times a number is 46.8.
   $5.2n = 46.8$
3. 128 less than a number is 452.
   $n - 128 = 452$
4. Four fifths of a number equals 11.
   $\frac{4}{5}n = 11$
5. The product of a number and 6 is 138.
   $6p = 138$
6. The number of miles decreased by 29.8 is 139.
   $m - 29.8 = 139$

Name ______________________

Lesson 60
CC.6.EE.7

1. Dora was born in 1981. Her son Tanner was born 25 years after Dora. Which equation could be used to find the year y in which Tanner was born?
   - (A) $y + 25 = 1981$
   - **(B) $y - 25 = 1981$**
   - (C) $y \times 25 = 1981$
   - (D) $y \div 25 = 1981$
2. During a school fundraiser, Dominic sold boxes of greeting cards for $7 each and earned a total of $364. Which equation could be used to find the number of boxes n Dominic sold?
   - (A) $n + 7 = 364$
   - (B) $n - 7 = 364$
   - **(C) $n \times 7 = 364$**
   - (D) $n \div 7 = 364$
3. A video game is on sale for $40. The sale price is $10 less than the regular price p. Which equation could be used to find the regular price of the video game?
   - (A) $p + 10 = 40$
   - **(B) $p - 10 = 40$**
   - (C) $p \times 10 = 40$
   - (D) $p \div 10 = 40$
4. Rowan started school in 1999. Kira started school 8 years after Rowan. Which equation could be used to find the year y in which Kira started school?
   - **(A) $y - 8 = 1999$**
   - (B) $y + 8 = 1999$
   - (C) $y \div 8 = 1999$
   - (D) $y \times 8 = 1999$

Problem Solving

5. An ostrich egg weighs 2.9 pounds. The difference between the weight of this egg and the weight of an emu egg is 1.6 pounds. Write an equation that could be used to find the weight w, in pounds, of the emu egg.
   $2.9 - w = 1.6$
6. In one week, the number of bowls a potter made was 6 times the number of plates. He made 90 bowls during the week. Write an equation that could be used to find the number of plates p that the potter made.
   $6p = 90$

Answer Key

Name ______________________

Lesson 61
COMMON CORE STANDARD CC.6.EE.7
Lesson Objective: Use models to solve addition equations.

Model and Solve Addition Equations

You can use algebra tiles to model and solve equations. Use a long rectangle to represent the variable, and a square to represent 1.

Model and solve the equation $x + 9 = 11$.

Step 1 Model the equation using algebra tiles.

Step 2 Get the variable by itself on one side of the equation. Remove the same number of tiles from each side.

Step 3 Write the solution.

$x = 2$

Solve the equation by using algebra tiles or by drawing a picture. Check students' models.

1. $x + 4 = 10$ — $x = 6$
2. $8 = x + 2$ — $x = 6$

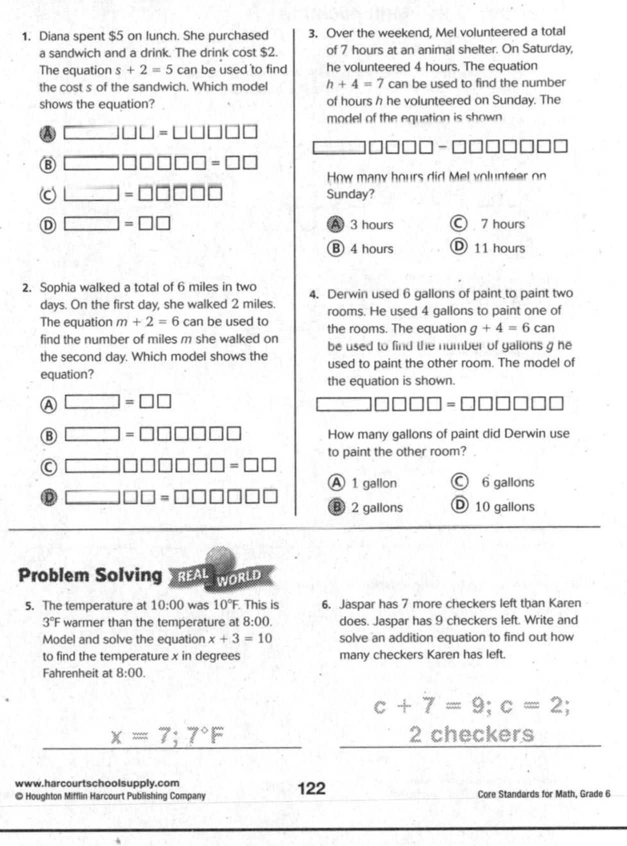

Name ______________________

Lesson 61
CC.6.EE.7

1. Diana spent \$5 on lunch. She purchased a sandwich and a drink. The drink cost \$2. The equation $s + 2 = 5$ can be used to find the cost s of the sandwich. Which model shows the equation?
   - **(A)** (marked)
   - (B)
   - (C)
   - (D)

2. Sophia walked a total of 6 miles in two days. On the first day, she walked 2 miles. The equation $m + 2 = 6$ can be used to find the number of miles m she walked on the second day. Which model shows the equation?
   - (A)
   - (B)
   - (C)
   - **(D)** (marked)

3. Over the weekend, Mel volunteered a total of 7 hours at an animal shelter. On Saturday, he volunteered 4 hours. The equation $h + 4 = 7$ can be used to find the number of hours h he volunteered on Sunday. The model of the equation is shown.

   How many hours did Mel volunteer on Sunday?
   - **(A) 3 hours** (marked)
   - (B) 4 hours
   - (C) 7 hours
   - (D) 11 hours

4. Derwin used 6 gallons of paint to paint two rooms. He used 4 gallons to paint one of the rooms. The equation $g + 4 = 6$ can be used to find the number of gallons g he used to paint the other room. The model of the equation is shown.

   How many gallons of paint did Derwin use to paint the other room?
   - (A) 1 gallon
   - **(B) 2 gallons** (marked)
   - (C) 6 gallons
   - (D) 10 gallons

Problem Solving REAL WORLD

5. The temperature at 10:00 was 10°F. This is 3°F warmer than the temperature at 8:00. Model and solve the equation $x + 3 = 10$ to find the temperature x in degrees Fahrenheit at 8:00.

   $x = 7$; 7°F

6. Jaspar has 7 more checkers left than Karen does. Jaspar has 9 checkers left. Write and solve an addition equation to find out how many checkers Karen has left.

   $c + 7 = 9$; $c = 2$; 2 checkers

Name ______________________

Lesson 62
COMMON CORE STANDARD CC.6.EE.7
Lesson Objective: Use algebra to solve addition and subtraction equations.

Solve Addition and Subtraction Equations

To solve an equation, you must isolate the variable on one side of the equal sign. You can use **inverse operations**: undoing addition with subtraction or subtraction with addition. These actions are made possible by the **Addition and Subtraction Properties of Equality.**

Solve and check.

Example 1: $y + 6.7 = 9.8$ **Example 2:** $57 = x - 8$

Step 1 Look at the side with the variable. Subtract the number that is added to the variable, or add the number that is subtracted from the variable. Be sure to perform the same operation on both sides of the equation.

Example 1		Example 2	
$y + 6.7 = 9.8$		$57 = x - 8$	
$y + 6.7 - 6.7 = 9.8 - 6.7$	Subtract 6.7 from both sides.	$57 + 8 = x - 8 + 8$	Add 8 to both sides.

Step 2 Simplify both sides of the equation.

Example 1	Example 2
$y + 6.7 = 9.8$	$57 = x - 8$
$y + 6.7 - 6.7 = 9.8 - 6.7$	$57 + 8 = x - 8 + 8$
$y + 0 = 3.1$	$65 = x + 0$
$y = 3.1$	$65 = x$

Step 3 Check your answer in the original equation.

Example 1	Example 2
$y + 6.7 = 9.8$	$57 = x - 8$
$3.1 + 6.7 \stackrel{?}{=} 9.8$	$57 \stackrel{?}{=} 65 - 8$
$9.8 = 9.8$	$57 = 57$
So, $y = 3.1$ is the solution.	So, $x = 65$ is the solution.

Solve and check.

1. $x + 13 = 27$ — $x = 14$
2. $38 = d - 22$ — $d = 60$
3. $12.4 = a + 7.9$ — $a = 4.5$
4. $w - 2\frac{3}{5} = 4\frac{2}{5}$ — $w = 7$

Name ______________________

Lesson 62
CC.6.EE.7

1. The temperature rose 9 degrees between 11:00 A.M. and 4:00 P.M. yesterday. The temperature at 4:00 P.M. was 87°F. Xin Xin used the following equation to find the temperature t at 11:00 A.M.

   $t + 9 = 87$

   What was the temperature at 11:00 A.M.?
   - (A) 68°F
   - (B) 76°F
   - **(C) 78°F** (marked)
   - (D) 96°F

2. José used the equation $h - 125 = 75$ to find the height in feet h of a hot air balloon before it began to come down. What was the height of the hot air balloon before it began to come down?
   - (A) 50 feet
   - (B) 100 feet
   - (C) 150 feet
   - **(D) 200 feet** (marked)

3. Dina adds $1\frac{1}{2}$ cups of sugar to some flour to make $4\frac{1}{4}$ cups of a baking mix. She solves the equation $f + 1\frac{1}{2} = 4\frac{1}{4}$ to find the amount of flour f in the baking mix. How much flour is in the baking mix?
   - (A) $1\frac{1}{4}$ cups
   - (B) $2\frac{1}{4}$ cups
   - **(C) $2\frac{3}{4}$ cups** (marked)
   - (D) $5\frac{3}{4}$ cups

4. Kelsey used the equation $h - 135 = 25$ to find the height in feet h of a kite before she began to reel it in. What was the height of the kite before Kelsey began to reel it in?
   - **(A) 160 feet** (marked)
   - (B) 130 feet
   - (C) 110 feet
   - (D) 55 feet

Problem Solving REAL WORLD

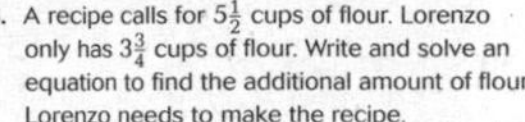

5. A recipe calls for $5\frac{1}{2}$ cups of flour. Lorenzo only has $3\frac{3}{4}$ cups of flour. Write and solve an equation to find the additional amount of flour Lorenzo needs to make the recipe.

   $3\frac{3}{4} + a = 5\frac{1}{2}$; $a = 1\frac{3}{4}$; $1\frac{3}{4}$ cups

6. Jan used 22.5 gallons of water in the shower. This amount is 7.5 gallons less than the amount she used for washing clothes. Write and solve an equation to find the amount of water Jan used to wash clothes.

   $a - 7.5 = 22.5$; $a = 30$; 30 gallons

Answer Key

Name ______________________

Lesson 63

COMMON CORE STANDARD CC.6.EE.7

Lesson Objective: Use models to solve multiplication equations.

Model and Solve Multiplication Equations

You can use algebra tiles or a drawing to model and solve equations. Use a rectangle to represent the variable and a square to represent 1.

Model and solve the equation $3x = 9$.

Step 1 Model the equation using rectangles and squares.

$3x = 9$

Step 2 Divide the squares into equal groups. The number of groups should be the same as the number of rectangles.

$3x = 9$

Step 3 Find the number of squares in each group.

$x = 3$

So, $x = 3$ is the solution.

Solve the equation by using algebra tiles or by drawing a picture. Check students' models.

1. $4x = 12$ — $x = 3$
2. $2x = 16$ — $x = 8$

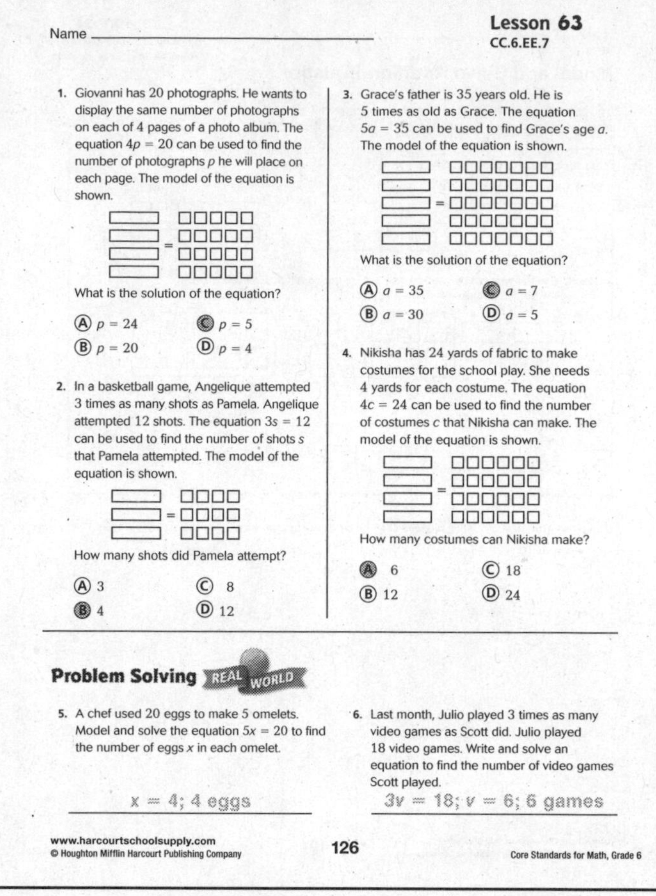

Name ______________________

Lesson 63

CC.6.EE.7

1. Giovanni has 20 photographs. He wants to display the same number of photographs on each of 4 pages of a photo album. The equation $4p = 20$ can be used to find the number of photographs p he will place on each page. The model of the equation is shown.

   What is the solution of the equation?

   Ⓐ $p = 24$ Ⓑ $p = 20$ **Ⓒ $p = 5$** Ⓓ $p = 4$

2. In a basketball game, Angelique attempted 3 times as many shots as Pamela. Angelique attempted 12 shots. The equation $3s = 12$ can be used to find the number of shots s that Pamela attempted. The model of the equation is shown.

   How many shots did Pamela attempt?

   Ⓐ 3 **Ⓑ 4** Ⓒ 8 Ⓓ 12

3. Grace's father is 35 years old. He is 5 times as old as Grace. The equation $5a = 35$ can be used to find Grace's age a. The model of the equation is shown.

   What is the solution of the equation?

   Ⓐ $a = 35$ Ⓑ $a = 30$ **Ⓒ $a = 7$** Ⓓ $a = 5$

4. Nikisha has 24 yards of fabric to make costumes for the school play. She needs 4 yards for each costume. The equation $4c = 24$ can be used to find the number of costumes c that Nikisha can make. The model of the equation is shown.

   How many costumes can Nikisha make?

   Ⓐ 6 Ⓑ 12 Ⓒ 18 Ⓓ 24

Problem Solving REAL WORLD

5. A chef used 20 eggs to make 5 omelets. Model and solve the equation $5x = 20$ to find the number of eggs x in each omelet.

   $x = 4$; 4 eggs

6. Last month, Julio played 3 times as many video games as Scott did. Julio played 18 video games. Write and solve an equation to find the number of video games Scott played.

   $3v = 18$; $v = 6$; 6 games

Name ______________________

Lesson 64

COMMON CORE STANDARD CC.6.EE.7

Lesson Objective: Use algebra to solve multiplication and division equations.

Solve Multiplication and Division Equations

A multiplication equation shows a variable multiplied by a number. A division equation shows a variable divided by a number. To solve a multiplication equation, you use the **Division Property of Equality**. To solve a division equation, you use the **Multiplication Property of Equality**. These properties state that both sides of an equation remain equal when you multiply or divide both sides by the same number.

Solve and check.

Example 1: $\frac{a}{5} = 6$ **Example 2:** $2.5x = 10$

Step 1 Look at the side with the variable. Use the inverse operation to get the variable by itself.

Example 1		Example 2	
$\frac{a}{5} = 6$	a is divided by 5.	$2.5x = 10$	x is multiplied by 2.5.
$5 \times \frac{a}{5} = 6 \times 5$	Multiply both sides by 5.	$\frac{2.5x}{2.5} = \frac{10}{2.5}$	Divide both sides by 2.5.

Step 2 Simplify both sides of the equation.

Example 1	Example 2
$\frac{a}{5} = 6$	$2.5x = 10$
$5 \times \frac{a}{5} = 6 \times 5$	$\frac{2.5x}{2.5} = \frac{10}{2.5}$
$a = 30$	$x = 4$

Step 3 Check your answer in the original equation.

Example 1	Example 2
$\frac{a}{5} = 6$	$2.5x = 10$
$\frac{30}{5} \stackrel{?}{=} 6$	$2.5 \times 4 \stackrel{?}{=} 10$
$6 = 6$	$10 = 10$
So, $a = 30$ is the solution.	So, $x = 4$ is the solution.

Solve and check.

1. $3x = 42$ — $x = 14$
2. $4c = 48$ — $c = 12$
3. $12.8 = 3.2d$ — $d = 4$
4. $12 = 1.5w$ — $w = 8$
5. $\frac{z}{6} = 9$ — $z = 54$
6. $\frac{d}{4} = 5$ — $d = 20$
7. $11 = \frac{n}{2.4}$ — $n = 26.4$
8. $12 = \frac{4}{5}k$ — $k = 15$

Name ______________________

Lesson 64

CC.6.EE.7

1. Spencer divided his baseball cards equally among 4 friends. Each friend received 16 cards. To find the number of cards c that Spencer had originally, he solved the equation $\frac{c}{4} = 16$. How many baseball cards did Spencer originally have?

   Ⓐ 4 Ⓑ 32 **Ⓒ 64** Ⓓ 72

2. Stephanie has a ball of dough that weighs 20.8 ounces. She divides the dough into 8 equal amounts to make rolls. To find the weight w of each amount of dough, Stephanie solves the equation $8w = 20.8$. What is the weight of each amount of dough?

   Ⓐ 2.6 ounces Ⓑ 12.8 ounces Ⓒ 28.8 ounces Ⓓ 166.4 ounces

3. Jenna earns $8 per hour. Her paycheck for one week was $136. The equation $8h = 136$ can be used to find the number of hours h she worked during the week. How many hours did she work?

   Ⓐ 17 hours Ⓑ 19 hours Ⓒ 24 hours Ⓓ 27 hours

4. Jasmine gave away her stuffed animal collection to 3 of her younger cousins. Each cousin got 18 stuffed animals. To find the number of stuffed animals s that Jasmine originally had, she solved the equation $\frac{s}{3} = 18$. How many stuffed animals did Jasmine originally have?

   Ⓐ 3 Ⓑ 6 Ⓒ 21 **Ⓓ 54**

Problem Solving REAL WORLD

5. Anne runs 6 laps on a track. She runs a total of 1 mile, or 5,280 feet. Write and solve an equation to find the distance, in feet, that she runs in each lap.

   $6d = 5{,}280$; $d = 880$; 880 feet

6. DeShawn uses $\frac{3}{4}$ of a box of rice to cook dinner. The portion he uses weighs 12 ounces. Write and solve an equation to find the weight of the full box of rice.

   $\frac{3}{4}w = 12$; $w = 16$; 16 ounces

Name ______

Lesson 65

COMMON CORE STANDARD CC.6.EE.7

Lesson Objective: Solve equations involving fractions by using the strategy *solve a simpler problem.*

Problem Solving • Equations with Fractions

After driving 25 miles, Kevin has traveled $\frac{2}{3}$ of the distance from his house to his friend's house. Use the equation $25 = \frac{2}{3}d$ to find the total distance d in miles to his friend's house.

Read the Problem

What do I need to find?	What information do I need to use?	How will I use the information?
I need to find the distance in miles from Kevin's house to his friend's house	I need to use the equation $25 = \frac{2}{3}d$	I can use multiplication to change the equation to an equation with only whole numbers not fractions. Then I can solve the new equation.

Solve the Problem

Step 1 Write the original equation.	$25 = \frac{2}{3}d$
Step 2 Write a simpler equation without fractions. Multiply both sides by the denominator of the fraction.	$3 \times 25 = (3 \times \frac{2}{3})d$ $75 = \frac{6}{3}d$ $75 = 2d$
Step 3 Solve the simpler equation. Use the Division Property of Equality.	$\frac{75}{2} = \frac{2d}{2}$ $37.5 = d$
So, the total distance is 37.5 miles.	

Solve.

1. Alyssa's cat weighs 12 pounds, which is $\frac{3}{8}$ of the weight of her dog. Use the equation $\frac{3}{8}d = 12$ to find the weight of Alyssa's dog.

   32 pounds

2. Randall bought 16 baseball cards from Max, which is $\frac{2}{5}$ of Max's collection. Use the equation $16 = \frac{2}{5}c$ to find the number of cards that were in Max's collection.

   40 cards

Name ______

Lesson 65

CC.6.EE.7

1. A track is $\frac{3}{4}$ mile in length. Milton jogged a total of 6 miles around the track. The equation $\frac{3}{4}n = 6$ can be used to find the number of times n he jogged around the track. How many times did he jog around the track?
   - Ⓐ 2
   - Ⓑ 8 (filled)
   - Ⓒ 18
   - Ⓓ 24

2. Janae paid \$12 for a shirt that was on sale. The sale price of the shirt was $\frac{1}{3}$ of the original price p. The equation $\frac{1}{3}p = 12$ can be used to find the original price of the shirt. What was the original price of the shirt?
   - Ⓐ \$3
   - Ⓑ \$4
   - Ⓒ \$15
   - Ⓓ \$36 (filled)

3. Jimmy has saved \$375 to purchase a new guitar. This is $\frac{3}{4}$ of the total price of the guitar. What is the price of the guitar?
   - Ⓐ \$125
   - Ⓑ \$500 (filled)
   - Ⓒ \$1,125
   - Ⓓ \$1,500

4. Sylvia has read 136 pages of a novel. She has read $\frac{2}{5}$ of the novel. The equation $\frac{2}{5}p = 136$ can be used to find the number of total pages p in the novel. How many total pages are there?
   - Ⓐ 340 (filled)
   - Ⓑ 136
   - Ⓒ 68
   - Ⓓ 54

Problem Solving REAL WORLD

5. Adele is taking a road trip. She has driven 160 miles, which is $\frac{5}{8}$ of the total distance she plans to travel. How far will she travel in all? Explain how you know.

   256 miles; Possible explanation: I wrote the equation $\frac{5}{8}m = 160$ to represent the situation, where m represents the total distance Adele will drive. Then, I multiplied both sides of the equation by 8 to write a simpler equation without a fraction: $5m = 1,280$. Finally, I used the Division Property of Equality to solve for m by dividing both sides of the equation by 5. So, $m = 256$.

Name ______

Lesson 66

COMMON CORE STANDARD CC.6.EE.8

Lesson Objective: Write algebraic inequalities.

Write Inequalities

Here are some ways to express each inequality symbol in words:

<	less than	under	not as much as
≤	less than or equal to	at most	no more than

>	greater than	over	more than
≥	greater than or equal to	at least	no less than

Passengers at least 12 years old pay full price for train tickets. Write an inequality to represent the situation.

Step 1 Choose a variable. Use a to represent "age."	a
Step 2 Choose an inequality symbol. "At least 12 years old" means "greater than or equal to 12."	≥
Step 3 Write the inequality.	$a \geq 12$

Write two word sentences to represent $y < 9$.

Step 1 Identify the inequality symbol.	< means "less than."
Step 2 Write a word sentence that uses the variable and integer.	y is less than 9.
Step 3 Write another word sentence with the same meaning.	y is under 9.

Write an inequality for the word sentence.

1. The distance d Mr. Chin drove was no more than 65 miles.

   $d \leq 65$

2. The amount of juice c in the punch is more than 3 cups.

   $c > 3$

3. The age a of Mia's sister is less than 8 years.

   $a < 8$

4. The temperature t was at least 30°F.

   $t \geq 30$

Write two word sentences to represent the inequality.

5. $n \geq 23$

   n is greater than or equal to 23; n is at least 23.

6. $p > 16$

   p is greater than 16; p is more than 16.

Name ______

Lesson 66

CC.6.EE.8

1. An MP3 player can store less than 240 songs. Which inequality represents the possible number of songs s the MP3 player can store?
   - Ⓐ $s \geq 240$
   - Ⓑ $s \leq 240$
   - Ⓒ $s > 240$
   - Ⓓ $s < 240$ (filled)

2. After-school activities are cancelled at Kurt's school if there are at least 2.5 inches of snow on the ground. Which inequality shows the number of inches of snow s for which after-school activities are cancelled?
   - Ⓐ $s < 2.5$
   - Ⓑ $s > 2.5$
   - Ⓒ $s \geq 2.5$ (filled)
   - Ⓓ $s \leq 2.5$

3. A ship can carry no more than 6 tons of cargo. Which inequality represents the number of tons t that the ship can carry?
   - Ⓐ $t < 6$
   - Ⓑ $t > 6$
   - Ⓒ $t \leq 6$ (filled)
   - Ⓓ $t \geq 6$

4. The repairs to Ryan's bike cost more than \$50. Which inequality represents the cost of repairs r?
   - Ⓐ $r > 50$ (filled)
   - Ⓑ $r < 50$
   - Ⓒ $r \geq 50$
   - Ⓓ $r \leq 50$

Possible answers are given.

Problem Solving REAL WORLD

5. Tabby's mom says that she must read for at least 30 minutes each night. If m represents the number of minutes reading, what inequality can represent this situation?

   $m \geq 30$

6. Phillip has a \$25 gift card to his favorite restaurant. He wants to use the gift card to buy lunch. If c represents the cost of his lunch, what inequality can describe all of the possible amounts of money, in dollars, that Phillip can spend on lunch?

   $c \leq 25$

Answer Key

Name ____________________

Lesson 67
COMMON CORE STANDARD CC.6.EE.8
Lesson Objective: Represent solutions of algebraic inequalities on number line diagrams.

Graph Inequalities

You can graph the solutions of an inequality on a number line.

Graph the inequality $n \geq 9$.

Step 1 Determine the meaning of the inequality. $n \geq 9$ means "n is greater than or equal to 9."

Step 2 Draw a number line and circle the number given in the inequality.

Step 3 Decide whether to fill in the circle. For ≤ or ≥, fill in the circle to show "or equal to." For < or >, do not fill in the circle.
Since the inequality uses ≥, 9 is a possible solution. So, fill in the circle.

Step 4 Shade from the circle in the direction of the remaining solutions.
Since the inequality symbol is ≥, the shading covers all numbers greater than 9.

Graph the inequality.

1. $k < 8$
2. $r \geq 6$
3. $w \leq 3$
4. $x > 3$

Write the inequality shown by the graph.

5. $x \geq 7$
6. $x > 5$

Name ____________________

Lesson 67
CC.6.EE.8

1. The East Park football team must gain at least 5 yards for a first down. The inequality $y \geq 5$ represents the number of yards y that the team must gain. Which graph represents the solutions of the inequality?
   Answer: A

2. The graph shows the possible ages a of children in a daycare center.
   Which inequality represents this graph?
   A $a > 6$ C $a \geq 6$
   B $a < 6$ D $a \leq 6$

3. The inequality $a < 4$ represents the ages a of children who are admitted into the aquarium at no charge. Which graph represents the solutions of the inequality?
   ** D**

4. The graph shows the temperatures t in degrees Celsius for which a certain substance is frozen.
   Which inequality represents this graph?
   A $t \leq {}^-3$ C $t < {}^-3$
   B $t \geq {}^-3$ D $t > {}^-3$

Problem Solving REAL WORLD

5. The inequality $x \leq 2$ represents the elevation x of a certain object found at a dig site. Graph the solutions of the inequality on the number line.

6. The inequality $x \geq 144$ represents the possible scores x needed to pass a certain test. Graph the solutions of the inequality on the number line.

Name ____________________

Lesson 68
COMMON CORE STANDARD CC.6.EE.9
Lesson Objective: Write an equation to represent the relationship between an independent variable and a dependent variable.

Independent and Dependent Variables

An equation with two variables shows a relationship between two quantities. The value of the **dependent variable** changes according to the value of the **independent variable.**

Sam rides the bus almost every day. He pays $2.50 for each bus ride.

Identify the dependent and independent variables in this situation. Then write an equation to represent the relationship between the total cost and the number of bus rides.

Step 1 Understand the relationship and identify variables.
Each bus ride costs $2.50. The total cost c for Sam's bus rides depends on the number of rides r he takes. The value of c will change when the value of r changes.

So, c is the dependent variable and r is the independent variable.

Step 2 Write an equation. The total cost will be $2.50 multiplied by the number of rides.
$c = 2.50 \times r$ (or $c = 2.50r$)

Use your equation to find out how much it would cost for Sam to take 4 bus rides.

Step 1 Think: 4 bus rides means $r = 4$.

Step 2 Substitute 4 for r in the equation.
$c = 2.50 \times r$
$c = 2.50 \times 4$
$c = 10.00$

So, Sam's total cost will be $10.00 for 4 rides.

Identify the dependent and independent variables. Write an equation to show the relationship between them. Then solve for the given value.

1. Janna is buying a netbook with a flash drive. The total cost c will include the price p of the netbook, plus $12.50 for the flash drive.
   Find the total cost if the price of the netbook is $375.00.

   The total cost depends on the netbook price
   dependent variable: c independent variable: p
   equation: $c = p + 12.50$
   Total cost: $c = 375.00 + 12.50$
   $c = 387.50$

Name ____________________

Lesson 68
CC.6.EE.9

1. Kenneth earns $9 per hour mowing lawns. The total amount earned t equals the amount earned per hour times the number of hours h. Which equation gives the total amount earned t if Kenneth works h hours?
   A $t = 9h$
   B $h = 9t$
   C $t = 9 + h$
   D $h = 9 + t$

2. Hakeem wants to rent a bike. Bike rental costs $1.25 per hour plus a one-time fee of $3. Which equation represents the relationship between the number of hours h Hakeem rents the bike and the total cost c?
   A $h = 1.25c + 3$
   B $c = 1.25h + 3$
   C $h = 3c + 1.25$
   D $c = 3h + 1.25$

3. Neema purchases a gallon of milk for $3 and some tomatoes for $2 per pound from the grocery store. Which equation represents the relationship between the number of pounds p of tomatoes purchased and the total amount a Neema spent at the grocery store?
   A $p = 3a + 2$
   B $a = 3p + 2$
   C $p = 2a + 3$
   D $a = 2p + 3$

4. Oscar uses a 20-dollar bill to purchase an item that costs x dollars. Which equation represents the amount of change y that he should receive from his purchase?
   A $y = 20 - x$
   B $y = 20 + x$
   C $x = 20 \div y$
   D $x = 20y$

Problem Solving REAL WORLD

5. Maria earns $45 for every lawn that she mows. Her earnings e in dollars depend on the number of lawns n that she mows. Write an equation that represents this situation.
   $e = 45n$

6. Martin sells cars. He earns $100 per day, plus any commission on his sales. His daily salary s in dollars depends on the amount of commission c. Write an equation to represent his daily salary.
   $s = 100 + c$

Name ______________________

Lesson 69
COMMON CORE STANDARD CC.6.EE.9
Lesson Objective: Translate between equations and tables.

Equations and Tables

You can use tables and equations to represent the relationship between two quantities.

Use the equation to complete the table.

$y = x \div 4$

Step 1 Look at the equation to find the rule. The rule for finding y is $x \div 4$.

Step 2 Apply the rule and fill in the missing values. Divide each x-value by 4.
$44 \div 4 = 11$ $36 \div 4 = 9$ $28 \div 4 = 7$ $20 \div 4 = 5$

x	y
44	
36	
28	
20	

Write an equation for the relationship.

Input, x	30	35	40	45	50
Output, y	6	7	8	9	10

Find a pattern.
Think: "What can I do to each x-value to find its corresponding y-value?"
The y-values are less than the x-values, so try dividing or subtracting.

$30 \div 5 = 6$ $35 \div 5 = 7$ $40 \div 5 = 8$ $45 \div 5 = 9$ $50 \div 5 = 10$

The pattern is to divide x by 5 to get y. The equation is $y = x \div 5$.

Write an equation for the relationship shown in the table. Then find the missing value in the table.

1.

x	20	40	60	80
y	23	43	63	83

$y = x + 3$

2.

x	3	4	5	6
y	18	24	30	36

$y = 6x$

Use the equation to complete the table.

3. $y = 7x$

Input, x	1	2	3	4
Output, y	7	14	21	28

4. $y = x - 2$

Input, x	5	8	11	14
Output, y	3	6	9	12

Name ______________________

Lesson 69
CC.6.EE.9

Use the table for 1–2.

The table shows the number of people n seated in each section of the gym depending on the total number of people p in the gym.

Total Number of People, p	9	10	27	36
People in Each Section, n	3	6	?	12

1. Which equation could be used to find the number of people n that are seated in each section of the gym?

Ⓐ $n = 3p$ Ⓒ $n = p - 6$
Ⓑ $n = \frac{p}{3}$ Ⓓ $n = p - 12$

2. How many people n would be seated in each section if there were 27 total people in the gym?

Ⓐ 7 Ⓒ 9
Ⓑ 8 Ⓓ 10

Use the table for 3–4.

A bowling alley charges \$1.50 for shoe rental and \$2 per game. The table shows the total cost y of bowling x games.

Number of Games, x	Cost (dollars), y
1	3.50
2	5.50
3	?
4	9.50

3. Which equation could be used to find the total cost y of bowling x games?

Ⓐ $y = 2x + 1.5$ Ⓒ $y = x + 2$
Ⓑ $y = 1.5x + 2$ Ⓓ $y = x + 1.5$

4. What is the total cost y of bowling 3 games?

Ⓐ \$7.50 Ⓒ \$5.00
Ⓑ \$6.50 Ⓓ \$4.50

Problem Solving 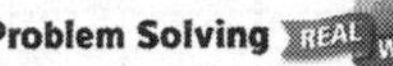

5. Tickets to a play cost \$11 each. There is also a service charge of \$4 per order. Write an equation for the relationship that gives the total cost y in dollars for an order of x tickets.

$y = 11x + 4$

6. Write an equation for the relationship shown in the table. Then use the equation to find the estimated number of shrimp in a 5-pound bag.

Weight of bag (pounds), x	1	2	3	4
Estimated number of shrimp, y	24	48	72	96

$y = 124x$; 120 shrimp

Name ______________________

Lesson 70
COMMON CORE STANDARD CC.6.EE.9
Lesson Objective: Solve problems involving relationships between quantities by using the strategy *find a pattern*.

Problem Solving • Analyze Relationships

The table shows the number of miles an overnight train travels. If the pattern in the table continues, how far will the train travel in 10 hours?

Overnight Train Travel Rate				
Time (hours)	1	2	3	4
Distance (miles)	60	120	180	240

Use the graphic organizer to help you solve the problem.

Read the Problem

What do I need to find?	What information do I need to use?	How will I use the information?
I need to find the number of miles the train will travel in 10 hours.	I need to find the relationship between time and distance shown in the table.	I will find a pattern in the table and use the pattern to write an equation.

Solve the Problem

Look for a pattern between the number of hours and the number of miles.

Overnight Train Travel Rate				
Time in hours, h	1	2	3	4
Distance in miles, m	60	120	180	240

1×60 2×60 3×60 4×60

Then write an equation to show the pattern. **Equation:** $m = 60 \times h$

To find the miles the train will travel in 10 hours, substitute 10 for h.
$m = 60 \times 10$
$m = 600$

1. The table shows how much a restaurant pays for coffee. How much will the restaurant pay for 100 pounds of coffee?

\$400

Coffee Purchasing				
Pounds, p	5	10	30	60
Cost, c	\$20	\$40	\$120	\$240

Name ______________________

Lesson 70
CC.6.EE.9

1. Mr. Ramirez is filling his swimming pool with water. The table shows the number of gallons of water w in the swimming pool after t minutes.

Water in Swimming Pool

Time (minutes), t	1	2	3	4
Water (gallons), w	60	120	180	240

If the pattern in the table continues, how many gallons of water w will be in the pool after 10 minutes?

Ⓐ 6 gallons Ⓒ 600 gallons
Ⓑ 69 gallons Ⓓ 2,400 gallons

2. The table shows the amount of flour x that a baker uses for y dozen cookies.

Flour Needed to Bake Cookies

Amount of Flour Used (cups), x	3	4	5	6
Number of Dozens, y	4	8	12	16

If the pattern in the table continues, how many cups of flour x does the baker use for 20 dozen cookies?

Ⓐ 6 cups Ⓒ 17 cups
Ⓑ 7 cups Ⓓ 24 cups

Problem Solving REAL WORLD

3. An employee at a home improvement store is mixing a certain shade of green paint. The table shows the number of gallons of yellow paint y needed for x gallons of blue paint.

Green Paint

Gallons of Blue Paint, x	2	4	6	8
Gallons of Yellow Paint, y	3	6	9	12

If the pattern in the table continues, how many gallons of yellow paint y are needed to mix with 12 gallons of blue paint to get the same shade of green paint? Explain how you know.

18 gallons; Possible explanation: I identified a pattern in the table. The ratio of yellow paint to blue paint is $\frac{3}{2}$. So, I used the equation $y = \frac{3}{2}x$. Then I substituted 12 for x in the equation: $y = \frac{3}{2}(12) = 18$ gallons.

Answer Key

Name ______________________

Lesson 71
COMMON CORE STANDARD CC.6.EE.9
Lesson Objective: Graph the relationship between two quantities.

Graph Relationships

You can use a graph to represent a relationship.

Graph the relationship represented by the table to find the unknown value of *y*.

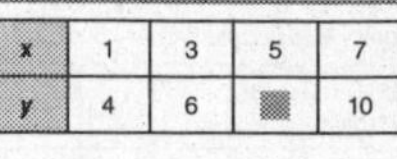

x	1	3	5	7
y	4	6	■	10

Step 1 Write ordered pairs that you know.
(1, 4), (3, 6), (7, 10)

Step 2 Plot the points.

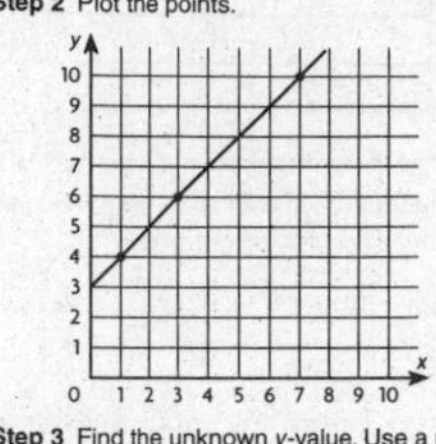

Step 3 Find the unknown *y*-value. Use a ruler to draw a line through the points. Find the *y*-value that corresponds to an *x*-value of 5.

So, when the *x*-value is 5, the *y*-value is 8.

Graph the relationship represented by the table to find the unknown value of *y*.

1.

x	1	2	3	4	5
y	3	4	■	6	7

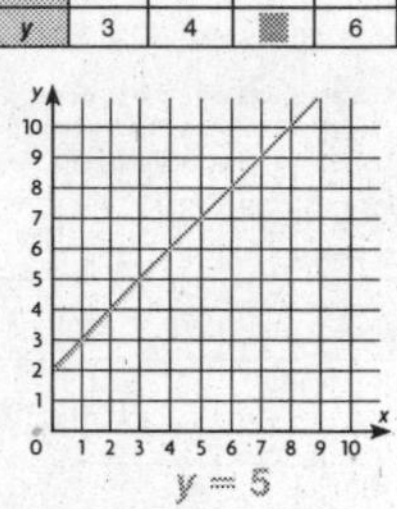

$y = 5$

2.

x	2	4	6	8	10
y	8	7	■	5	4

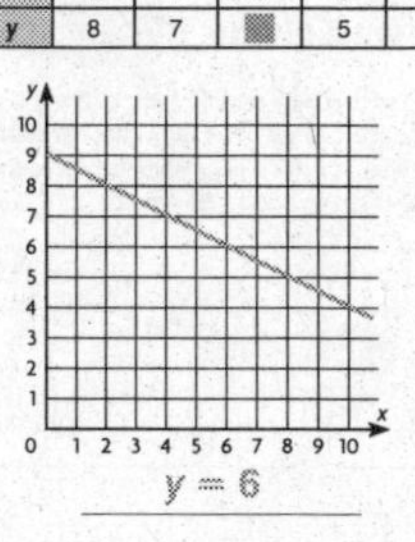

$y = 6$

Name ______________________

Lesson 71
CC.6.EE.9

1. Nicholas drives at a rate of 60 miles per hour. He lets *x* represent the time in hours and *y* represent the number of miles driven. Which ordered pair is a point on the graph of the relationship?
   - Ⓐ (60, 1)
   - Ⓑ (4, 240)
   - Ⓒ (3, 120)
   - Ⓓ (2, 60)

2. DVDs cost $15 each. Mariah graphs the relationship that gives the cost *y* in dollars of buying *x* DVDs. Which ordered pair is a point on the graph of the relationship?
   - Ⓐ (0, 15)
   - Ⓑ (2, 3)
   - Ⓒ (3, 45)
   - Ⓓ (15, 3)

3. Posters cost $7 each. Rafael graphs the relationship that gives the cost *y* in dollars of buying *x* posters. Which ordered pair is a point on the graph of the relationship?
   - Ⓐ (3, 10)
   - Ⓑ (5, 15)
   - Ⓒ (8, 52)
   - Ⓓ (9, 63)

4. Tiedra reads 3 books each month. Which ordered pair is a point on the graph that shows the relationship between the total number of books *y* Tiedra reads in *x* months?
   - Ⓐ (9, 3)
   - Ⓑ (5, 15)
   - Ⓒ (4, 7)
   - Ⓓ (3, 1)

Problem Solving REAL WORLD

5. Graph the relationship represented by the table.

DVDs Purchased	1	2	3	4
Cost ($)	15	30	45	60

6. Use the graph to find the cost of purchasing 5 DVDs.

$75

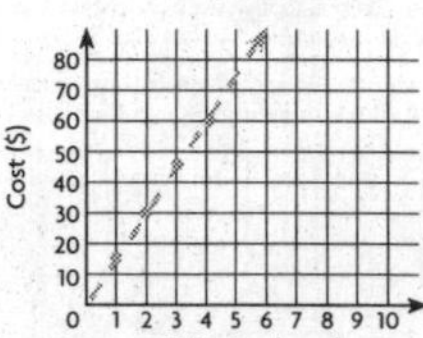

Name ______________________

Lesson 72
COMMON CORE STANDARD CC.6.EE.9
Lesson Objective: Translate between equations and graphs.

Equations and Graphs

You can make a table of values for any equation. Use the table to write ordered pairs. Plot points to help you graph the equation. The graph of a **linear equation** is a straight line.

Graph the linear equation.

$y = x + 1$ $y = 3x - 2$

Step 1 Find ordered pairs that are solutions of the equation.

Choose four values for *x*. Substitute each value for *x* in the equation and find the corresponding value of *y*. Use easy values for *x*, such as 1, 2, 3, 4.

x	*x* + 1	*y*	Ordered Pair
1	1 + 1	2	(1, 2)
2	2 + 1	3	(2, 3)
3	3 + 1	4	(3, 4)
4	4 + 1	5	(4, 5)

x	3*x* − 2	*y*	Ordered Pair
1	3 · 1 − 2	1	(1, 1)
2	3 · 2 − 2	4	(2, 4)
3	3 · 3 − 2	7	(3, 7)
4	3 · 4 − 2	10	(4, 10)

Step 2 Graph the equation.

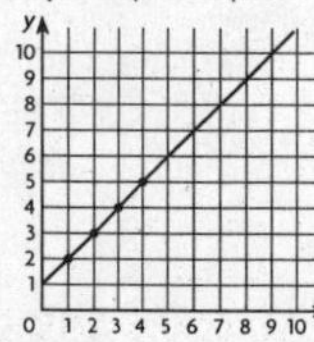

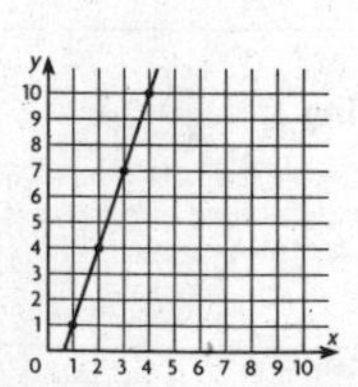

Graph the linear equation.

1. $y = x - 1$

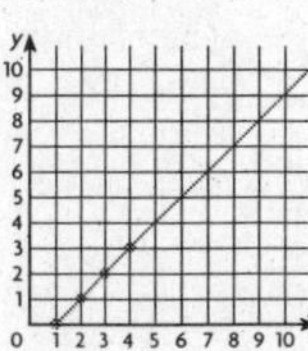

2. $y = 2x - 1$

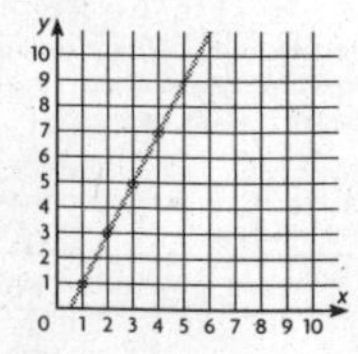

Name ______________________

Lesson 72
CC.6.EE.9

1. The graph shows the distance *y* a cyclist traveled over a period of time *x* in hours.

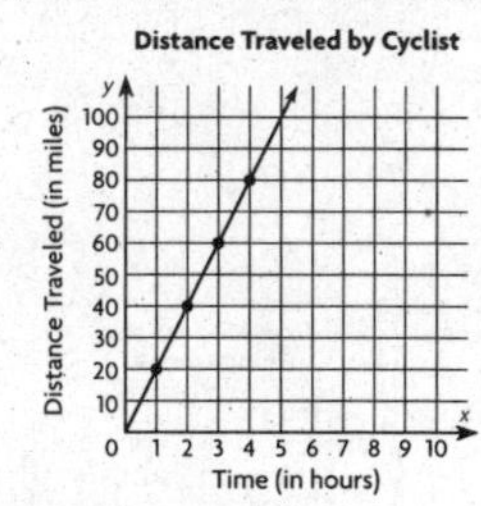

Which linear equation represents the relationship shown by the graph?
   - Ⓐ $y = x + 19$
   - Ⓑ $y = x + 20$
   - Ⓒ $y = \frac{x}{20}$
   - Ⓓ $y = 20x$

2. The linear equation $y = 5x$ represents the cost *y* in dollars of *x* pounds of dog food. Which ordered pair lies on the graph of the equation?
   - Ⓐ (3, 15)
   - Ⓑ (3, 10)
   - Ⓒ (2, 3)
   - Ⓓ (2, 12)

3. The linear equation $p = 10n$ represents the total number of points *p* scored on a quiz if *n* questions are correct. Which ordered pair lies on the graph of the equation?
   - Ⓐ (10, 1)
   - Ⓑ (7, 70)
   - Ⓒ (5, 2)
   - Ⓓ (4, 15)

4. Rod earns $12 per hour at his summer job. The linear equation $y = 12x$ represents his earnings *y* for *x* hours of work. Which ordered pair lies on the graph of the equation?
   - Ⓐ (0, 12)
   - Ⓑ (4, 16)
   - Ⓒ (8, 96)
   - Ⓓ (12, 1)

Problem Solving REAL WORLD

5. Dee is driving at an average speed of 50 miles per hour. Write a linear equation for the relationship that gives the distance *y* in miles that Dee drives in *x* hours.

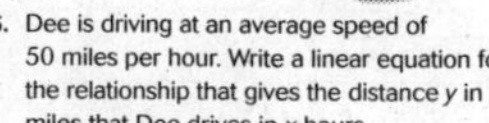

$y = 50x$

6. Graph the relationship from Exercise 5.

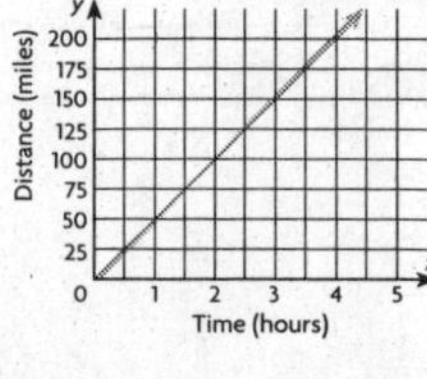

Answer Key

Name ______________________

Lesson 73

COMMON CORE STANDARD CC.6.G.1

Lesson Objective: Find the area of parallelograms.

Algebra • Area of Parallelograms

The formula for the area of a parallelogram is the product of the base and height.

height = h

base = b

$A = bh$

The formula for the area of a square is the square of one of its sides.

side = s

$A = s^2$

Find the area.

2 yd

$5\frac{1}{2}$ yd

Step 1 Identify the figure. The figure is a parallelogram, so use the formula $A = bh$.

Step 2 Substitute $5\frac{1}{2}$ for b and 2 for h. $A = 5\frac{1}{2} \times 2$

Step 3 Multiply. $A = 5\frac{1}{2} \times 2 = \frac{11}{2} \times \frac{2}{1} = 11$

So, the area of the parallelogram is 11 yd^2.

Find the area.

1. 4.7 m, 13 m

Figure: parallelogram

Formula: $A =$ bh

$A =$ 13 $\times$ 4.7 $=$ 61.1 m^2

2. 12 mi, 12 mi

144 mi^2

3. 3 yd, $7\frac{1}{5}$ yd

$21\frac{3}{5}$ yd^2

Name ______________________

Lesson 73

CC.6.G.1

1. The roof on Mrs. Vega's house is shaped like a parallelogram. The base of the roof is 16.7 meters and the height is 9 meters. What is the area of the roof?

Ⓐ 7.7 square meters
Ⓑ 25.7 square meters
Ⓒ 114.4 square meters
Ⓓ 150.3 square meters

2. Nishelle's backyard is in the shape of a parallelogram. The parallelogram has an area of 224 square feet and a base of 14 feet. What is the height of the parallelogram?

Ⓐ 8 feet
Ⓑ 16 feet
Ⓒ 238 feet
Ⓓ 3,136 feet

3. The windows in an office building are shaped like parallelograms. The base of each window is 1.8 meters and the height is 1.5 meters. What is the area of each window?

Ⓐ 1.35 square meters
Ⓑ 2.7 square meters
Ⓒ 3.3 square meters
Ⓓ 6.6 square meters

4. Leeza is making labels in the shape of parallelograms. Each label has an area of 18 square centimeters and a base of 6 centimeters. What is the height of each label?

Ⓐ 3 centimeters
Ⓑ 24 centimeters
Ⓒ 48 centimeters
Ⓓ 108 centimeters

Problem Solving REAL WORLD

5. Ronna has a sticker in the shape of a parallelogram. The sticker has a base of 6.5 cm and a height of 10.1 cm. What is the area of the sticker?

65.65 cm^2

6. A parallelogram-shaped tile has an area of 48 $in.^2$. The base of the tile measures 12 in. What is the measure of its height?

4 in.

Name ______________________

Lesson 74

COMMON CORE STANDARD CC.6.G.1

Lesson Objective: Investigate the relationship among the areas of triangles, rectangles, and parallelograms.

Explore Area of Triangles

You can use grid paper to find a relationship between the areas of triangles and rectangles.

Step 1 On grid paper, draw a rectangle with a base of 8 units and a height of 6 units. Find and record the area of the rectangle.

$A =$ 48 square units

Step 2 Cut out the rectangle.

Step 3 Draw a diagonal from the bottom left corner up to the top right corner.

Step 4 Cut the rectangle along the diagonal.

You have made 2 triangles

- Are the triangles congruent? yes
- How does the area of one triangle compare to the area of the rectangle?

The area of the triangle is half the area of the rectangle.

If l is the length and w is the width, you can use a rectangle to find the area of a triangle.

Find the area of the triangle.

4 m, 7 m

Area of rectangle: $A = lw = 7 \times 4 = 28$ m^2

Area of triangle: $A = \frac{1}{2} \times$ area of rectangle $= \frac{1}{2} \times 28 = 14$ m^2

So, the area is 14 square meters.

Find the area of the triangle.

1. 8 in., 10 in.

40 $in.^2$

2. 4 ft, 10 ft

20 ft^2

3. 6 m, 9 m

27 m^2

Name ______________________

Lesson 74

CC.6.G.1

1. A diagram of part of a Navajo rug is shown.

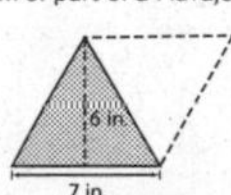

What is the area of the shaded triangle?

Ⓐ 13 square inches
Ⓑ 21 square inches
Ⓒ 35 square inches
Ⓓ 42 square inches

2. A rectangular school flag has a base of 25 inches and a height of 32 inches. The flag is divided into 2 congruent triangles formed by 2 sides and a diagonal of the flag. What is the area of each triangle?

Ⓐ 800 square inches
Ⓑ 400 square inches
Ⓒ 57 square inches
Ⓓ 41 square inches

3. A diagram of a patch on Max's quilt is shown.

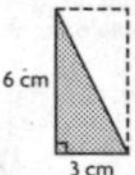

What is the area of the shaded triangle?

Ⓐ 2 square centimeters
Ⓑ 3 square centimeters
Ⓒ 9 square centimeters
Ⓓ 18 square centimeters

4. Kendra is sewing a pattern of parallelograms on her backpack. Each parallelogram has a base of 5 centimeters, a height of 18 centimeters, and is divided into two congruent triangles. What is the area of each triangle?

Ⓐ 45 square centimeters
Ⓑ 46 square centimeters
Ⓒ 90 square centimeters
Ⓓ 92 square centimeters

Problem Solving REAL WORLD

5. Fabian is decorating a triangular pennant for a football game. The pennant has a base of 10 inches and a height of 24 inches. What is the total area of the pennant?

120 $in.^2$

6. Ryan is buying a triangular tract of land. The triangle has a base of 100 yards and a height of 300 yards. What is the area of the tract of land?

15,000 yd^2

Answer Key

Name ____________________

Lesson 75
COMMON CORE STANDARD CC.6.G.1
Lesson Objective: Find the area of triangles.

Algebra • Area of Triangles

To find the area of a triangle, use the formula $A = \frac{1}{2} \times \text{base} \times \text{height}$.

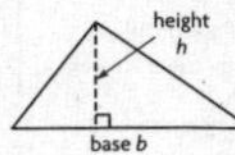

Find the area of the triangle.

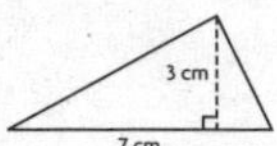

Step 1 Write the formula. $A = \frac{1}{2}bh$

Step 2 Rewrite the formula. Substitute the base and height measurements for b and h. $A = \frac{1}{2} \times 7 \times 3$

Step 3 Simplify by multiplying. $A = \frac{1}{2} \times 21$
$A = 10.5$

Step 4 Use the appropriate units. $A = 10.5 \text{ cm}^2$

Find the area of the triangle.

1. Write the formula. $A = \frac{1}{2} \times$  bh
Substitute for b and h. $A = \frac{1}{2} \times$ 6 $\times$ 17
Simplify. $A = \frac{1}{2} \times$ 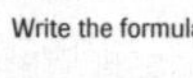 102
$A =$ 51 ft²

(17 ft, 6 ft)

2. 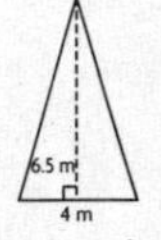

$A =$ 13 m²

3. 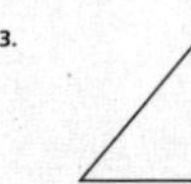

$A =$ 49.5 in.²

Name ____________________

Lesson 75
CC.6.G.1

1. Farah cut triangular pieces of felt to use in her art project. The size of one of the triangular pieces is shown.

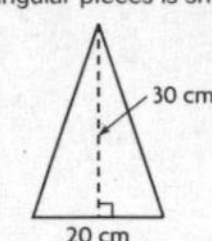

What is the area of this piece of felt?

Ⓐ 600 square centimeters
Ⓑ 300 square centimeters
Ⓒ 50 square centimeters
Ⓓ 25 square centimeters

2. Liang used 75 square inches of fabric to make a triangular pennant to take to a football game. The base of the pennant was 6 inches. What was the height of the pennant?

Ⓐ 3 inches **Ⓒ 25 inches**
Ⓑ 12.5 inches Ⓓ 37.5 inches

3. Marta drew this diagram of a triangular window at the art museum.

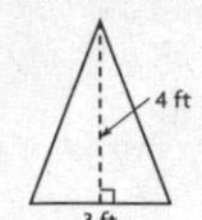

What is the area of the window?

Ⓐ 14 square feet
Ⓑ 12 square feet
Ⓒ 7 square feet
Ⓓ 6 square feet

4. Hiro used 60 square inches of fabric to make a triangular sail for his model sailboat. The base of the sail was 8 inches. What was the height of the sail?

Ⓐ 15 inches Ⓒ 5 inches
Ⓑ 7.5 inches Ⓓ 2.5 inches

Problem Solving REAL WORLD

5. Bayla draws a triangle with a base of 15 cm and a height of 8.5 cm. If she colors the space inside the triangle, what area does she color?

63.75 cm²

6. Alicia is making a triangular sign for the school play. The area of the sign is 558 in.². The base of the triangle is 36 in. What is the height of the triangle?

31 in.

Name ____________________

Lesson 76
COMMON CORE STANDARD CC.6.G.1
Lesson Objective: Investigate the relationship between the areas of trapezoids and parallelograms.

Explore Area of Trapezoids

Show the relationship between the areas of trapezoids and parallelograms.

Step 1 On grid paper, draw two copies of the trapezoid. Count the grid squares to make your trapezoid match this one.

Step 2 Cut out the trapezoids.

Step 3 Turn one trapezoid until the two trapezoids form a parallelogram.

Step 4 Find the length of the base of the parallelogram. Add the lengths of one shorter trapezoid base and one longer trapezoid base. $4 + 7 = 11$ units

Step 5 Find the area of the parallelogram. Use the formula $A = bh$. $A = 11 \times 3 = 33$ square units

Step 6 The parallelogram is made of two congruent trapezoids. So, divide by 2 to find the area of one trapezoid. $33 \div 2 = 16.5$ square units

Find the area of the trapezoid.

1. Trace and cut out two copies of the trapezoid. Arrange them to form a parallelogram.

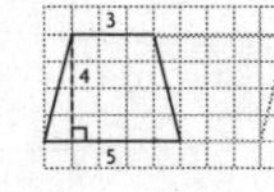

a. Find the base of the parallelogram. 3 + 5 = 8
b. Find the area of the parallelogram, using $A = bh$.
$A =$ 8 $\times$ 4 $=$ 32 square units
c. Find the area of the trapezoid.
32 $\div 2 =$ 16 square units

2. 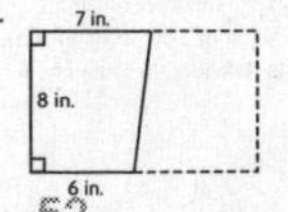

52 in.²

3. 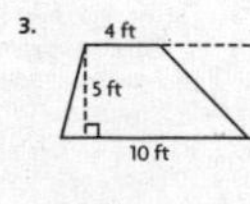

35 ft²

4. 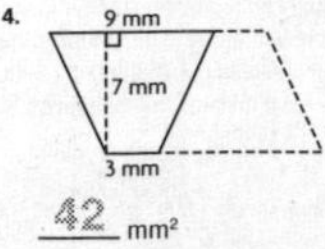

42 mm²

Name ____________________

Lesson 76
CC.6.G.1

1. Tamara made a copy of a trapezoid to make a design in the shape of a parallelogram.

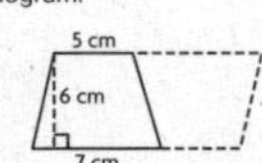

What is the area of each trapezoid?

Ⓐ 9 square centimeters
Ⓑ 18 square centimeters
Ⓒ 36 square centimeters
Ⓓ 72 square centimeters

2. Leon makes a rectangular logo for his skateboarding club. He cuts from fabric two copies of the trapezoid shown and joins them to form a rectangle.

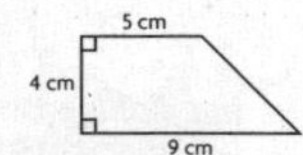

What is the area of the rectangular logo?

Ⓐ 56 square centimeters
Ⓑ 28 square centimeters
Ⓒ 18 square centimeters
Ⓓ 9 square centimeters

3. Josh constructs a banner in the shape of a parallelogram by making a copy of a trapezoid.

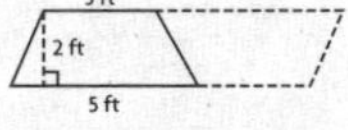

What is the area of each trapezoid?

Ⓐ 8 square feet
Ⓑ 10 square feet
Ⓒ 16 square feet
Ⓓ 20 square feet

4. Glenda cuts a trapezoid with the shown dimensions from construction paper. She uses a copy of the trapezoid to create a rectangular design.

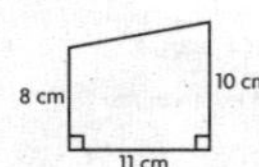

What is the area of the rectangular design?

Ⓐ 29 square centimeters
Ⓑ 40 square centimeters
Ⓒ 99 square centimeters
Ⓓ 198 square centimeters

Problem Solving REAL WORLD

5. A cake is made out of two identical trapezoids. Each trapezoid has a height of 11 inches and bases of 9 inches and 14 inches. What is the area of one of the trapezoid pieces?

126.5 in.²

6. A sticker is in the shape of a trapezoid. The height is 3 centimeters, and the bases are 2.5 centimeters and 5.5 centimeters. What is the area of the sticker?

12 cm²

Answer Key

Name ______________________

Lesson 77
COMMON CORE STANDARD CC.6.G.1
Lesson Objective: Find the area of trapezoids.

Algebra • Area of Trapezoids

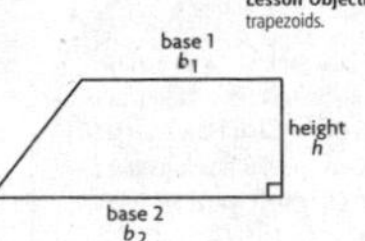

To find the area of a trapezoid, use the formula
Area $= \frac{1}{2} \times (\text{base}_1 + \text{base}_2) \times$ height.

Find the area of the trapezoid.

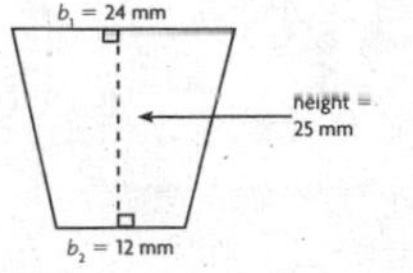

Step 1 Write the formula to find the area. $A = \frac{1}{2}(b_1 + b_2)h$

Step 2 Replace the variable b_1 with 24, b_2 with 12, and h with 25. $A = \frac{1}{2} \times (24 + 12) \times 25$

Step 3 Use the order of operations to simplify. $A = \frac{1}{2} \times 36 \times 25$
$A = 18 \times 25$
$A = 450$

Step 4 Use the appropriate units. $A = 450 \text{ mm}^2$

Find the area.

1.

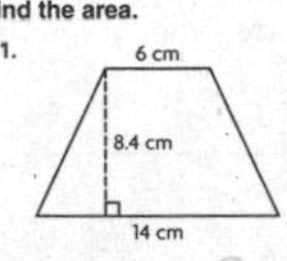

Write the formula. $A = \frac{1}{2}(b_1 + b_2)h$
Replace the variables. $A = \frac{1}{2} \times (\underline{6} + \underline{14}) \times \underline{8.4}$
Simplify. $A = \frac{1}{2} \times \underline{20} \times \underline{8.4}$
$A = \underline{84 \text{ cm}^2}$

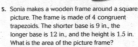

2.

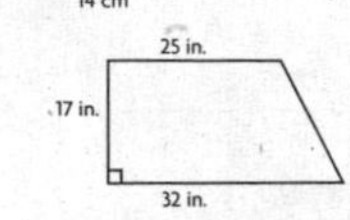

$A = 484.5 \text{ in.}^2$

3.

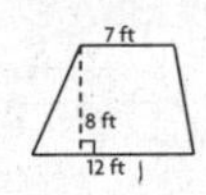

$A = 76 \text{ ft}^2$

Name ______________________

Lesson 77
CC.6.G.1

1. Olivia's father is going to build a new deck in the backyard. He draws this design for the deck.

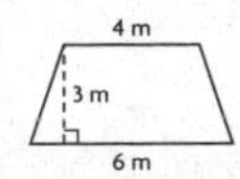

What is the area of the deck?

(A) 72 square meters
(B) 36 square meters
(C) 30 square meters
(D) 15 square meters

2. The lid on a ceramic box is in the shape of a trapezoid. The area of the lid is 36 square inches. The bases of the lid are 5 inches and 7 inches. What is the height of the lid?

(A) 48 inches
(B) 24 inches
(C) 6 inches
(D) 1 inch

3. Mr. Wen has a desk that is shaped like a trapezoid. The diagram shows the dimensions of the desk.

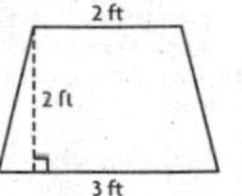

What is the area of the desk?

(A) 5 square feet (C) 10 square feet
(B) 7 square feet (D) 12 square feet

4. Rita is making a large poster for an art project. The shape and dimensions of her poster are shown.

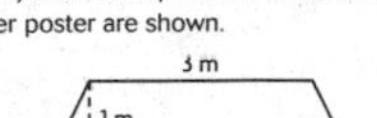
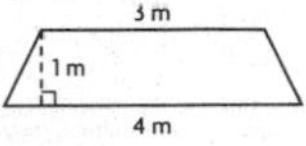

What is the area of the poster?

(A) 3.5 square meters
(B) 7 square meters
(C) 8 square meters
(D) 12 square meters

Problem Solving REAL WORLD

5. Sonia makes a wooden frame around a square picture. The frame is made of 4 congruent trapezoids. The shorter base is 9 in., the longer base is 12 in., and the height is 1.5 in. What is the area of the picture frame?

63 in.^2

6. Bryan cuts a piece of cardboard in the shape of a trapezoid. The area of the cutout is 43.5 square centimeters. If the bases are 6 centimeters and 8.5 centimeters long, what is the height of the trapezoid?

6 cm

Name ______________________

Lesson 78
COMMON CORE STANDARD CC.6.G.1
Lesson Objective: Find the area of regular polygons.

Area of Regular Polygons

In a regular polygon, all sides have the same length and all angles have the same measure. To find the area of a regular polygon, divide it into triangles.

Step 1 Draw line segments from each vertex to the center of the regular polygon.

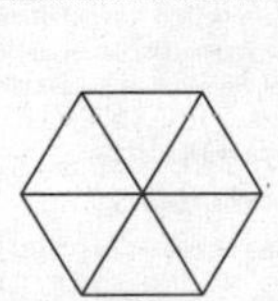

Step 2 Examine the figure.

The line segments divide the polygon into congruent triangles. This polygon is a hexagon. A hexagon has 6 sides, so there are 6 triangles.

Step 3 Find the area of one triangle. Use the formula $A = \frac{1}{2}bh$.

The base of the triangle (or one side of the hexagon) is 14 in. The height of the triangle is 12.1 in.

$A = \frac{1}{2} \times 14 \times 12.1 = \frac{1}{2} \times 169.4 = 84.7 \text{ in.}^2$

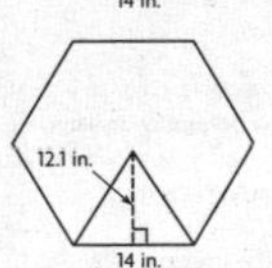

Step 4 Multiply by 6, because there are 6 triangles. $84.7 \times 6 = 508.2$

So, the area of the regular hexagon is 508.2 square inches.

Find the area of the regular polygon.

1. Number of congruent triangles inside the pentagon: $\underline{5}$

Area of each triangle:
$A = \frac{1}{2} \times \underline{8} \times 5.5 = \frac{1}{2} \times \underline{44} = \underline{22} \text{ mm}^2$

Area of the pentagon: $\underline{22} \times \underline{5} = \underline{110} \text{ mm}^2$

5.5 mm
8 mm

2.

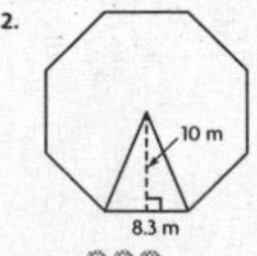

$\underline{332} \text{ m}^2$

3. 6.2 ft, 4 ft

$\underline{124} \text{ ft}^2$

4. 16.5 cm, 19 cm

$\underline{940.5} \text{ cm}^2$

Name ______________________

Lesson 78
CC.6.G.1

1. Marcia has a regular hexagonal patch on her backpack. A diagram of the patch is shown.

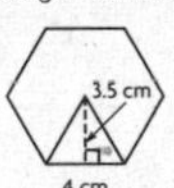

What is the area of the patch?

(A) 7 cm^2 **(C) 42 cm^2**
(B) 14 cm^2 (D) 84 cm^2

2. Radimir is paving his driveway using brick pavers. The brick pavers that he is using are in the shape of regular pentagons as shown.

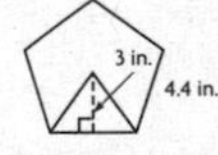

What is the area of the pentagon shown?

(A) 6.6 in.^2 **(C) 33 in.^2**
(B) 13.2 in.^2 (D) 66 in.^2

3. Giselle has a pendant on her necklace that is shaped like a regular hexagon. On the pendant, there are lines from the center to each vertex that divide it into congruent triangles. Each triangle has an area of 2 square centimeters. What is the area of the pendant?

(A) 10 cm^2 (C) 20 cm^2
(B) 12 cm^2 (D) 24 cm^2

4. Amira's bathroom floor is made of regular octagon tiles and square tiles. A diagram of one of the octagon tiles is shown.

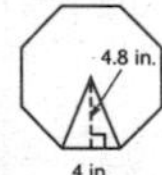

What is the area of one of the octagon tiles?

(A) 9.6 in.^2 (C) 38.4 in.^2
(B) 19.2 in.^2 **(D) 76.8 in.^2**

Problem Solving REAL WORLD

5. Stu is making a stained glass window in the shape of a regular pentagon. The pentagon can be divided into congruent triangles, each with a base of 8.7 inches and a height of 6 inches. What is the area of the window?

130.5 in.^2

6. A dinner platter is in the shape of a regular decagon. The platter has an area of 161 square inches and a side length of 4.6 inches. What is the area of each triangle? What is the height of each triangle?

16.1 in.^2; 7 in.

Answer Key

Name ______________________

Lesson 79

COMMON CORE STANDARD CC.6.G.1

Lesson Objective: Find the area of composite figures.

Composite Figures

A **composite figure** is made up of two or more simpler figures, such as triangles and quadrilaterals.

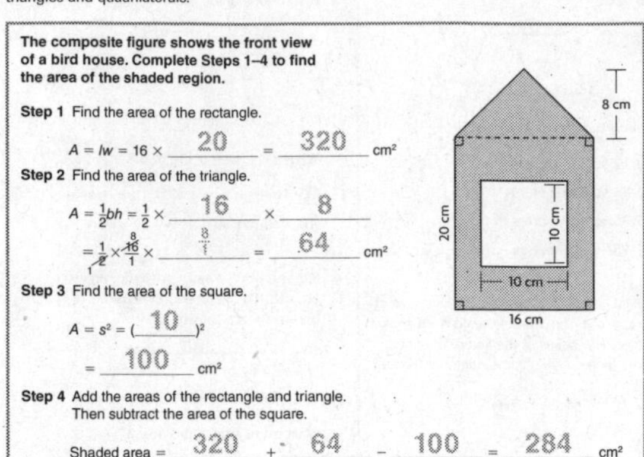

The composite figure shows the front view of a bird house. Complete Steps 1–4 to find the area of the shaded region.

Step 1 Find the area of the rectangle.

$A = lw = 16 \times$ 20 = 320 cm²

Step 2 Find the area of the triangle.

$A = \frac{1}{2}bh = \frac{1}{2} \times$ 16 × 8

$= \frac{1}{2} \times \frac{16}{1} \times \frac{8}{1}$ = 64 cm²

Step 3 Find the area of the square.

$A = s^2 = ($ 10 $)^2$

= 100 cm²

Step 4 Add the areas of the rectangle and triangle. Then subtract the area of the square.

Shaded area = 320 + 64 − 100 = 284 cm²

So, the area of the shaded region is 284 cm².

Find the area of the shaded region.

1. 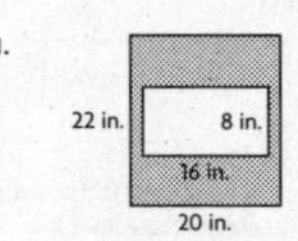

312 in.²

2. 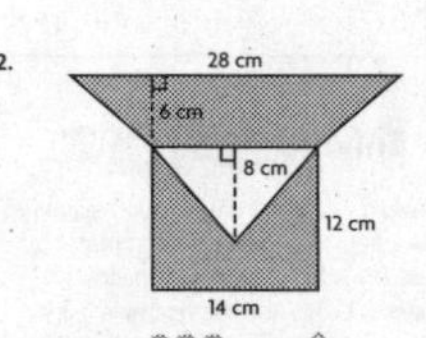

238 cm²

Name ______________________

Lesson 79

CC.6.G.1

1. Melvin wants to install new carpet in his basement. He needs to know the area of the basement to determine how much carpet he will need to purchase. The figure shows the dimensions of Melvin's basement.

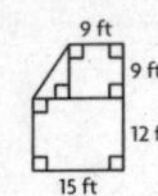

What is the area of his basement?

Ⓐ 315 ft²
Ⓑ 288 ft²
Ⓒ 189 ft²
Ⓓ 180 ft²

2. Jacob is constructing a model of a spacecraft for his science project. The design of the wing of the spacecraft is shown.

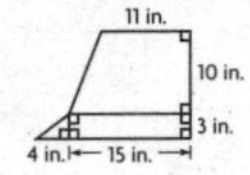

What is the area of the wing?

Ⓐ 70 in.²
Ⓑ 130 in.²
Ⓒ 150 in.²
Ⓓ 181 in.²

3. Mrs. Webster cut a triangle with a height of 4 inches and a base of 6 inches out of a sheet of paper measuring 10 inches by 12 inches. She recycled the unused paper. What is the area of the paper she recycled?

Ⓐ 12 in.²
Ⓑ 24 in.²
Ⓒ 108 in.²
Ⓓ 120 in.²

4. Sofia wants to remodel some rooms in her home. She needs to know the total area of the rooms before she can begin. The figure shows the dimensions of the rooms she wants to remodel.

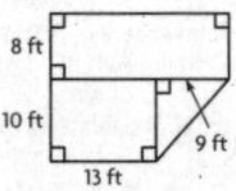

What is the total area of the rooms she is going to remodel?

Ⓐ 130 ft²
Ⓑ 279 ft²
Ⓒ 351 ft²
Ⓓ 396 ft²

Problem Solving REAL WORLD

5. Janelle is making a poster. She cuts a triangle out of poster board. What is the area of the poster board that she has left?

9 in.
10 in.
20 in.

155 in.²

Name ______________________

Lesson 80

COMMON CORE STANDARD CC.6.G.1

Lesson Objective: Determine the effect of changing dimensions on the area of a polygon by using the strategy *find a pattern.*

Problem Solving • Changing Dimensions

Amy is sewing a quilt out of fabric pieces shaped like parallelograms. The smallest of the parallelograms is shown at the right. The dimensions of another parallelogram she is using can be found by multiplying the dimensions of the smallest parallelogram by 3. How do the areas of the parallelograms compare?

6 cm
4 cm
5 cm

Read the Problem		
What do I need to find?	**What information do I need to use?**	**How will I use the information?**
I need to find how the areas of the different parallelograms compare	I need to use the dimensions of the smallest parallelogram and the number by which the dimensions are multiplied	I can draw a sketch of each parallelogram and calculate the areas. Then I can look for patterns in my results

Solve the Problem		
Sketch	**Multiplier**	**Area**
	none	$A = 6 \times$ 4 = 24 cm²
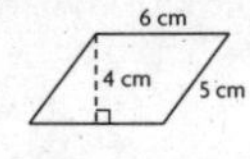 18 cm, 12 cm, 15 cm	3	$A =$ 18 × 12 = 216 cm²

When the dimensions are multiplied by 3, the area is multiplied by 9.

1. Sunni drew a parallelogram with area 20 in.². If she doubles the dimensions, what is the area of the new parallelogram?

80 in.²

2. Abe drew a square with side length 20 mm. If he draws a new square with dimensions that are half that of the previous square, what is the area of the new square?

100 mm²

Name ______________________

Lesson 80

CC.6.G.1

1. Jeremy wants to enlarge his younger brother's 5-foot by 5-foot sandbox by multiplying its dimensions by 3. How will the area of the sandbox be affected?

Ⓐ It will be multiplied by 9.
Ⓑ It will be multiplied by 3.
Ⓒ It will be multiplied by $\frac{1}{3}$.
Ⓓ It will be multiplied by $\frac{1}{9}$.

2. Malcolm wants to enlarge a 2-inch by 3-inch photograph by multiplying its dimensions by 5. How will the area of the photograph be affected?

Ⓐ It will be multiplied by $\frac{1}{25}$.
Ⓑ It will be multiplied by $\frac{1}{5}$.
Ⓒ It will be multiplied by 5.
Ⓓ It will be multiplied by 25.

3. Katie wants to shrink this triangle by multiplying its dimensions by $\frac{1}{2}$.

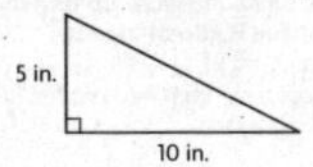

How will the area of the triangle be affected?

Ⓐ It will be multiplied by $\frac{1}{16}$.
Ⓑ It will be multiplied by $\frac{1}{8}$.
Ⓒ It will be multiplied by $\frac{1}{4}$.
Ⓓ It will be multiplied by $\frac{1}{2}$.

Problem Solving REAL WORLD

4. Kimberly wants to enlarge her 5-foot by 10-foot rectangular patio by multiplying its dimensions by 2. How will the area of the patio be affected? Explain how you know.

The area will be multiplied by 4; Possible explanation: The area of the patio is $A = 5 \text{ ft} \times 10 \text{ ft} = 50 \text{ ft}^2$. The dimensions of the patio become 10 ft by 20 ft when multiplied by 2. The area of the patio with the new dimensions is $A = 10 \text{ ft} \times 20 \text{ ft} = 200 \text{ ft}^2$. That is 4 times the area of the original patio.

Name ______________________

Lesson 81

COMMON CORE STANDARD CC.6.G.2

Lesson Objective: Investigate the volume of rectangular prisms with fractional edge lengths.

Fractions and Volume

Find the volume of a rectangular prism that is $2\frac{1}{2}$ units long, 2 units wide, and $1\frac{1}{2}$ units high.

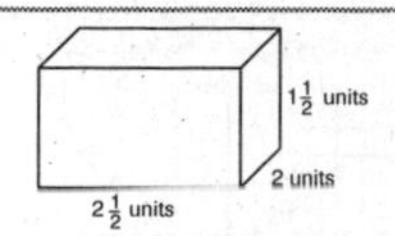

Step 1 Stack cubes with $\frac{1}{2}$-unit side length to form a rectangular prism.

Length: 5 cubes = $\frac{1}{2}+\frac{1}{2}+\frac{1}{2}+\frac{1}{2}+\frac{1}{2} = 2\frac{1}{2}$ units

Width: 4 cubes = $\frac{1}{2}+\frac{1}{2}+\frac{1}{2}+\frac{1}{2} = 2$ units

Height: 3 cubes = $\frac{1}{2}+\frac{1}{2}+\frac{1}{2} = 1\frac{1}{2}$ units

Step 2 Count the total number of cubes.

60 cubes

Step 3 It takes 8 cubes with $\frac{1}{2}$ unit side lengths to make 1 unit cube. So, each smaller cube has $\frac{1}{8}$ the volume of a unit cube.

Divide 60 by 8 to find how many unit cubes it would take to form the prism. Write the remainder as a fraction and simplify.

$60 \div 8 = 7\frac{4}{8}$ $7\frac{4}{8} = 7\frac{1}{2}$

So, the volume of the prism is $7\frac{1}{2}$ cubic units.

1. Find the volume of the rectangular prism.

a. Stack cubes with $\frac{1}{2}$-unit side lengths to form the prism.

b. Count the cubes. 36

c. Divide by 8. 36 ÷ 8 = $4\frac{4}{8}$

d. The prism has a volume of $4\frac{1}{2}$ cubic units.

Name ______________________

Lesson 81

CC.6.G.2

1. What is the volume of the rectangular prism shown?

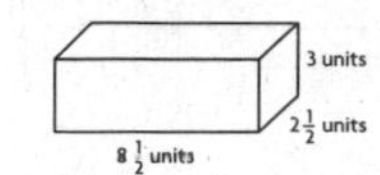

Ⓐ $63\frac{3}{4}$ cubic units (answer)
Ⓑ $42\frac{1}{2}$ cubic units
Ⓒ 28 cubic units
Ⓓ 14 cubic units

2. A prism is filled with 25 cubes with $\frac{1}{2}$-unit side lengths. What is the volume of the prism in cubic units?

Ⓐ $3\frac{1}{8}$ cubic units (answer)
Ⓑ $3\frac{1}{3}$ cubic units
Ⓒ $12\frac{1}{8}$ cubic units
Ⓓ $12\frac{1}{2}$ cubic units

3. A box measures 4 units by $2\frac{1}{2}$ units by $1\frac{1}{2}$ units. What is the greatest number of cubes with a side length of $\frac{1}{2}$ unit that can be packed inside the box?

Ⓐ 16
Ⓑ 30
Ⓒ 64
Ⓓ 120 (answer)

4. What is the volume of the box shown?

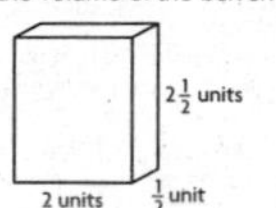

Ⓐ $6\frac{1}{2}$ cubic units
Ⓑ 5 cubic units
Ⓒ $2\frac{1}{2}$ cubic units (answer)
Ⓓ 1 cubic unit

Problem Solving REAL WORLD

5. Miguel is pouring liquid into a container that is $4\frac{1}{2}$ inches long by $3\frac{1}{2}$ inches wide by 2 inches high. How many cubic inches of liquid will fit in the container?

$31\frac{1}{2}$ in.^{3}

6. A shipping crate is shaped like a rectangular prism. It is $5\frac{1}{2}$ feet long by 3 feet wide by 3 feet high. What is the volume of the crate?

$49\frac{1}{2}$ ft^3

Name ______________________

Lesson 82

COMMON CORE STANDARD CC.6.G.2

Lesson Objective: Use formulas to find the volume of rectangular prisms with fractional edge lengths.

Algebra • Volume of Rectangular Prisms

You can find the volume of a prism by using the formula $V = Bh$. V stands for volume, B stands for the area of the base, and h stands for the height.

For a rectangular prism, any face can be the base, since all faces are rectangles.

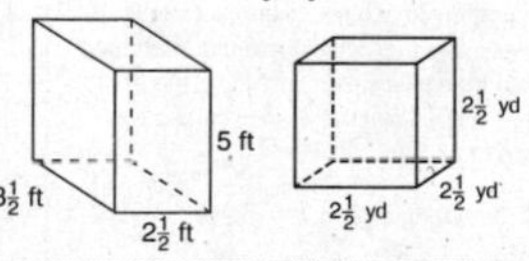

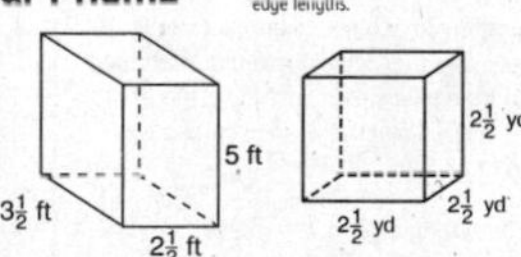

Find the volume of the rectangular prism.

Step 1 Find the area of the base. The base is $2\frac{1}{2}$ ft by $3\frac{1}{2}$ ft.

$A = l \times w$

$A = 2\frac{1}{2}\text{ ft} \times 3\frac{1}{2}\text{ ft} = 8\frac{3}{4}\text{ ft}^2$

Step 2 Multiply the area of the base by the height.

$V = Bh$

$V = 8\frac{3}{4}\text{ ft}^2 \times 5\text{ ft} = 43\frac{3}{4}\text{ ft}^3$

So, the volume of the rectangular prism is $43\frac{3}{4}$ ft^3.

Find the volume of the cube.

Step 1 Because the length, width, and height are all equal, you can use a special formula.

$V = Bh = l \times w \times h$

$V = s^3$

Step 2 Substitute $2\frac{1}{2}$ for s.

$V = s^3 = \left(2\frac{1}{2}\right)^3 = \left(\frac{5}{2}\right)^3$

$V = \frac{5}{2}\text{ yd} \times \frac{5}{2}\text{ yd} \times \frac{5}{2}\text{ yd} = \frac{125}{8}\text{ yd}^3$

$= 15\frac{5}{8}\text{ yd}^3$

So, the volume of the cube is $15\frac{5}{8}$ yd^3.

Find the volume.

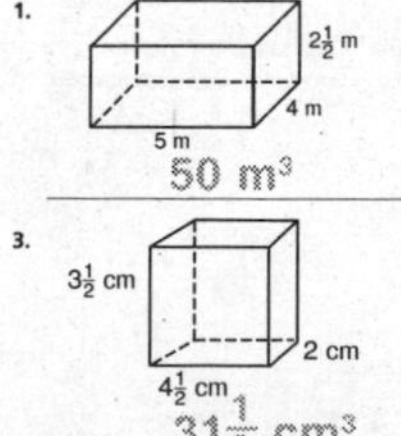

1. 50 m^3

2. ($1\frac{1}{2}$ in. by $1\frac{1}{2}$ in. by $1\frac{1}{2}$ in.) $3\frac{3}{8}$ in.^{3}

3. ($4\frac{1}{2}$ cm by 2 cm by $3\frac{1}{2}$ cm) $31\frac{1}{2}$ cm^3

4. (16 ft by 30 ft by $12\frac{1}{2}$ ft) 6,000 ft^3

Name ______________________

Lesson 82

CC.6.G.2

1. A moving box is a rectangular prism with a width of 24 inches and a height of $18\frac{1}{2}$ inches. The volume of the box is 10,656 cubic inches. What is the length of the box?

Ⓐ 12 inches
Ⓑ 24 inches (answer)
Ⓒ 42 inches
Ⓓ 432 inches

2. Marci bought a box of energy-efficient light bulbs. The box had dimensions of 10 inches by $5\frac{1}{2}$ inches by 6 inches. What is the volume of this box?

Ⓐ 330 cubic inches (answer)
Ⓑ $300\frac{1}{2}$ cubic inches
Ⓒ 296 cubic inches
Ⓓ $21\frac{1}{2}$ cubic inches

3. Mr. Jackson rented a storage unit in the shape of a rectangular prism. The volume of the unit is 230 cubic yards. The storage unit is $5\frac{3}{4}$ yards wide and 10 yards long. What is the height of the storage unit?

Ⓐ 2 yards
Ⓑ 4 yards (answer)
Ⓒ 14 yards
Ⓓ 50 yards

4. A rectangular box is 20 inches long, $10\frac{1}{2}$ inches wide, and $24\frac{1}{2}$ inches high. What is the volume of the box?

Ⓐ $1,086\frac{1}{8}$ cubic inches
Ⓑ $2,173\frac{1}{4}$ cubic inches
Ⓒ $4,532\frac{1}{2}$ cubic inches
Ⓓ 9,065 cubic inches (answer)

Problem Solving REAL WORLD

5. A cereal box is a rectangular prism that is 8 inches long and $2\frac{1}{2}$ inches wide. The volume of the box is 200 in.^{3}. What is the height of the box?

10 in.

6. A stack of paper is $8\frac{1}{2}$ in. long by 11 in. wide by 4 in. high. What is the volume of the stack of paper?

374 in.^{3}

Answer Key

Name ______________________

Lesson 83

COMMON CORE STANDARD CC.6.G.3

Lesson Objective: Plot polygons on a coordinate plane, and use coordinates to find side lengths.

Figures on the Coordinate Plane

The vertices of a parallelogram are A(⁻2, 2), B(⁻3, 5), C(4, 5), and D(5, 2). Graph the parallelogram and find the length of side AD.

Step 1 Draw the parallelogram on the coordinate plane. Plot the points and then connect the points with straight lines.

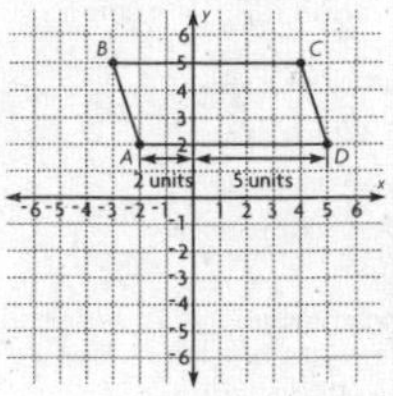

Step 2 Find the length of side *AD*.

Horizontal distance of *A* from 0: |⁻2| = 2
Horizontal distance of *D* from 0: |5| = 5

Points *A* and *D* are in different quadrants, so add to find the distance from *A* to *D*.
2 + 5 = 7 units

So, the length of side *AD* is 7 units.

Graph the figure and find the length of the given side.

1. Triangle *JKL*
J(⁻3, ⁻3), *K*(⁻3, 5), *L*(5, 2)

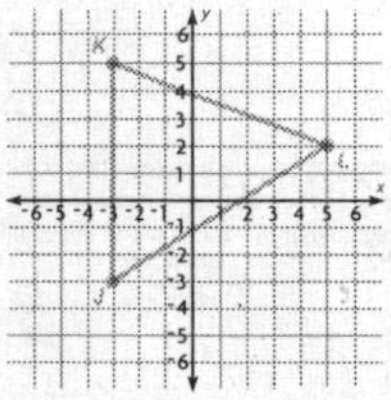

length of $\overline{JK}$ = 8

2. Trapezoid *WXYZ*
W(⁻2, ⁻3), *X*(⁻2, 3), *Y*(3, 5), *Z*(3, ⁻3)

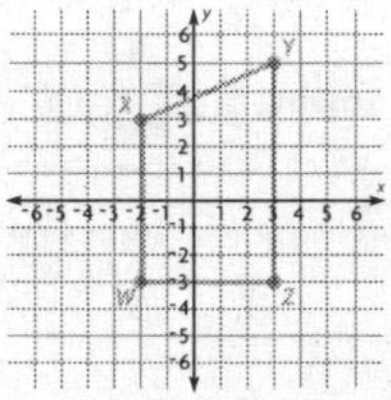

length of $\overline{WZ}$ = 5

Name ______________________

Lesson 83

CC.6.G.3

1. Andrew is drawing a sketch of the garden he is going to plant. Line segments *JK* and *KL* are two sides of parallelogram *JKLM*.

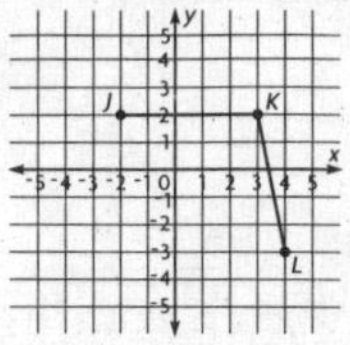

What are the coordinates of vertex *M*?

Ⓐ (1, 3)
Ⓑ (⁻1, 3)
Ⓒ (1, ⁻3)
Ⓓ (⁻1, ⁻3)

2. Mrs. Moy is building a rectangular garden in her yard. She already has placed stakes to mark 3 of the corners of the garden. She needs to place the final stake. The map shows the location of the 3 stakes she has already placed.

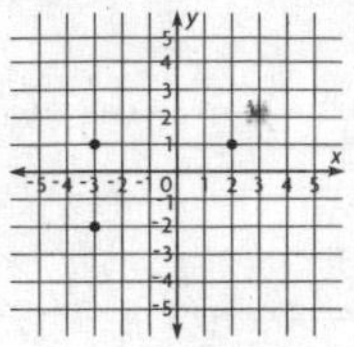

What are the coordinates for the final stake?

Ⓐ (2, ⁻2)
Ⓑ (⁻1, ⁻2)
Ⓒ (⁻2, ⁻1)
Ⓓ (2, 2)

Problem Solving REAL WORLD

3. On a map, a city block is a square with three of its vertices at (⁻4, 1), (1, 1), and (1, ⁻4). What are the coordinates of the remaining vertex?

(⁻4, ⁻4)

4. A carpenter is making a shelf in the shape of a parallelogram. She begins by drawing parallelogram *RSTU* on a coordinate plane with vertices *R*(1, 0), *S*(⁻3, 0), and *T*(⁻2, 3). What are the coordinates of vertex *U*?

(2, 3)

Name ______________________

Lesson 84

COMMON CORE STANDARD CC.6.G.4

Lesson Objective: Use nets to represent three-dimensional figures.

Three-Dimensional Figures and Nets

Solid figures have three dimensions–length, width, and height. They can be named by the shapes of their bases, the number of bases, and the shapes of their lateral faces.

Identify and draw a net for the solid figure.

Step 1 Describe the base of the figure.
The base is a square.

Step 2 Describe the lateral surfaces.
The lateral surfaces are triangles.

So, the figure is a square pyramid.

Step 3 Name the shapes to be used in the net. Then make a sketch. Draw a square for the base, and four triangles for the lateral faces.

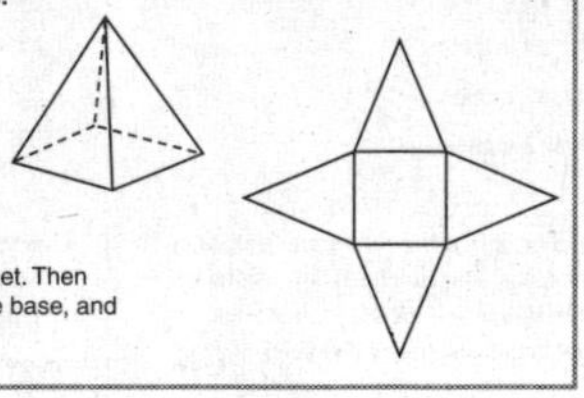

Identify and draw a net for the solid figure.

1.

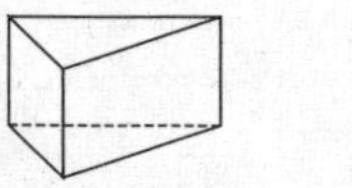

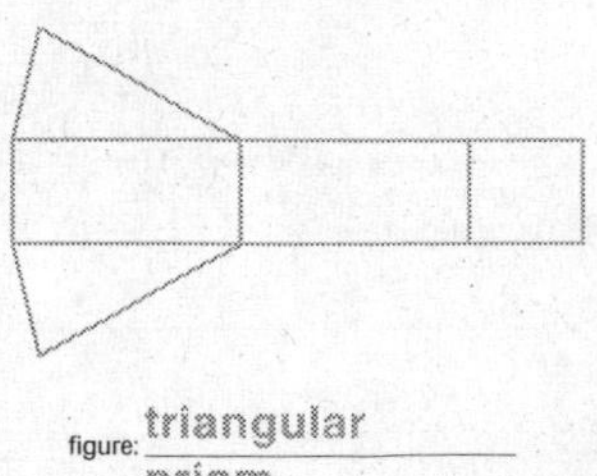

figure: triangular prism

2.

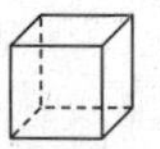

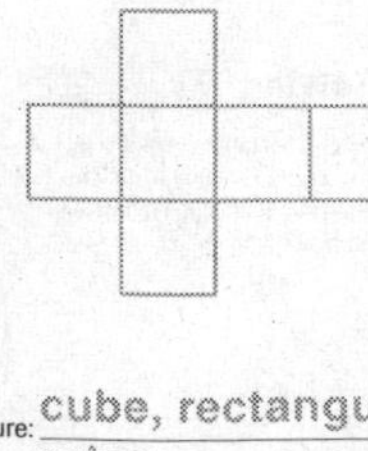

figure: cube, rectangular prism

Name ______________________

Lesson 84

CC.6.G.4

1. An employee at a tent manufacturer is sewing together tents. Each tent is shaped like a triangular prism (including the floor). What shapes can the employee use for each tent?

Ⓐ 3 rectangles and 2 triangles
Ⓑ 2 rectangles and 3 triangles
Ⓒ 4 rectangles and 1 circle
Ⓓ 3 triangles and 1 rectangle

2. Wilson cut open a packing box that was shaped like a rectangular prism to see the net. What shapes did Wilson see?

Ⓐ 1 triangle and 2 rectangles
Ⓑ 1 square and 3 rectangles
Ⓒ 6 rectangles only
Ⓓ 6 triangles only

3. Georgette's computer came in a box shaped like a cube. How many square faces does the box have?

Ⓐ 2
Ⓑ 4
Ⓒ 6
Ⓓ 8

4. Julio made a triangular pyramid out of wood. What shapes did he use?

Ⓐ 3 triangles only
Ⓑ 4 rectangles only
Ⓒ 3 triangles and 1 rectangle
Ⓓ 4 triangles only

Problem Solving REAL WORLD

5. Hobie's Candies are sold in triangular-pyramid-shaped boxes. How many triangles are needed to make one box?

4

6. Nina used plastic rectangles to make 6 rectangular prisms. How many rectangles did she use?

36

Answer Key

Name ____________________

Lesson 85
COMMON CORE STANDARD CC.6.G.4
Lesson Objective: Use nets to recognize that the surface area of a prism is equal to the sum of the areas of its faces.

Explore Surface Area Using Nets

The net of a solid figure shows you all of the faces or surfaces of the figure. A net can help you find the **surface area** of a figure.

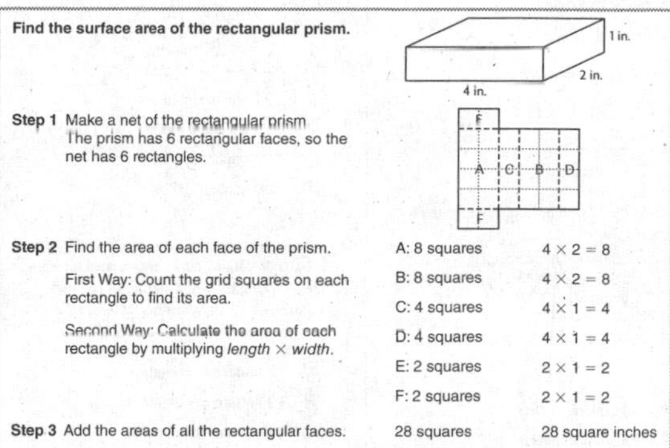

Find the surface area of the rectangular prism.

Step 1 Make a net of the rectangular prism. The prism has 6 rectangular faces, so the net has 6 rectangles.

Step 2 Find the area of each face of the prism.

First Way: Count the grid squares on each rectangle to find its area.

Second Way: Calculate the area of each rectangle by multiplying *length* × *width*.

A: 8 squares	$4 \times 2 = 8$
B: 8 squares	$4 \times 2 = 8$
C: 4 squares	$4 \times 1 = 4$
D: 4 squares	$4 \times 1 = 4$
E: 2 squares	$2 \times 1 = 2$
F: 2 squares	$2 \times 1 = 2$

Step 3 Add the areas of all the rectangular faces. 28 squares 28 square inches

So, the surface area of the rectangular prism is 28 square inches (in.^{2}).

Use the net to find the surface area of the prism.

1.

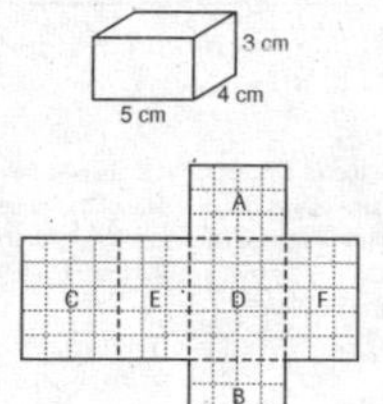

a. Find the area of each face.

A: 12 B: 12
C: 20 D: 20
E: 15 F: 15

b. Add: A + B + C + D + E + F = 94

c. The surface area is 94 cm^2.

Name ____________________

Lesson 85
CC.6.G.4

1. Jami covered the lateral faces of the wooden box shown with felt.

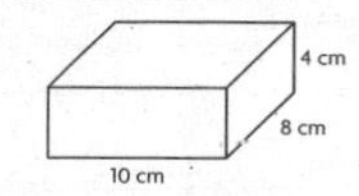

Which expression shows the amount of felt, in square centimeters, that she used to cover the lateral faces?

Ⓐ $2(8 \times 4) + 2(8 \times 10)$
Ⓑ $2(8 \times 4) + 2(10 \times 4)$
Ⓒ $2(10 \times 8) + 2(10 \times 4)$
Ⓓ $2(10 \times 8) + 2(10 \times 4) + 2(8 \times 4)$

2. The net of a rectangular prism is shown.

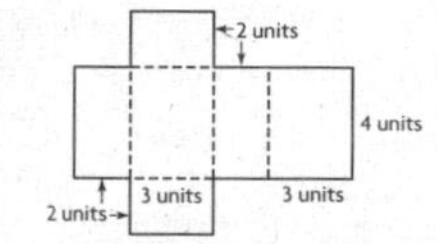

What is the surface area of this prism?

Ⓐ 24 square units Ⓒ 52 square units
Ⓑ 26 square units Ⓓ 58 square units

3. Darrell is decorating the top and lateral faces of this box with collages made of pictures from his favorite magazines.

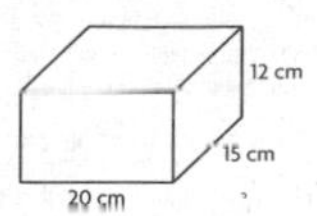

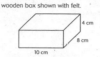

Which expression shows the amount of surface area, in square centimeters, that Darrell will cover with collages?

Ⓐ $2(20 \times 15) + 2(15 \times 12) + (20 \times 12)$
Ⓑ $2(20 \times 12) + 2(15 \times 12) + (20 \times 15)$
Ⓒ $2(20 \times 12) + 2(20 \times 15) + (12 \times 15)$
Ⓓ $2(20 \times 12) + 2(20 \times 15) + 2(12 \times 15)$

Problem Solving REAL WORLD

4. Jeremiah is covering a cereal box with fabric for a school project. If the box is 6 inches long by 2 inches wide by 14 inches high, how much surface area does Jeremiah have to cover?

248 in.^{2}

5. Tia is making a case for her calculator. It is a rectangular prism that will be 3.5 inches long by 1 inch wide by 10 inches high. How much material (surface area) will she need to make the case?

97 in.^{2}

Name ____________________

Lesson 86
COMMON CORE STANDARD CC.6.G.4
Lesson Objective: Find the surface area of prisms.

Algebra • Surface Area of Prisms

You can find the surface area of a figure by adding the lateral surface area to the sum of the areas of the bases.

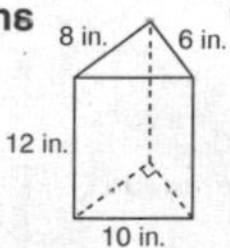

Use a net to find the surface area.

Step 1 Draw a net.

Note any faces that have equal areas.

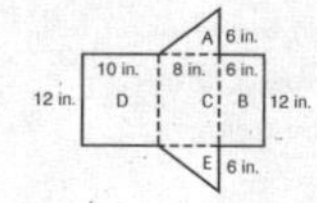

Step 2 Both triangular bases have the same area.

Base A: $A = \frac{1}{2}bh = \frac{1}{2} \times 6 \times 8 = 24$ in.^{2}
Base E: $A = 24$ in.^{2}

Step 3 Find the areas of the rectangular faces.

Face B: $A = lw = 6 \times 12 = 72$ in.^{2}
Face C: $A = lw = 8 \times 12 = 96$ in.^{2}
Face D: $A = lw = 10 \times 12 = 120$ in.^{2}

Step 4 Add the areas: A + B + C + D + E $24 + 72 + 96 + 120 + 24 = 336$ in.^{2}

So, the surface area of the triangular prism is 336 square inches (in.^{2}).

Use a net to find the surface area.

1.

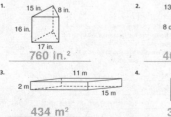

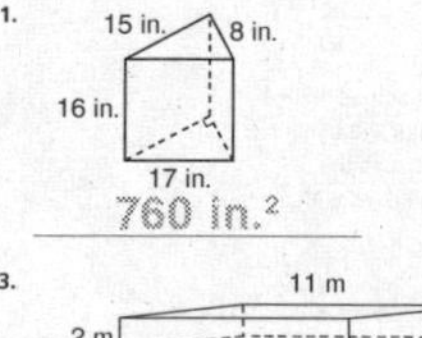

760 in.^{2}

2.

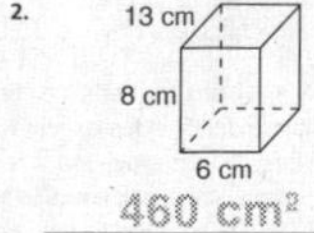

460 cm^2

3. (11 m, 2 m, 15 m)

434 m^2

4.

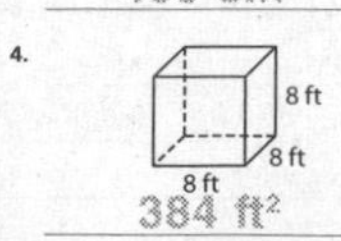

384 ft^2

Name ____________________

Lesson 86
CC.6.G.4

1. A rectangular prism measures 10 inches by 6 inches by 6 inches. What is its surface area?

Ⓐ 360 square inches
Ⓑ 312 square inches
Ⓒ 240 square inches
Ⓓ 192 square inches

2. A rectangular gift box measures 8 inches by 10 inches by 3 inches. What is its surface area?

Ⓐ 184 square inches
Ⓑ 214 square inches
Ⓒ 240 square inches
Ⓓ 268 square inches

3. Liam made a music box. The box is a rectangular prism that measures 12 centimeters by 8 centimeters by 5 centimeters. What is the surface area of the box?

Ⓐ 196 square centimeters
Ⓑ 240 square centimeters
Ⓒ 392 square centimeters
Ⓓ 480 square centimeters

4. Emily's decorative box is shaped like a cube and measures 5 inches by 5 inches by 5 inches. What is its surface area?

Ⓐ 75 square inches
Ⓑ 100 square inches
Ⓒ 125 square inches
Ⓓ 150 square inches

Problem Solving REAL WORLD

5. A shoe box measures 15 in. by 7 in. by $4\frac{1}{2}$ in. What is the surface area of the box?

480 in.^{2}

6. Vivian is working with a styrofoam cube for art class. The length of one side is 5 inches. How much surface area does Vivian have to work with?

150 in.^{2}

Answer Key

Name ______________________

Lesson 87

COMMON CORE STANDARD CC.6.G.4

Lesson Objective: Find the surface area of pyramids.

Algebra • Surface Area of Pyramids

To find the surface area of a pyramid, add the area of the base to the **lateral area**. The lateral area is the combined area of the triangular faces.

Find the surface area of the square pyramid.

Step 1 The base is a square with side length of 6 in. Use the formula $A = s^2$ to find the area. Substitute 6 for the variable s.

$A = 6^2 = 36$ in.^{2}

8 in.
6 in.

Step 2 The lateral faces are four triangles with base of 6 in. and height of 8 in. Find the area of one triangular lateral face using the formula $A = \frac{1}{2}bh$. Substitute 6 for b and 8 for h.

$A = \frac{1}{2}(6)(8) = 24$ in.^{2}

8 in.
6 in.
6 in.

Step 3 Multiply by 4 to find the total lateral area. $L = 24 \times 4 = 96$ in.^{2}

Step 4 Add the area of the base and the lateral area. $S = 36$ in.$^2 + 96$ in.$^2 = 132$ in.^{2}

So, the surface area of the square pyramid is 132 square inches (in.^{2}).

Use a net to find the surface area of the square pyramid.

1.

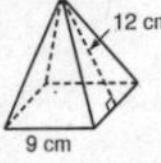

a. Area of the base: 81 cm^2

b. Area of one triangular lateral face: 54 cm^2

c. Total lateral area: 216 cm^2

d. Total surface area: 297 cm^2

2.

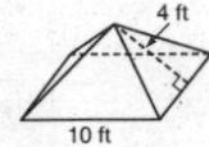

a. Area of the base: 100 ft^2

b. Area of one triangular lateral face: 20 ft^2

c. Total lateral area: 80 ft^2

d. Total surface area: 180 ft^2

Name ______________________

Lesson 87

CC.6.G.4

1. A square pyramid has a base with a side length of 7.5 feet and lateral faces with heights of 16 feet. Which expression could be used to find the surface area, in square feet, of the pyramid?

Ⓐ $7.5^2 \times \frac{1}{2} \times 7.5 \times 16$

Ⓑ $7.5^2 + \frac{1}{2} \times 7.5 \times 16$

Ⓒ $7.5 \times 4 \times \frac{1}{2} \times 7.5 \times 16$

Ⓓ $7.5^2 + 4 \times \frac{1}{2} \times 7.5 \times 16$

2. What is the lateral area of the triangular pyramid shown?

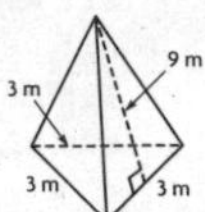

Ⓐ 40.5 square meters

Ⓑ 49.5 square meters

Ⓒ 81.0 square meters

Ⓓ 85.5 square meters

3. What is the lateral area of the square pyramid shown?

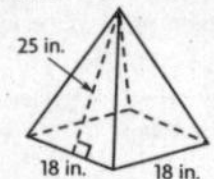

Ⓐ 2,124 square inches

Ⓑ 1,525 square inches

Ⓒ 1,224 square inches

Ⓓ 900 square inches

4. A triangular pyramid has a base with an area of 7 square centimeters and lateral faces with bases of 4 centimeters and heights of 12 centimeters. What is the surface area of the pyramid?

Ⓐ 72 square centimeters

Ⓑ 79 square centimeters

Ⓒ 103 square centimeters

Ⓓ 151 square centimeters

Problem Solving REAL WORLD

5. Cho is building a sandcastle in the shape of a triangular pyramid. The area of the base is 7 square feet. Each side of the base has a length of 4 feet and the height of each face is 2 feet. What is the surface area of the pyramid?

19 ft^2

6. The top of a skyscraper is shaped like a square pyramid. Each side of the base has a length of 60 meters and the height of each triangle is 20 meters. What is the lateral area of the pyramid?

2,400 m^2

Name ______________________

Lesson 88

COMMON CORE STANDARD CC.6.G.4

Lesson Objective: Solve problems involving area, surface area, and volume by applying the strategy *use a formula*.

Problem Solving • Geometric Measurements

Leslie stores gardening supplies in this shed shaped like a rectangular prism. What is the area of the ground covered by the shed?

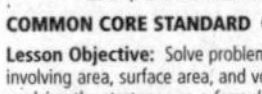

Read the Problem	Solve the Problem
What do I need to find? I need to find the area of the ground covered by the shed.	Choose the measure—area, surface area, or volume—that gives the area of the ground covered by the barrel. Explain. area; The area covered by the shed is the same as the area of the base of the shed.
What information do I need to use? I need to use the dimensions of the shed.	Choose an appropriate formula. $A = l \times w$
How will I use the information? First, I will decide which measure to use. Then I will choose a formula I can use to calculate this measure. Finally, I will replace the variables and evaluate the formula.	Replace the variables l and w in the area formula with their values in the dimensions of the shed. l = 12 ft w = 8 ft Evaluate the formula. A = 12 × 8 = 96 ft^2

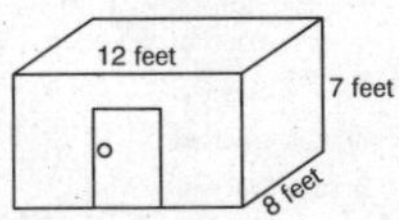

Solve.

1. Leslie is covering bricks with paint. Each brick is 8 in. long, 4 in. wide, and 2 in. high. How many square inches will Leslie paint on each brick?

112 in.^{2}

2. Leslie's planting box is shaped like a rectangular prism. It is 60 cm long, 35 cm wide, and 40 cm high. How many cubic cm of soil will Leslie need to fill the box?

84,000 cm^3

Name ______________________

Lesson 88

CC.6.G.4

1. As part of her art project, Sarah is painting the lateral faces of 2 identical triangular pyramids. Each lateral face has a base of 6 centimeters and a height of 8.5 centimeters. What is the total area that she will paint?

Ⓐ 25.5 square centimeters

Ⓑ 51 square centimeters

Ⓒ 76.5 square centimeters

Ⓓ 153 square centimeters

2. Albert wants to know how much water a fish tank shaped like a rectangular prism can hold. What geometric measure does Albert need to find?

Ⓐ the volume of the fish tank

Ⓑ the surface area of the fish tank

Ⓒ the area of the base of the fish tank

Ⓓ the perimeter of the base of the fish tank

3. Miguel is painting a cabinet shaped like a rectangular prism. He is going to paint all of the exterior sides except the top and the bottom. The cabinet is 6 feet tall, 4 feet wide, and 2 feet deep. What is the surface area of the portion of the cabinet that Miguel is going to paint?

Ⓐ 36 square feet

Ⓑ 48 square feet

Ⓒ 72 square feet

Ⓓ 88 square feet

4. Ms. Jessup is planning to lay new sod on her front yard. Her rectangular front yard is 85 feet long by 32 feet wide. What is the area of Ms. Jessup's front yard?

Ⓐ 117 square feet

Ⓑ 234 square feet

Ⓒ 1,360 square feet

Ⓓ 2,720 square feet

Problem Solving REAL WORLD

5. Lourdes is decorating a toy box for her sister. She will use self-adhesive paper to cover all of the exterior sides except the bottom of the box. The toy box is 4 feet long, 3 feet wide, and 2 feet high. What is the surface area of the portion of the box Lourdes is going to cover with self-adhesive paper? Explain how you found your answer.

40 square feet; Lourdes is covering the top of the box and the lateral faces of the box. So, I multiplied to find the area of each rectangular face, and then added the areas together to find the area that she will cover with self-adhesive paper: $(4 \times 3) + 2(2 \times 3) + 2(2 \times 4) = 40$ square feet.

Answer Key

Name ______________________

Lesson 89

COMMON CORE STANDARD CC.6.SP.1

Lesson Objective: Recognize statistical questions.

Recognize Statistical Questions

A **statistical question** is a question about a set of **data** that can vary. To answer a statistical question, you need to collect or look at a set of data.

Identify the statistical questions about Jack's homework time.

A. How many times did Jack spend longer than an hour on homework this week?
Statistical question. Jack is unlikely to do homework for the same amount of time each day, so the question asks about a set of data that can vary. You could answer it with data about Jack's homework time for a week.

B. How long did Jack do homework today?
Not a statistical question. It asks about Jack's homework time on one day. It does not refer to a set of data that varies.

Write a statistical question about your school's cafeteria.

Think of what kind of data could vary in the situation. In this situation, it might be menu items, students, or activities.

These are both statistical questions:

A. How many students were in the cafeteria during fourth period each day for the past two weeks?

B. What was the greatest number of entrees served in one day in the cafeteria last month?

Identify the statistical question. Circle the letter of the question.

1. A. How many people flew from New York to San Francisco yesterday?
   (B.) How many people flew from New York to San Francisco each day this month?

2. (A.) How many siblings does each of your classmates have?
   B. How many siblings does your best friend have?

Write a statistical question you could ask in the situation.

3. Hannah recorded the temperature in her yard every day for a week.
   Possible answer: Which day had the highest temperature?

4. Ian knows his scores for each time he has bowled this year.
   Possible answer: What was Ian's lowest score?

Name ______________________

Lesson 89

CC.6.SP.1

1. The number of points a basketball player scored each game for one week is recorded. Which is a **not** a statistical question for the situation?
   (A) What is the greatest number of points the basketball player scored?
   (B) What is the least number of points the basketball player scored?
   (C) How many points did the basketball player score in the first game of the week?
   (D) How many total points did the basketball player score during the week?

2. Which is a statistical question that could be asked about the data shown in the table?

Trail Lengths

Trail	Length (miles)
Pinkney	1.75
Armstead	2.34
Oak	1.69

   (A) What is the length of the longest trail?
   (B) In what state is the shortest trail?
   (C) Who uses the trails?
   (D) How are the trails used?

3. The length of each movie in a DVD collection is recorded. Which is a **not** a statistical question for the situation?
   (A) What is the length of the shortest movie?
   (B) What is the length of the longest movie?
   (C) What movie is more than 2 hours long?
   (D) What actors star in the longest movie?

4. Students at Meghann's school participate in a recycling program for one month. The amount of paper that is recycled each day as well as the number of students who participated each day is recorded. Which is a **not** a statistical question for the situation?
   (A) On what day did the recycling program begin?
   (B) What is the least amount of paper recycled per day?
   (C) What is the average number of students who participated each day?
   (D) What is the greatest amount of paper recycled per day?

Problem Solving REAL WORLD

5. The city tracked the amount of waste that was recycled from 2000 to 2007. Write a statistical question about the situation.
   Possible answer: In which year was the least amount of waste recycled?

6. The daily low temperature is recorded for a week. Write a statistical question about the situation.
   Possible answer: What was the highest daily low temperature?

Name ______________________

Lesson 90

COMMON CORE STANDARD CC.6.SP.2

Lesson Objective: Describe the distribution of a data set collected to answer a statistical question.

Describe Distributions

When interpreting data, it helps to make a graph and then analyze the distribution of data.

Mr. Chen asked all of his students how long it takes them to clean their rooms. He displayed the information in a histogram. Describe the data distribution.

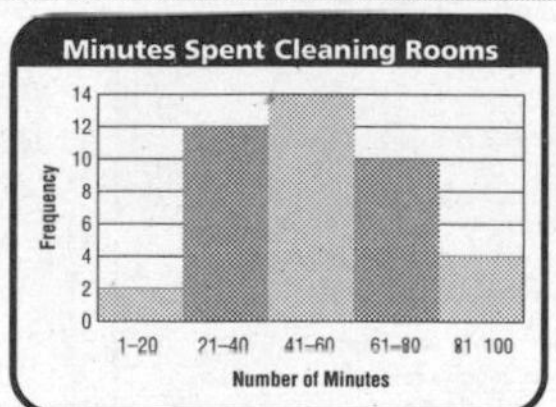

Step 1 Look for clusters. — There are no groups of data that are separated from the rest, so there are no clusters of data.

Step 2 Look for gaps. — There are no intervals that contain no data, so there are no gaps in the data.

Step 3 Look for peaks. — There is one peak, at the interval 41–60.

Step 4 Look for symmetry. — Imagine folding the graph in half vertically, along the interval 41–60. The halves are not identical, but they are close. The graph has symmetry.

1. Sally has a restaurant. She recorded the cost of each person's dinner on Friday. Describe the distribution.
   There are peaks at \$8 and \$11. There is a cluster from \$8 to \$13 and a gap at \$14–\$15. There is no symmetry.

Cost (in dollars) of Dinners Ordered Friday

Name ______________________

Lesson 90

CC.6.SP.2

1. The ages of people at a movie theater were recorded and displayed in a histogram.

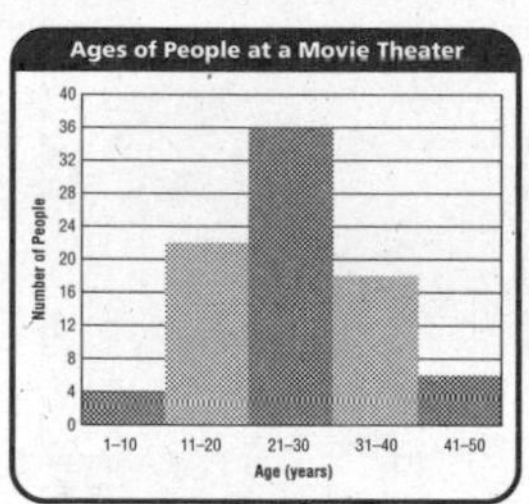

   Which interval represents a peak in the data?
   (A) 1–10 **(C)** 21–30
   (B) 11–20 (D) 31–40

2. Mr. Cruz used a dot plot to display the number of questions that each student answered correctly on the math quiz.

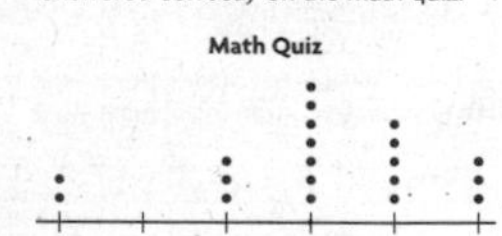

   Which statement correctly describes the data?
   (A) There is a cluster from 5 to 7.
   (B) The median of the data is 7.5
   (C) The mode of the data is 9.
   (D) There is a gap at 6.

Problem Solving REAL WORLD

3. Mr. Carpenter teaches five classes each day. For several days in a row, he kept track of the number of students who were late to class and displayed the results in a dot plot. Describe the data.
   There are peaks at 6 and 8 students and gaps at 4 and 7 students. There are clusters between 0 and 3, 5 and 6, and 8 to 11.

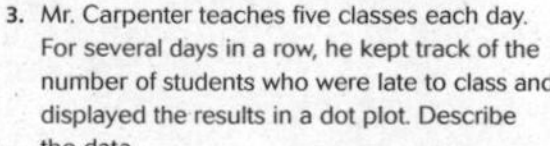

Number of Students Late to Class Each Day

Answer Key

Name ______

Lesson 91

COMMON CORE STANDARD CC.6.SP.2

Lesson Objective: Draw conclusions about the distribution of a data set by using the strategy *work backward.*

Problem Solving • Misleading Statistics

Zaire wants to move to a town where the annual snowfall is no more than 5 inches. A real estate agent tells her that the mean annual snowfall in a certain town is 4.5 inches. Other statistics about the town are given in the table. Does this location match what Zaire wants? Why or why not?

Town Statistics for Annual Snowfall (in.)	
Minimum	0.5
Maximum	12
Median	8
Mean	4.5

Read the Problem

What do I need to find?	What information do I need to use?	How will I use the information?
I need to decide if the annual snowfall in the town is typically less than 5 inches	I need the statistics in the table.	I will work backward from the statistics to draw conclusions about the annual snowfall

Solve the Problem

The minimum annual snowfall is 0.5 in.
The maximum annual snowfall is 12 in.
The median annual snowfall is 8 in.
The mean annual snowfall is 4.5 in.

Think: The median is 8 in., which means that half of the data is equal to or greater than 8 in.

So, the annual snowfall is usually greater than 5 inches because at least half of the annual snowfall values are greater than 5 inches. This location does not match what Zaire wants.

1. Mack says he typically spends 4 hours per week practicing his piano. For the past 6 weeks, he has practiced for 1, 1, 1, 2, 10, and 9 hours. Do you agree with Mack? Explain.

Possible answer: No; Although the mean is 4, he has two outliers that help him get this mean. For 4 weeks out of 6, he practiced less than 4 hours.

Name ______

Lesson 91

CC.6.SP.2

1. Mrs. Cho recorded statistics about her students' scores on the history exam in the table shown.

Scores on History Exam	
Minimum	70
Maximum	98
Median	92
Mean	85
Lower Quartile	88
Upper Quartile	95

Which statement is **not** true?

(A) Most students scored 85 on the exam.
(B) The range of the scores is 28.
(C) The interquartile range of the scores is 7.
(D) Half of the students scored 92 or higher on the exam.

2. The box plot shows statistics for the daytime temperatures in a city for two weeks.

Daytime Temperatures

40 41 42 43 44 45 46 47 48 49 50 51 52 53

Temperature (°F)

Which conclusion can be drawn using the statistics?

(A) The daytime temperature in the city is usually around 46°F.
(B) On half of the days during the two weeks, the temperature was at least 46°F.
(C) The range of the daytime temperatures is 10°F.
(D) The interquartile range of the data is 4°F.

Problem Solving REAL WORLD

3. Cynthia has 5 books with heights of 5 inches, 6 inches, 7 inches, 11 inches, and 11 inches. She says that her books are about 8 inches high. Do you agree or disagree with Cynthia's claim? Explain your answer.

Possible explanation: I disagree with Cynthia's claim. The mean height of Cynthia's books is 8 inches. However, none of the books are exactly 8 inches in height, and more than half of the books are shorter than 8 inches.

Name ______

Lesson 92

COMMON CORE STANDARD CC.6.SP.3

Lesson Objective: Recognize what measures of center and variability indicate about a data set.

Apply Measures of Center and Variability

You can use measures of center and variability to compare sets of data.

Two math groups were given the same test.

Test Scores	Mean	Interquartile range
Group A	76.9	30
Group B	81.1	8

Compare the data.

Step 1 Compare the means. Group B's scores are higher on average than Group A's scores because it has a greater mean.

Step 2 Compare the interquartile ranges. Group B has a smaller interquartile range, which means their scores do not vary as much as Group A's scores.

Compare the data.

1.

Bowling Scores	Median	Range
Team X	66	11
Team Y	70	19

Since Team Y's median is greater, they typically score higher. Since Team X's range is less, their scores vary less.

2.

Cantaloupe Weights in Pounds	Mean	Range
Farm 1	4	1.5
Farm 2	7	3

Since Farm 2's mean is greater, they typically have heavier cantaloupes. Since Farm 1's range is less, their cantaloupes vary less in weight.

Name ______

Lesson 92

CC.6.SP.3

1. The prices of MP3 players at Electronic City and Best Electronics are shown in the table.

Prices of MP3 Players	
Electronic City	\$24, \$108, \$30, \$44, \$62, \$80
Best Electronics	\$69, \$42, \$120, \$59, \$66, \$76

Which statement is true?

(A) The variation between the prices at each store is the same.
(B) The mean price at Electronic City is greater than the mean price at Best Electronics.
(C) The interquartile range of the prices at Electronic City is greater than the interquartile range of the prices at Best Electronics.
(D) The median price at Electronic City is greater than the median price at Best Electronics.

2. The table shows the number of Jimmy and Darnell's shot attempts in 7 basketball games.

Number of Shot Attempts	
Jimmy	5, 3, 2, 4, 0, 1, 6
Darnell	4, 6, 3, 4, 7, 5, 6

Which statement is true?

(A) The mean of Jimmy's shot attempts is the same as the mean of Darnell's shot attempts.
(B) The number of Jimmy's shot attempts varied more from game to game than the number of Darnell's shot attempts.
(C) The mean of Jimmy's shot attempts is greater than the mean of Darnell's shot attempts.
(D) The range of Jimmy's shot attempts is the same as the range of Darnell's shot attempts.

Problem Solving REAL WORLD

3. Mrs. Mack measured the heights of her students in two classes. Class 1 has a median height of 130 cm and an interquartile range of 5 cm. Class 2 has a median height of 134 cm and an interquartile range of 8 cm. Write a statement that compares the data.

The average height in Class 2 is greater, but the heights of the students in Class 2 vary more.

4. Richard's science test scores are 76, 80, 78, 84, and 80. His math test scores are 100, 80, 73, 94, and 71. Compare the medians and interquartile ranges.

Both sets of tests have a median of 80. The interquartile range of the math scores, 25, is greater than science, which is 5.

Name ____________________

Lesson 43

COMMON CORE STANDARD CC.6.SP.4

Lesson Objective: Display data in dot plots and frequency tables.

Dot Plots and Frequency Tables

A **dot plot** displays data by placing dots above a number line. Each dot represents one data value.

Paloma sells produce at the farmers' market. The chart shows the number of pounds she sells each day. What was the most common number of pounds that Paloma sold?

Produce Sold (pounds)			
15	19	15	16
20	16	17	20
11	12	15	20
15	13	11	15

Step 1 Draw a number line with an appropriate scale. The chart contains numbers from 11 to 20, so use a scale from 10 to 20.

Step 2 For each data value in the chart, plot a dot above the number on the number line. The first data value in the chart is 15, so the dot is placed above 15 on the number line.

Complete the dot plot for the other values in the table. Since there are 16 data values, there should be 16 dots in all.

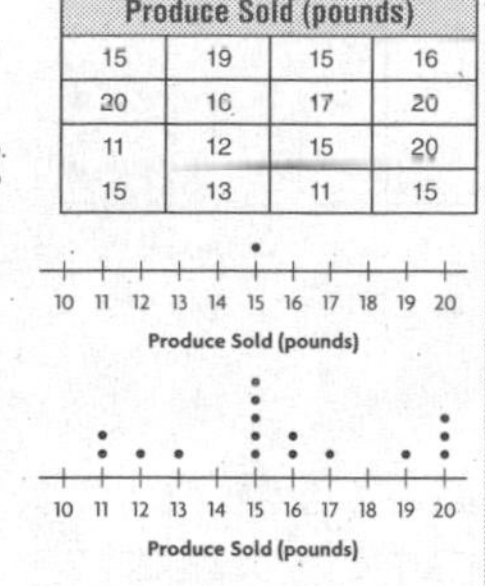

Step 3 The number of pounds Paloma sells most often is the value with the most dots. The stack with the most dots is at 15 pounds.

So, Paloma most often sells 15 pounds of produce.

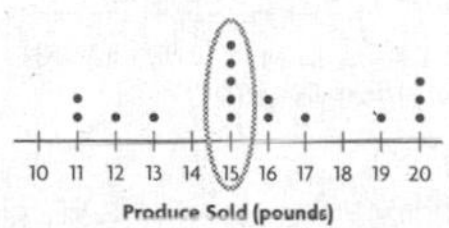

Use the data in the chart at right.

Number of Cars Sold per Month					
26	32	35	29	30	26
25	29	28	31	29	26
35	26	26	28	26	30

1. Complete the dot plot.

25 26 27 28 29 30 31 32 33 34 35

Number of Cars Sold per Month

2. What is the most common number of cars sold per month?

26 cars

Name ____________________

Lesson 43

CC.6.SP.4

The dot plot shows how many hours members of the band practiced last week. Use the dot plot for 1–2.

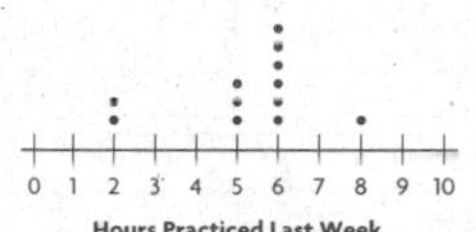

1. What is the most common number of hours that the band members practiced?

Ⓐ 2 Ⓒ 6 Ⓑ 5 Ⓓ 8

2. What is the total number of hours the band members practiced last week?

Ⓐ 12 hours Ⓒ 55 hours Ⓑ 36 hours Ⓓ 63 hours

The frequency table shows Mrs. Cho's students' scores on a recent English test. Use the frequency table for 3–4.

English Test Scores

Score	Frequency
41–50	1
51–60	2
61–70	8
71–80	12
81–90	20
91–100	7

3. What percent (%) of the students received a score of 71–80?

Ⓐ 36% Ⓒ 12% Ⓑ 24% Ⓓ 8%

4. What percent (%) of the students received a score **greater** than 80?

Ⓐ 27% Ⓒ 54% Ⓑ 39% Ⓓ 78%

Problem Solving REAL WORLD

5. The frequency table shows the ages of the actors in a youth theater group. What percent of the actors are 10 to 12 years old?

55%

Actors in a Youth Theater Group	
Age	**Frequency**
7–9	8
10–12	22
13–15	10

Name ____________________

Lesson 44

COMMON CORE STANDARD CC.6.SP.4

Lesson Objective: Display data in histograms.

Histograms

A **histogram** looks like a bar graph without spaces between bars. When you have data to organize, it is helpful to group the data into intervals and let each bar show the frequency, or number of data, in that interval.

Complete the frequency table below, using the data to the right. Then make a histogram.

Number of Hours of TV Watching per Week				
4	14	24	17	10
21	21	15	20	23
5	22	19	18	8
24	19	20	22	24

Step 1 Sort the data into each interval.
Only the 4 (1 item) is in the interval 1–4.
8 and 5 (2 items) are in 5–9.
10 and 14 (2 items) are in 10–14.
17, 15, 19, 18, 19 (5 items) are in 15–19.
24, 21, 21, 20, 23, 22, 24, 20, 22, 24 (10 items) are in 20–24.

Hours of TV/week	1–4	5–9	10–14	15–19	20–24
Frequency	1	2	2	5	10

Step 2 Check that all 20 items in the table are in the frequency table by adding.
1 + 2 + 2 + 5 + 10 = 20

Step 3 Make the histogram of the data.
Use a vertical scale from 0 to 12.
Title and label the histogram.
Draw a bar for each interval.
Draw bars the same width.
Draw the bar as high as the frequency.

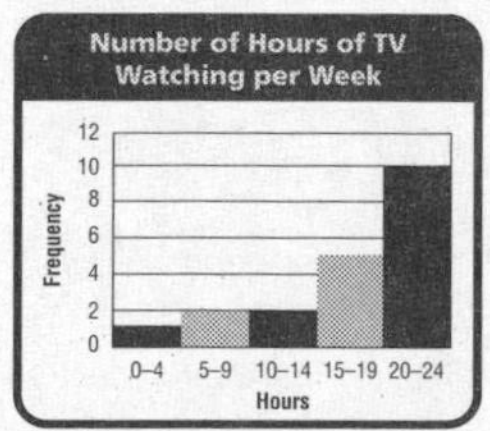

For 1–2, use the table shown.

Minutes on Treadmill Each Day				
28	28	24	52	35
43	29	34	55	21
38	60	71	59	62
19	64	39	70	55

1. Complete the frequency table of the data.

Number of Minutes	0–19	20–39	40–59	60–79
Frequency	1	9	5	5

2. Make a histogram of the data.

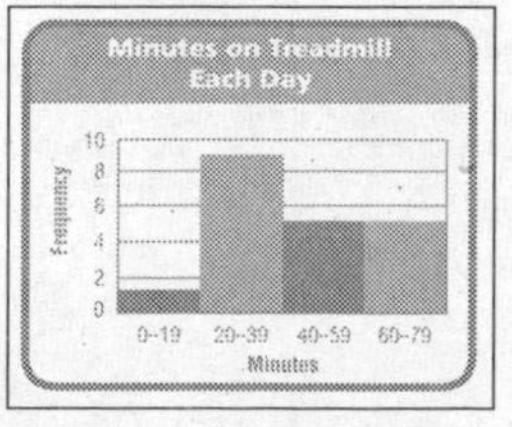

187

Name ____________________

Lesson 44

CC.6.SP.4

The histogram shows the ages of the runners who participated in a marathon. Use the histogram for 1–2.

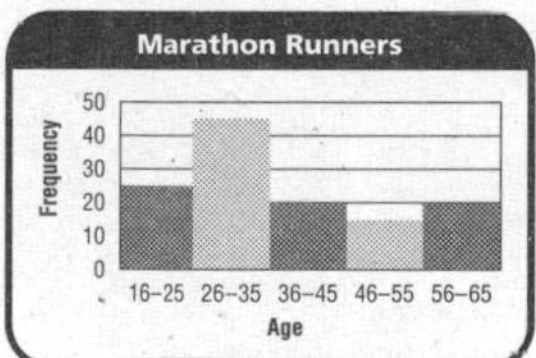

1. How many runners are in the 26–45 age group?

Ⓐ 65 Ⓒ 25 Ⓑ 45 Ⓓ 20

2. What fraction of the runners are in the 16–25 age group?

Ⓐ $\frac{1}{10}$ Ⓒ $\frac{1}{5}$ Ⓑ $\frac{1}{8}$ Ⓓ $\frac{1}{4}$

The school nurse recorded the heights, in inches, of the sixth-grade students. The histogram shows the results. Use the histogram for 3–4.

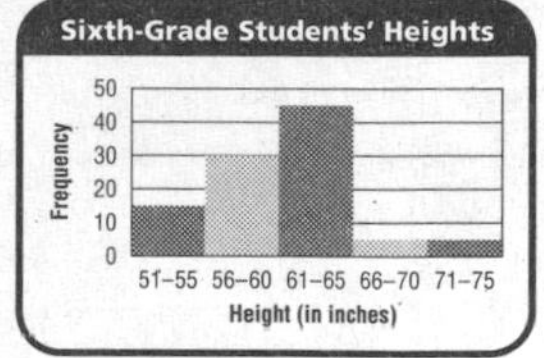

3. How many students are in the 56–60 inch group?

Ⓐ 5 Ⓒ 30 Ⓑ 15 Ⓓ 45

4. What fraction of the students are in the 61–65 inch group?

Ⓐ $\frac{9}{10}$ Ⓒ $\frac{13}{40}$ Ⓑ $\frac{9}{20}$ Ⓓ $\frac{3}{20}$

Problem Solving REAL WORLD

For 5–6, use the histogram.

5. For which two age groups are there the same number of customers?

10–19 and 50–59

6. How many customers are in the restaurant? How do you know?

63; add the frequencies for all of the intervals

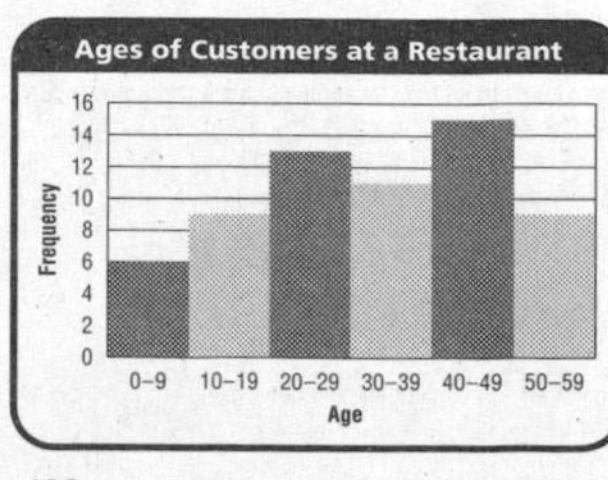

Answer Key

Name ____________________

Lesson 95

COMMON CORE STANDARD CC.6.SP.4

Lesson Objective: Solve problems involving data by using the strategy *draw a diagram.*

Problem Solving • Data Displays

The table shows the highest state populations in 2007, rounded to the nearest million. What percent of the states had at least 15 million residents?

2007 State Populations (in millions)					
18	10	6	9	6	9
6	37	13	12	6	11
24	8	6	6	19	6
10	6				

Read the Problem

What do I need to find?	What information do I need to use?	How will I use the information?
I need to find the percent of states that had at least 15 million people.	I will use the state population data	I will pick intervals for the data, find the frequency for each interval and use the frequencies to make a histogram. I will use the information from the histogram to find a percent

Solve the Problem

Make a frequency table.

Millions	5–9	10–14	15–19	20–24	25–29	30–34	35–40
Frequency	15	5	2	1	0	0	1

Use the frequency table to make a histogram.

States with at least 15 million: 2 + 1 + 1 = 4

Total states: 20

Percent with at least 15 million: $\frac{4}{20} = 0.20 = 20\%$

So, 20% of the states have populations over 15 million.

2007 Population of States

Frequency: 0, 2, 4, 6, 8, 10, 12

5–9, 10–14, 15–19, 20–24, 25–29, 30–34, 35–40

Population (in millions)

Use the data in the histogram above.

1. What percent of the states had between 5 million and 14 million residents?
   States with 5–14 million: 16
   Percent with 5–14 million: 80 %

2. What percent of the states had less than 10 million residents?
   States with less than 10 million: 11
   Percent with less than 10 million: 55 %

Name ____________________

Lesson 95

CC.6.SP.4

1. The data shows the number of siblings for each student in a class. What is the most common number of siblings among the students in the class?

Number of Siblings				
4	0	5	3	1
4	3	2	2	0
1	2	1	6	1
1	5	2	2	2

Ⓐ 0 Ⓑ 1 **Ⓒ 2** Ⓓ 3

2. Tabitha records the number of books she reads each month.

Books Read Each Month					
4	2	2	1	3	3
3	5	1	3	5	3

For what percent (%) of the months does she read **more** than 3 books?

Ⓐ 15% **Ⓑ 25%** Ⓒ 33% Ⓓ 66%

3. The manager at a clothing store recorded the number of customers each hour for one day.

Number of Customers Each Hour					
10	12	2	13	6	4
4	15	11	4	8	10

What is the most common number of customers per hour?

Ⓐ 4 Ⓑ 10 Ⓒ 11 Ⓓ 12

4. Shantelle works in a music store. She records the number of CDs purchased by each customer in one day.

Number of CDs Purchased				
1	3	1	2	1
3	4	2	2	2
1	3	4	2	2

What is the most common number of CDs purchased by each customer?

Ⓐ 1 **Ⓑ 2** Ⓒ 3 Ⓓ 4

Problem Solving REAL WORLD

5. The ages of the players on a baseball team are recorded in the table.

Ages of Players (years)				
8	11	13	12	14
12	10	11	9	11

What percent (%) of the players are younger than 10 years old? Explain how you know.

20%; Possible explanation: I made a relative frequency table using the intervals of ages 8–9, 10–11, 12–13, and 14–15. There are 2 values in the interval 8–9 and 10 players altogether. So, $\frac{2}{10} = 20\%$.

Name ____________________

Lesson 96

COMMON CORE STANDARD CC.6.SP.4

Lesson Objective: Display data in box plots.

Box Plots

The weights in ounces of 12 kittens are 20, 18, 22, 15, 17, 25, 25, 23, 13, 18, 16, and 22.

A **box plot** for the data would show how the values are spread out.

Make a box plot for the data.

Step 1 Write the numbers in order from least to greatest. Find the median and the least and greatest values.

13 15 16 17 18 (18 20) 22 22 23 25 25

Since there is an even number of values, the median is the mean of the two middle values. The median is 19. The least value is 13, and the greatest value is 25.

Step 2 Find the lower and upper quartiles.

The **lower quartile** is the median of the lower half of the data.

The **upper quartile** is the median of the upper half of the data.

(13 15 16 17 18 18) | (20 22 22 23 25 25)

lower quartile — upper quartile

Draw a line where the median should be. Now the data set has been split into halves. (If there were an odd number of values in the data set, the median would be one of the data values, but you would not include it in the upper or lower half.) The lower quartile is 16.5, and the upper quartile is 22.5.

Step 3 Plot the five points on a number line, and construct the box and whiskers. Use an appropriate scale.

11 13 15 17 19 21 23 25 27

Weights of Kittens (ounces)

The numbers of laps completed on a track are 4, 5, 2, 7, 6, 8, 9, 8, and 6. Use the data for 1–4.

1. What is the median? 6
2. What is the lower quartile? 4.5
3. What is the upper quartile? 8
4. Make a box plot for the data.

1 2 3 4 5 6 7 8 9

Number of Laps Completed

Name ____________________

Lesson 96

CC.6.SP.4

1. The chart shows the number of items purchased by customers in an express check-out line at the grocery store.

Number of Items
15, 1, 9, 7, 11, 12, 13, 13, 3

What is the lower quartile of the data?

Ⓐ 5 Ⓑ 7 Ⓒ 11 Ⓓ 13

2. The box plot displays data for the ages of students in a dance class.

Dance Class Students

10 11 12 13 14 15

Age

What is the median of the data?

Ⓐ 10 Ⓑ 11.5 **Ⓒ 12.5** Ⓓ 13.5

3. The chart shows points scored by a basketball team in their last several games.

Points Scored
76, 62, 75, 88, 84, 89, 71

What is the upper quartile of the data?

Ⓐ 71 Ⓑ 76 **Ⓒ 88** Ⓓ 89

4. The prices of a football jersey at several different stores are shown.

Football Jersey Prices
\$55, \$78, \$63, \$82, \$70

What is the median price?

Ⓐ \$80 **Ⓑ \$70** Ⓒ \$59 Ⓓ \$21

Problem Solving REAL WORLD

5. The amounts spent at a gift shop today are \$19, \$30, \$28, \$22, \$20, \$26, and \$26. What is the median? What is the lower quartile?

\$26; \$20

6. The weights of six puppies in ounces are 8, 5, 7, 5, 6, and 9. What is the upper quartile of the data?

8 ounces

Name ______________________

Lesson 97

COMMON CORE STANDARDS CC.6.SP.5a, CC.6.SP.5b

Lesson Objective: Describe a data set by stating what quantity was measured and how it was measured.

Describe Data Collection

To describe a set of data, describe these features:

Attribute: the characteristic being recorded or measured
Unit: the unit of measurement, such as inches or grams
Means: the tool used for the observations or measurements
Observations: the number of observations or measurements

Describe the data set shown in the chart.

Daily Dog Walks

Day	Time (min)	Day	Time (min)
1	35	5	60
2	40	6	25
3	25	7	90
4	55	8	20

Step 1 What attribute is measured?
The attribute is *length of time* spent walking a dog.

Step 2 What unit of measurement is used?
The time is shown in *minutes*.

Step 3 What means was likely used to obtain the measurements?
To measure time, you use a *clock*, *timer*, or *stopwatch*.

Step 4 How many observations were made?
Count the number or observations: 8

Describe the data set by listing the attribute measured, the unit of measure, the likely means of measurement, and the number of observations.

1. Attribute: weight
Unit of measurement: pounds
Means: scale
Number of observations: 10

Pet Weights (lb)

5.2	8	9.5	48.4	0.9
4.7	10.5	32	18	12

2. Attribute: volume
Unit of measurement: cups
Means: measuring cup
Number of observations: 5

Serving Volume (cups)

Lettuce	2	Soup	1.5
Cheese	0.25	Ice Cream	0.75
Sauce	0.5		

Name ______________________

Lesson 97

CC.6.SP.5a, CC.6.SP.5b

1. The table shows data collected by an electricity supplier.

Monthly Electricity Usage (kilowatt-hours)		
917 kWh	1,129 kWh	1,007 kWh
837 kWh	983 kWh	924 kWh

What is the attribute being measured?

(A) monthly electricity usage
(B) kilowatt-hours
(C) electricity meter
(D) electricity

2. How many observations are in the data set shown?

Heights of Television Towers (meters)			
457	502	498	526
678	619	564	642

(A) 2
(B) 4
(C) 6
(D) 8

3. What is the unit of measure for the data set shown?

Heights of Plants (inches)				
10.1	7.3	8.6	6.4	7.7
7.9	8.4	9.3	7.9	8.1
0.5	7.5	8.2	8.8	9.8

(A) heights of plants
(B) inches
(C) plants
(D) ruler

4. What was the likely means of measurement for the data set shown?

Distance Driven Daily for a Week (miles)						
22	103	47	31	56	124	45

(A) measuring tape
(B) odometer
(C) yardstick
(D) ruler

Problem Solving

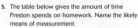

5. The table below gives the amount of time Preston spends on homework. Name the likely means of measurement.

Amount of Time Spent on Homework (hours)								
5	3	1	2	4	1	3	2	

clock or watch

6. The table below shows the speed of cars on a highway. Name the unit of measure.

Speeds of Cars (miles per hour)							
71	55	53	65	68	61	59	62
70	69	57	50	56	66	67	63

miles per hour

Name ______________________

Lesson 98

COMMON CORE STANDARD CC.6.SP.5c

Lesson Objective: Understand the mean as a fair share and as a balance point.

Mean as Fair Share and Balance Point

Five students brought 3, 4, 5, 3, and 5 cups of flour to the cooking club. They divided it evenly so that each student got the same amount for cooking. Use counters to show how many cups each student got.

Step 1 Make 5 stacks of counters: one stack for each student.
Use one counter for each cup of flour.

Step 2 Take counters from taller stacks and put them on shorter stacks. Move counters until all the stacks are the same height.

Step 3 Count the counters in each stack. There are 4 counters in each stack.

So, 4 is the mean of the data. When you divide the flour equally, each student gets 4 cups.

Use counters to find the mean of the data set.

1. 3, 5, 7, 5 — Draw 4 stacks to show the data set. — Make the stacks the same height.
5 counters in each stack
Mean: 5

2. 5, 7, 4, 3, 4, 1 — Draw 6 stacks to show the data set. — Make the stacks the same height.
4 counters in each stack
Mean: 4

Name ______________________

Lesson 98

CC.6.SP.5c

1. Khalifa has a bookcase with 5 shelves. There are 11, 12, 9, 11, and 7 books on each of the 5 shelves. If she rearranges the books so that each shelf has the same number of books, how many books will be on each shelf?

(A) 10
(B) 11
(C) 12
(D) 13

2. The sixth graders raised money to fund a field trip. The five classes raised $42, $51, $38, $49, and $40. The classes decided to combine their money so that each class would have the same amount. What is the fair share, in dollars ($), raised by each class?

(A) $12
(B) $42
(C) $44
(D) $51

3. The desks in a classroom are arranged in 3 rows. There are 6 desks in the first row, 3 desks in the second row, and 6 desks in the third row. If the desks are rearranged so that each row has the same number of desks, how many desks will be in each row?

(A) 2
(B) 3
(C) 5
(D) 6

4. Alivia goes to lunch with 3 of her friends. The costs of their meals are $8, $4, $7, and $5. If they split the bill evenly, how much should each person pay?

(A) $3
(B) $6
(C) $9
(D) $15

Problem Solving REAL WORLD

5. Three baskets contain 8, 8, and 11 soaps. Can the soaps be rearranged so that there is an equal whole number of soaps in each basket? Explain why or why not.

Yes; Possible explanation: If I move counters around, I can fit 9 in each group.

6. Five pages contain 6, 6, 9, 10, and 11 stickers. Can the stickers be rearranged so that there is an equal whole number of stickers on each page? Explain why or why not.

No; Possible answer: There is no way to rearrange 5 stacks of counters with heights 6, 6, 9, 10, and 11 so that there is an equal number in each stack.

Answer Key

Name ______________________

Lesson 99
COMMON CORE STANDARD CC.6.SP.5c
Lesson Objective: Summarize a data set by using mean, median, and mode.

Measures of Center

A **measure of center** is a single value that describes the middle of a data set.

The **mean** is the sum of all items in a set of data divided by the number of items in the set.

The **median** is the middle number or the mean of the middle two numbers when the items in the data set are listed in order.

The **mode** is the data value that is repeated more than other values. A data set can have more than one mode, or no mode.

Find the mean, median, and mode for the set of data.
80, 74, 82, 77, 86, 75

Find the mean.

Step 1 Find the sum of the data.
80 + 74 + 82 + 77 + 86 + 75 = 474

Step 2 Count the number of data items.
There are 6 items.

Step 3 Divide.
$\frac{\text{sum}}{\text{number of items}} = \frac{474}{6} = 79$

So, the mean is 79.

Find the median.

Step 1 Order the data.
74, 75, 77, 80, 82, 86

Step 2 Find the middle number.
There are two middle numbers: 77 and 80.

Step 3 Find their mean.
$\frac{77 + 80}{2} = 78.5$

So, the median is 78.5.

Find the mode.

Use the ordered list and look for numbers that repeat.
No numbers repeat. So, there is no mode.

Find the mean, median, and mode.

1. 31, 3, 14, 31, 11
mean: 18 median: 14
mode: 31

2. 95, 18, 51, 1, 22, 5
mean: 32 median: 20
mode: none

3. 14, 22, 15, 7, 14, 0, 12
mean: 12 median: 14
mode: 14

4. 67, 103, 94, 65, 18, 114, 94, 63, 94, 27
mean: 73.9 median: 80.5
mode: 94

Name ______________________

Lesson 99
CC.6.SP.5c

1. Every day for one week, Keller recorded the number of customers who bought blueberry muffins at his cafe. The customer counts are 13, 8, 12, 15, 11, 20, and 19. What is the mean of the data?

Ⓐ 11
Ⓑ 12
Ⓒ 13
Ⓓ 14 (marked)

2. Carmen is training for a swim meet. The table shows the number of laps she swims each day.

Carmen's Training Log

Day	Number of Laps
Monday	40
Tuesday	45
Wednesday	55
Thursday	45
Friday	40
Saturday	50

Which shows the mode(s) of the data?

Ⓐ 40 and 45 (marked)
Ⓑ 45 and 50
Ⓒ 45
Ⓓ 40

3. Todd and his friends collect coins. The numbers of coins in their collections are 45, 73, 86, 24, 57, 100, 58, 86, 68, and 74. What is the median of the data?

Ⓐ 67.1
Ⓑ 70.5 (marked)
Ⓒ 76
Ⓓ 86

4. Michelle recorded the number of customers who bought plain bagels at her bakery each day for one week. The customer counts are 15, 7, 6, 9, 10, 12, and 11. What is the mean of the data?

Ⓐ 6
Ⓑ 9
Ⓒ 10 (marked)
Ⓓ 15

Problem Solving 

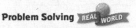

5. An auto manufacturer wants their line of cars to have a median gas mileage of 25 miles per gallon or higher. The gas mileage for their five models are 23, 25, 26, 29, and 19. Do their cars meet their goal? Explain.

Yes; the median gas mileage for their five models is 25 miles per gallon.

6. A sporting goods store is featuring several new bicycles, priced at \$300, \$250, \$325, \$780, and \$350. They advertise that the average price of their bicycles is under \$400. Is their ad correct? Explain.

No; the mean price of their bicycles is \$401, which is greater than \$400.

Name ______________________

Lesson 100
COMMON CORE STANDARD CC.6.SP.5c
Lesson Objective: Describe overall patterns in data, including clusters, peaks, gaps, and symmetry.

Patterns in Data

The histogram shows the number of minutes a caller had to be placed on hold before talking to a representative.

According to the graph, there were 10 people who were on hold for 0 to 4 minutes.

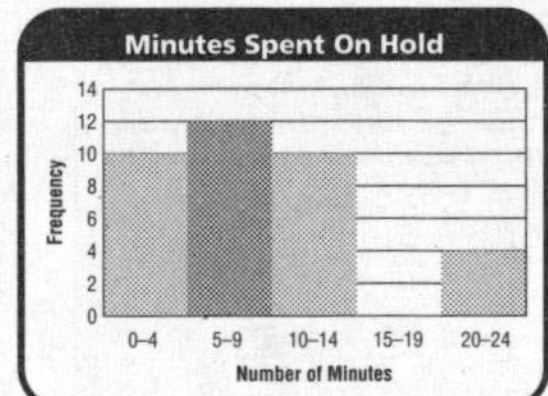

Does the graph contain any clusters or gaps? If so, where? Does the graph have symmetry?

Step 1 Look for a group of data points that lie within a small interval. These are clusters.	The bars for 0–4, 5–9, and 10–14 are in a group. This is a cluster of data.
Step 2 Look for an interval that contains no data. These are gaps.	There is no bar above the interval 15–19. This is a gap in the data. This means there were no people who were on hold for 15 to 19 minutes.
Step 3 Look for symmetry. If you draw a vertical line in the graph, the bars on the left and right sides will match if the graph has symmetry.	A line cannot be drawn anywhere on the graph and have the bars on either side match. There is no symmetry.

Use the dot plot to answer the questions.

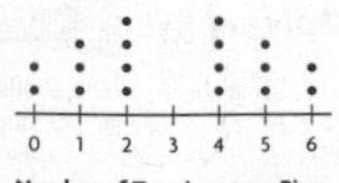

1. Are there any clusters? If so, where?
Yes, at 0-2 and 4-6

2. Are there any gaps? If so, where?
Yes, at 3

3. Is there symmetry? If so, where can the line of symmetry be drawn?
Yes, the line can be drawn at 3.

Name ______________________

Lesson 100
CC.6.SP.5c

1. The histogram shows the amount of monthly allowance for the students in Linda's class.

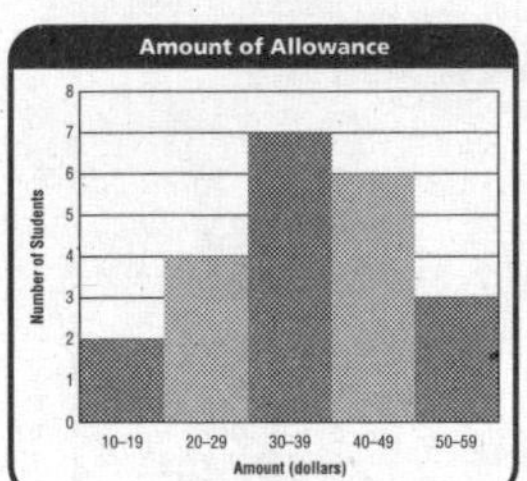

Which interval of dollar amounts represents the peak of the histogram?

Ⓐ 10–19
Ⓑ 20–29
Ⓒ 30–39 (marked)
Ⓓ 40–49

The dot plot shows the number of students in each sixth-grade class at Hilltop Middle School. Use the dot plot for 2–3.

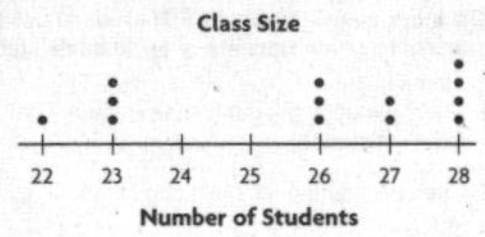

2. For which interval is there a gap in the data?

Ⓐ 26 to 28
Ⓑ 24 to 25 (marked)
Ⓒ 23 to 26
Ⓓ 22 to 23

3. Which interval names a cluster in the data?

Ⓐ 23 to 25
Ⓑ 24 to 25
Ⓒ 24 to 28
Ⓓ 26 to 28 (marked)

Problem Solving REAL WORLD

4. Look at the dot plot at the right. Does the graph have line symmetry? Explain.

Yes; there is a peak near the middle, and the two halves are roughly mirror images.

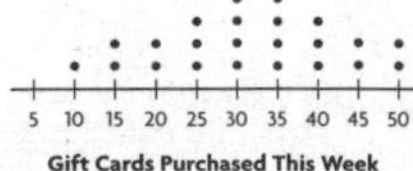

Name ______________________

Lesson 101

COMMON CORE STANDARD CC.6.SP.5c

Lesson Objective: Understand mean absolute deviation as a measure of variability from the mean.

Mean Absolute Deviation

The **mean absolute deviation** tells how far away the data values are from the mean. A small mean absolute deviation means that most values are close to the mean. A large mean absolute deviation means that the data values are more spread out.

The prices of 8 lunches are $10, $8, $3, $5, $9, $6, $7, and $8. The mean is $7. Find the mean absolute deviation.

Step 1 Determine how far each data value is from the mean. You can use a number line.

Plot a value on the number line. Then count how many spaces you must move to reach the mean, 7.

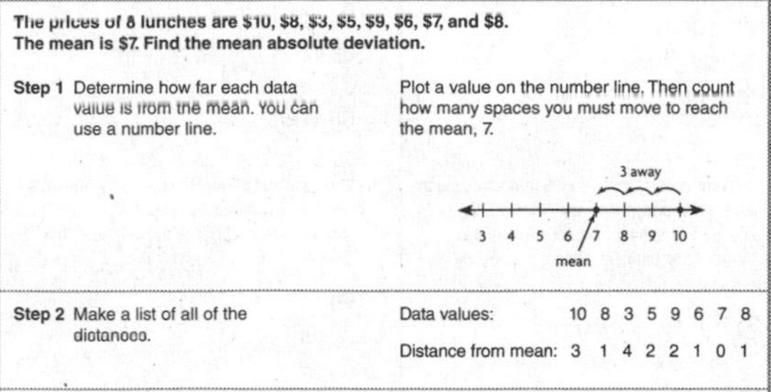

Step 2 Make a list of all of the distances.

Data values: 10 8 3 5 9 6 7 8

Distance from mean: 3 1 4 2 2 1 0 1

Step 3 Find the mean of the distances by finding the sum and dividing by 8. The quotient is the mean absolute deviation.

$\frac{3+1+4+2+2+1+0+1}{8} = \frac{14}{8} = 1.75$

So, on average, each data value is 1.75 away from the mean.

Use counters or a number line to find the mean absolute deviation.

1. ages of people on a team in years: 9, 12, 10, 8, 11
   mean = 10 years
   distances from mean = 1, 2, 0, 2, 1
   mean absolute deviation = 1.2

2. Sam's test scores: 86, 71, 92, 84, 76, 95
   mean = 84
   mean absolute deviation = 7

3. prices of dinner menu items: $15, $10, $13, $19, $20, $12, $9, $14
   mean = $14
   mean absolute deviation = 3

4. daily low temperatures, °F, in a city: 45, 39, 40, 52, 44
   mean = 44°F
   mean absolute deviation = 3.6

Name ______________________

Lesson 101

CC.6.SP.5c

1. The dot plot shows the number of history books borrowed from the library each day during a 10-day period. The mean of the number of books borrowed each day is 8.

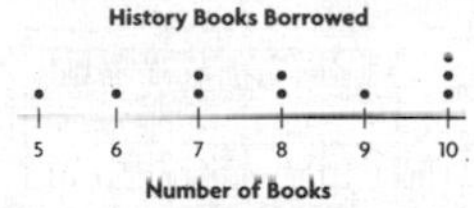

What is the mean absolute deviation of the data?

Ⓐ 14 Ⓑ 10 Ⓒ 1.5 **Ⓓ 1.4**

2. Angie plays the violin. The number of hours she practiced each week for 5 weeks are 2, 3, 5, 7, and 8. The mean number of hours per week she practiced is 5. What is the mean absolute deviation of the data?

Ⓐ 2 Ⓑ 5 Ⓒ 10 Ⓓ 25

3. The table shows the mean absolute deviation of the number of canned goods collected per person for a food drive by 4 sixth-grade classes.

Number of Canned Goods

Class	Mean Absolute Deviation
Mr. Williams	2.5
Mrs. Chung	3.6
Mrs. Singh	4.2
Mr. Scott	1.3

In which class did the number of canned goods that were collected per student vary the **most**?

Ⓐ Mr. Williams
Ⓑ Mrs. Chung
Ⓒ Mrs. Singh
Ⓓ Mr. Scott

Problem Solving

4. In science class, Troy found the mass, in grams, of 6 samples to be 10, 12, 7, 8, 5, and 6. What is the mean absolute deviation?

   2 grams

5. Five recorded temperatures are 71°F, 64°F, 72°F, 81°F, and 67°F. What is the mean absolute deviation?

   4.4°F

Name ______________________

Lesson 102

COMMON CORE STANDARD CC.6.SP.5c

Lesson Objective: Summarize a data set by using range, interquartile range, and mean absolute deviation.

Measures of Variability

A **measure of variability** is a single number that describes how far apart the numbers are in a data set. **Range, interquartile range,** and mean absolute deviation are all measures of variability.

The box plot shows the cost of various concert tickets. Find the range and interquartile range of the data in the box plot.

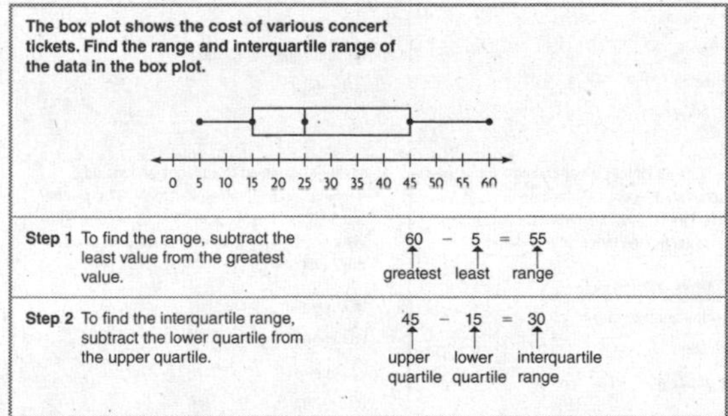

Step 1 To find the range, subtract the least value from the greatest value.

60 − 5 = 55
greatest least range

Step 2 To find the interquartile range, subtract the lower quartile from the upper quartile.

45 − 15 = 30
upper quartile lower quartile interquartile range

Make a box plot for the data. Then find the range and interquartile range.

1. number of free throws made: 8, 13, 9, 4, 1, 6, 2, 2, 14, 6, 9, 11
   0 2 4 6 8 10 12 14
   range = 13
   interquartile range = 7

2. minutes spent cooking dinner: 45, 38, 52, 29, 28, 31, 44, 40, 25
   20 25 30 35 40 45 50 55
   range = 27
   interquartile range = 16

Name ______________________

Lesson 102

CC.6.SP.5c

1. The chart shows the toll rates to drive across several different bridges.

Toll Rates ($)
1.00, 6.50, 4.50, 3.25, 2.25, 1.50, 2.00

What is the mean absolute deviation of the data?

Ⓐ $1.50 Ⓑ $3.00 Ⓒ $5.50 Ⓓ $10.50

2. Mrs. Gupta displayed the highest scores on the history quiz in the box plot shown.

Highest Scores on History Quiz
80 82 84 86 88 90 92 94 96 98 100
Quiz Score

What is the range of the data?

Ⓐ 11 **Ⓑ 20** Ⓒ 89 Ⓓ 100

3. The box plot displays data for the number of shoe brands sold by several department stores.

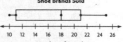

Shoe Brands Sold
10 12 14 16 18 20 22 24 26
Number of Brands

What is the interquartile range of the data?

Ⓐ 10 Ⓑ 11 Ⓒ 15 Ⓓ 21

4. The chart shows the prices of cell phone plans that a company offers.

Cell Phone Plan Prices
$49, $70, $55, $100, $85, $35

What is the interquartile range of the prices?

Ⓐ $85 Ⓑ $65 Ⓒ $49 **Ⓓ $36**

Problem Solving

REAL WORLD

5. The following data set gives the amount of time, in minutes, it took five people to cook a recipe. What is the mean absolute deviation for the data?

   33, 38, 31, 36, 37

   2.4 minutes

6. The prices of six food processors are $63, $59, $72, $68, $61, and $67. What is the mean absolute deviation for the data?

   $4

Answer Key

Name ______________________

Lesson 103

COMMON CORE STANDARD CC.6.SP.5d

Lesson Objective: Determine the effects of outliers on measures of center and variability.

Effects of Outliers

Sometimes a data set contains a number that is much less or much greater than the rest. This number is called an **outlier.** Taking note of outliers can help you understand a data set.

Use a dot plot to find the outlier for the quiz scores. Then tell how the outlier affects the mean and median.

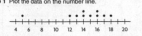

Scores on 20-question Quiz				
15	16	17	13	18
12	5	14	14	16

Mean: 14 Median: 14.5

Step 1 Plot the data on the number line.

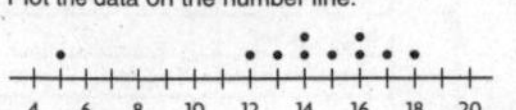

Step 2 Find the outlier.

Most of the points are between 12 and 18. 5 is much less than the rest, so it is an outlier.

Step 3 Find the median and mean without the outlier.

Median: Make an ordered list and find the middle value.

12, 13, 14, 14, (15), 16, 16, 17, 18

The new median is 15.

Mean: One value has been removed. Add the new list of values and divide by 9.

$\frac{12 + 13 + 14 + 14 + 15 + 16 + 16 + 17 + 18}{9} = 15$

The new mean is 15.

Step 4 Describe the effect of the outlier.
Without the outlier, the mean went up from 14 to 15.
The median went up from 14.5 to 15.

Use the table for Problems 1–3.

Shirt Prices ($)				
29	33	24	14	29
31	31	33		

Mean: $28 Median: $30

1. Find the outlier by drawing a dot plot of the data.

15 18 21 24 27 30 33

Outlier: 14

2. Find the mean and median without the outlier.

Median: $ 31 Mean: $ 30

3. Without the outlier, the mean rose from $28 to $30

The median rose from $30 to $31

Name ______________________

Lesson 103

CC.6.SP.5d

1. The prices of karaoke machines at 6 different stores are $77, $85, $78, $72, $80, and $118. What is the outlier in the data set?

Ⓐ $74
Ⓑ $79
Ⓒ $85
Ⓓ $118

2. The amounts of money Gillian earned each week from babysitting are $5, $10, $20, $10, $15, $5, $42, and $5. How is the mean of the data set affected when the outlier is removed?

Ⓐ The mean is unchanged.
Ⓑ The mean increases by $4.
Ⓒ The mean decreases by $4.
Ⓓ The mean increases by $1.

3. The low temperatures for the week in Carrollton, in degrees Fahrenheit (°F), were 17, 41, 11, 14, 11, 13, and 15. What is the mean of the temperatures **without** the outlier?

Ⓐ 11.6°F
Ⓑ 13.5°F
Ⓒ 14.5°F
Ⓓ 17.4°F

4. The number of points scored by a football team in 6 different games are 26, 38, 33, 20, 3, and 28. What is the outlier in the data set?

Ⓐ 3
Ⓑ 25
Ⓒ 27
Ⓓ 38

Problem Solving REAL WORLD

5. Duke's science quiz scores are 99, 91, 60, 94, and 95. Describe the effect of the outlier on the mean and median.

The outlier is 60. It decreases the mean from about 94.8 to 87.8. It slightly decreases the median from 94.5 to 94.

6. The number of people who attended an art conference for five days was 42, 27, 35, 39, and 96. Describe the effect of the outlier on the mean and median.

The outlier is 96. It increases the mean from about 36 to about 48. It increases the median from 37 to 39.

Name ______________________

Lesson 104

COMMON CORE STANDARD CC.6.SP.5d

Lesson Objective: Choose appropriate measures of center and variability to describe data, and justify the choice.

Choose Appropriate Measures of Center and Variability

Sometimes one measure of center or variability represents the data better than another measure of variability. For example, the median might be a better representation than the mean.

Cheeseburger prices at several different restaurants are $5, $3, $2, $6, $4, and $14. Should the mean, median, or mode be used to describe the data? Should the range or interquartile range be used?

Measure of Center	Measure of Variability
Step 1 Find the mean, median, and mode. Mean: $\frac{5 + 3 + 2 + 6 + 4 + 14}{6} \approx \$5.67$ Median: 2 3 4 | 5 6 14 $\frac{4 + 5}{2} = \$4.50$ Mode = none	**Step 1** Find the range and interquartile range. Range: 14 − 2 = $12 Interquartile range: 6 − 3 = $3 2 (3) 4 | 5 (6) 14
Step 2 Compare. There are six data values, and the mean is greater than four of them. The outlier of $14 is causing this. So, the median is a better measure of center.	**Step 2** Compare. All of the data values except one are between $2 and $6. The interquartile range is a better measure.

1. The times, in minutes, spent cleaning a room are 60, 50, 33, 28, and 44. Decide which measure(s) of center best describes the data set. Explain your reasoning.

mean, 43, and median, 44; They are very close, and there are no outliers.

2. The amounts of snowfall, in inches, are 4, 3, 20, 6, 8, and 2. Decide which measure(s) of variability best describes the data set. Explain your reasoning.

interquartile range; Most values are from 3 to 8.

Name ______________________

Lesson 104

CC.6.SP.5d

1. Brianna received pledge amounts of $89, $35, $22, $36, $32, $31, and $28 for her participation in a walkathon. Which measure of center **best** describes the pledge amounts?

Ⓐ median
Ⓑ mode
Ⓒ mean
Ⓓ range

2. The number of lunch specials on the menus of several different restaurants are 11, 14, 2, 10, 14, 10, and 12. What measure **best** describes the variation in the data?

Ⓐ lower quartile
Ⓑ interquartile range
Ⓒ range
Ⓓ upper quartile

3. The hockey team's scores for several games were 4, 2, 3, 0, 0, 1, and 10. What measure **best** describes the variation of the data?

Ⓐ lower quartile
Ⓑ upper quartile
Ⓒ interquartile range
Ⓓ range

4. Vishal compared the prices of a video game at several different stores. The prices are $43, $64, $38, $36, $37, $34, and $28. Which measure of center **best** describes the prices?

Ⓐ median
Ⓑ mode
Ⓒ mean
Ⓓ range

Problem Solving REAL WORLD

5. Brett's history quiz scores are 84, 78, 92, 90, 85, 91, and 0. Decide which measure(s) of center best describes the data set. Explain your reasoning.

mean = 74.3 median = 85

mode = none

The median; there is no mode, and the mean is less than almost all of the data values.

6. Eight students were absent the following number of days in a year: 4, 8, 0, 1, 7, 2, 6, and 3. Decide if the range or interquartile range better describes the data set, and explain your reasoning.

range = 8 interquartile range = 5

The range; there are several low values, but several high values also.

Ratios and Proportional Relationships CC.6.RP

Understand ratio concepts and use ratio reasoning to solve problems.

1. Understand the concept of a ratio and use ratio language to describe a ratio relationship between two quantities.
2. Understand the concept of a unit rate a/b associated with a ratio $a{:}b$ with $b \neq 0$, and use rate language in the context of a ratio relationship.
3. Use ratio and rate reasoning to solve real-world and mathematical problems, e.g., by reasoning about tables of equivalent ratios, tape diagrams, double number line diagrams, or equations.
   a. Make tables of equivalent ratios relating quantities with whole-number measurements, find missing values in the tables, and plot the pairs of values on the coordinate plane. Use tables to compare ratios.
   b. Solve unit rate problems including those involving unit pricing and constant speed.
   c. Find a percent of a quantity as a rate per 100 (e.g., 30% of a quantity means 30/100 times the quantity); solve problems involving finding the whole, given a part and the percent.
   d. Use ratio reasoning to convert measurement units; manipulate and transform units appropriately when multiplying or dividing quantities.

Common Core State Standards

The Number System CC.6.NS

Apply and extend previous understandings of multiplication and division to divide fractions by fractions.

1. Interpret and compute quotients of fractions, and solve word problems involving division of fractions by fractions, e.g., by using visual fraction models and equations to represent the problem.

Compute fluently with multi-digit numbers and find common factors and multiples.

2. Fluently divide multi-digit numbers using the standard algorithm.
3. Fluently add, subtract, multiply, and divide multi-digit decimals using the standard algorithm for each operation.
4. Find the greatest common factor of two whole numbers less than or equal to 100 and the least common multiple of two whole numbers less than or equal to 12. Use the distributive property to express a sum of two whole numbers 1–100 with a common factor as a multiple of a sum of two whole numbers with no common factor.

Apply and extend previous understandings of numbers to the system of rational numbers.

5. Understand that positive and negative numbers are used together to describe quantities having opposite directions or values (e.g., temperature above/below zero, elevation above/below sea level, credits/debits, positive/negative electric charge); use positive and negative numbers to represent quantities in real-world contexts, explaining the meaning of 0 in each situation.
6. Understand a rational number as a point on the number line. Extend number line diagrams and coordinate axes familiar from previous grades to represent points on the line and in the plane with negative number coordinates.
   a. Recognize opposite signs of numbers as indicating locations on opposite sides of 0 on the number line; recognize that the opposite of the opposite of a number is the number itself, e.g., $-(-3) = 3$, and that 0 is its own opposite.
   b. Understand signs of numbers in ordered pairs as indicating locations in quadrants of the coordinate plane; recognize that when two ordered pairs differ only by signs, the locations of the points are related by reflections across one or both axes.
   c. Find and position integers and other rational numbers on a horizontal or vertical number line diagram; find and position pairs of integers and other rational numbers on a coordinate plane.
7. Understand ordering and absolute value of rational numbers.
   a. Interpret statements of inequality as statements about the relative position of two numbers on a number line diagram.
   b. Write, interpret, and explain statements of order for rational numbers in real-world contexts.

The Number System *(continued)* CC.6.NS

c. Understand the absolute value of a rational number as its distance from 0 on the number line; interpret absolute value as magnitude for a positive or negative quantity in a real-world situation.

d. Distinguish comparisons of absolute value from statements about order.

8. Solve real-world and mathematical problems by graphing points in all four quadrants of the coordinate plane. Include use of coordinates and absolute value to find distances between points with the same first coordinate or the same second coordinate.

Expressions and Equations CC.6.EE

Apply and extend previous understandings of arithmetic to algebraic expressions.

1. Write and evaluate numerical expressions involving whole-number exponents.
2. Write, read, and evaluate expressions in which letters stand for numbers.

   a. Write expressions that record operations with numbers and with letters standing for numbers.

   b. Identify parts of an expression using mathematical terms (sum, term, product, factor, quotient, coefficient); view one or more parts of an expression as a single entity.

   c. Evaluate expressions at specific values of their variables. Include expressions that arise from formulas used in real-world problems. Perform arithmetic operations, including those involving whole-number exponents, in the conventional order when there are no parentheses to specify a particular order (Order of Operations).
3. Apply the properties of operations to generate equivalent expressions.
4. Identify when two expressions are equivalent (i.e., when the two expressions name the same number regardless of which value is substituted into them).

Reason about and solve one-variable equations and inequalities.

5. Understand solving an equation or inequality as a process of answering a question: which values from a specified set, if any, make the equation or inequality true? Use substitution to determine whether a given number in a specified set makes an equation or inequality true.
6. Use variables to represent numbers and write expressions when solving a real-world or mathematical problem; understand that a variable can represent an unknown number, or, depending on the purpose at hand, any number in a specified set.

Common Core State Standards

Expressions and Equations *(continued)* CC.6.EE

7. Solve real-world and mathematical problems by writing and solving equations of the form $x + p = q$ and $px = q$ for cases in which p, q and x are all nonnegative rational numbers.
8. Write an inequality of the form $x > c$ or $x < c$ to represent a constraint or condition in a real-world or mathematical problem. Recognize that inequalities of the form $x > c$ or $x < c$ have infinitely many solutions; represent solutions of such inequalities on number line diagrams.

Represent and analyze quantitative relationships between dependent and independent variables.

9. Use variables to represent two quantities in a real-world problem that change in relationship to one another; write an equation to express one quantity, thought of as the dependent variable, in terms of the other quantity, thought of as the independent variable. Analyze the relationship between the dependent and independent variables using graphs and tables, and relate these to the equation.

Geometry CC.6.G

Solve real-world and mathematical problems involving area, surface area, and volume.

1. Find the area of right triangles, other triangles, special quadrilaterals, and polygons by composing into rectangles or decomposing into triangles and other shapes; apply these techniques in the context of solving real-world and mathematical problems.
2. Find the volume of a right rectangular prism with fractional edge lengths by packing it with unit cubes of the appropriate unit fraction edge lengths, and show that the volume is the same as would be found by multiplying the edge lengths of the prism. Apply the formulas $V = l\,w\,h$ and $V = b\,h$ to find volumes of right rectangular prisms with fractional edge lengths in the context of solving real-world and mathematical problems.
3. Draw polygons in the coordinate plane given coordinates for the vertices; use coordinates to find the length of a side joining points with the same first coordinate or the same second coordinate. Apply these techniques in the context of solving real-world and mathematical problems.
4. Represent three-dimensional figures using nets made up of rectangles and triangles, and use the nets to find the surface area of these figures. Apply these techniques in the context of solving real-world and mathematical problems.

Statistics and Probability CC.6.SP

Develop understanding of statistical variability.

1. Recognize a statistical question as one that anticipates variability in the data related to the question and accounts for it in the answers.
2. Understand that a set of data collected to answer a statistical question has a distribution which can be described by its center, spread, and overall shape.
3. Recognize that a measure of center for a numerical data set summarizes all of its values with a single number, while a measure of variation describes how its values vary with a single number.

Summarize and describe distributions.

4. Display numerical data in plots on a number line, including dot plots, histograms, and box plots.
5. Summarize numerical data sets in relation to their context, such as by:
   a. Reporting the number of observations.
   b. Describing the nature of the attribute under investigation, including how it was measured and its units of measurement.
   c. Giving quantitative measures of center (median and/or mean) and variability (interquartile range and/or mean absolute deviation), as well as describing any overall pattern and any striking deviations from the overall pattern with reference to the context in which the data were gathered.
   d. Relating the choice of measures of center and variability to the shape of the data distribution and the context in which the data were gathered.